"Roy Richard Grinker's insightful book reveals that mental illness stigma isn't wired into our genes. *Nobody's Normal* interweaves culture, history, and incredible, readable commentary to reveal that people with mental disorders can be accepted into the mainstream, especially when the going gets tough—as in times of war. A must-read."

—Stephen P. Hinshaw, author of *Another Kind of Madness*

"From time immemorial, we have averted our eyes rather than face the cold, hard facts of the impact of war on the human psyche. Within our military today, we are beginning to come to terms with those facts and striving to do better for our soldiers and their families. Roy Richard Grinker, with the wide-ranging eye and objectivity of a brilliant anthropologist, has written a must-read book for those seeking to understand, prevent, and treat the wounds of war to the heart, mind, and soul."

—Pete Geren, former congressman and former US Secretary of the Army

"Roy Richard Grinker's remarkable history of psychiatry reveals how culture has stigmatized those who deviate from the pernicious illusion of normality. He shows that we will always need culture to fully understand those who think differently, and to reveal and resist stigma."

—Professor Simon Baron-Cohen, director of the Autism Research Centre, University of Cambridge

"*Nobody's Normal* is a breathtaking tour de force. With lively illustrations across the centuries, and spanning the United States, England, Namibia, South Korea, and Nepal, Roy Richard Grinker shows how our shifting models of mental illness can only be fully appreciated by using different frames of reference. This fascinating book weaves together stories of mental illness during war, Grinker's grandfather's psychoanalysis by Sigmund Freud, and a focus on post-traumatic stress disorder and autism. The net result is a compelling global panorama. An invaluable book."

—Sir Graham Thornicroft, professor of community psychiatry, King's College London

NOBODY'S NORMAL

Also by Roy Richard Grinker

A Companion to the Anthropology of Africa (coeditor)

Perspectives on Africa:
A Reader in Culture, History, and Representation (coeditor)

Unstrange Minds:
Remapping the World of Autism

In the Arms of Africa:
The Life of Colin M. Turnbull

Korea and Its Futures:
Unification and the Unfinished War

Houses in the Rainforest:
Ethnicity and Inequality Among Farmers and Foragers in Central Africa

NOBODY'S NORMAL

How Culture Created the
Stigma of Mental Illness

ROY RICHARD GRINKER

W. W. NORTON & COMPANY
Independent Publishers Since 1923

Copyright © 2021 by Roy Richard Grinker

Excerpt from "The Double Image" from *The Complete Poems* by Anne Sexton. Copyright © 1981 by Linda Gray Sexton and Loring Conant Jr., executors of the will of Anne Sexton. Reprinted by permission of SLL / Sterling Lord Literistic, Inc.

Some passages in this book appear in different form in Grinker, R. R. 2020. "Autism, 'Stigma,' Disability: A Shifting Historical Terrain." *Current Anthropology* 61 (supplement 21), S55–S68.

For information about permission to reproduce selections from this book, write to Permissions, W. W. Norton & Company, Inc., 500 Fifth Avenue, New York, NY 10110

For information about special discounts for bulk purchases, please contact W. W. Norton Special Sales at specialsales@wwnorton.com or 800-233-4830

Manufacturing by Lake Book Manufacturing
Production manager: Lauren Abbate

Library of Congress Cataloging-in-Publication Data

Names: Grinker, Roy Richard, 1961– author.
Title: Nobody's normal : how culture created the stigma of mental illness / Roy Richard Grinker.
Description: First Edition. | New York : W. W. Norton & Company, 2021. | Includes bibliographical references and index.
Identifiers: LCCN 2020030381 | ISBN 9780393531640 (hardcover) | ISBN 9780393531657 (epub)
Subjects: LCSH: Mental illness—History. | Mentally ill—History. | Stereotypes (Social psychology)—History.
Classification: LCC RC455 .G75 2021 | DDC 616.89—dc23
LC record available at https://lccn.loc.gov/2020030381

W. W. Norton & Company, Inc., 500 Fifth Avenue, New York, N.Y. 10110
www.wwnorton.com

W. W. Norton & Company Ltd., 15 Carlisle Street, London W1D 3BS

1 2 3 4 5 6 7 8 9 0

To the Chicago Grinkers

Part way back from Bedlam
I came to my mother's house in Gloucester,
Massachusetts. And this is how I came
to catch at her; and this is how I lost her.
I cannot forgive your suicide, my mother said.
And she never could. She had my portrait
done instead.

Anne Sexton, "The Double Image"

CONTENTS

PART THREE

Body and Mind

THE ROAD OUT OF BEDLAM

*The concept of the normal is properly a variant of
the concept of the good. It is that which society has
approved.*

Ruth Benedict (1934)

When I was six years old, my grandfather gave me a copy of his newest publication, a book about how to diagnose borderline personality disorder. He signed it: "To my grandson, who will carry on." I didn't know how to read full sentences, so he told me what it meant: I would be a psychiatrist, just like him—the fourth generation of psychiatrists named Grinker.

I am not a psychiatrist.

My family was deeply disappointed, of course, but I eventually earned some redemption by marrying a psychiatrist and by becoming an anthropologist who studies mental health. And inasmuch as this book is about both psychiatry and my family, I do "carry on" their legacy. The lives and work of those generations infuse the pages below—from my great-grandfather, Julius, a late-nineteenth-century neurologist and psychoanalyst who believed people with mental illnesses were biologically inferior, to my own cross-cultural research on autism in sub-Saharan Africa and East Asia that rejects such antiquated views.

This book chronicles the many cultural and historical threads that have brought us to the present, a time when societies throughout the world are challenging the stigma that has, for centuries, shadowed mental illnesses. We haven't put it into words, but most of the people I encounter, even in low-income countries with inadequate health care, sense that something positive is happening. Although 60 percent of people with a mental illness in the United States still receive no mental health treatment,[1] mental illness is fast becoming a more accepted and visible part of the human condition. We are acknowledging that mental illnesses are more common than we used to think, and that they affect us all—either individually or because of our relationships to others. Indeed, it is impossible to imagine that there is anyone unconnected to mental illness. In the twenty-first century, many of the people we most admire—celebrities like Lady Gaga and swimmer Michael Phelps, for example—speak publicly about their own emotional struggles. Also, in comparison to their parents, millennials are more willing to disclose a diagnosis and seek treatment. Many people, like my daughter Isabel, who is autistic, even celebrate forms of differences that just a few decades ago were a mark of shame.

These developments show us that we need not surrender to stigma, as if it were natural to marginalize otherness and difference. Stigma isn't in our biology; it's in our culture. It is a process we learn from within our communities, and we can change what we teach. But only if we know the history of stigma can we target the social forces that created it in the first place, strengthen those that reduce stigma, and say "enough" to the many barriers that keep so many people from getting care.

My grandfather, also named Roy Grinker, did not share his father's objectionable views, and he spent much of his career trying to eradicate stigma. I was fortunate to grow up across the street from him. Occasionally, he would reminisce about the time he spent in Vienna as one of Freud's patients, and I remember how often he talked about Freud's wishes. One was that doctors could help lead people out of misery, not into a perfect life but into ordinary unhappiness. Another was to prove that emotional distress was universal. Perhaps, Freud told him, if people understood that we are all neurotic, they might eventually feel no shame seeking psychological care for their problems. Perhaps some psychiatric conditions could even become like the common cold, something everyone gets from time to time. And maybe students would be more eager to choose a career in psychiatry.

I was raised in a family that believed everyone had a little mental illness, that emotional pain was a normal part of life, and that mental illnesses existed within a hierarchy of all diseases. Anxiety, for example, was more serious than the common cold and less serious than cancers, but still in the range of what typical human beings confronted throughout their lives. I wasn't ignorant of the stigma of mental illnesses since, outside my home, most people talked about them in a whisper. But people also whispered about cancer, dementia, and sexually transmitted diseases. It just took me a while to figure out the difference between the stigma of mental versus physical illness.

That realization came after I finished the tenth grade, when my grandfather helped arrange a summer job for me in a psychiatric hospital, cleaning and filing. One day I bumped into an emaciated girl who was my classmate. She was a patient, and simply seeing her caused an uproar. I was so harshly admonished by so many people—our school principal, her parents, my parents, my grandfather, her doctors, my supervisor at work—to keep her hospitalization confidential that I felt as if I had committed a crime. I can only imagine how uncomfortable she felt as she struggled with both her illness and the commotion around her.

I recognized then the extent to which our society had made psychiatric conditions frightening and shameful, a double illness: first, the ailment itself, and second, society's negative judgment.

In any given year, nearly 20 percent of American adults—more than 60 million people—meet the criteria for a mental illness.[2] Many of these con-

ditions are mild, short-term, and self-limiting. But others have serious consequences. Anorexia nervosa, perhaps the most fatal of all, has a mortality
rate of as high as 10 percent, by some measures.[3] Suicide, almost always
associated with mental illnesses, is the third leading cause of death among
American teenagers, and most who die never received any mental health
care. In 2013, a Centers for Disease Control and Prevention (CDC) survey
of American high school students nationwide showed that more than 13
percent said they had at some time in their lives created a plan to commit
suicide, and 17 percent "seriously considered suicide."[4] But many felt too
ashamed to tell anyone in their family. Every year, mental illnesses account
for at least 12 percent of the total disease burden worldwide, and many people with serious mental illnesses and intellectual disabilities in low-income
countries like South Sudan, Somalia, and Uganda are condemned to a life
of confinement and abuse in their villages.[5]

Why don't more people seek treatment? It is true that many barriers to
care are inherent in the conditions themselves. People who are seriously
depressed, for example, may simply not have the will to see a doctor, or they
may believe they deserve to be depressed. Because the person with anorexia
nervosa may welcome the extreme weight loss, they may not want to seek
care. But, for the most part, the experts say that stigma is the biggest problem. According to the U.S. Department of Health and Human Services,
stigma remains "the most formidable obstacle to future progress in the
area of mental illness and health."[6] Steven Hyman, former director of the
National Institute of Mental Health (NIMH), has called stigma an international "public health crisis."

But what exactly is "stigma"? Even in the academic literature, stigma
has become a default concept that condenses a multitude of different kinds
of fears, prejudices, and shame into a single and often amorphous word.
Scholars speak of stigma in conditions as different as AIDS, Alzheimer's,
and schizophrenia, in locations as different as rural Namibia and downtown Chicago, and among populations as different as hunter-gatherers
and college students. But at a very general level they are all referring to the
process through which people who think or behave in ways that diverge

from a society's norms are alienated and abhorred. The word *stigma* actually comes from the ancient Greek word meaning a mark or branding on the body made with a sharp instrument, and it has long been associated in its plural form (*stigmata*) with Christ's crucifixion wounds. Stigma in our times, however, has come to connote something else. The stigma of mental illness is when your psychological state defines your identity; when people see you as flawed and incompetent; when you are invisible to others; or when people see your suffering but blame you for it. It is the unwanted shadow of a person, produced when a society casts a certain light on human differences. It is also the process of hiding or denying emotional hardship in a vain effort to preserve an ideal—as the poet Anne Sexton described in her autobiographical poem, "The Double Image," which serves as the epigraph of this book. In the aftermath of her own suicide attempt, her mother refuses to see her for who she really is. She accepts her only as the portrait she constructs herself, of the child she wished she had.

In any society that reveres conformity, the sociologist Erving Goffman said in 1963, all people will at some point in their lives experience the pain of stigma. And in the relatively intolerant social context in which Goffman was writing, everyone would be afflicted by stigma except, he said, the "young, married, white, urban, northern, heterosexual Protestant father of college education, fully employed, of good complexion, weight, and height, and a recent record in sports."[7] Everyone else (which included all women!) was vulnerable to discrimination and prejudice. Of course, some form of stigma exists everywhere in the world, but what is stigmatized always varies according to place and time. Under the right circumstances, virtually anything—skin color, religion, poverty, sexuality, medical illnesses, physical disabilities, disfigurement, being a victim of rape, having a child out of wedlock, and even being divorced—can lead to a discredited identity. Certainly, having a mental illness has been an embarrassment, something people were ashamed of and hid; and when they could not hide their illnesses, they could hear the sounds of stigma in murmurs, or feel its potency as they were bullied, harassed, assaulted, and denied work, housing, and other opportunities.

However, there is evidence that we are reducing the shame and secrecy that exacerbates emotional suffering and breaking down the barriers to care. Seeking treatment for post-traumatic stress disorder (PTSD), for example, is increasingly seen more as evidence of strength and resilience than weakness.[8] Greater recognition of conditions that begin in childhood has led to early-intervention programs and academic supports. According to the U.S. Department of Education, about 13 percent of all children in American public schools now receive some kind of special education. People with both mental and physical disabilities are also beginning to reject old norms and developmental milestones, like the expectation that a person is an adult at the arbitrary ages of eighteen or twenty-one and should live independently. Being gay, transgender, or gender fluid are fast becoming personal, social, and political identities rather than signs of pathology. When Isabel uses the word "autism" to describe her talents—like the uncanny ability to assemble complex jigsaw puzzles, picture-side down—I sometimes wonder what Julius would think of her.

Celebrities acknowledge their mental illnesses today. Athletes are now thanking their therapists after they win big games, and comedian David Letterman's psychiatrist joined him on stage in 2017 when he received the Kennedy Center's Mark Twain Prize for American Humor. Musician Bruce Springsteen speaks and writes about his psychiatric treatment for major depression, and about how his father's mental illnesses were neither discussed nor diagnosed. We now know that Pope Francis was once in therapy with a psychoanalyst in Argentina. Black hip-hop artists, especially in the new genre called "emo Rap," rap about mental illnesses, trauma, and suicide, topics that have long been silenced in African American communities.[9]

Current movies and television programs also shine a light on mental illnesses. Take "autism spectrum disorder" (ASD), for example, the meanings of which continue to change. Autism has not only ceased to be a source of shame, in some cases it's become somewhat cool. Autistic characters pervade children's and adult television. There is an autistic Sesame Street character, an autistic Power Ranger, and other protagonists with obvious autistic traits in television shows such as *The Big Bang Theory, Silicon Valley, Community,* and *The Good Doctor.* The hero of the book and award-winning play *The Curious Incident of the Dog in the Night-Time* is autistic.

We need only listen to millennials to get a sense of the changes underway. A student in one of my classes described her struggle to find treatment for attention deficit hyperactivity disorder (ADHD) when she was in high school. Her father told her she did not have ADHD, that she simply wasn't working hard enough to get good grades. She begged to see a psychiatrist, but she had to wait until she went to college to act on her own. "Getting diagnosed with ADHD," she told our class, "was one of the best days of my freshman year because someone actually saw that I wasn't stupid or lazy, that I just needed treatment to help me do better."[10] Another student even wore a T-shirt that read "I hate normal people." The shirt is a statement of her support of neurodiversity, the movement that argues that neurological and cognitive differences and "deficits," especially those that characterize autism, are a universal aspect of human variation. From this perspective, many human differences are pathological or disabling only if society makes them so—like the person in a wheelchair who is "disabled" only when the environment has no ramps or elevators. In fact, the contemporary term for normal that comes from the neurodiversity movement, "neurotypical," doesn't really mean "normal." It refers, critically, to people who conform to society's definition of the normal.

Recently, I reeled off some prevalence estimates for my students: between 8 percent and 9 percent of American children have ADHD; in some states the prevalence estimate for autism is over 2 percent; 8–10 percent of children have an anxiety disorder; approximately 1 percent of adults have schizophrenia; more than 2.5 percent of adults have bipolar disorder; and the prevalence of major depression for adults between the ages of eighteen and twenty-five is about 11 percent. A student asked in jest, "Isn't anyone normal anymore?"

I answered no. Nobody's normal. And since we have for so long used the concept of "normal" to decide who we accept into our social worlds and who we reject, it's about time we recognize that normal is a damaging illusion.

Stigma has diminished, my students often say, because we now value diversity, including neurodiversity, more than sameness, and "because people are more open today about their lives." But when I ask them why people are more open, they answer "because there is less stigma." Their circular reasoning points to the fact that we still have not been able to explain the changes we are witnessing.

Few scholars have explored in depth the underlying historical and cultural forces that shape stigma over time.[11] Under the presumption that stigma already and always exists, the many compassionate researchers who have devoted their careers to studying stigma have focused more on the present: on how labels and stereotypes alienate sufferers; how people with mental illnesses lose status and are discriminated against; and how, by necessity, individuals manage their differences, often by assimilating as much as possible to a perceived norm and covering their stigmatizing attributes, as when people keep their troubling emotions secret or isolate themselves from social interactions. However, we know less about why particular kinds of stigma emerged, or what forms of power sustain them.[12] Why, for example, does one society consider homosexuality a form of insanity, while another sees it as a crime, and yet another sees it as a normal part of human development? How can one condition, such as the psychological trauma of war, denote weakness and femininity among male soldiers in one historical period, while in another war it denotes patriotism? What can modern industrialized societies in Europe and North America learn from the history of the stigma of mental illness? How can we use that knowledge to improve the care and treatment of people with the most stigmatizing illnesses? And how can we, in turn, help people in other societies, with other histories, reduce their suffering?

The answers to these questions are unlikely to be found in the basic sciences. We cannot and probably never will see mental illnesses in a microscope, or test for them in a laboratory. They are experiences shaped by more factors than we can imagine—genes, childhood, wealth, poverty, friendships, education, and so on. Yet leading mental health professionals, like the former directors of NIMH, contemplate a day when we will discover the precise biological causes of mental illnesses, develop more effective treatments, and as a result reduce stigma. As National Institutes of Health director Francis Collins put it when he was director of the National Human Genome Research Institute, "The time is right for a focused effort to understand, and potentially to reclassify, all human illnesses on the basis of detailed molecular characterization."[13] In this view, mental illnesses would be the product of genetic mutations and neurological diseases—sicknesses of the brain, not of the self or society.

We shouldn't rule out the possibility that we might eventually discover the causes of specific mental illnesses and, as a result, diminish stigma. Certainly, the fear and concealment of HIV/AIDS began to decrease as we learned more about the virus and its transmission and developed treatments effective enough to transform it from a fatal to a chronic illness. Given the success of chemotherapy and immunotherapy in oncology, the same is true for many cancers. Obituaries for people who die of cancer are no longer purposely vague, as they were two decades ago when cancer was more mysterious and death notices read simply, "she died after a long illness." But given the complexity of the brain, psychiatry is nowhere near that point. After all, no truly novel psychiatric medications have been developed for decades, and any improvements doctors can claim for existing medicines have been incremental at best.

Not only do scientists know very little about what causes most mental illnesses, mental illnesses are, almost by definition, illnesses *without* a known cause. They are patterns of behaviors associated with significant distress or disability in a person's life. Since 1980, the various versions of the psychiatrist's manual, the *Diagnostic and Statistical Manual of Mental Disorders* (DSM), mention causes for only a few conditions out of several hundred—post-traumatic disorder as the result of trauma, bereavement disorder after the loss of a loved one, or reactive attachment disorder as the result of pathological caretaking during childhood. And when a specific cause is identified (as was the case with Rett's disorder, caused by a mutation in a specific gene called MECP2), the disorder is removed from the

DSM and placed in the domain of genetics and neurology. The American Psychiatric Association (APA) actually tells clinicians to make a psychiatric diagnosis *only* after ruling out the possibility that the symptoms are due to a "nonpsychiatric medical condition" or the "direct physiological effects of a substance."

I must also point out that, unlike cancer and AIDS, there is no proof that any biological explanation has ever reduced the stigma of a neurological or mental disorder. Epilepsy, for example, remains one of the most stigmatized conditions throughout Asia, Central America, and sub-Saharan Africa, despite widespread awareness of its biological bases and physiology and the presence of beneficial therapies.[14] Finding a cause and a treatment for an affliction does not necessarily remove its stigma, especially afflictions of the brain. As we'll see later, even an effective and safe brain-based medical treatment like electroconvulsive therapy continues to be met with fear and secretiveness, if not hostility. Indeed, biological models of human variation sometimes do more harm than good.

My field, cultural anthropology, was born as a reaction against the early evolutionary efforts in Europe to define humankind in biological terms. Nineteenth-century thinkers used science as a weapon to argue that if laws of nature governed all people everywhere, then the diverse peoples in non-Western societies were naturally different from Europeans and therefore naturally inferior. By the same token, they believed that Europeans who were poor, mentally ill, or had developmental disabilities were also naturally inferior. By illuminating the extraordinary range of beliefs and practices in the world, anthropology challenges the mechanisms of exclusion—race, class, sex, and the institutionalization of the "insane," for example—that doctors, scientists, and policy makers once justified with biological arguments.[15] Culture itself constructed the illusion of innate differences on which so much discrimination is based. If there is anything that truly counts as human *nature*, it is our unique ability to transcend nature through culture.

This book is therefore not a history of the progress of scientific knowledge, though it is a history of progress. Over the past several centuries, neither medical nor scientific advances have lessened the stigma of mental illness. Stigma is a social process that can be explained through cultural history, in the forms of exclusion humans create. Our judgments about mental illnesses have come from our definitions of what, at different times and places, people consider the ideal society and the ideal person. Stigma ebbs and flows as the result of deep structural conditions—in particular, capitalism, ideologies of individualism and personal responsibility, and the complicated legacies of war, racism, and colonialism. Our dynamic conceptions of mental illness ride on the waves of broader cultural changes, and when science or medicine does appear to lessen the shame of suffering it does so as the servant of culture.

Like all histories, the history of the stigma of mental illness doesn't move in only one direction. There are twists and turns, unintended consequences, great progress and disturbing setbacks. For example, many minority communities in the United States receive less mental health care not only because of low access to services but also because of cultural tendencies to keep mental disturbances a family secret and a learned mistrust of medical institutions. Alcoholics Anonymous remains anonymous. And the very phrase "mental health" is designed to avoid the connotations of sickness. Even the National Institute of Mental Health, the lead federal agency for research on mental illness, does not call itself an institute of mental *illness*, though most of the other national institutes are named for diseases (e.g., the National Cancer Institute, the National Institute of Allergy and Infectious Diseases). In the media, soldiers discuss PTSD openly, but the persistent belief that mental illness is a sign of weakness prevents many soldiers on active duty from seeking help.[16] The Church of Scientology maintains a free museum on Sunset Boulevard in Los Angeles, named Psychiatry: An Industry of Death, that blames psychiatry for everything from the Holocaust to September 11.

The persistence of stigma also inhibits people from seeking help. Even for the most seriously mentally ill today, the time from the onset of symptoms to psychiatric care is startling. In the United States, the average time from first psychosis to first treatment is seventy-four weeks.[17] Despite the recent acceptance and appreciation of human differences, many conditions, such as schizophrenia and substance abuse, are still highly stigmatized and feared because both threaten our modern ideals of self-control and autonomy.

But I want to show you in this book just how much has changed for the better. I will take you to 1941 when, in an effort to cure John F. Kennedy's twenty-three-year-old sister, Rosemary, of her mood swings and rebelliousness, her family made her undergo a lobotomy. It caused severe and permanent brain damage. You will meet Erik Erikson, one of the most famous figures in the history of psychology, who in 1944 whisked his son, Neil, born with Down syndrome, to an institution, telling his friends and his other children that the baby had been stillborn. He was afraid that having a child with Down syndrome would hurt his reputation. And in 1949 there was James Forrestal, the former secretary of war. Efforts to shield him from the shame of a diagnosis of depression cost him his life: without prompt and appropriate treatment, he committed suicide. In the 1960s, doctors blamed autism on pathological caretaking, characterized a generation of warm and loving parents as cold and abusive, and institutionalized autistic children in order to remove them from what psychoanalyst Bruno Bettelheim called "their mothers' black milk."[18] Actress Glenn Close, a staunch advocate for mental health care, wrote that silence nearly led her sister to commit suicide. "I come from a family that had no vocabulary for mental illness," she said. Distinguished scholar of stigma Stephen Hinshaw told me that he never knew why his father left home for months at a time during the 1960s and 1970s. Only as an adult did he learn that his father had bipolar disorder and was frequently hospitalized. "As a child and teenager," he said, "I just knew that I wasn't supposed to ask about it."[19]

In the pages that follow, I trace the history of how people with mental illnesses have been judged as abnormal, marginalized, discriminated against, and even experimented on. Stigma and illness are, of course, very different concepts, but for hundreds of years in Europe and North America mental illnesses have been inextricably bound up with stigma, and so their two histories can be told as one. We begin at the onset of the industrial revolution, when a march to conformity first begins, and proceed to the present, a time when many mental illnesses and diverse ways of being are less stigmatizing than at any point in our history. Mental illnesses, we'll see, are modern phenomena, stigmatized from the moment of their invention.

This book chronicles several historical patterns that can help us understand the dynamics of the stigma of mental illnesses. One of them is *capitalism*. In capitalism, the inability to work became the quintessential disease of modernity, and the source of the stigma of mental illness. Stigma does not derive from ignorance or lack of knowledge, but rather from the conception of mental illness as the sign of the idle, a personality incapable of achieving the ideal: producing for oneself and the economy.[20] In order to be named and stigmatized, mental illnesses had to be defined first as diseases of the failed worker and then as diseases of one's character rather than one's body. They had to be seen as objects of study rooted in the individual and individual responsibility, and not just as the inevitable outcome of one's race, sex, or social class. They had to define a person, to represent more than simply a lack of fit with the social order, but a lasting and dehumanizing mark of inferiority.

Much of this redefinition was carried out in asylums, like the famous Bethlem Royal Hospital (locally pronounced "Bedlam," from which we get the word *bedlam*, meaning chaos), in which people who, for whatever reason, were incapable of participating in the emerging economy were confined and disciplined. This is *not* to suggest that capitalism created psychological impairments; rather, psychological impairments acquired new meanings in capitalism. Only in confinement could doctors for the first time observe large numbers of people with mental illnesses and develop a vocabulary to name and classify their sicknesses.

Because in most of North America and western Europe we created our concept of the person within a framework of capitalism, the most stigmatized people tend to be those who do not conform to the ideal modern worker: the autonomous, self-reliant individual. In a country like the United States, with minimal hereditary distinctions, we place a high value on independence, social and economic mobility, and self-sufficiency.[21] As early as 1835, Alexis de Tocqueville noted that the American was ideally his own master, accountable and dependent to no one else (except perhaps God), that he "exists only in himself and for himself alone."[22] It's not surprising, then, that many people with disabilities that limit their ability to work often want to be invisible, and that many don't even seek care. Socialist countries do no better, since the ideals of independence and productivity fostered by capitalism were in place long before socialism emerged.

It follows that if an economic force like capitalism created mental illness stigma as the antithesis of the ideals of the modern worker, then changes in capitalism might also affect stigma and our ideas about our selfhood. Indeed, economic shifts have led to new accommodations and greater accessibility for people who were previously marginalized from both education and the workplace—including the people we increasingly call the "neurodiverse," "not normal," or "on the spectrum." The valued twenty-first-century worker can be self-employed, work from home, work part-time, combine paid work with family care or volunteerism, interact virtually rather than in person, and even live with his or her parents. They might be socially awkward, have restricted interests in science and technology, and be more comfortable interacting with others online than face-to-face. They might enjoy the repetitive tasks of administrative and technical work that others find difficult or dislike. Many of the people who might have been demeaned in the past for their narrow interests in science and computers—like Bill Gates and the other entrepreneurs the writer Steve Silberman once described as having the "geek syndrome"[23]—are today among our heroes. The high-tech economy is truly the revenge of the nerds.

Another historical pattern I follow is war. World War I, World War II, the Korean War, and the Vietnam War illuminated many mental illnesses and, like the asylums in which the very idea of mental illness as we know it emerged, provided the context in which psychiatry and psychology emerged as bona fide disciplines. Indeed, the history of the mental health professions should not be characterized by the slow, incremental growth of knowledge, but by bursts of knowledge generated during wars, as well as sustained periods of forgetting between wars, in which clinicians and researchers remained ignorant of the lessons learned in previous conflicts.

Whereas asylums exacerbated the shame of psychological problems, wars reduced it, in both military and civilian life. In wartime, psychiatric disturbances became an acceptable response to stress, whether inside or outside of combat. And because soldiers were, in effect, employed by the military, many of those who might have been unemployed and stigmatized in the civilian sector were integrated into a new community, their personality differences often muted by conformity to military structure. In both the United States and the United Kingdom, record numbers of previously unemployed disabled people found work in positions vacated by those who joined the war effort. But wars and their aftermaths also show us that success in the battle against stigma can be precarious, as progress is often followed by a regression back into the prewar shame of mental illnesses. In a pattern repeated throughout the twentieth century, stigma gradually returned in postwar years when the economic costs of chronic mental illnesses strained government budgets, and when people with mental and physical disabilities yielded their jobs to veterans. That pattern is disrupted only when a war is sustained for many years, as in the current conflicts in Iraq and Afghanistan. Since those wars began, the US military has focused more intensively on the stigma of mental illness than at any other time in American history, and its efforts to eliminate barriers to mental health care have continued unabated.

Military psychiatry serves as a kind of microcosm through which we can see, in sometimes exaggerated form, broad trends in the diagnosis, treatment, and moral judgments of mental illnesses. In WWII, for example, scientists like my grandfather, who was stationed in North Africa, realized for the first time how common mental illnesses were in American society, how stressors that originate outside of one's body cause or exacerbate emotional problems, that many more doctors needed to be trained as psychiatrists, and, most importantly, that mental illnesses were treatable outside of asylums and hospitals. As a direct response to the war, President Harry S. Truman established NIMH and ordered the military to write a manual for the diagnosis of mental disorders to ensure a degree of standardization among clinicians and researchers. That manual, the *Diagnostic and Statistical Manual of Mental Disorders-I* (DSM-I), was first written by the military during WWII (then called Medical 203) and was then adapted by the military in 1953 for civilian use.

However, by 1973, the civilian psychiatric establishment—in line with general opposition to the Vietnam War—had developed resolutions to ban military psychiatrists from the APA. Many argued that military psychiatry was at best irrelevant to mainstream psychiatry and at worst an immoral effort to persuade psychologically traumatized men to return to combat. They had already forgotten, or perhaps never knew, that their own ideas and practices, such as the therapeutic community, group therapy, psychiatric screening as a preventive measure, the treatment of acute stress reactions, short-term psychotherapy, and community psychiatry, had all begun in the military.

A third historical pattern I follow is the increasing medicalization of mental illness. Medicalization is the process whereby we construe aspects of everyday life, including nonmedical problems, as if they were medical— as when being transgender becomes "gender dysphoria," when having a certain body mass becomes "obesity," or when childbirth falls almost completely under the purview of the doctor in a hospital.[24] When we describe and think about ourselves through a language of disease, and when we seek technical or scientific solutions to our problems, we can lose sight of the social origins of disease and stigma. Every society and every historical moment, as we'll see, has its own way of making sense of physical and emotional pain. Economics, kinship, politics, and technology, among other aspects of society, all shape the way we experience, talk about, and judge illnesses and disabilities. Medicalization is itself a product of culture, an ideological position grounded first in the belief that we can separate the body and the mind, and second in the belief that we can separate the mind from the environments in which we live, as if culture is just a bothersome factor that obscures biological realities.

The separation of body and mind is one of the more problematic legacies of Western philosophy. Without it we might never have produced the idea that the mind, though seated in the brain, could have its own disorders, or might never have developed a specialization like psychiatry. It is possible that without the body/mind distinction, mental illnesses would be less stigmatizing today, and that lifesaving psychiatric treatments that act directly on the brain—like electroconvulsive therapy, for example—would be no more stigmatizing than the jolt of electricity from a defibrillator that rescues someone from a life-threatening cardiac event.

The division between body and mind continues to impede mental health care for people who have physical complaints that do not conform to a medical model, as when a doctor tells a patient who suffers from headaches or back pain that the X-rays or lab tests show nothing "physically" wrong with him and that he might benefit from psychological treatment. Many patients feel insulted by such a suggestion, as if the doctor is giving up on them, or saying "it's just stress" or "snap out of it!" Who knows how many people who suffer from physical ailments could benefit from mental health care and yet do not seek treatment because they are convinced that bodily symptoms are unrelated to the mind, and also because physical illnesses are more socially acceptable while mental illnesses are stigmatized. It's possible that the stigma of psychiatric conditions leads many patients to unconsciously experience their emotional distress through the body, like the WWI soldiers who had been nowhere near combat and yet had the identical symptoms of shell shock as someone who had endured weeks of gunfire. They had the symptoms that were socially acceptable and made sense to themselves and to the people around them.

Despite the fact that all of us, every day, temporarily express emotions through the body—like having butterflies in one's stomach or sweaty palms when nervous—there is a tendency in the United States to resist psychological explanations for persistent bodily complaints. Uncontrollable movements, nonepileptic seizures, impairments like partial blindness, mutism, and paralysis, skin rashes, diarrhea, and chronic pain can all be psychiatric symptoms. Most people outside of Western industrial societies do not question this fact because they tend to suffer through the body. They feel

anxiety as stomach pain, sadness and hopelessness as a burning or pricking
sensation in one's limbs, and so on.

Finally, a note on terminology. You may have noticed that I use the term
"mental *illness*" rather than the psychiatrist's term of art, "mental *disorder*."
My reasoning is as follows. First, "disorder" is a word that suggests there is
such a thing as an "ordered" mind, even though we know virtually nothing
about what an ordered mind looks like. Disorder also evokes the old characterization of people with mental illnesses as having disorganized or disintegrated minds, and it reinforces many nontechnical and derogatory words
and phrases for psychiatric conditions. Many of these are metaphors for disorder and fragmentation, like "screw loose," "going to pieces," "not all there,"
"one can short of a six-pack," "cracking up," and "split personality." Second,
whereas disorder connotes a disease that has disrupted the normal and systematic functioning of the body or mind, "illness" connotes the *experience*
of sickness or impairment. As the anthropologist and psychiatrist Arthur
Kleinman argued, disease and disorder are clinicians' terms, the medical
frameworks through which to comprehend a patient's complaint; illness,
however, is the personal and social meaning of that disease, the "experience
of symptoms and suffering . . . how the sick person and the members of the
family or wider social network perceive, live with, and respond to symptoms and disability."[25] Disease draws our attention to biological processes
whereas illness illuminates the facets of an actual life.

Ultimately, mental illnesses may never lend themselves to the same
sorts of rational, objective, impersonal disease models we expect of science
and medicine. That's not because psychiatry has failed, but because we
want it to be something it isn't, something no branch of medicine is either.
Once considered an art centuries ago, medicine now clothes itself in numbers and images, as if they represent truths.[26] This is a fallacy. Pediatricians
make estimates about what constitutes "normal" growth and development;
cardiologists make judgments about what blood pressure level is high, normal, or low; and internists make lifestyle recommendations such as the
number of alcoholic beverages a person should have per week or how many

hours one should exercise to be "healthy." A particular quantitative measure of blood pressure in 2020, for example, is considered an objective sign of hypertension only in comparison to a number that physicians in 2020 happen to agree is "normal," not because there exists in nature any absolute number for low, normal, or high blood pressure. In fact, hypertension isn't even a disease; it is a measurement of risk for disease. Primary care physicians spend much of their time treating fatigue and bodily pain, but fatigue and pain are not diagnoses, and they are certainly not measurable.

Psychiatry is thus emulating a false idol, something that doesn't actually exist. Doctors don't discover realities as much as they characterize what they observe with the models they've developed and accepted by consensus. They also treat symptoms far more often than actual diseases. Psychiatric conditions appear to us to be less objective or fact-based only because we don't yet have the numbers or images to trick us into believing they are.

Consider a woman who has just been diagnosed with breast cancer. She has a disease doctors can see with the naked eye, and so we assume that it has a certain empirical reality that a mental illness does not. The technician can study the tumor and its cells under a microscope and describe its characteristics through lab tests. But this is just the beginning. It is likely that, upon diagnosis, this woman's vision of the future will change. Relationships she thought were the most stable and intimate, such as with her partner or other close family members, may change. Friends she thought were close become distant because of their own anxiety about cancer; others, who were just acquaintances, become close and supportive friends. At any rate, the social network mobilized around her will be different from the one before her diagnosis.

Depending on the society in which she lives, this woman may think that a malevolent force like a sorcerer or witch produced the cancer, or that she or someone close to her has done something wrong that caused a god or gods to afflict her. She may believe that she has inherited a genetic predisposition to cancer from her parents, and will now be concerned about her daughters' futures. Even the kind of medical treatment she seeks will be affected by her culture—whether she prays in a church for her health, has surgery, chemotherapy, or radiation, uses herbal remedies, or consults a shaman. If she lives in a society in which the breast is closely related to one's ideas of femininity and attractiveness, her sense of being a woman—and perhaps others' views of her femininity—will change. Throughout the world, the values and meanings of breast cancer are thus sometimes best understood under the magnifying glass of the visual arts and poetry.

The experience of disease—in other words, a disease as *illness*—is not written in the cells of a tumor, the molecules of a bacterium or a virus, or the DNA in our genome. And if, one day, we do succeed in reducing mental illnesses to biological materials and mechanisms, the meanings of those conditions will still be of our own making.

PART ONE

CAPITALISM

CHAPTER 1

EVERY MAN FOR HIMSELF

*The past is a foreign country: they do things differ-
ently there.*

L. P. Hartley, *The Go-Between* (1953)

The Jun/oansi hunter-gatherers live in remote villages in the Kalahari Desert of Namibia, in southwestern Africa. When I was last there, in 2017, I met a man named Tamzo who sometimes hears angry voices in his head. Once a month, he walks to a clinic, twelve miles each way, to get his anti-psychotic medicine, chlorpromazine. As I sat with Tamzo, his wife, and two children outside his hut, all of the twenty or so people who live in his village gathered to talk. Without hesitation, and with no discomfort I could discern on her part, Tamzo's wife said, "Everyone knows that if he doesn't take his medicines the voices in his head will return; they tell him that he can kill people with his thoughts." Those voices come not from within Tamzo but from spirits sent to him as revenge from a nearby village where, some years ago, one of his cousins allegedly raped a young woman. The spirits her relatives sent to Tamzo's village settled in him, not because of anything

Tamzo himself had done wrong but simply at random. Tamzo's sickness is not his fault.

A traditional healer was able to quiet the spirits but could not remove them entirely, so Tamzo sought Western medicines as well. The clinic staff who provide the medicine write the diagnosis of "schizophrenia" in their records. But that technical word is useful only for them. Other than a slang word that means "odd" or "crazy," the Jun/oansi have no term for schizophrenia or psychosis, and regardless, even someone who is crazy is crazy only when he shows signs of it. Because Tamzo, at least for the time being, no longer has delusions or auditory hallucinations, he is not crazy and he is not stigmatized. He almost certainly has the same condition that we call schizophrenia in North America and Europe. It's just that the Jun/oansi conceptualize the symptoms differently. At home, Tamzo is a victim of malevolence; only at the clinic does he have schizophrenia.

In another village, nine-year-old Geshe cannot speak. He puts his tongue under his front teeth, repeatedly makes the sound "th . . . ," and often drools while doing so. He moves his fingers in unusual ways in front of his face, makes little eye contact, and likes to be alone. There is a ratty suitcase in the village of these hunter-gatherers, but while the other children ride on it, pretending it is a donkey, Geshe just likes to move the zipper back and forth. His peers sometimes tease him because he is so different, but they also look out for him. Parents teach their children not to bully and also not to fight back. The Jun/oansi are such a peaceful society that they are known in the anthropological literature as "the harmless people."[1]

Geshe's parents told me that his problems started when he was a toddler and nearly died from measles. They have never taken him to a clinic, but were he to show up in an American doctor's office, he would probably be diagnosed with autism, since he has all the classic symptoms. His parents and neighbors spoke warmly about him. "Why should we take him to a doctor?" his father asked me. "He survived measles, and he is great herding the goats. He always knows where they are in the day or night." His father also said Geshe has a great memory, that he finds whatever they lose in the bush, like knives or arrows. When I asked his father if he is concerned about who will take care of Geshe when he and his wife pass away, he looked confused and then pointed to his neighbors. "We won't all die at once," he said.

I would never pretend that Jun/oansi society is idyllic, yet we can learn from it. The Jun/oansi have fashioned a society that accepts differences we have shunned. No one there expects a condition like schizophrenia or autism to define a person as a whole. No one in these villages expects anyone to live on their own and be completely responsible for their own successes and failures. In Europe and North America, however, we've long idealized the autonomous individual, dignified those who produce the most capital, and stigmatized those who produce the least. It is, in fact, because of this obsession with independence that Europeans first invented mental illness categories during the early industrial revolution. The idea was to separate out unproductive workers into distinct identities. In capitalism, mental illnesses and dependence on one's family became signs of disgrace. Geshe's father's view, in contrast, stems from the kind of society in which he lives, a society in which there are multiple caretakers and a range of social supports. No one in these villages expects to become the self-reliant individual we associate with the ideal person and worker in Western capitalism, and so people with disabilities live with less stigma. In a society like Geshe and Tamzo's, one would never ask the question nearly every American parent with an autistic child is, at some point, asked: Will your child be able to live independently?

We can also learn from how people in the past have prevented the stigma of physical disabilities, like the first British settlers on the island of Martha's Vineyard.

The island today is an affluent vacation spot, just a forty-five-minute ferry ride from Woods Hole, Massachusetts, or about eighty miles from Boston. But for two and a half centuries, it was home to a small population of English settlers and their descendants. The British first came to the island in the early 1600s, when it was still occupied by a native community of several thousand Wampanoag Indians. As it was in the colonies as a whole, the number of Indians there diminished quickly, while the British population grew. For generations, the settlers married each other and rarely traveled even to the neighboring island of Nantucket, just thirty-eight miles away, let alone to Boston.[2] By the mid-1700s, there were only thirty different surnames among 3,100 British residents, and the consequences of years of inbreeding began to take their toll.

In this closed gene pool, a genetic disorder emerged. By the end of the 1800s, almost a quarter of the residents in some villages had some degree of hereditary deafness. But the deaf, the partially deaf, and the hearing devised their own sign language so that they could communicate, and the islanders, with no other population to compare themselves to, assumed deafness was just a part of human variation. In fact, deafness was so common that in oral histories collected in the twentieth century, descendants of the settlers had trouble recalling who among their friends and family was deaf or hearing. "You see," one of the elders said in 1980, "everyone here spoke sign language."

This community was unlike anything on the mainland. By the end of the nineteenth century, American schoolteachers prohibited children from using sign language. They believed that sign language was a primitive, almost savage, form of communication that would inhibit children's intellectual and social growth and prevent them from becoming productive members of society. Doctors also strongly discouraged deaf people from marrying, so they would be less likely to have children, pass on their defects, and hinder evolutionary progress. On Martha's Vineyard, deafness was a kind of ordinary difference. Everywhere else, it was a deficit; deaf children were educated separately from other children, with a curriculum that promoted lip-reading instead. By the end of World War I, about 80 percent of deaf children in the United States were taught without sign language.[3]

Over time, as people left Martha's Vineyard, and new residents arrived, hereditary deafness disappeared.[4] But the locals remembered, and many hearing people continued to use sign language with other hearing people, out of habit, years after the last islander with hereditary deafness died in 1952.[5] They remembered that, unlike on the mainland, the deaf were not singled out, that because everyone spoke sign language deafness was, therefore, not a disability and was never stigmatized. And since they weren't distinguished as a group, people who could not hear were never even classified as "deaf." The beauty of the invention of their sign language was that the islanders developed a cultural adaptation to a physical condition. They provide one of the best examples of how culture, and not nature, produces and defines what is considered normal and abnormal. It was culture—social isolation and intermarriage—that created the biological condition, but then culture was strong enough and creative enough to eclipse it. Because people who could not hear were fully integrated into their communities and were able to communicate with everyone, we could even say that no one was really "deaf" on Martha's Vineyard.

Most research on stigma is inspired to some degree by the sociologist Erving Goffman's book *Stigma: Notes on the Management of Spoiled Identity* (1963). Actually, I cannot think of another major concept in social science that is so tied to a single text. Goffman conceived of stigma as interactional and performative, meaning that it unfolds in the interactions of everyday life as the result of public intolerance, ignorance, and fear. In his view, individuals whose personal attributes diverge from what their society expects carry the burden of stigma. They are compelled to hide or mitigate the exposure of their discrediting conditions. But because Goffman was concerned mainly with studying daily social activities—a kind of micro-sociology—his work inadvertently deflected attention away from the larger historical or cultural differences, within or outside the United States, that produce stigma.

Yet, as the examples from Namibia and Martha's Vineyard illustrate, stigma is highly variable across time and place. It does not derive from ignorance or an individual's inability to navigate everyday life and public exposure, but rather from a given society's definitions of the ideal person. Just as Tamzo's and Geshe's illness experiences are shaped by their society and its history, so too are illness experiences in the United States. Because we live in an industrial society, the answer to many questions about why stigma increases or decreases over time can therefore be found in the history of capitalism. Indeed, in North America and Europe, stigma resulted from a modern, capitalist brand for the idle. Doctors, politicians, and other "experts" on public health isolated people they deemed economically unproductive, including those who were unable to work because of serious intellectual or behavioral disabilities.

Most of us may not believe in evil spirits like Tamzo, but we do worship the commodity, and we've built a shrine to capital accumulation and infinite needs.[6] We adore the maximizer, the producer, and the free market, and we privilege self-sufficiency above care from the state, church, or community. Market values now pervade all aspects of our lives, crossing over the boundaries of what we usually think of as "the economy"—as when universities value chemistry more than Shakespeare because large research grants bring more money, and when insurance companies determine the monetary value of our lives and body parts. If capitalism can shape such a diverse array of phenomena, then it makes sense to ask how capitalism also shapes our attitudes toward health and illness.

Mental illnesses, as we'll see, are just as much a product of our culture as Tamzo's illness is a product of Jun/oansi culture. We all give an aura of truth to the explanations that make sense to us, even though no mental illness can be validated by a lab test and Tamzo can't prove that he is the victim of supernatural malevolence. In North America, most of us assume that because the experts create and classify mental illness names, they must be based on more than just consensus. We give power and authority to the scientists, as if "expertise" is a real thing that a person or an institution can possess (like a diploma or a PhD after one's name), and conveniently forget that the practice, and the spirit, of science is best understood as trial and error, best guesses and fallibility. Mental illnesses are also anchored in the many activities we carry out, and the billions of dollars we spend, in their name—diagnostic interviews, publications, therapies, research funding, insurance reimbursement, and academic conferences, for example, all of which depend on diagnostic labels for their continued existence. The more these practices become tradition, the more they become embedded in our everyday lives and the business of health care and education, and the more likely we are to reproduce the diagnoses that support them. One can't very well maintain foundations, clinics, therapies, research programs, schools, and conferences for a specific condition unless we believe the condition actually exists, unless we can manufacture a steady supply of diagnoses.

But mental illness categories are just temporary names or frameworks to help us understand patterns of behavior that cause suffering. Someone with a diagnosis of autism, like my daughter Isabel, will have challenges with language, social communication, and repetitive behaviors no matter what anyone calls her. We have called her autistic because we currently live in a society in which that concept makes sense, and that provides—at least for now—a relatively nonstigmatizing model for understanding Isabel's kind of difference and for organizing services that we think benefit her. But no one knows how long the concept of autism will last. There are many illness names, now defunct, that the smartest scientists once believed would last forever—hysteria, neurasthenia, and even the recently eliminated category of Asperger's disorder, for example. Of course, people still convert emotional distress into often-debilitating bodily symptoms (what used to be called hysteria); people still have headaches, fatigue, and feel irritable when anxious or depressed (what used to be called neurasthenia); and there are still people who have all the symptoms of autism except a language delay (what used to be called Asperger's). Those illnesses are just as real as they've ever been. We just call them something else.

Much of what we know about mental illnesses before capitalism comes from descriptions of psychological problems in ancient Islamic medical texts, many of them Arabic translations of ancient Greek texts. These texts suggest that there was no difference between an illness of the mind and an illness of the body. One tenth-century document, written in northern Africa by Ibn Imran, is devoted to the topic of "black thoughts," "panics," and "feelings of misfortune," and prescribes treatments like herbal concoctions to purge black bile from the body, exercise, and a reduction in alcohol consumption. Medieval Islamic societies appear, for the most part, to have been quite tolerant of human differences. In the fourteenth century, a chronicle by al-Maqrizi describes men in Egypt who claimed to be sultans known to have died long ago, but typically they were punished only if they posed an actual political risk.[7] From the 1500s through the work of the nineteenth-century Finnish anthropologist Edvard Westermarck, scholarly and popular texts repeatedly describe the existence of the *majdhub*, the "madman," who is mad because he is divine and who is respected and venerated as long as he does no harm.

Many people with mental illnesses in North Africa and the Middle East were also thought to be possessed by demons like *jinns* (beliefs that still exist today, and from which the English word "genie" derives) or afflicted by a host of other spirits, including God, the evil eye, or magic employed by an enemy.[8] By the fifteenth century, an asylum for the "insane" had been established in Fez (present-day Morocco), where patients were frequently bound and whipped. But the patients were also brought to the mosque regularly, and the goal was cure rather than lifelong institutionalization. In addition to prayer, patients were treated with baths, herbs, leeches, opium, fragrant plants, and conversations with doctors to reassure the patients about their future.

In Korea, during the late Chosŏn dynasty (1392–1897), the Daily Records of the Royal Secretariat recorded the political activities of various royal families (between 1413 and 1865) and also aspects of health that we would today call "psychiatric." One Chosŏn dynasty condition even has nearly the identical symptoms today: *hwa-byung* (fire-illness),[9] though at that time the name was slightly different; Koreans referred to it using the Chinese phrase *hua-tseung* or "fire symptoms."[10] The Chosŏn dynasty illness also comprised many more symptoms than it does in the twenty-first century, including psychosis. It's listed as a sickness in the DSM-5 glossary of "cultural concepts of distress" and is especially common among middle-aged Korean or diasporic Korean women. Some scholars call it Korea's "national illness."[11] Hwa-byung combines the Chinese belief that fire causes sickness with the long-standing Korean belief that anger, especially unresolved and unexpressed anger, leads to both physical and mental woes, including palpitations, insomnia, and the feeling of a mass in one's abdomen.

One notable person who suffered from hwa-byung was the Crown

Prince Sado (1735–1762). Debilitated by anxiety, and publicly humiliated by his father, King Yeongjo, Sado became prone to sudden rages. In local terms, he could not contain his internal fire.[12] In her 1805 memoir, Sado's wife, Lady Hyegyeong, wrote that he began to rape and murder palace workers, compulsively change his clothes, and threaten to kill the king. In the summer of 1762, recognizing that, by law, Sado's execution would also require the palace to execute Sado's mother, wife, and son, the king devised a plan to spare their lives. He arranged for Sado to be locked in a trunk for eight days during the summer as a treatment for his condition, during which time Sado died.[13] Both elites and commoners experienced symptoms similar to Sado's, but anger, hate, and depressed mood, among other feelings, were thought to be caused by social injustices, or an imbalance between the spiritual and human worlds. Shamans believed that if you were emotionally distressed, it was because something was wrong in the world, not just in your body or mind.

"Mental illness" didn't appear in Korea as a distinct category until the 1880s, when a Korean newspaper reported on the existence of something called "insanity" in a British article entitled "The Mental Institution in England."[14] Korean doctors soon acquired British and German psychiatric texts, and in 1913, at the beginning of the Japanese colonization of Korea, European and American missionaries opened the first psychiatric ward in a Korean hospital. The Korean doctors' primary concern in these units was suicide, one of the many tragic consequences of the colonial period. The Japanese treated Koreans like second-class citizens, suppressed Korean culture and religion, forced Koreans to take Japanese names and speak only Japanese, and conscripted Korean women as sex slaves. And when the number of suicides began to increase in tandem with Japanese atrocities, the colonial authorities were unconcerned. The Japanese administrators said that suicides were simply a natural by-product of modernization and industrialization, as those incapable of competing successfully in the marketplace would be marginalized, or would marginalize themselves through suicide, from the rest of society.[15]

In Europe too, where psychiatry first began as a branch of medicine, mental illnesses were not separated out into a distinct category from other kinds of sicknesses or problematic behavior until the turn of the nineteenth century. As a result, even though there had been asylums for centuries— well before there were people who were classified as insane—the asylums were also the prisons. The first places of confinement exclusively for criminals were not constructed in England until the 1700s, amid humanitarian efforts to end large-scale public dissections and executions of serious offenders[16] and to build "houses of correction" for their potential rehabilitation. And prisons did not become common until reformers decided to separate the mentally ill from the criminal toward the end of the 1700s.

By the early 1800s, these prison/asylums in western Europe were, therefore, populated mostly by criminals, drunkards, heretics and the blasphemous, the unemployed, the homeless, and the physically handicapped, but only occasionally by the people we today would think of as having mental illnesses or intellectual disabilities. The only thing the residents had in common was that they didn't work. In England and France, people with serious mental illnesses went to asylums only if they were too dangerous to live at home, or if they provided no labor to the household. For noncriminals, incarceration was a last resort. This is not to suggest that a person with a mental illness was treated kindly at home. Many families kept their sick relatives in chains. But if such a person was treated badly, it was not because they had something their family and neighbors called a *mental* illness. Before the turn of the nineteenth century, there was no distinct category of "mental illnesses" and no distinct disciplines of psychology or psychiatry. Nor were there *insane* asylums, just general asylums for the lawless and unproductive.

Some of the first insanity laws in Italy and England during the nineteenth century stipulated that harmless mentally ill patients should live with their families, even if it meant they were confined to a small outbuilding or chained to a tree.[17] It was not only the moral responsibility of the family to care for its own, especially children; it was an economic requirement because they could work at home. Someone who did not have the use of his legs was more likely to end up in an asylum than someone who heard voices in his head but was still able to contribute to the household. Before capitalism, rural European families were ideally self-sufficient because communities were organizations of interdependent individuals. Even impoverished · people who owned no land at least had customary rights to the local plots and pastures where they were born, raised, and lived.

Imagine the European farmer before capitalism. A feudal lord, if the farmer has one, might care for him and his dependents, but most farmers produce mainly for the family and trade only some surplus. The farmer's world is ordained by God and enforced by both the church and the state. The eighteenth-century Enlightenment idea that man's perfection comes from free will has yet to emerge, so the farmer has only a limited concept of human choice and mobility. It is God and not the human who is the center of the world. One would have been hard-pressed to find an ethos of self-improvement, autonomy, or personality development driven internally by an individual himself. In the absence of the "every man for himself" secular ideology of capitalism, with its emphasis on personal striving and success, the farmer does not pursue great profit. There were certainly greedy people. But if someone was greedy, he was greedy because of his character and not because he was fighting for himself in a competitive marketplace of individuals.[18]

European governments would eventually build asylums to house people who didn't work, but first the economy had to change. The gradual transition from feudalism to capitalism motivated governments to begin a massive land-privatization movement, in Europe and in the Spanish colonies in the Americas, to uproot subsistence farmers. Because the farmers produced mostly for themselves, the emerging bourgeoisie believed that the farmers were a barrier to economic growth and progress. By the seventeenth century, the British evicted tenants, raised rents, increased taxes, and initiated a policy called "enclosure" with the goal of ending subsistence farming and eliminating small farms.[19] "Enclosure" was the process of fencing off privately held lands to prevent people from using their customary rights of access to them. Non-landowners and other poor people had previously been able to eke out a subsistence in the countryside because, by tradition (but with no formal legal rights), they were permitted to hunt on or cultivate land within their communities. Enclosure ended those rights. It disenfranchised the poor, and the higher taxes compelled many smaller landholders to sell their land to wealthier owners who could produce food for urban markets and export.

Entire villages were razed. Many people who were unable to provide for themselves because they were poor or had serious mental illnesses or intellectual disabilities left their communities to search for work in fast-growing cities. The eighteenth-century economist Sir James Steuart eloquently described this uprooting in both capitalist and gendered terms: "Their parent, Earth, has in a manner banished them from her bosom; they have her no more to suckle them in idleness; industry has gathered them together, labour must support them, and this must produce a surplus for bringing up children."[20] Kinship relations eroded as people moved to towns and cities, away from their extended families. And, over time, urban-industrialized society would become increasingly responsible for controlling people whose differences might have been tolerated at home.[21]

The life of the poor person was just as wretched under capitalism as it was under feudalism, but wretched in a different way. Because capitalist economies can exist only in capitalist societies, a new kind of social being developed during the industrial revolution: the modern individual, a person with freedoms only capitalism could have devised. Workers were free to break from tradition, to begin to imagine themselves as competing individuals, and with the false belief that, as individuals, all people were equal from the start. Governments would promise liberty, the ability to own private property, and the freedom to communicate directly with God in whatever language a person spoke, even if one could not read or write.[22] The period known as "the Enlightenment" or "the Age of Reason," which spanned roughly the entire eighteenth century, bequeathed to Europe a new hierarchy for the emerging industrial economy and for science: work over inactivity, reason over faith, individual freedoms over political and religious authority.

Outside of the communal farm or the household, the individual was now also free to be his own mode of surveillance, free to discipline himself and not require discipline from an external coercive force. Moral capacity was supposed to reside within the individual, a person "true to himself" and capable of improving and perfecting both his character and his economic productivity. And if he could not be responsible for himself—whether he was psychologically or physically impaired due to illness, injury, or age— he would be exiled to an institution. In a world in which everyone ideally controlled his own destiny, no one suffered by accident. Every individual was accountable for his own misfortunes. Accordingly, asylums would be designed to segregate and punish the idle, often brutally and in squalid cells, and prisons were designed to produce guilt.[23] Modernity blames the victim.

At this point in European history, the question of whether people were treated better in confinement or at home is irrelevant, as they could live terrible lives in both places. The important point is that at home they were just family members, not examples of a disease. At home, a disabled person might be known simply as "Crazy John" or "Mute Jane." In the asylum, over time, the idle would become new types of people: the "insane," the "cripple," the "idiot." Doctors came to define mental and physical disabilities primarily in terms of the failure to function properly in the economy, a view that lives on in the contemporary definition of mental illnesses and unexplained neurological symptoms as "functional impairments," and also in the World Health Organization's definition of mental health, which includes the phrase "productive work."

I'm not suggesting that anyone devised a plan to value people in capitalist terms. Historical transformations are rarely the product of deliberate action; they are the result of a multitude of factors that act in concert to shape our beliefs and behaviors, often without our ever being aware of what is happening until it has already happened. This is why the great thinkers of the modern age, like Freud, Weber, Spinoza, and Marx, argued that the goal of social science is to expose the powerful but hidden forces that shape our assumptions about the world. As Marx famously put it, "It is not the consciousness of men that determines their existence but their social existence that determines their consciousness."[24] It follows that we cannot purposefully change our consciousness unless we unmask the historical processes that created it.

In his monumental book, *History of Madness*, the philosopher Michel Foucault identified a single year as a turning point in France, when French society's treatment of the poor changed from tolerance to large-scale confinement and control. It was 1656, when by royal decree, the Hôpital Général opened in a group of Parisian buildings where a powerful administrative staff would oversee idle and poor inmates. The buildings included the Salpêtrière, where, more than three hundred years later, in 1984, Foucault himself would die. The hospital's mandate read that it had been established "to prevent begging and idleness, the sources of all disorder."[25]

The hospital was not a medical or charitable institution. It was a mechanism for removing people who, for whatever reason, did not support the industrial revolution with their labor. People who worked deserved to be free; people who did not work, even people maimed in an accident, deserved only to be excluded. Nor was the hospital itself, or the other asylums that would soon be built, of much economic value. Asylum residents performed some menial municipal tasks, but their incarceration wasn't intended to provide cheap labor; incarceration was the right and moral thing to do to people who were so irrational and morally defective that they didn't work. Many elites also welcomed the confinement of the poor as a way of stemming a potential revolt by the lower classes.[26] Less than a year after the hospital opened, thousands of jobless poor French men and women would be put there, and just a few decades later, after more asylums were built, nearly one percent of the population of Paris was confined.

In Renaissance Europe, a common way to visually represent the exclusion of social misfits was the "ship of fools," an image from a late-fifteenth-century satire by German writer Sebastian Brant. In text, and in illustrations attributed to Albrecht Dürer, Brant's book, *Narrenschiff* (*The Ship of Fools*), depicts eccentric figures—symbols of people who were probably too dangerous to remain at home—crammed on a boat, headed away from shore, since there was no place on land in which to confine them. Just a few years after Brant's publication, Dutch artist Hieronymus Bosch painted another, and now more well-known, ship of fools.[27] It shows a monk and a nun sitting in a boat with a group of eight peasants in front of a picturesque landscape. The "fool" in the picture is clothed in the stereotypical costume of the court jester—leggings and a hood. One peasant balances a glass on his head, another uses a ladle as an oar; one is poised to strike another; and two are in the water, one of whom is hanging on to the boat, perhaps in danger of drowning, though the rest of the crew remains oblivious. The passengers do not appear to have any common purpose, because they lack reason and rationality.

As in Brant's work, on which Bosch's painting is likely based, the image wasn't completely disparaging because artists and writers often employed the fool or the madman to criticize society, government, and the church. Like a court jester, the fool was free to challenge authority, and so the boat filled with fools symbolized "society seemingly adrift in its madness."[28] The fool was not yet the insane person. He might be merely a "simpleton," or he might be a holy fool headed on a path to salvation. But he was certainly purer than any ordinary person, unadulterated by earthly corruption and reason, perhaps blessed by God, and someone who should be cared for.[29] Similarly, throughout the Middle Ages, people generally treated the poor with some kindness, if only because they expected that their generosity would lead to their salvation.[30] But with the growth of capitalism and scientific reason in Europe, the charitable work of the church gradually waned, replaced by an ethic of individualism and personal responsibility. Once asylums were created to house the idle, the poor person's identity changed. He was no longer just someone in need. He was a pauper—a new and shameful category of being.

It would take a bit longer for the concepts of the "insane" or the "lunatic" to emerge. Before the mid-1700s, the words "lunacy" and "insanity" were seldom noted in British hospital records (despite long-standing suspicion that insanity was a common but unspoken cause of death),[31] in large part because there was no separate medical category for the mentally ill. By the end of the 1700s, there were still few categories of deviancy, with the seriously mentally impaired included in the more general group of vagrants, physically handicapped, and criminals.

Even by the mid-1800s, when the asylum population of England was at its peak, the "insane" continued to be only crudely classified. In 1838, the American doctor Isaac Ray proposed that insanity could be divided into only two categories: "idiots" and "imbeciles." Idiocy, he said, was caused by congenital abnormalities; imbecility was caused by disorders of the mind that developed over one's life.[32] In Ireland, the approximately 500 patients in residence at the Limerick asylum in 1866 were classified as "Lunatics Probably Curable," "Lunatics Probably Incurable," "Lunatics, Idiots," and "Lunatics Epileptics."[33] The nineteenth-century Poor Laws in England, which provided welfare to the poor only in the context of workhouses (institutions where poor, unemployed men, women, and children could exchange manual labor for food and lodging), used all of these terms, and more, without defining any of them.[34] The words "normal" and "abnormal" would not be available as categories of human behavior until the mid-nineteenth century when mathematicians coined them to describe statistical averages.

The word "insanity" comes from the Latin *insānitātem*, and simply means "not healthy." In the eighteenth century, for example, someone could have "insanity of the mind" or "moral insanity," but "insanity" itself wasn't a specific diagnosis, and the word did not define a person's individual identity. As for "lunacy," it too was not yet a singular diagnosis. It was, instead, a symptom of something else. It was either a symptom of the degeneration of the brain or a temporary loss of reason caused by the phases of the moon—which is why the word "lunatic" comes from the Latin *lūna*, meaning moon. And with the exception of the most serious conditions, like psychosis, most people experienced and described emotional distress not in psychological terms but as bodily symptoms like fatigue, sweating, paralysis, uncontrollable movements, and insomnia.

While there have always been people who experienced chronic sadness, mood swings, and anxiety, who inexplicably stopped eating to the point of starvation, who had delusions and hallucinations, or who were addicted to alcohol, they were not defined completely by their differences. Only in the last century did men who were sexually attracted to men become "homo-sexuals," people addicted to alcohol become "alcoholics," the person who heard voices become a "schizophrenic." Only recently did mental illnesses brand the whole person, not just his or her behavior, with what Goffman called a "spoiled identity." To be sure, there had been names for sadness or depression, like melancholy or love melancholy, but these were feelings not identities, and talk of such problems was for the wealthy, the educated, and the titled, such as dukes, earls, and Shakespeare's Prince Hamlet. "By the time 'Hamlet' was first performed in 1609," writer Andrew Solomon notes, "melancholy was almost as much of a privilege as a disease."[35] For everyone else, purely *mental* afflictions were inconceivable—like the old, apocryphal story about the poor peasant who, after reading a book by Immanuel Kant, said, "I wish I had *his* problems."

European scientists had long struggled to understand what separated humans from other animals. The asylum and its residents—who appeared to have diverged from the ideals of humanity—now provided an answer. Humans, unlike animals, had reason. As early as 1609, we find these lines in *Hamlet*, where Shakespeare says, in the context of Ophelia's madness, that humans without reason may not be humans at all.

> *Divided from herself and her fair judgment,*
> *Without the which we are pictures, or mere beasts.*
> [Act 4, Scene 5]

For the staff of the new seventeenth-century asylums, the inability to work and govern oneself properly was caused by a lack of reason—that is, an individual's inability to think and behave in a way that conformed to the social order.[36] In their records, asylum workers often described the residents as beasts capable of incredible physical strength and impervious to intense heat, cold, and pain. They were animals who needed to be tamed and controlled, who in return for accepting discipline would receive free food and lodging.[37]

Throughout the eighteenth century, the mentally ill appeared in all media, from medical textbooks to the fine arts, as half human, half animal, as in William Blake's 1795 painting of Nebuchadnezzar, the ancient king whom God punishes with madness in the Book of Daniel. Blake shows him naked, crawling on all fours in a jungle, with long hair and nails resembling talons, eating grass.[38] The asylum resident had become a symbol of inhumanity and irrationality, a trope that writers and pamphleteers could use in their critiques of political unreason. In the poem "The Legion Club" (1736), for example, Jonathan Swift employed the asylum as a metaphor with which to expose the injustices of the Irish parliament:

> Tie them keeper in a tether
> Let them starve and stink together;
> Both are apt to be unruly,
> Lash them daily, lash them duly,
> Though 'tis hopeless to reclaim them'
> Scorpion Rods perhaps may tame them.[39]

Physical deformity also suggested a predisposition to animality and mental disease. Because there was as yet no clear separation between body and mind, the deformed individual was likely also insane. This is the sort of stigma we see in Shakespeare's plays, in which the villain's body is marked. *Richard III* thus begins as Richard—short and with the curvature of the spine that was once pejoratively called a "hunchback"—tells the audience that he is both a physical and a mental monster. Given the dominant beliefs at the time when he wrote the play—that one's criminal tendencies were inscribed on the body—Shakespeare certainly intended Richard to be fated by his nature: "I am determined to prove a villain," Richard says. Seventeenth-century physicians used physical traits to distinguish between different kinds of human beings, almost as if they were different species. Distinct sorts of people tended to appear, behave, or talk in certain ways, and some even had distinct odors; thus, for example, Christians widely believed that Jews smelled bad.[40]

Control of the body was crucial to the control of deviance. Some communities, such as the Puritans in the American colonies, believed that anyone without reason—and that included babies—was an animal that required appropriate discipline in order to be properly integrated into society. The Puritans placed babies in wooden go-carts to keep them from crawling like animals, employed neck stays to keep a baby's head upright, and sometimes placed wooden rods on toddlers' spines to make sure they acquired a fully human posture as early as possible.[41]

When the great seventeenth-century philosopher René Descartes argued that one's mind is distinct from one's body, he gave the upper classes of European societies an excuse for controlling the poor. If the mind and the body of the human were separate, elites reasoned, then perhaps elites were driven by their minds while the uneducated peasants laboring in the fields or in factories were driven, like animals, by instinct and appetite. Hence, authorities would have little compunction punishing the bodies of the poor when they did not do what their superiors demanded, or when they committed even minor crimes, like stealing a loaf of bread. For the poor, therefore, discipline for behavioral problems—whether crimes or any other kind of disorder—was administered against the body rather than the mind. As one result of this objectification of the body of the lower-class worker, during much of the 1700s in England there were more than 150 different crimes for which a person could be executed. The countless people who were hanged or beheaded in England were often referred to as "dead commodities"—the casualties of both "capital punishment and the punishment of capital."[42]

Witch hunts directed at women were another form of bodily control crucial to the development of capitalist societies during the time of enclosures. In England during the sixteenth and seventeenth centuries, the period in which witchcraft accusations reached their peak—and when the stage was just being set for capitalism to emerge—the responsibility to take care of one's poor neighbors was shifting from local communities to institutions like asylums and workhouses. Even in the earliest stages of capitalism, charity was frowned upon. Witch hunting and executions thus pitted the poor against the wealthy, men against women, neighbors against neighbors. You refuse a poor elderly widow who asks for food. The next day, one of your horses dies. You refuse a woman who asks for seeds to plant, and for the next week there is no rain. Your refusal to give violates a traditional moral duty to help your neighbor. You feel conflicted and blame her for your misfortune. Witchcraft fears thus became a kind of defense mechanism against guilt, as you were now the victim rather than the sinner.[43]

Witch hunts were central to a struggle over both class and gender. Thousands of people were killed, the vast majority of them poor women. In the transition to capitalism, there was an intensified patriarchal order aimed at maximizing wealth, which included the number of children one had. Confident that population growth was the key to personal and national wealth, men were afraid of anything that interfered with reproduction and their power to control women's bodies. Women were considered, at best, morally inferior to men and, at worst, conspirators plotting to undermine economic progress. In England, France, and Spain, men suspected that women were preventing pregnancies, killing infants, causing childhood diseases, or making sexual pacts with the devil. "In a village or small town of a few thousand people," one historian wrote, "where at the peak of the witch-hunt dozens of women were burned in the space of a few years or even a few weeks, no man could feel safe and be sure that he did not live with a witch."[44] And the lower a woman's status, the more likely she was to be ruled by her body, like an automaton, without reason. The transition to capitalism was thus, in a phrase, an attack on the body.[45]

Scientists would soon argue that women were more closely connected to nature than men, that their bodies were naturally designed to function for the reproduction and feeding of babies. Even menstruation paralleled the movement of the moon. In contrast, men were designed to control nature (including women). And because, in their view, women were also governed more by their bodies than by reason and rationality, women were also more susceptible than men to mental illnesses. It wouldn't be long before the process of harnessing women's bodies for capitalism changed the language of medicine. Doctors would call childbirth a process of "labor and delivery," menstruation "failed production," and menopause "a factory in decline."[46]

CHAPTER 2

THE INVENTION OF MENTAL ILLNESS

*Behind prison walls are those who transgress the
laws that imprison society.*

Destroy Yourselves (1968), Serge Bard, director

Mental illnesses were not named or classified because there was any
new scientific knowledge about the mind or because the mentally ill were
singled out for confinement. "It was the depths of confinement itself," Foucault writes, "that generated the phenomenon."[1] Until confinement, doctors had never before seen so many deviant individuals in a single space.
Confinement thus created the conditions in which doctors could observe
people, generate the concept of mental illness, separate diseases of the body
from diseases of the mind, and attempt to establish psychiatry as a new
branch of medicine. And in this world into which mental illness would soon
emerge as a distinct object of study, mostly well-meaning doctors believed
that confinement represented real progress.

The mentally ill were a society's undesirable, physically excluded from the community as a novel kind of human being, but now conceptually included into the new world of science and rationality. Doctors believed that patients could improve and eventually rejoin society only if first separated from their communities and placed in new homes with new rules and routines. Susan Sontag noted that the same was true with tuberculosis (TB) during the nineteenth century. "Like TB," she wrote, "insanity is a kind of exile." It is no accident, she added, that "the most common metaphor for an extreme psychological experience viewed positively—whether produced by drugs or by becoming psychotic—is a trip."[2] Not surprisingly, by the beginning of the twentieth century, once TB was contained and on the decline in the United States and Europe, TB sanatoriums were converted into asylums for the insane.

Foucault chose the ship of fools as the dominant image for his history of madness. Though rare, there were indeed a few such ships; one of the earliest left Frankfurt in 1399 to carry a man, who had walked the streets naked, away from the city. But what really mattered was not how many ships there were but how the ship served as a metaphor of exclusion. As a metaphor, the ship and its madmen embodied the contradiction of confinement in asylums: the madman at sea disappeared, yet never really left. He remained in the imagination of the society that created him as a powerful symbol of unreason.

In both England and France, exile and unreason figured prominently in art and literature. Since 1330, England's most famous asylum, Bethlem, had been a home for a small number of the most impoverished residents of London. Despite the fact that, until the late 1600s, Bethlem had at any one time only two to three dozen inmates, everyone in England knew the name. Parents warned their children that if they were naughty they'd be sent there. Bethlem appears in Shakespeare's *King Lear*, when Edgar of Gloucester disguises himself as a "Bethlam beggar," a "poor Tom." A 1637 English ballad called "Love's Lunacie" mentioned the horror:[3]

> *This Bethlem is a place of torment;*
> *Heere's fearfull notes still sounding;*

Here minds are fil'd with discontent,
And terrors still abounding.
Some shake their chaines in wofull wise,
Some sweare, some curse, some roaring,
Some shrieking out with fearfull cries,
And some their cloaths are tearing.

A century later, people sang songs about "Mad Tom o'Bedlam"[4] and continued to mention Bethlem in fiction and poetry.

Were you to look through seventeenth- and eighteenth-century paintings of asylums, you'd see images of not only petty criminals but also caged
people with what appear to be mania, depression, and hallucinations. There
are contorted and suffering bodies, sometimes violent, sometimes sexually
provocative. Throughout the eighteenth century, asylums were miserable
places. Reports from France, written in the late 1700s, told of patients in
the Bicêtre Hospital just south of Paris sleeping in wet rooms on nothing
but straw. Inmates at the Salpêtrière Hospital in Paris occupied cells located
near sewers that frequently flooded. The inspector of hospitals, M. Des-
portes, wrote of the Salpêtrière that "cells are invaded by hordes of rats . . .
mad women have been found with bites all over their feet, hands, and
faces."[5] In England, tourists to Bethlem at the end of the eighteenth century paid a small fee to get a glimpse of the insane, and many described the
horrors. They saw inmates without clothes, even during winter, and men
and women chained to walls and beds. One man wore an iron collar tied
to a chain that extended up the wall so that guards could control his movements, like an animal on a leash. In 1799, a four-year-old child was among
the residents, diagnosed with insanity and kept from her mother for four
months—probably not an extraordinary occurrence since doctors did not
believe young children had developed reason.[6]

In the late 1770s, when British prison reformer John Howard visited the
vast network of asylums that had emerged throughout Europe, he was dis-
turbed to find that hardened criminals were often kept in the same space
as the bankrupt and the insane.[7] He understood that the goal of confine-

ment was to create a new space for people who diverged dramatically from what had become the ideal person in emerging capitalism.[8] But he, and others throughout Europe, proposed a more efficient and humane policy of separating people into different categories so they could be controlled more precisely and perhaps even cared for. The criminal, the beggar, and the person hearing voices each needed different identities, kinds of discipline, and institutions. The British built the first prisons because they wanted to separate the criminals from the insane. In other words, prisons couldn't really be invented until a category of mental illness had been invented.

In the context of the asylum, "insanity" gradually took shape as a distinct label and a stigma—an actual and deplorable social identity apart from other kinds of difference. The profession of psychiatry also slowly emerged, along with insanity, melancholia, and a small number of other labels, though the first psychiatrists were not really doctors. They were, for the most part, administrators and caretakers. Even by the turn of the nineteenth century, when my great-grandfather Julius tried his hand at psychoanalysis, most doctors, and all medical schools, did not yet consider psychiatry a legitimate branch of medicine. Psychiatrists were sometimes stigmatized as if they had the same diseases as their patients. Even throughout the twentieth century, Hollywood writers and film producers would stereotype psychiatrists as flawed, duplicitous, and neurotic.

In the late 1700s, the famous French physician Philippe Pinel— sometimes called "the father of psychiatry"—led the charge to make asylums better places for both inmates and doctors. He treated his patients with discipline, but also with conversation and kindness when possible. He wrote treatises on "madness" to document the various forms of cognitive and emotional impairment among the thousands of people confined in Paris. Pinel's approach became known as "moral treatment," but not in the sense that we use the word "moral" today. We usually think moral means the right and the good. Moral for Pinel actually meant psychological. The moral denoted a person's mind and character as opposed to his physical or material existence.[9]

Through this concept of the moral came a new definition of unreason.

The French word for madness, *folie*, had previously meant an inability to follow the rules of social and economic life. Now madness referred not only to the alienation of the person from society but also to the alienation of the mind from the body: *aliénation mentale*.[10] In a major break from the past, doctors argued that the mind, though seated in the brain, could have its own disorders. And that is exactly what insanity became—not just any kind of deviance but a set of diseases in its own right for doctors of the mind, soon called "alienists," to study and treat.

Well before insane asylums were conceived, Descartes provided the first inklings of the modern concept of stigma when he argued that the only thing he could be certain of in the world was that he wasn't mad. He said he was rational and didn't look or think like people who were mad. As my grandfather would write in the 1970s, Descartes set the stage for mental illnesses to be stigmatized by isolating the "mental" from all the other factors that shape us. Although doctors stressed the unity of the body and mind well into the mid-nineteenth century,[11] to say that body and mind always influenced each other was still to accept that they were two distinct entities.[12]

But it was the new doctors and asylum administrators, not the philosophers, who first defined mental *illnesses* as discrete conditions and created institutions as a mechanism to marginalize and silence the mentally ill in the name of science. Mental illness and stigma were born together.

In the Enlightenment, science wasn't just a search for knowledge. It was also a search for how to use knowledge and reason to improve humanity. If the right techniques were employed, the asylum could discipline the inmate, control the passions that might undermine society and the nation at large in a time of rapid change, and help heal the disordered mind. Asylum administrators thus used their institutions as laboratories for imaginative and experimental therapies.

Take the cat piano. German physician Johann Reil came up with the idea of a *katzenclavier* to help repair the vitality of patients whose senses had been dulled or were—pun intended—catatonic:

[Cats would be placed] in a row with their tails stretched behind them. And a key board fitted out with sharpened nails would be set over them. The struck cats would provide the sound. A fugue played on this instrument—when the ill person is so placed that he cannot miss the expressions of their faces and play of these animals—must bring Lot's wife herself from her fixed state into conscious awareness.[13]

Reil explicitly advocated torture on humans as well, including the use of red-hot irons, bullwhips, and submersion in water to resemble drowning.[14] Even as late as the mid-nineteenth century, Belgian physician Joseph Guislain described his "Chinese Temple," a cage containing the patient that would be lowered into a pool of water. Believing he was drowning, the patient would be shocked into a new condition, a new life. If we are to believe his reports, the Swedish physician Georg Engström placed depressed patients in sacks full of ants to animate their senses. And in Germany, J. H. Lehmann claimed to have placed similar patients in tubs filled with eels.[15]

Regardless of whether these devices were ever constructed or used—and there is no proof they were—the relevant point is that psychiatry originated in multiple sites as an attempt to shock the mind. Although this might sound like a precursor to modern electroconvulsive therapy, the two have little in common. The rationale behind the inventions does, however, bear some similarity to mid-twentieth-century psychoanalytic theories that convulsive and frightening therapies somehow help the patient recognize and release pent-up aggressive thoughts that can then be discussed in psychotherapy. The "fear of annihilation," my grandfather and a coauthor wrote, can create a sense of "infantile helplessness" that compels patients to accept the therapist as a caring, parental figure.[16] Reil and others similarly used fear to "awaken" the person from a state of senselessness or melancholy, to make them acutely aware of their senses and become more self-conscious of their absence of reason.

There was, in what sounds so cruel to the twenty-first-century reader, a therapeutic intention. For Reil, the insane were people to be treated, not feared. In addition to harsh therapies, he also recommended sexual intercourse, exercise, and a good diet. In a sentiment that foreshadowed Freud, Reil seemed more afraid of civilization than of the insane, and he aimed to show that the insane were actually no madder than the rest of the world—perhaps less so. In 1803, he wrote of what he called the "maelstrom" of the "madhouse."

> *Pride of ancestry, egoism, vanity, greed, and all the other idols of human weakness guide the rudder in this maelstrom, just as in the ocean of the large world. Yet every fool in Bicêtre and Bedlam stands more open and innocent than those from the great madhouse of the world. In the world, the vengeful ravage.... But [within the madhouse] no villages smolder, and no men whimper in their own blood.*[17]

In fact, it was Reil who, in 1808, coined the word "psychiatry" (literally, "mind doctor," from the ancient Greek *psukhē*, meaning mind and soul, and the ancient Greek *iatros*, meaning doctor). Sometimes called "the German Pinel," Reil intended psychiatry to be the branch of medicine that addressed the complicated relationship between the body and the mind.[18]

Alongside capitalism, a new vocabulary of the mind arose that denoted control: words like "order," "laws," and "regulation." The old images of chaos in the madhouse in the sixteenth-century paintings by Bosch and Hogarth were, in the late eighteenth century, replaced by images of order and serenity, as if the asylum were a well-run hospital or a sanctuary. Regulation and classification were vital to proper social functioning, whether inside or outside the asylum. For capitalists at the beginning of the industrial revolution, there was a natural order of things in which humans existed; it was a hierarchical order that required some people and some communities to be subordinated to others, their bodies managed and organized. Elites and slave owners could not conceive that their servants or slaves were unfree or discriminated against; they were where they naturally belonged. (As we all know, when the writers of the U.S. Declaration of Independence wrote that "all men are created equal," they were speaking only of white male landowners.) Nor could elites imagine that the people in asylums were being mistreated. When Pinel released the residents of his asylum from chains, he replaced the chains with straitjackets and truly thought he was liberating them.[19]

When European countries did enact significant asylum reforms, it wasn't because of guilt. It was because capitalism required those reforms. Since low-wage workers were increasingly important to the economy, the growing bourgeoisie, Foucault tells us, began to realize that confinement was "an economic mistake."[20] Why keep or hide people in an asylum when they could be put to work as a cheap labor force, and could perform some of the menial labor no one else wanted to do in the city or in the countryside? Most of the people confined in France in the early 1800s were still either criminals or the insane, but the purpose of confinement had begun to shift. Severe discipline still dominated asylum and prison life, but increasingly less so, in favor of a more humane approach that would restore the inmate's health and his or her capacity to work.

One impetus for this change was the emerging consensus that mental illnesses could not be understood solely as medical or biological diseases. They were also illnesses of the mind and spirit and were therefore more responsive to human intervention than were the more purely physical ailments.[21] This sentiment was reproduced in England and in the United States, where by the mid-1800s asylum administrators started to believe that all patients had the ability to regain sanity. Asylum stays shortened significantly, to two years or fewer, so that patients could return to work and family.[22] Toward the end of the nineteenth century, the staffing of asylums would change too, as administrators gradually yielded authority to the alienists (the predecessors of the doctors we today call psychiatrists), who treated rather than simply managed madness.[23] But that important shift required an intermediate step, often called the era of moral treatment.

In 1790, the sixty-year-old Quaker businessman and philanthropist William Tuke, from Yorkshire, England, learned that another Quaker in his community, Hannah Mills, had inexplicably died after living just six weeks in an asylum for the insane. No one knew for sure whether Hannah had been mistreated, but Tuke's daughter Ann was troubled enough by the news to implore her father to open his own, more humane asylum, which he did in 1796. He called it, simply, the Retreat.[24]

The Tuke family retreat in England, like Pinel's hospital in France, was part of the piecemeal movement away from confinement and shelter to care and treatment. However, Tuke's method, known as "moral treatment," did not initially involve kindness and emotional support. Moral treatment began with the presumption that all patients, like all human beings, had the capacity for reason, but only if their bodies could regain control over their minds. New arrivals had to surrender themselves to the asylum authorities. One strategy was to first weaken the afflicted completely, to remove their ability to resist the asylum keeper—indeed, to frighten them if necessary. Though free to move around the hospital grounds, they were under constant surveillance and were not allowed to leave.

There were countless rules of behavior to ensure that the retreat was a place of order and self-control, and residents were physically restrained and disciplined if they failed to do their chores. Each resident was, quite literally, a "patient," meaning a passive recipient of treatment—hence the double usage of the word, an adjective to describe tolerance of suffering and a noun to denote the sufferer. But the ultimate goal was to replace external coercion with self-constraint. Residents, called "friends" in the manner of the Quakers, would be granted new freedoms if they showed self-discipline, responded positively to a system of rewards and punishments, and began to defeat their symptoms.

As a Quaker, Tuke discouraged violent therapies, but in most asylums during the era of moral treatment physicians continued to induce vomiting, cause starvation and dehydration, carry out blood lettings, and administer acids on the scalp to create blisters. One of Tuke's contemporaries, the reformer Francis Willis, even treated his famous patient, King George III of England, as a beast that needed to be subdued. In order to heal the king (who had become "insane" with recurrent manic episodes), Willis chained him to a stake and beat and starved him. Even in the age of moral treatment, the "mad" person required discipline and dread, even if he was the king of Great Britain and Ireland.

In addition to running their hospitals, administrators such as Tuke and Pinel also wrote detailed observations of their patients and published scientific articles. They then drew on this growing literature to recommend that knowledge gained from within the asylum could be applied to society at large. By virtue of their amassed knowledge, they had now become experts on how to control human behavior in a range of places—at work, in the home, on the street, in schools and prisons. The psychiatrist's domain of expertise gradually included anything that was not in order—from divorce to delusions, mania to masturbation. Pinel, in fact, wrote that the same differences one sees among ordinary people, like melancholy or hypochondriasis, were present in the asylum as well, only in a more extreme form.[25] A visionary, he suggested both that mental illnesses, including those that involved delusions and hallucinations, were distributed through the general population and that they could be seen as existing on a spectrum. He noted that some people who were depressed, manic, or heard voices went on with their lives unimpaired while others were seriously disabled.

In this new view of mental disturbance, doctors encouraged one another to study even the most common and private acts as evidence of the functioning of the mind. Sex was a special curiosity because so many doctors believed that the sex organs held the key to understanding and treating mental illnesses. Even the ancient Greeks believed that emotional disturbances were caused by problems of sexual passion and anatomy, especially one's uterus—hence the term "hysteria," which comes from the Greek word for uterus, *hystera*—an organ the Greeks believed existed in both men and women, though in women this pouch was inside the body while in men it was outside (what anatomists would later call the scrotum). One historian wrote that, during the first decades of the 1800s, "physicians and educators became obsessed with the personal sexual habits of those in their charge."[26] Some of the earliest developments in plastic surgery derive from efforts to alter sexual desire and behavior by operating on the genitals, or on parts of the body believed to be related to sex, like the nose. By the end of the 1800s, most scientists believed that the shape of the nose reflected a person's character, and that there were similarities between nasal and vaginal tissues and between the periodicity of nosebleeds and menstruation. In Europe, many psychoanalysts—including Freud—sent their patients to surgeons to have their noses operated on. So when doctors criticized the early German plastic surgeon Johan Jacobs for needlessly changing the shape of his patients' noses, he countered that he wasn't doing cosmetic surgery; he was not operating on the nose at all, but on the mind.[27]

Few aspects of sex aroused as much intellectual passion in the emerging medical professions as masturbation, because it was widely believed to be the primary cause of mental illnesses. Masturbation was also associated with antisocial behavior since people tended to do it when they were alone, and in secret. Doctors in France, England, and Germany during the nineteenth century believed that masturbation was the basis for all sexual perversions and self-destructive behaviors and called it "self-abuse." As an example of how the logic of capitalism extended to the body and mind, one doctor compared wasting sperm through masturbation to "throwing money out of the window."[28]

Abnormal sex—like masturbation—was not just the root of mental illnesses but a crime against nature and a threat to the nation. It could cause an entire country to degenerate—a belief that persists to this day among some evangelists and political conservatives. As early as 1775, in Paris, J. F. Bertrand opened a wax museum that depicted "masturbators" with various diseases and stages of physical deterioration—a boy without a penis, a woman with ulcers on her vagina—all caused by masturbation. The museum remained open for four decades and in some years was a popular destination for school field trips. Masturbators were not just antisocial. They were potential conspirators against the state. Jews, for example, were stereotyped as both enemies of the state and compulsive masturbators. Only marriage and proper sex and love could protect against what Dr. Balthazar Bekker called the "heinous sin of self-pollution," and prevent all the sicknesses caused by masturbation, including diarrhea, acne, paralysis, spinal deformity, epilepsy, memory loss, fatigue, and suicide.[29]

Writing in 1854, a French physician named T. Parvin did not think he was exaggerating when he said, "Neither the plague, nor war, nor smallpox, nor a crowd of similar evils have resulted more disastrously for humanity, than the habit of masturbation: it is the destroying element of civilized society."[30] In England, several residents of insane asylums were admitted for "masturbation,"[31] and "masturbator" became a diagnosis. Well into the twentieth century, some American doctors even advocated circumcision of both boys and girls as a way to reduce the frequency of masturbation, and there is considerable consensus among historians that circumcision became commonplace for boys born in Anglophone countries precisely for this reason.[32]

Today, few people sitting at a table eating their Kellogg's Corn Flakes or granola know, or even want to know, that their breakfast was invented and marketed to prevent masturbation. Nutritionist John Harvey Kellogg (1879–1920) and his brother Will Keith Kellogg ran a sanatorium in Battle Creek, Michigan, where people with chronic illnesses could recover their health through relaxation and prescribed diet—so-called rest-cures, a term coined by the great Civil War physician Weir Mitchell. The Kelloggs believed that a dysfunction of excess sexual desire and activity was the basis of nearly all diseases, mental and physical. Any use of the sexual organs for pleasure was toxic and shocked the entire body. They also believed that diet was the key to curing such excess. Spicy foods created sexual desire, including the desire to masturbate, while bland foods inhibited it. In addition to insanity, John Kellogg listed thirty-nine signs that someone was masturbating. They included bashfulness, fickleness, sleeping too little, sleeping too much, love of solitude, and acne. He also named common sites for the transgression, such as barns, garrets, and secluded places in the woods. One suspects that Kellogg turned many parents into spies.[33]

The brothers devised a concoction of corn, oat, and wheat flour, which they baked and then split off into flakes. At the time, they insisted no sugar be added; it was intentionally tasteless. They called the cereal "Granula," until they discovered that another manufacturer of cereal was already using that name. So they changed it to "Granola." To prevent masturbation, Kellogg also advocated vegetarianism, exercise, yogurt enemas, binding a man's foreskin with silver wire to make masturbation painful, and burning off a woman's clitoris with carbolic acid.[34] John Harvey Kellogg was not shy about telling audiences that he had never consummated his own marriage and that all of his children were adopted.[35] For the same reason—to prevent what he called copulatory insanity and "sexual solitaire"—the Presbyterian minister Sylvester Graham (1794–1851) created the Graham cracker, also without sugar. Bland foods and moderation in all forms would reduce sexual stimulation. Graham believed that masturbation caused short stature, bad posture, baldness, tooth decay, idiocy, and ulcers, among other afflictions.[36]

Graham and Kellogg were not unusual thinkers in their day. From the mid- to late nineteenth century, one way that poor urban dwellers in the United States reacted to their plight was to protest the industrial world as secular, evil, and impure. In England, doctors and journalists compared industrial cities to Sodom and Gomorrah, "jungles" that were "breeding grounds of homosexuality and masturbation."[37] The proof was obvious to the scientists who had begun counting the number of "insane" Americans. The insane were concentrated in the cities, living in slums, jails, or asylums. Furthermore, well-known writers and physicians at the time wrote that "self-abuse" was a form of sexual excess that depleted human beings of their strength and reason. Having surrendered their minds to their instincts, masturbators were no better than the "animals" in asylums. No wonder masturbation has long evoked a sense that one has done something wrong. Because people internalize the values of their time, they no longer need society to shame them; they can do it on their own. Guilt needs no audience—only the reflex to stigmatize oneself.

Ultimately, from these changes in economics and social thought came one of the greatest and least-known of revolutions. It was just as important to the development of the social order as madness was, just as crucial to the creation and alienation of the "abnormal." I am talking about the invention of the female, a category of person that didn't exist before the late 1700s. I know it sounds unbelievable but, until then, the world had been populated only by males.

CHAPTER 3

THE DIVIDED BODY

For those that have the strictest searchers been,
Find women are but men turned outside in.

Aristotle's Masterpiece (1684)

The great sixteenth-century writer Michel de Montaigne told the story of Marie Garnier, a teenager who lived on the banks of the Marne river in the north of France. She was unremarkable, except that she had a little hair on her chin. The other girls teased her, calling her "the beard." It came to pass one day, Montaigne said, that she was chasing after a pig in a wheat field and came to a wide ditch. "When she put forth all her strength in taking a leap," he wrote, "the distinctive signs of manhood showed themselves."[1] Marie ran home, crying. She told her mother that her guts were coming out of her body. The perplexed doctors examined her but could only conclude that what she called guts were actually a penis and a scrotum; they said she had exerted so much energy that the heat of her body turned her into a man. The Cardinal of Lenoncourt renamed her Germain, since she now needed a masculine name, and gave her boy's clothes. In the village, the girls composed a song to warn of the dangers of jumping too far and getting overheated. When Germain reached adulthood, stocky and with a thick red beard, he joined the army of the king at Vitry-le-François in Champagne.

Long ago, there were many such stories of women who became men. There were also tales of men who became women. The stories don't make sense to us today because scientists no longer believe, as they did in every Western civilization until the late 1700s, that men and women were different manifestations of a single underlying sex: male. Just as Eve's body came from Adam's rib, or Eve and Adam came from one God, the male body and the female body were superior and inferior versions of the same sex.

Economic imperatives during the industrial revolution played an important part in halting the sexual fluidity of the past and fixing male and female identities and social roles. Capitalism would also become a tool to reinforce the subordination of women. Men encouraged women to remain in their homes and justified their isolation as a way to protect women from illegitimate pregnancies and to support the health and productivity of the worker. Moreover, doctors began to see nonproductive or nonprocreative kinds of sex, such as masturbation, oral, anal, and homosexual sex, as pathological and dangerous because they limited population growth and industry.[2]

The story of the stigma of mental illness cannot be fully told without the story of this transition from a one-sex to a two-sex world. The first psychiatrists quickly embraced the topic of what was women's most dangerous and least understood quality—their unique sex and sexuality—and began to consider as insane those women who resisted their now biologically defined sex roles, such as women who read too much, wanted jobs, or disobeyed their husbands. As a result, both the study of a specifically female sexuality and the effort to control unruly women would become cornerstones of modern psychiatric thought.

Until the late 1700s, there wasn't even a separate anatomical lexicon for the female genitalia. The clitoris was called a penis, the uterus an internal scrotum. The ovaries were testicles, the vulva and labia were foreskin, the vagina was an inverted penis, and the fallopian tubes were the epididymis.

In fact, as any twenty-first-century biologist will tell you, these are indeed homologous pairs of organs, and the male and female genitalia look virtually identical in the first trimester of a fetus. There were, of course, two genders—man and woman—but those identities came from society not nature. When Marie Garnier became a man, her gender changed but not her sex. It is likely that many of the people who changed their gender over time were what we today call intersex—a condition well described in the medical literature—raised as a girl or a boy until puberty changed the course of their development and social identity. In this one-sex world, Queen Elizabeth I could refer to herself as both a feeble virgin and the nation's husband, and artists could represent Eve's partner, Adam, as pregnant.[3] Before the Enlightenment, there were even paintings of Christ with breasts.

The belief in western Europe that men and women were all members of just one sex was the result of centuries of thought in which writers proposed that all living things were linked together in a hierarchy, in harmonious opposition. Man might be opposed to woman in myriad ways, just as the narwhal with its single tusk was opposed to the unicorn, but they were just different expressions of life along a continuum. In this world, men and women both bled, but women menstruated only because they had a cooler temperature and thus had a surplus of blood that needed to be released. Moreover, all the fluids of the body—milk, blood, semen, and fat—were interchangeable. For example, a pregnant or nursing woman would not menstruate because her body turned her surplus blood into milk.[4] A man with too much blood might have a nosebleed, but he would then suffer from a lack of semen. Such correspondence exists today in societies that use the same word for semen and menstrual blood.[5]

By the early 1800s, the reverse was true in European thought. Society had previously defined sex; now sex would define society. In the precapitalist one-sex world, one could move, like Marie Garnier, along the continuum of maleness. In the two-sex world, populated by both males and females, sex was fixed and inscribed in medical texts with new words to describe the female anatomy. Today we tend to think about sexual fluidity as something modern, but the reality is that sex has been fixed for only two centuries of the long history of Western civilization, and a number of non-Western societies have, for generations, recognized three, four, or five sexes, and with little or no stigma. The *hijras* in India are neither male nor female—though most were born with male genitalia—and are generally revered.[6] In Indonesia, on the island of Sulawesi, the Bugi ethnic group recognizes five genders: man, woman, trans woman, trans man, and androgynous or intersex individuals.[7] In Polynesia, the *mahu* are also neither male nor female, and they engage in sex with both men and women, without any sort of sexual stigma.[8]

This rather abrupt change from one sex to two sexes was not the result of any new knowledge of the female or male body. Scientists knew little more about human anatomy in 1800 than they did in 1700. What changed was the demand for a division of human beings into stable categories, a demand that was essential for social order in an increasingly industrialized Europe. Science, in other words, didn't change anything on its own but rather did the work of culture by defining a new reality. And in this world, there was little room for any idea that sex was a spectrum or continuum along which humans could move. A clear-cut distinction between male and female roles, and between the home and work, the private and public spheres, was essential, even if in most industrial English working-class families both men and women worked. An ideology of manliness, male privilege, and superiority also fit well with the new image of the strong, independent male worker who was at no risk of becoming as soft and vulnerable as men believed women to be. In the one-sex world, women were thought to be passionate, with healthy sexual appetites. In the two-sex world, the ideal woman was a weak, passive vessel, prone to the illnesses, such as hysteria and lunacy, that came from being female.

Criminals, the insane, and others who had previously been grouped together in an undifferentiated mass of idle workers now had fixed and distinct identities, and so did men and women. Women were denied the opportunity to claim that they were by nature just like males, even if imperfect males, and the male sex had become the ideal, "the measure of all things."[9] But early capitalism did more than just separate men and women into distinct sexes. It made it possible for men to subordinate women in a new kind of hierarchical social order. The world was now comprised of males who gained prestige by killing (for example, as hunters or soldiers), and females who were destined by nature to give life; creative males who altered the earth through agriculture, art, architecture, and other kinds of production, and procreative females who merely reproduced. Women, in the words of Simone de Beauvoir, were "more enslaved" to the animality of the human species.[10]

As "proof" of their closer connection to nature, menstruation followed the lunar cycles in nature; and just as "lunacy" came from the Latin *lūna*, "menstruation" came from another word for moon, the Latin *mensis* (month). From the perspective of the biologist, "the ovary . . . became the driving force of the whole female economy."[11] The female body, and therefore the woman, was reduced to its natural functions, whether described in the mechanistic terms of the biologist or the capitalist. The ovaries soon became a factory that produced eggs to be shipped and fertilized before labor and delivery, and that, in the case of slavery, could produce more human property.[12] Commenting on how women's biology led to emotional turmoil, one nineteenth-century doctor wrote that woman is "the victim of periodicity."[13] And now that sexual difference was determined by the body and not by the community, women were born stigmatized.

By the early 1800s, according to historians, "in moral discourse there was hardly any overlap between the active, rational, resolute male and the emotional, nurturing, malleable female. Woman was constructed as 'other' in a more absolute sense than ever before."[14] This separation made it even easier for experts to fix stereotypes of femaleness, including a tendency to equate women with mental illness. In 1798, the French philosopher Pierre-Jean-Georges Cabanis claimed that because women appeared to be physically weaker, and tended to have smaller brain volume than men (even when corrected for mens' larger body size), their health was always at risk and that in their daily lives "suffering dominates."[15] A woman should therefore be confined to the home where she is "best equipped for the care of children and the infirm who, like her, are of underdeveloped reasoning and/or destined for confinement."[16] Cabanis was certain that unmarried women were at even greater risk for both dementia and idiocy; marriage was like an asylum that protected women from these diseases.

The expansion of slavery, capitalism, and political power into Africa reinforced European efforts to see women's bodies, and especially non-European bodies, as fixed by their nature. In 1810, a South African show-man named Hendrik Cesars exhibited a southern African woman, Sara Baartman (whom Cesars called the "Hottentot Venus"), on a London stage.[17] Baartman would continue to be displayed, both clothed and naked, singing for a gawking public—an example of the "primitive" anatomy—in British and French theaters for five years until her death. After she died, and following her dissection by the famed zoologist Georges Cuvier, her genitalia were displayed at the Musée de l'Homme in Paris, before finally being repatriated in 2002.[18] Other African women were also exhibited, if not in freak shows then in laboratories, in the name of a new science of race. By reducing these women to their bodies and, in particular, to their sex organs, some scientists could even make the claim that Africans and Europeans were entirely different species.[19] The physical characteristics of the African woman—which the European doctors deemed to be an exaggerated form of the European genitalia—predisposed her to be promiscuous, and rooted her to her fate. Civilization was about controlling oneself, but also about a "superior race" controlling the sexual impulses of "others" (including women) for their own good. In British colonial literature, the entirety of sub-Saharan Africa (what the explorer Henry Morton Stanley called "the dark continent") was often likened to a mysterious, unknown female body waiting to be dominated and penetrated by Europe.[20] Freud himself called female sexuality "the dark continent" of psychology.[21]

If love in the nineteenth century was moral and sacred, sex was profane; if love was uniquely human and spiritual, sex was animalistic and material. As psychiatry continued to grow in Europe, in societies that separated the mind and the body, love became associated with the mind, and sex with the body. It followed that disorders of love then became mental rather than bodily disorders.[22] In fact, one of the first mental illnesses to have a name other than simply "madness," "lunacy," or "insanity" was "erotomania": madness from unrequited and sometimes delusional love. Approximately ten percent of the more than two thousand cases of madness in the records of the early-seventeenth-century English physician Richard Napier were caused by love.[23] Diseases of the body, in contrast, were caused not by disturbances of love but by the body's sexual needs. By the late 1800s, doctors had begun to explain tuberculosis as a disease that preferentially afflicted people who had lost the desire for sex. Doctors even prescribed sex as a treatment for tuberculosis. Cancer, conversely, became a disease caused by too much of a sex drive.[24]

In Britain during the late 1800s, the majority of asylum residents were women—in large part because of unprecedented poverty and unemployment. As a rule, the more poverty there was in a city, the more people one would find in asylums, and women had far fewer work options than men. Doctors began to link women's bodies with particular kinds of mental conditions: hysteria, nymphomania, "lactational insanity" (caused by weakness and malnutrition among mothers who nursed too much), and "ovarian insanity."[25] Believed to be governed more by nature than by culture, women were more susceptible to a lack of reason, and to lack of control over their emotions and behavior. In 1872, out of 58,640 certified lunatics in England and Wales, 31,822 (54 percent) were women.[26] At the same time, in the United States, institutionalized women, like those committed to the New York State Asylum for Idiots, were kept in custody for significantly longer periods of time than men.[27]

The behaviors that characterized female insanity were those that were incompatible with the idealized image of the Victorian woman. Women with insanity were distinguished by their lack of passivity, by their rebelliousness against the sexual order of the two-sex world. Insane women disliked being women. They rebelled against their subordination by men, and they enjoyed sex too much. Doctors (all men of course!) warned parents to look for signs of the onset of insanity, such as the desire to leave home and become a nurse.[28]

Like the invention of the two-sex world, the division between heterosexuality and homosexuality also emerged out of capitalism. If, in capitalism, the family was no longer the anchor for all productive work, then men and women were free to sell their labor outside of their kinship network and thus outside of the heterosexual family. Capitalism, historian John D'Emilio wrote, "created conditions that allowed some men and women to organize a personal life around their erotic/emotional attraction to their own sex."[29] The "traditional" family, D'Emilio argued, became more unstable. As a result, people were more invested in protecting it, and demonizing nonconformists. Eventually, doctors would develop the concepts of homosexuality/homosexual and heterosexuality/heterosexual to define people who either deviated from or adhered to the ideals of the family.

The words "homosexuality" and "heterosexuality" are thus recent inventions. Of course, men have had sex with men, and women with women, for as long as we know, and both churches and states condemned same-sex sex. But as the renowned historian of European sexuality George Mosse noted of the Catholic Church, "it judged the individual sex act rather than drawing consequences for an entire personality or way of life."[30] In fact, neither heterosexuals nor homosexuals (nor "heterosexuality" and "homosexuality") existed until psychologists coined those terms in 1892 and, in so doing, created a new kind of modern individual (and a new kind of "abnormality") defined in terms of a person's sexual preferences. As one consequence, doctors began to think of homosexuality as a kind of psychopathology, rather than just a form of deviance, only in the early twentieth century. The word "homosexuality" is so new that it did not even enter the *Oxford English Dictionary* until a 1976 revision.

Similarly, the ancient Greeks did not classify people as homosexual or heterosexual. They only classified as "sexual deviants" people who committed sexual acts deemed inappropriate. Same-sex sex was more often than not totally acceptable. It was acceptable if the dominant or insertive partner was of higher status than the passive or receptive partner. For example, if a man had *insertive* sex with a boy, a male slave, or a woman, the act was not distinguished from any other kind of appropriate sex.[31] On the other hand, if a citizen (and only men were citizens) had *receptive* sex with a boy, slave, or any other noncitizen, he was committing a perverse act. Sex was thus not something people did *together* but what one person of higher status did *to another* of lower status. Sexual passivity was incompatible with the ideals of virility and patriarchy, and one can still find this hierarchical logic in many parts of Latin America today, and in most American jails, where engaging in same-sex sex does not always mean one is a "homosexual."[32]

Even for the Puritans in the New World, sex between men was much more often tolerated than prosecuted, seen as an undesirable practice but not one that turned a person into an outcast. When the Puritans in New England did execute someone for a sexual abnormality—as far as historians know, this occurred only twice—it was not because he was a "homosexual" but because he had sex with men.[33] When Henry VIII passed his anti-buggery law in 1533 (which made nonvaginal sex illegal), men were certainly afraid of being caught having sex with other men, but they were just as afraid of being caught having nonvaginal sex with a woman. And they were certainly not afraid of being called homosexuals since that category did not yet exist. Through the end of the nineteenth century, it was therefore simply impossible for physically intimate men, or women, to be afraid that the discovery of their behavior would turn them into an entirely new kind of person—the "homosexual" as opposed to just someone who violated cultural norms. This is why, despite all the information about the young Abraham Lincoln's romantic relationship with his friend Joshua Speed,[34] it makes no sense to even ask whether Lincoln was gay or straight.

But once the identity was created, homosexuals could become scapegoats for social instability—which they were even well into the twentieth century when, in the McCarthy era, homosexuals were linked to conspiracy against the state and the economy. In fact, homosexuality was one of the key psychological conditions that helped psychiatry remain a method to regulate behavior. By turning homosexuality into a mental illness in the first half of the twentieth century, psychologists and psychiatrists would highlight the dangers of sex and sexuality, as a watch tower in the center of a prison yard illuminates everything around it. Psychopathology was the alibi for surveillance and discipline.

Capitalism and industrialization generated not only mental illness categories, heterosexuality, and homosexuality, but also a passion for science and scientific measurement. Nineteenth-century doctors began to keep statistics on all sorts of "diseases" that might signal the degeneration of civilization, including insanity (also called lunacy), prostitution, and other forms of criminality. One could argue that the history of statistics as an academic discipline began with the study of behavioral pathology.[35] The more scientists gathered statistics, the more sickness there seemed to be. And the statistics themselves, in turn, were understood as truths that answered epidemiological questions. For example, if there were more women in asylums, then naturally, they reasoned, women must be more prone to sickness. Experts were at a loss to explain the apparent epidemic created by the illnesses they themselves had invented and were now counting.

After the passage of the 1845 Lunatics Act in England, intended to provide beneficial social services to every citizen, all British counties and boroughs were required to build asylums for lunatics.[36] The result was a rapid marginalization of the so-called mentally ill from their communities. Within fifteen years after passage of the law, the number of lunatics in England had doubled. And not just in England. By the 1870s, in the United States, "the very founding of a hospital in an area . . . made families more receptive to institutionalizing troubled relatives."[37] There weren't very many agreed-upon terms in England or in other countries, but historians who have studied the symptom descriptions in old records suggest that most of these cases would today be called mania, depression, obsession-compulsion, and psychosis.[38] Statisticians reported that in 1844 one in 802 people in England and Wales was "insane," but the rate rose to one in 400 by 1870.[39]

In 1871, British psychiatrist Henry Maudsley, a medical celebrity at the time, delivered a paper entitled "Is Insanity on the Increase?" Maudsley didn't have a definitive answer, but he told skeptical audiences that the increase was caused by factors other than an increase in the incidence of

the disease itself. Among other reasons, such as longevity and better counting methods, he stressed that with the rise of capitalism there was increasing popular and government support for individuals to be cared for outside
of the home and family so that family members could be free to engage
in productive labor. A decade earlier, the British Commission of Lunacy
attributed the increase to better surveillance, and they were probably right.
Since economic growth required workers, it was important to keep track
of, and try to rehabilitate, nonworkers.[40] A similar process was visible in the
United States, where the care of the mentally ill had shifted away from the
community toward state-run institutions. In thirty years, the proportion of
Americans classified as insane doubled. Statistics from 1850 showed 15,610
insane people in the United States out of a total population of 21,000,000;
the 1880 US census listed 91,997 insane people out of a total population of
50,000,000.[41]

What was happening, of course, was that the stresses of industrialization on families made it increasingly difficult for relatives and neighbors
to care for, or to be willing to care for, those who were too ill or too old to
work. Throughout England, most of the admissions to asylums came not
from vagrants living on the streets but from households whose members
petitioned their local governments to commit an unproductive relative.[42]
Continuing the same policies of the late 1700s, people were being confined
not because doctors had devised any cures or demonstrated useful therapies but wherever the removal of an individual from the household facilitated economic productivity. And once removed from society, they had to
be classified in some way both to comprehend and to justify the removal.

From 1790 to 1820, the US government gathered census data on asylum
residents, but only the most basic information like age, race, sex, and residence. It was not until 1830 that the US government began to count people
with physical disabilities, like blindness and deafness. And only in 1840 did
the US government add to the census the phrase "insane and idiotic," with
a combined count that did not separate the two categories, but noted only
whether the individual was in public or private hands. Statisticians hated

the lack of standardization in the 1840 census. Each census taker decided by himself who was insane and idiotic based on whatever records were available to him. In addition, the census didn't even define those words, or any other words for disabilities, including "blind" and "deaf." In 1843, the new American Statistical Association, founded in 1839, told the U.S. House of Representatives that the census data were invalid.

Nonetheless, the structure of the census remained the same for fifty years, with only three exceptions. First, beginning in 1850, the census distinguished between mental *illness* (insanity) and mental *retardation* (idiocy). Second, by 1860, the census listed causes of insanity in certain hospitals. All told, there were nearly 300 different terms for the causes of insanity (poverty, masturbation, childbirth, epilepsy, suppressed menstruation, love, etc.). Third, by the 1880 census, the 300 causes had been reduced to only a handful, as doctors began to name and describe specific disorders (e.g., mania, melancholia, and dementia) and paid less attention to speculative causes.[43] These changes were a matter of trial and error, the haphazard approaches of a medical specialization in its infancy. In the process, however, psychiatric classification was starting to look more like it does today. The DSM, and the mental health section of the World Health Organization's International Classification of Diseases, or ICD (which largely conforms to the DSM), are both descriptive manuals that are concerned not with causality but with cataloging symptoms.

Doctors were unsure whether their characterizations of mental illnesses held true for all human beings—male, female, white, Black, rich, poor—and whether confinement was justifiable for all sufferers. During the nineteenth century, debates about confinement of the mentally ill thus intersected with debates about a different kind of confinement: slavery. Proslavery advocates from a range of professions argued strongly against emancipation and looked for scientific data to support their views. Proslavery economists, for example, believed emancipation would have drastic consequences for the American economy, which depended so much on plantation production; philosophers and religious leaders argued that the enslavement of so-called inferior races was a natural institution that, like a law of human nature, should never be abolished. In the view of many doctors, African Americans were inherently prone to insanity because they could not constrain their impulses and instincts; slavery, they argued, provided a structure to prevent that loss of control.[44] In 1843, the *Boston Courier* reported that in the free states of Ohio, Indiana, and Illinois, the prevalence of insane "Negroes" was one in every eighty-eight. The average rate across the states of Massachusetts, Maine, New Hampshire, and Vermont was one in thirty-four, and in Maine alone the rate was one in fourteen. In some towns, all "colored people" were listed as insane. The free states together had an insanity prevalence of one in every 144.5 Negroes. But in the southern slave states as a whole, the rate of insanity among Negroes was only one in 1,558.[45]

In short, the proportion of free Blacks with insanity was eleven times greater than it was among enslaved Blacks, and there was no difference in the insanity rate between whites in free or slave states. The fact that the rate of white insanity was the same in both free and slave states supported doctors' claims that mental illness and slavery were related. The proslavery advocate John Calhoun told the U.S. Congress: "Here is proof of the necessity of slavery. The African is incapable of self-care and sinks into lunacy under the burden of freedom. It is a mercy to him to give him the guardianship and protection from mental death."[46] In 1851, doctors began using a new mental illness term for disobedient slaves: "drapetomania," a disorder defined by the urge to violate the laws of nature and the Bible by running away from one's masters.

Dr. Edward Jarvis, a statistician and physician, demolished Calhoun's argument (though it did not stop Calhoun and other politicians from continuing to make the same case for decades to come).[47] Initially, Jarvis had accepted the idea that slaves were mentally healthy because their minds were not taxed by sophisticated mental activity. He wrote, "In the highest state of civilization and mental activity there is the greatest derangement; for here, where there is the greatest mental torpor, we find the least insanity."[48] This was the same logic British doctors used in the colonies to justify slavery and to explain the higher rate of insanity among the "lower classes" in England. (One wonders why doctors didn't prescribe slavery to treat white people with mental illnesses!)

But Jarvis soon found widespread errors. For example, many of the patients reported as Negro were, in fact, white. Worcester, Massachusetts, was said to have 133 Negro lunatics and idiots, but they actually had 133 *white* lunatics and idiots. Jarvis also noted that nearly all the statistics in the census came from institutions. First, the North had, proportionally, many more mental institutions (and doctors) than the South. Second, in the North, the state paid for a Negro's care; in the South, if a slave owner wanted his slave to go to a mental institution he would have to pay for it, and thus part with both his money and his slave's labor. It was economically unwise to institutionalize slaves, and as a result fewer slaves were in institutions, and fewer cases were reported in the census. Virginia even had a law that stated "no insane slave should be received or retained" in an asylum.[49]

Nonetheless, such beliefs persisted long after abolition. In a 1921 article, a psychiatrist from St. Elizabeth's Hospital in Washington, DC, made the audacious and racist suggestion that the transition from slavery to freedom might have been more difficult than the transition from living free in Africa to becoming a slave in the American South.

> *Less than three hundred years ago the alien ancestors of most of the families of this race were savages or cannibals in the jungles of Central Africa.... In later years, citizenship with its novel privileges (possibly a greater transition than the first) was thrust upon the race finding it poorly prepared, intellectually, for adjustment to this new social order.... With their low moral level and as free agents, no wrong is felt in gratifying their natural instincts and appetites. The untoward effects of their excesses and vices are potent factors in the production of mental diseases.*[50]

Three decades later, American mental health professionals still thought of African Americans in terms of a contrast between the civilized and the savage. As a psychiatrist wrote in 1953: "In the South the presence of a large group of Negroes not long removed from a primitive society ... complicated the mental health picture."[51]

The linking of race and mental illness not only harmed African Americans but also supported stereotypes of all populations based on their supposed nature. It was scientists, doctors, and other highly educated "experts" and not, as is often assumed, ignorant or uneducated lay people who generated and reproduced racist ideologies.[52] Prejudice and discrimination often start at the top. Well into the mid-twentieth century, white doctors described African American men as irritable, aggressive, relatively impervious to pain, and prone to the so-called negative symptoms of schizophrenia: monosyllabic speech, few gestures, lack of interest in the world, physical and verbal unresponsiveness, and lack of will, spontaneity, and initiative. American doctors started a tradition of misdiagnosing depressed and suspicious African American patients with schizophrenia. And because World War II–era psychoanalysts, like my grandfather, believed that people labeled "schizophrenic" lacked the cognitive ability to benefit from "talk therapy," these men received little or no psychiatric treatment after diagnosis. My grandfather's most influential book, *Men Under Stress*, popularized the psychoanalytic concept of post-traumatic stress by describing the successful treatment of hundreds of war-weary soldiers. But every one of the patients he wrote about was white, and he saw no reason to ever mention why.[53]

One prominent but lonely voice stressing the cultural factors behind the alleged psychological differences between Blacks and whites was the anthropologist and psychiatrist Abram Kardiner. In a 1951 book, *The Mark of Oppression*, he argued that the stereotype of the sullen and angry African American male was indeed based in reality, but in the reality of cultural experience, not biology. The "black personality," Kardiner said, was the result of repeated traumatic and racist insults, beginning in childhood, and perpetuated by American social and economic inequality. Racial prejudice, he proposed, caused the person to believe he was inferior and to alienate himself—what we today sometimes call self-stigma—to withdraw from a world he rightfully mistrusts, to become what Ralph Ellison called "the invisible man."[54] This kind of internalized stigma is what W. E. B. Du Bois meant by a double consciousness—when one sees oneself, but only through the eyes of others.

White southerners used their power both to scar and to silence, to disfigure the Black body and also the Black mind.[55] Slaves could be whipped and mutilated for a gesture, a look of dissatisfaction, for speaking too much or too loudly. For the Western observer, Sara Baartman and other African women displayed as "marvels of nature" were, after all, never really individuals with their own identities. They were bodies that Europeans turned into metaphors. The African American social reformer Frederick Douglass noted long ago that the Black body was itself an act of communication. And when the great abolitionist and suffragist Sojourner Truth bared her breasts in public protest to proclaim how many of the white men who became estate owners had been nurtured on her milk, she was using her body as an act of resistance. In demanding to be seen, she was at once representing herself as someone used and violated, a woman, a mother, a slave, a thinking and feeling person, and the source of white men's masculinity.[56] As scholar Carol Henderson has noted, well into the civil rights era of the twentieth century, the Black body remained a kind of "speech act," a mechanism of resistance, in marches and sit-ins.[57]

Remarkably, the legacy of the white fascination with the Black body as a marker of difference could even be seen in the image of the Black Power fist featured in a 1974 advertisement by McNeil Laboratories for Haldol, the antipsychotic medication for schizophrenia that was marketed, it seems, for the treatment of the angry Black man. Whereas schizophrenia had once been a disease of white middle-class men and women, in the civil rights era it became an African American disease. Advertisements in medical journals for another antipsychotic medicine during the 1970s, Stelazine, included images of African masks or figurines, portraying schizophrenia as a primitive condition. Schizophrenia was what, in 1968, psychiatrists Walter Bromberg and Franck Simon termed the "protest psychosis," a disease of paranoia and delusion caused by civil disobedience and activism.[58] Schizophrenia, a "black disease,"[59] became one of the stigmata of racism. And in a cruel sleight of hand, psychiatrists justified their views on schizophrenia with Du Bois's own words about double consciousness: "One ever feels his two-ness, an American, a Negro; two souls, two thoughts, two unreconciled strivings; two warring ideals in one dark body, whose dogged strength alone keeps it from being torn asunder."[60] This view of schizophrenia is still with us in the name itself: "schizo," from the Greek *skhizein* or "split," and "phrenia," from the Greek *phren* or "mind."

The tradition of preferentially diagnosing depression and other conditions as schizophrenia in African American men is still alive today. Although there is no evidence that schizophrenia is more prevalent in any particular ethnic group, one review of more than 130,000 files in the Veterans Administration showed that during the 1990s, African Americans were diagnosed with schizophrenia four times as often as their white counterparts, and other studies have found even more disproportionate rates.[61] African American psychiatrists are also more likely to diagnose African American men with schizophrenia. Even Martin Luther King Jr. reiterated the resemblance between psychosis and African American identity when he said that "a persistent schizophrenia leaves so many of us tragically divided against ourselves."[62]

CHAPTER 4

THE DIVIDED MIND

It has been said that the great events of the world
take place in the brain. It is in the brain, and the
brain only, that the great sins of the world take
place also.

Oscar Wilde, *The Picture of Dorian Gray* (1890)

O n Saturday mornings, when I was a teenager, my grandfather used to give me what he called "seminars." I wanted to do other things with him, like art, music, or sports, but he was color-blind, tone-deaf, and had chronic back pain. Dressed in a suit, even on weekends, clean shaven and with a cigar in his mouth, he talked to me as if I were an adult. One thing he told me was that "to know the history of schizophrenia is to know the history of psychiatry." Though the prevalence of schizophrenia is only about one percent in any population, it was, he said, the foundation of modern psychiatry: severe, progressive insanity characterized by a dissociation from reality. If the first psychiatrists could claim any expertise at all, it was the ability to know who was "sane" and who was "insane." Writing about schizophrenia, historian Roy Porter said, "Jeopardize the reality of this polar distinction between reason and unreason, mental health and mental disorder, and the very state of psychiatry totters."[1] In 1973, psychologist David Rosenhan thus used schizophrenia as the disorder with which to challenge the validity of psychiatric diagnosis as a whole. He began his infamous paper, "On Being Sane in Insane Places," on how he fooled clinicians into diagnosing healthy patients with schizophrenia by asking: "If sanity and insanity exist, how shall we know them?"[2]

In the mid-1970s, in the run-up to the DSM-III, my grandfather bitterly opposed any effort to conceive of schizophrenia as a spectrum, an argument he would eventually lose. "You either have it or you don't," he said. In 1976, in Toronto, he joined ten other mental health leaders who had come to listen to the APA's defense of the organizational principles and content of the latest draft of the DSM. As a sign of how important schizophrenia was to the American psychiatric establishment, the debates over schizophrenia were among the most heated. My grandfather said angrily, "You can't be borderline [in the sense of there being a continuum] schizophrenic."[3] He also objected to a proposal to define schizophrenia in biological and genetic terms and to exclude psychological and social variables as causes. "Sometimes at a meeting like this," he said, "I feel as if I'm in a never-never land . . . no psychological factors in the aetiology of the schizophrenias? Now, can anybody believe that?"[4]

Where did such serious concern over the meanings of a relatively rare mental illness come from? When he said that schizophrenia was the foundation of psychiatry, I think my grandfather meant that in a world in which we seek to draw sharp lines between normal and abnormal behavior, we should start by looking at the most easily differentiated forms. If chemists want to analyze the properties of an element, they study it in its purest form. Similarly, from the earliest days of the profession, psychiatrists defined their work as the study of "insanity"—chronic, debilitating mental disorder. Schizophrenia was the psychiatrist's most dependable source of work before the onset of the psychotherapeutic culture of the second half of the twentieth century when psychiatrists began to treat much less severe conditions—the so-called common disorders, like anxiety, compulsions, and obsessions. The spectrum of mental illness that most of us recognize today, from the very mild to the life-threatening, was unsatisfying to the scientist because continua, by definition, defy easy classification. So it made sense to look at the extreme, schizophrenia, the quintessential—albeit uncommon—mental illness that appeared to represent the opposite of order and reason.

We saw that the end of the Enlightenment marked the transition from a single-sexed body to a divided body, with women stigmatized as driven by instinct and predisposed to mental illness. The Enlightenment also marked the development of a divided mind, precariously held together in the brain of the modern, rational worker. This view of the mind, still with us today in the highly stigmatized diagnosis of schizophrenia, was the glue that held stigma and mental illness together. But the study of schizophrenia would inform more than just psychiatry. It also informed a powerful Eurocentric critique of the poor, the nonwhite, and the colonized, and became a tool for branding certain people as potential dangers to society. Even by the twentieth century, doctors sometimes called schizophrenia "the most sinister of mental disorders."[5]

For eighteenth- and nineteenth-century European thinkers, schizophrenia was not just a window into a disordered mind. It was also a way to study human variation in general. Why did some humans, such as the people that explorers, missionaries, and colonists encountered in Africa, believe in things that Europeans were certain could not possibly exist, like witchcraft and sorcery? Could schizophrenia help us understand why humans—even apparently mentally healthy humans—did not all think and act in the same way?

The first psychiatrists referred to what we today call schizophrenia as *dementia praecox* ("early dementia"), because it was characterized by a gradual deterioration in cognition beginning in early adulthood. They sought to explain its existence with two theories, generally known as *degeneration* and *disintegration*. Both of these concepts were integral to the description of insanity as a split mind and, ultimately, to the stigma of mental illnesses in general.

Degeneration and disintegration derived from the observations of eighteenth-century psychiatrists—like Philippe Pinel in France, Bénédict Augustin Morel in Austria, and John Haslam in England—who noticed that some men and women who did not seem to exhibit any worrisome behaviors as children began to deteriorate in their young adulthood rather than flower into productive citizens. Their emotions were blunted, they withdrew from social interaction, even with close family members, and were unable to maintain jobs. They didn't seem to care how they looked or smelled, responded to voices no one else could hear, and sometimes believed things that seemed unreasonable, such as being in direct contact with God or evil spirits. Of such people, Haslam wrote, "In the interval between puberty and manhood, I have painfully witnessed this hopeless and degrading change, which in a short time has transformed the promising and vigorous intellect into a slavering and bloated idiot."[6] One of the men Haslam studied was named James Tilly Matthews, and many historians consider Haslam's account of Matthews to be the first detailed description of paranoid schizophrenia—though that term had yet to be coined. Matthews was unremarkable as a child, but in his late teens he became convinced that he was under attack by a group of four men and three women who lived in an apartment somewhere in London. They were conspiring against the government and had placed throughout the city "air-looms" that could harm a person from a distance of a thousand feet.

Working in mid-nineteenth-century France, Viennese psychiatrist Morel proposed the term *démence précoce* (early or rapid dementia) to describe the course of this disease. He reported on one highly intelligent boy who in his teenage years slowly became ever more emotionally and socially withdrawn. Morel believed the boy was an example of hereditary degeneration since both his mother and his grandmother had reportedly exhibited eccentric behaviors. For Morel, mental illness was "a degradation of the progeny."[7] He suggested that this boy would likely be the last in his family line since he would probably neither marry nor reproduce. Morel said of him: "The young patient progressively forgot everything he had learned; his intellectual faculties, formerly so brilliant, underwent a very disturbing period of stoppage ... when I revisited him, I judged that the fatal transition to the state of *démence précoce* was in progress...."[8]

At the same time Haslam and Morel were writing, doctors also noticed that there was more crime and disease (especially alcoholism and syphilis) in the cities than in the countryside. Concerned that society as a whole was decaying, scientists proposed that the deterioration of individuals like Matthews was caused by widespread degeneration in cities from the pure form of humanity embodied by Adam and Eve and that this was a threat to the growth of civilization. Because the afflicted were unable to work, dementia praecox represented the opposite of progress and economic achievement. Thus the disorder that we now call schizophrenia was "the antithesis of the idealized person."[9]

Haslam and Morel were not especially bigoted or racist by the standards of their day, but they believed that degeneration could explain why Africans and other nonwhite people still existed in the world. Perhaps, scientists thought, Europeans had evolved but had left non-Europeans behind in a state of arrested development at earlier stages of evolution—the people who still hunted with bows and arrows, who believed in multiple gods, and who practiced polygamy. Or perhaps, the proponents of degeneration reasoned, Europeans had remained as they were originally made by God while non-Europeans had degenerated. Scientists who were committed to both the ideology of progress and pre-Darwinian views on heredity believed— or at least they hoped—that eventually these lower races (including poor Caucasians) would disappear from the earth. Morel was pessimistic about the possibility of helping degenerating individuals or populations, but he was optimistic "for society as a whole, which would soon be cleansed of these self-limiting strains."[10]

In numerous European countries, scientists championed the concept of degeneration, not only because it promised to rid the world of what they saw as "primitive races" but also because it justified laws preventing the migration of "lower racial types" and intermarriage between classes and races.[11]

But the more the asylum population grew, the more psychiatrists started to think that, rather than disappearing from the earth, there were more degenerates than ever, even in white wealthy families. It looked as if there were an epidemic of degeneration. Perhaps, they thought, all humans were degenerating, but Europeans were degenerating at a slower rate than non-Western peoples. If scientists could agree on which physical signs (or "stigmata," as they were called) indicated degeneration, then they could also help authorities detect real or future criminals. In a review of the existing literature in 1898, one scientist found the stigmata of degeneracy (for example, bushy eyebrows, aquiline noses, and thick lips) in 75 percent of 3,000 insane individuals in asylums, and in 82 out of 128 men counted in a billiard hall (a den of immorality). Scientist Eugene S. Talbot assured Americans, however, that while England and France were degenerating, there was nothing wrong with the American lineage. Most of the degenerates in the United States, he said, were recent immigrants from Europe.[12]

The theory of degeneration helped validate the emerging field of psychiatry. Because most doctors believed degeneracy was an inherited brain disease, they could also argue that psychiatry was a genuine medical specialization. But Morel was dismayed when he failed to find lesions in the brains of deceased insane patients. He and his colleagues were afraid that scientists would interpret the absence of visible damage to the tissue of the brain as evidence that mental illnesses were purely psychological. If mental illnesses were not physical ailments, then anyone—even someone with no knowledge of medicine—could claim the authority to treat them.[13] In 1862, the philosopher Albert Lemoine warned that insanity must be "always a diseased body whose reason had become unhinged as a consequence of the general and close union of the body and soul."[14] In response, Morel redefined the word "lesion." He said that the lesions at the root of insanity were not anatomical injuries but hereditary injuries to the nervous system as a whole.

Following closely in Morel's footsteps, in the 1880s and 1890s German psychiatrist Emile Kraepelin provided the most detailed descriptions of what we today call schizophrenia, though he still called it dementia praecox. These descriptions, based largely on the records of about 700 patients, as well as his method of classification (such as distinguishing between affective disorders and schizophrenia), set the precedent for the way we classify mental illnesses today. Kraepelin believed that the patients with dementia praecox had inherited their illness, and that it was characterized by physical and mental deterioration over time. He described them with words and phrases like "gradual failure," "a tree whose roots no longer find nurture in the available soil," "sink into a languishing state," "decline," and "decay." But he went beyond Morel to state that their condition was marked less by long-term degeneration than by the short-term deterioration of the mind in weak-willed individuals, such as the residents of asylums, or soldiers who suffered emotional trauma after battle.[15] For Kraepelin, the signs of mental decay were visible in the customs of "wild tribal people," the "spineless submission" of children, and the emotional volatility of women.[16]

In focusing on schizophrenia, psychiatrists were therefore also providing, perhaps unwittingly, a cultural description of the Western self. As Australian psychiatrist Robert Barrett noted, "In as much as the ideal person (the adult Caucasian male) epitomized the pinnacle of evolution, development, power and strength, schizophrenia, like a negative photographic image, was characterized in terms of degeneration and weakness."[17] Schizophrenia thus became a multipurpose tool. The eugenicist used it to justify the regulation of sex, marriage, and reproduction among supposedly inferior groups; the biologist used it to support the evolutionary theories of cultural differences that demeaned non-Caucasians as "primitive"; and the politician used it to rationalize racism, colonialism, and other forms of social and economic inequality. Schizophrenia epitomized the effort to preserve the status quo.

The second concept, disintegration, was fueled by the widespread nineteenth-century European belief that within each person there is an integrated, coherent assemblage of numerous parts. Kraepelin reflected this view by describing dementia praecox as the premature "loss of the inner unity of the activities of intellect, emotion and volition."[18] Later, in the 1920s, Swiss psychiatrist Eugen Bleuler popularized the word "schizo-phrenia" to refer to the "splitting of psychic functions" in dementia prae-cox, and over the next three decades "schizophrenia" gradually replaced the now-obsolete term "dementia praecox." For Bleuler, thought and mood, for example, had become separated in dementia praecox; memory, a sense of self, consciousness, and unconsciousness were no longer integrated.

Thinking in someone with such splitting—as manifested by the patient's speech and writing—often involved a seemingly random grouping of words (what became known in the twentieth century as "word salad") and a rapid leap from idea to idea ("flight of ideas") that Bleuler referred to as *associations*. The person with schizophrenia, he said, combines ideas in unusual ways, so the listener is often unable to comprehend their connec-tions. A man might observe a painting of whales and say something like "There are whales in the picture. My eyes are blue. You need sperm to make a baby." One might guess that the person is thinking of blue whales and sperm whales, but that association is not immediately clear to the listener.[19] Even people who are deaf and have schizophrenia sometimes express such loosely organized thinking in their sign language. In addition, Bleuler said, people with schizophrenia have confused *affect*. They express emotions that seem inappropriate for the social context—like laughing at a funeral— or that seem to spontaneously occur with no obvious stimulus. People with schizophrenia, he said, also typically separate themselves from social inter-action. As they withdraw into their isolated world of thoughts, they often show little emotion or interest in other people, a feature of schizophrenia that Bleuler called *autism* (literally "self-ism")—the first usage of the word in any European language. For the person with schizophrenia, moreover, his or her thoughts could be contradictory (as when someone has two intentions so antithetical that they become unable to act), what Bleuler termed *ambivalence*. These four features—association, affect, autism, and ambivalence—became known as Bleuler's "four As" and, unfortunately, schizophrenia would become popularly known as a "split personality."

In all areas of intellectual inquiry, from philosophy to fiction to med-icine, Europeans believed that within human beings there existed two selves, the light and the dark, the good and the evil, the sane and the insane. Franz Anton Mesmer's late-eighteenth-century magnetic hypnosis therapy, from which we get the word "mesmerize," was based on the proposition that the mind consisted of two layers of consciousness. The well-known literary works *Frankenstein* (1823), *Faust* (1829), *Dr. Jekyll and Mr. Hyde* (1886), and *The Picture of Dorian Gray* (1890) are all examples of this view.[20]

I cannot imagine any reputable twenty-first-century psychiatrist describing schizophrenia so simplistically as a divided or disintegrated mind. It would wrongly suggest that schizophrenia is a split or multiple personality. Yet, remarkably, more than 150 years after Dostoevsky wrote about the "second self" as the sign of the disintegration of the mind in his book *The Double* (1846), current advertisements for antipsychotic pharmaceuticals still show images of young men breaking into pieces, or of the floor cracking beneath their legs. A twenty-first-century ad for the antipsychotic drug Invega shows a beautiful naked woman emerging from a man who appears to be dead or sleeping, and whose clothes and limbs are melting like wax. The tag reads: "For the person within." Other contemporary images of people with schizophrenia include a face, or simply two eyes, with a crack running vertically down the middle; two faces—one illuminated, the other one darkened in shadow; a collage composed of dozens of pieces of paper, held together only by a weak glue.

It would be foolish to think that the ideas Europeans generated about the mind stayed in Europe. After all, Europeans were fanning out across the globe, extracting resources, conquering communities, saving the souls of the "heathens" in Africa, and researching the question of why there were so many physical and cultural differences among humans. They carried with them the assumption that Europeans were biologically and culturally superior to all others, and that European rule in Africa was therefore only natural.[21] With their different customs and beliefs—whether polygamy, ancestor worship, witchcraft, or sorcery—the colonies provided a place where European doctors could extend the range of their search for unreason. Colonial scientists couldn't very well prove the theory of degeneration,

and justify racist ideologies at home, unless they also proved that degenerates actually existed. So one basic aim of colonialism was to find them.

Scholars debated whether there existed a distinct "primitive" mind and
a "modern" or "civilized" mind." For many, the African was like a living fos-
sil, reflecting the human mind at an earlier stage of evolution. When Carl
Jung traveled by train along the eastern coast of Kenya in 1925, he wrote
about seeing an African above the tracks, holding a long spear: "It was as
if I were this moment returning to the land of my youth, and as if I knew
that dark-skinned man who had been waiting for me over 5,000 years."[22]
The British psychiatrist John Colin Carothers believed he had found the
evidence of degeneration in Africans' spiritual beliefs. Like people with
schizophrenia, Carothers said, Africans lived in a fantasy world populated
by spirits, and when any misfortune occurred the Africans always blamed
it on external forces, like witches, never taking personal responsibility for
their problems. He wrote, "The normal African is not schizophrenic, but
the step from the primitive attitude to schizophrenia is but a short and easy
one."[23] Of course, he did not think that believing in Jesus, the resurrection,
or virgin birth was an indication of any mental pathology.

In the southern African region of Zululand in 1910, colonial officials
charged eleven teenage and adult unmarried women with practicing witchcraft, a criminal offense in the colonies. The women denied they were
witches. They spoke unintelligible words, were moody, and ate animals that
no one else wanted to eat, like dogs and cats. But they said they were victims, not perpetrators. They had what they called *mandike*, a condition in
which the spirit of a dead person (called *indike*) possesses you.

Officials at the resident magistrate's office said they had never heard of
mandike, but mandike was, in fact, known throughout southeastern Africa,
and was thought to be contagious. Among the symptoms was an apparent
lack of appreciation of money. Most sufferers were unmarried women who,
in the words of one colonial official, "not only fritter away their time, but
squander their little wealth."[24] Was this a particular kind of African insanity? The British couldn't decide if they were insane, had hysteria, were lying,
were employing witchcraft, or were victims of witchcraft.

The officials judging the Zulu girls and women were in a difficult position. If they called the illness "witchcraft," it might be tantamount to admitting that witches actually existed, and neither the authorities nor missionaries wanted to validate local customs. The whole purpose of the law against witchcraft was to eradicate false beliefs. But if the officials defined mandike as a mental illness, then they might be obliged to try to treat it. Just as problematic, when doctors began to diagnose mental illnesses in other parts of Africa, they wondered if perhaps colonialism itself was the cause. And if the hardships of being conquered led to insanity, did this suggest that insanity was caused by the social and political environment in which one lived, and not, as scientists believed, by a population's natural or evolutionary history? The confused officials ultimately reached a split decision. They sentenced five of the girls to hard labor, and simply reprimanded the rest.

The conflict between colonizer and colonized in Zululand brought into relief the assumptions in European psychological thought about cultural evolution and the natural causes of mental deterioration. Colonial doctors argued that insanity originated within an afflicted individual. They therefore interpreted the Zulu belief that a person or spirit can impinge on the minds of others as proof of a lack of individuation. That is, the African had failed to become the distinct, private, and autonomous individual that was the ideal of Western industrial society.[25] In addition, because doctors believed that mental illnesses were largely biological phenomena, they rejected any claim that a witch or sorcerer could cause them. From the perspective of the Zulu, however, the women were victims who should be supported, not lunatics to be punished. As unmarried young females, without the protection of a husband's clan, and in a transitional state between being girls and women, they were especially susceptible to malevolence. The Zulu were vexed by the colonists' inability to understand this obvious fact, and rightly so. After all, British physicians had long emphasized the importance of marriage to a woman's mental and physical health.

The Zulu women rejected being stigmatized either as witches or as insane, and they had a system of belief to back them up. But mentally ill

European colonists did not have the cultural vocabulary to mount the same resistance. Colonial authorities acknowledged that the greatest stigma associated with mental illness was among white settler families, for whom admission to an asylum was tantamount to being given the label "social refuse."[26] Europeans, and especially poor Europeans, with mental or physical illnesses were usually hidden from African view as much as possible, a common colonial practice, to preserve the image of white people as elites with healthy bodies and superior mentalities.[27]

In the end, the only really beneficial mental illness category for colonial administrations was "insanity," which could be used to commit Black patients to institutions and put them to work as unpaid laborers, as happened in the Cape Colony, in what is today South Africa.[28] Insanity could also be relabeled as "mass insanity" to explain and control anti-colonial protests,[29] not unlike the way Soviet leaders in the twentieth century committed political dissidents to asylums with diagnoses of schizophrenia, the Argentinian military state during the 1970s labeled mental health practitioners as subversive, and the Chinese government in the late 1970s branded members of religious minorities with *zhengzhi fenzi*, literally "political insanity."[30]

What colonial psychiatrists did not understand was that the symptoms of mental illnesses are inevitably local. Most societies view emotional and physical sicknesses as a problem of the community that therefore demands a social rather than an individual therapeutic response. Mandike might thus be better explained in terms of these Zulu women's social status as the victims were all unmarried women with little control over their bodies. In fact, whether in Africa or elsewhere, spirit possession is a way for unmarried women to respond to their own anxieties, as well as public anxieties, about their ambiguous social status. Spirit possession in Southeast Asia, for example, often afflicts unmarried female factory workers who, because they work outside the home, are stigmatized as sexually promiscuous.[31]

Systems of healing that do not hew to the orthodoxy of Western individualism have found ways to protect the sufferer. They deflect responsibility away from the individual and the individual's brain, and in the best of circumstances they harness the social supports that, even the most Eurocentric doctors will confess, lessen the pain of mental illness. As we now turn from the nineteenth to the twentieth century, we'll see that European and North American psychiatry continued to shame and discredit the individual sufferer, but that stigma decreases when a society accepts some of the blame.

PART TWO

WARS

CHAPTER 5

THE FATES OF WAR

The war that had promised so much in the way of "manly" activity had actually delivered "feminine" passivity, and on a scale that their mothers and sisters had scarcely known. No wonder they broke down.

Pat Barker, *Regeneration* (1991)

I never had the pleasure of meeting my great-grandfather Julius, who was by all accounts unlikable. He was caustic, hypercritical, and sexist, even by the standards of 1900. As difficult as it was for Jews in the United States those days, Julius became a nationally recognized neurologist, and audiences were eager to listen to his diatribes against women, idealists, and industrialization. Julius believed that insanity was caused by a person's inability to control their impulses—especially the desire to shop.

Although he was born into poverty, in what was then Prussia, Julius had little sympathy for the downtrodden. But his views were not radical. By the time he settled in Chicago in the late 1800s, the so-called ugly law was in place to warn the public of the dangers of the poor and the disabled. The ordinance, which the city repealed only in 1973, labeled as a criminal anyone who was obviously "diseased, maimed, mutilated, or in any way deformed" and who "expose[d] himself to public view."[1] Newspapers demeaned women and the disabled in the same breath, writing that women were so weak that they could be traumatized by coming into contact with someone with a disability: "The consequences to a lady in delicate health of having a repulsive deformity suddenly presented to her by an abrupt appeal for charity might be serious."[2] The overall influence of this and other ugly laws (also known as "unsightly beggar ordinances") was to bolster public opinion that physical deformity was a condition of nature, inherited over generations through diseased bloodlines.[3]

That argument also extended to the insane. There wasn't much one could do to help such perversions of nature except isolate them in their homes or treat them in asylums. For the wealthy, there were private sanatoriums in the countryside where people could escape the stresses of the city, and where some spent the rest of their lives. But doctors like Julius probably never thought much about whether psychiatrists could help people living outside of an institution. He thought that the only two psychiatric techniques available for the general population—hypnosis and persuasion— were quackery.[4] Moreover, psychiatry was an ignoble profession of asylum administrators. No ambitious doctor in his right mind would become a psychiatrist if he had other options, and especially if you were Jewish and had been able to succeed in a somewhat respected specialization like neurology.

Julius had no interest in taking a step backward. In Europe, the only discipline with lower status than psychiatry—and thus populated almost entirely by Jewish doctors—was dermatology, because it mostly involved treating syphilitic sores. In Vienna, dermatology had the nickname *Judenhaut* ("Jew skin").[5] As scholar Sander Gilman told me, "The first academic Jewish doctors were in the most disgusting professions." "Austrian universities didn't even permit Jews to study medicine until the mid-1800s," Gilman said. "And then it was okay only if they didn't take the other doctors' patients away, and stuck to their own community"—only if, like Freud, they would take care of the Jewish patients.

Given the fact that psychiatric care was carried out almost entirely in asylums, the psychiatric casualties of World War I surprised the medical establishment.[6] Most doctors didn't know how to treat, or even talk about, people who were not insane and yet were clearly distressed. The vocabulary of mental illness was still too deficient. Dissatisfied with "insanity" as a diagnosis for traumatized soldiers, doctors began to favor the term "mental alienation," but that term was no more precise, referring to everything from homesickness to psychosis. Soldiers affected by inexplicable illnesses brought on by the stresses of war, like partial paralysis, stuttering, and mutism, existed somewhere between sanity and insanity, and between physical and mental illness. But because they were soldiers, they deserved to be treated.

In fact, during WWI, people with mental illnesses were probably better cared for, more supported and nurtured, in the military than they would have been in civilian life. In the military, they remained potential combatants or at least individuals whose sacrifices the military recognized and to whom society owed a debt of gratitude. Had they not served, they might have been seen as idle parasites on the national economy. The military was indirectly teaching civilian society that mental illnesses included a wide range of symptoms that could afflict even the best men when faced with difficult circumstances. Indeed, the stigma of mental illness tends to lessen during wars and return during peacetime.

I can't think of a better example than WWI to show how patients and doctors drew on the limited medical knowledge and available idioms of distress in their societies to shape the symptoms and treatments of mental illnesses. The story of any sickness, of course, is one that doctors and patients weave together, in which they find consensus about what constitutes a culturally legitimate and sensible symptom at a particular moment in history.[7] By the time the war began, the majority of Americans and British still expressed their emotional distress through bodily symptoms like fatigue or paralysis. What we think of today as mental disorders were, in the past, problems of the nerves rather than the mind, and if anyone sought care for such conditions they went to their general practitioner, or perhaps a neurologist. Doctors had little interest in treating someone with emotional issues. At an unconscious level, patients knew to express their complaints through the body.

Precisely because the symptom has to make sense to the healer and the sufferer, symptom patterns can also tell us a great deal about the societies that create them. Although we tend to think of wars as chaotic upheavals, as separate from the normal functioning of a society, they can also make pre-existing social patterns more visible—phenomena like sexism, racism, economic inequality, and the repression of emotion among men. As historian Peter Barham writes, wars are not episodes distinct from civilian life but are "woven into the fabric of modernity."[8]

On December 8, 1900, Julius Grinker delivered a lecture at the Chicago Public Library entitled "American Nervousness: Its Cause and Cure." In the grandeur of this extraordinary building, amid inscriptions in praise of brotherly kindness and under Tiffany glass lights, he told an audience of urban professionals and journalists that there was an epidemic of insanity in America caused by indiscriminate marriages. "If the people of America," he said, "would keep the coming generations from inhabiting madhouses, they should abolish indiscriminate marriages, forget that hallucination called love, and choose their life partners on the same principle that a successful cattleman chooses his stock."[9] The next day, the headline of one newspaper article on the lecture, alluding to Molière's famous satire, said of Julius: "Occasionally the misanthrope appears in actual life exactly as in the play."[10]

Adding that capitalism was the root of mental illness, and displaying his misogyny, my great-grandfather bemoaned the "thousands and thousands of nervous women on the streets every day," of whom, he said, "ninety-nine out of a hundred should be in a sanitarium." "The shopping habit is one of the great causes," and "every family has at least one member with some form of nervousness." By "nervousness," he was probably referring to "hysteria" and "neurasthenia," two of the most common "neuroses" at the turn of the century—that is, neurological and emotional symptoms that could not be explained physiologically. In the United States and England, they were classified as "nervous diseases" because sufferers had no fever, localized pathology, or other comprehensible physical disease. Both were also classified in the United States and England as "functional diseases,"[11] meaning there was a disturbance of one or more organs without any discernible organic cause. Remarkably, doctors use a similar term today for such ailments: "functional neurological symptom disorder."

Hysteria was predominantly a female disease. During the latter half of the nineteenth century, doctors believed that women's reproductive anatomy caused insanity, and countless women underwent surgical procedures to cure them of it—removal of the clitoris or the ovaries, for example. One of the founders of the field of gynecology, German doctor Ernst Hegar, said that "gynecology represents the bridge between general medicine and neuropathology."[12] Hysteria was characterized by diverse symptoms such as lack of emotional control, extreme emotions, anxiety, and frigidity. Psychological stress and frustration in hysteria would also be converted into bodily symptoms—like partial paralysis, fainting, and difficulty breathing—that resembled a physical illness. The illness experience fit nicely with the stereotype of the emotionally, physically, and sexually frustrated Victorian woman, suffering as she tried to conform to the expectation that the ideal woman was dependent, passive, and passionless.

Neurasthenia (literally, "nervous weakness") was actually a fashionable disease for urban middle- and upper-class men because it was a sign that they were engaged in great intellectual work that sapped their nervous system of energy. Also occasionally known as "the American disease" or "Americanitis," neurasthenia involved fatigue and weakness associated with the stresses of urban life in America and with the mental struggles of writers, artists, and scientists. Henry James, William James, Charles Darwin, Sigmund Freud, Theodore Roosevelt, and Frederic Remington were all said to have neurasthenia, with symptoms like lethargy, vertigo, headaches, and other aches and pains. In 1903, Rexall drugs advertised a miracle potion for the diseases caused by rapid economic change: "We Guarantee Rexall Americanitis Elixir Will Make You Feel Younger."[13] Up until WWI, neurasthenia was the nonstigmatized catch-all term for feeling run-down, but only for the higher classes since doctors did not believe that physical labor—the work of the lower classes—taxed the brain or the nervous system. Neurasthenics suffered greatly, but the diagnosis was also a sign of privilege.[14]

Psychiatry in Chicago, Julius's hometown, resembled psychiatry elsewhere in the United States. Other than the expensive rural private hospitals, there were a few private rest-cure establishments in the city itself. Rest-cure proponents believed that insanity was caused by a "deficiency of fatty substances surrounding the nerve fibers," and was therefore treatable with rest and a high-calorie diet.[15] The county asylum in Chicago, popularly known as "Dunning Hospital," opened as a poorhouse (the equivalent of the British "workhouse") in 1851, and by 1881 there were about 250 new admissions per year of city residents (out of a total population of 600,000 Chicagoans), mostly impoverished young men brought to the asylum by the police after arrest.[16] The few records of the residents indicated a name and date of entry but little else.[17] At home, my grandfather and father remembered, parents admonished mischievous children by saying things like "Keep misbehaving and I'll send you to Dunning!" The majority of the residents stayed on the 160-acre campus for three to six months, but others stayed for years if their families deserted them, some dying there. Dunning, one historian noted, "became synonymous with the shame of poverty and the hopelessness of mental illness."[18]

Looking back, psychiatry should have been a more important profession in Europe and North America by the time WWI began, not because of any advances in science, but simply because of the large number of soldiers who had suffered in previous conflicts from emotional distress and ailments that could not be explained in medical terms: catatonia, depressions, sudden muteness or deafness, and an inability to walk. There are records of numerous psychiatric casualties in the American Civil War (1861–65), the

Spanish-American War (1898), the Boer War (1899–1902), and the Russo-Japanese War (1904–6). But during those wars, mental illnesses were still framed in physical terms. Civil War physicians, for instance, described the often-fatal disease of "nostalgia" or homesickness (from the Greek *nostos*, "return home," and *algia*, "pain") as a "mental disease," but only because the symptoms of depression and lethargy were psychological. Mental diseases at that time were still widely considered to be diseases of the entire body—hence, nostalgia caused people to have diarrhea, waste away, and die. Thousands of Civil War deaths were attributed to nostalgia.[19] As one doctor put it, "But be the nostalgia the cause or the result of diarrhea, dysentery, or typhoid fever, it is in either event a complication to be dreaded as one of the most serious that could befall the patient."[20] Thousands of deaths were also caused by "irritable heart" and "exhausted heart," conditions that sound a lot like the psychiatric symptoms of WWI.

At the beginning of the war, there were only fifty psychiatrists in the US military—though at the time, they were called "neuropsychiatrists"—for an army of more than four million. As a result, most of the people who treated soldiers had no psychiatric training at all. One couldn't expect that surgeons, neurologists, and internists would have any experience diagnosing psychiatric conditions, and so they focused more on the body than the mind. They treated physical symptoms, and patients described their complaints almost entirely in physical terms. A bodily ailment simultaneously validated a patient's inability to continue fighting the war, his need for care, and the vital role of the hospital and its staff as healers.

Many emotionally distressed soldiers and officers had paralysis and muscle contractures with restricted movement in the joints; sometimes their bodies were contorted. Some were mute, temporarily deaf, or blind; others lost the ability to smell or taste. Some had fatigue, insomnia, and vertigo. Doctors initially referred to all of these conditions as hysteria, but this was a troublesome term. They disagreed about whether hysteria was one or many diseases, or whether it was a real disease at all.[21] But more importantly, hysteria implied femininity and a lack of emotional control, and so the diagnosis almost always stigmatized soldiers.

Anthropologist-turned-psychologist Charles Myers put his anthropology to work in an effort to reduce that stigma. Myers and his colleagues, anthropologist W. H. R. Rivers and psychologist William McDougall, had traveled together on the legendary 1898 expedition to the Torres Strait islands separating northern Australia and southern New Guinea. There they learned about the complex relationship between culture and perception. They lived for four months on Murray Island, and with a sample of a few hundred "natives" they gathered data on a host of physical traits, such as sensitivity to light, hearing, muscle strength, and pain threshold. Although they didn't study intelligence, they concluded that the natives scored better than Europeans in several areas, especially eyesight. But it wasn't that the natives were *born* with good vision and visual perception; their culture demanded that they develop the ability to detect minute details at a distance.

Realizing that perception was a cultural process, and could therefore be changed, Myers and his colleagues promoted a new word for emotional distress in war—"shell shock"—to change soldiers' assumptions about sickness. Patients themselves had invented the term to characterize the effects of being close to an explosion without having experienced an external injury to the body. They found the word quite sensible since they believed that the wind generated by a bullet could cause "nervous instability."[22] But Myers was the first to realize its great symbolic value. The patients had invented it, albeit unconsciously, as a way to interpret their symptoms biologically rather than psychologically, and to reaffirm their sense of manhood. Myers reasoned that since war was linked to masculinity, and both masculinity and sanity were linked to the ability to control one's feelings, shell shock was an ideal replacement for the feminized term "hysteria."[23]

Myers described "shell shock" for the first time in a 1915 case report on three soldiers.[24] The first soldier reported that shells had exploded all around him for several hours; the second had been buried for eighteen hours in a trench; the third had fallen fifteen feet. They all had impairments in their field of vision and had lost almost all sense of taste. Two of the three lost their sense of smell, and all three were unable to defecate for five days after the traumatic events. Doctors in other European countries quickly followed with their own translations of the term.[25] By the summer of 1915, after the first year of the war, 112,000 German soldiers had been diagnosed with shell shock.[26] In May 1917, 15 percent of British soldiers had already been discharged from the military with the diagnosis.

In most professional discourse, it was clear that when you talked about shell shock you were really talking about hysteria. But at least soldiers were less ashamed of the diagnosis. Upon hearing the term, one's immediate association was to an injury sustained in or near combat, and not to lack of courage or fortitude. So although doctors in Europe and North America never achieved consensus on an exact definition of shell shock—one historian called it a term with a "quicksilver and shifting character"[27]—everyone seemed to agree that it served a useful purpose: it provided a way for society to legitimate suffering, to console the sufferer, and to do so in a way that avoided the feminizing stigma of hysteria.

Women serving as nurses and ambulance drivers in WWI also experienced shell shock, but they were typically not diagnosed or treated for their symptoms. If they were diagnosed, the diagnosis was hysteria, and they were immediately discharged from the war. Officials in France, Belgium, England, and the United States considered women of less value than combat soldiers and so made less effort to treat or retain them. In addition, when doctors thought about war trauma, they didn't include interpersonal trauma that occurred outside of combat, such as sexual violence and the trauma of witnessing the effects of warfare. Yet women were exposed to just as much violence, if not more, than many men. Nurses had to care for horrific injuries and participate in surgeries, including amputations for men with gangrene. A Canadian military nurse, M. Lucas Rutherford, wrote that among all the conditions, shell shock was the most distressing and difficult to treat because the afflicted soldiers were often unreachable, unable to communicate.[28]

When British nurses traumatized by the war did go to asylums, or when civilian women became "insane" after the death of family members in the war, they were often admitted as "pauper lunatics" rather than as "service patients," as the men with shell shock were called. In England, women received no official recognition that the war had an impact on their lives. In both the United States and England, the historical and psychological literature on WWI, and for that matter the literature on every war up to the current wars in Iraq and Afghanistan, pays little attention to women—more confirmation of how social inequality underwrites the history of the stigma of mental illness.[29]

If women were excluded and ignored, men were silenced. Because shell shock was experienced as symptoms of the body and not the mind, it became a way to talk about physical ailments but to mute expressions of the emotional consequences of war, and to keep robust discussions of the psychological effects of trauma out of the civilian world. Still, some highly respected physicians tried to unmask the political correctness of the category of shell shock. Doctors from Manchester University in England wrote in 1917 that shell shock was just a polite word "for nothing else but 'funk,'" and they accused sufferers of malingering.[30] People believed to have faked or exaggerated their symptoms to get out of the war were sometimes court-martialed and, in a few cases, when malingerers deserted the military, were sentenced to death by firing squad.

The doctors' challenge to differentiate "real" shell shock from faking, and emotional from physical illness, is captured magnificently in Pat Barker's *Regeneration* trilogy. In the first book of this historical fiction, *Regeneration*, the protagonist—psychiatrist and anthropologist W. H. R. Rivers—struggles to balance two opposing principles. Rivers, modeled on the actual anthropologist W. H. R. Rivers (1864–1922), knows that men stricken with shell shock can recover only if they can confront and integrate their emotions and physical symptoms, but he also knows that "they'd been trained to identify emotional repression as the essence of manliness."[31] The character adds, "fear, tenderness—these emotions were so despised that they could be admitted into consciousness only at the cost of redefining what it meant to be a man."[32]

People with shell shock didn't talk much about their feelings. They twisted their bodies in unusual ways, moved as if they were proceeding gingerly on a tightrope, or fell to the ground repeatedly as they tried unsuccessfully to walk. Some doctors described them as having had the life sucked out of them. One article in a 1914 issue of the *Lancet* said the men resembled "a group of waxwork bodies at Madame Tussaud's."[33] Shell shock did not involve flashbacks (*reliving* rather than just remembering a traumatic experience) or hyperarousal, the typical symptoms of what we today call PTSD. In addition, the symptoms of shell shock had their onset during the war, and not, as among the veterans of more recent wars, months or years after the war.

Remarkably, many other soldiers with the classic symptoms of shell shock had been nowhere near combat.[34] In the United States, Thomas Salmon, the American physician who led British and American efforts to screen recruits during WWI, wrote that "hundreds of soldiers who have not been exposed to battle conditions at all develop symptoms almost identical with those in men whose nervous disorders are attributed to shell fire."[35] In France, according to one of the leading psychiatrists of the day, almost all the psychiatric patients with war-related neuroses had physical *symptoms*, but only 20 percent of these patients actually had physical wounds.[36] By December 1918, one percent of American troops had been admitted to hospitals with the symptoms of shell shock.[37]

After each war, doctors, generals, and military historians complain that they failed to heed the lessons of the past, as if they knew nothing of how widespread physical responses to psychological pain had been in previous wars. Commenting on the apparent novelty of hysterical symptoms in WWI, German neurologist Hermann Oppenheim said, "Hysteria has now overflowed all banks, and nothing is safe from it."[38] With the exception of the most highly educated doctors familiar with European studies of hysteria or American studies of "railway spine" (in which people had bodily symptoms months or years after an accident), most clinicians had never seen anything like it. The Australian armed forces reflected that at Gallipoli the concept of a psychiatric disorder in the military "had simply not entered into the minds of the medical services."[39] Were bodily symptoms simply the only way people knew how to express their strong emotions? And what of the men with shell shock who had never left England or the United States? Did anxious soldiers unintentionally mimic the symptoms of the men who had been physically wounded?

Decades before the war, the French physician Jean-Martin Charcot, nicknamed "the Napoleon of Neuroses,"[40] had begun to popularize the concept of hysteria, which he defined as an organic condition caused by psychological trauma. "Hysteria," he claimed, was a distinct condition that operated according to different biological rules than the rest of human physiology, and could afflict both men and women. For doctors and patients throughout Europe, fixed physical signs, like paralysis and muteness, became the "stigmata" of hysteria. Even before the war, doctors were preoccupied with hysteria, and this is what so concerned Julius. In the words of one historian, "Doctors' offices from Paris to Vienna and as far away as New York and Buenos Aires were flooded with women suffering from such symptoms as sudden loss of speech, narrowing of the visual field, tics, tremors, and partial paralysis in the legs and arms."[41]

Later in the twentieth century, doctors would call such bodily symptoms "conversion disorders" rather than hysteria. Conversion is a universal process through which people both consciously and unconsciously articulate feelings and experiences in a culturally acceptable language, even if that language is physical rather than spoken. As military historian Ben Shephard told me about WWI, "It was astonishing. A few people starting twitching and two years later everyone is twitching." Whether or not they had been in combat, the soldiers unconsciously developed the same symptoms as those who they observed were getting positive attention and care. As Freud himself noted, the typical symptoms of an illness tend to be the same and thus blunt individual variation.[42] That's a good thing, I suppose; if symptoms lacked similarity and pattern, doctors would have no way of conceptualizing or classifying them.

So even though the term "shell shock" was new, the war did not create many new symptoms. It did create a new framework in which to understand them as a pattern. Shell shock was caused not by the passions, as in women, but by physical experience. The diagnosis, historian Peter Lerner writes, "once a taboo, was not only acceptable by the middle of the war but was turned into a rallying cry, a patriotic crusade inflected with nationalistic and military language."[43] The diminishing concern about the feminine connotations of hysterical symptoms was especially pronounced in Germany, where Hermann Oppenheim said that with the term "shell shock" he could now talk about a soldier's "nervous disturbances" without making him sound mentally diseased.[44] In the United States, Thomas Salmon remarked on the tenacity with which war veterans "clung to a diagnosis of 'shell shock.'"[45] And with this common diagnosis came a message for the public at large: anyone, soldier or civilian, could get a neurosis, and to have one should in no way be dishonorable.

But psychiatric symptoms varied according to rank. Enlisted men more commonly experienced the gross bodily symptoms like paralysis, mutism, and deafness. Many officers had the same symptoms, but the higher the rank the more likely they had the features of neurasthenia, like fatigue and insomnia, associated with mental disturbances among elites in civilian life. In England, the class system often eclipsed compassion. British doctors' moral and political sensibilities led them to preferentially apply a second-order category of shell-shock diagnoses that reinforced existing biases. They often used the words "malingering" and "hysteria" to describe shell shock in already marginalized populations: working-class soldiers, Jews, the Irish, and colonial subjects like West Africans.

In India, British colonial doctors separated out British psychiatric lunatics into two classes. First-class patients—that is, British citizens who represented the best image of British national character—were said to suffer from temporary weaknesses. Second-class patients—British laborers, alcoholics, and sex workers—were classified as "idiots" or "maniacs."[46] During the war, some of the poorest young British men—a significant portion of whom joined the war effort less out of passion for the war than to escape unemployment—were thought to be untreatable because, in addition to their sicknesses, they were inherently inferior by virtue of their birth and upbringing. As Lord Moran, Winston Churchill's personal physician, put it many decades after WWI, "Man's fate in battle is worked out before war begins." He was even more blunt in some handwritten notes: "bad stock paves way for shell shock."[47]

Class also influenced the way shell shock was described in Germany and France, where soldiers from poor backgrounds were more likely to "take flight into sickness."[48] In Germany, hysteria was more frequently used as a diagnosis for working-class men whose impairments were evidence of them being "work-shy."[49] In France, for example, "the violent event made neurosis manifest, but it did not cause neurosis. The problem was with the patient, not the war."[50] Shell shock didn't further diminish a person's social status. But in an unstable and chaotic world, the diagnosis could reinforce one's inferior position in a social hierarchy, and might prove that their sickness was predetermined by heredity.[51]

Despite its initial popularity, American military and civilian doctors eliminated the term "shell shock" by the end of 1918, in part because scientists found it vague and also because it was used so loosely as to be meaningless. However, doctors continued to use "neurasthenia," especially as a diagnosis for educated officers who, clinicians reasoned, were simply exhausted by the stress of war and needed rest and long baths; by most accounts, fewer than 15 percent of all American shell-shock cases were officers. With money, and a diagnosis with less stigma, officers relaxed in private homes or sanatoriums, and were sometimes treated with talk therapy (although it wasn't the long-term psychoanalytic kind of talking associated with Freud). In contrast, working-class soldiers with the same symptoms as their neurasthenic counterparts were sometimes punished for their hysteria. They suffered in miserable lodgings without proper heat, where they were sedated and often subjected to electric shocks without anesthesia.[52] The fact that they were no longer productive members of society and, unlike wealthier soldiers, made continued demands on the national budget for their care exacerbated their shame and alienation with the stigmatized label of "pauperism."

Soldiers were now, in effect, being asked to relinquish themselves to a bureaucratic system comprised of officers, experts, therapeutic practices, and methods of exclusion. Henri Barbusse, one of the great French novelists of WWI, wrote in 1919 that war was like the abduction of one's body, "like legal arrest, from which nothing that is poor and needy can escape." The new masters strip the soldier of his clothes, dress him in a uniform, and imprison him in barracks. He joins with other men to form a group that is at once powerful and impotent. And when the war ends, the masters bury the soldier or return him to the society that has to pay for the war and its consequences. Warning the veteran of his insignificance, Barbusse said, "This is the terrible fate which grips you . . . sharply unmasked, offensive, and complicated," the postwar condition being yet another form of abduction, not by war but by the industrial machine.[53] The soldier, though perhaps a servant, a laborer, or something else outside of war, was always destined to be under the control of some form of discipline. "Soldier of the wide world," Barbusse wrote, "you, the man taken haphazard from among men, remember—there was not a moment when you were yourself."

When the war finally came to a close, so too did the safe harbor of a shell-shock diagnosis. The causes, treatments, and value of shell shock had been debated throughout the war, as each observer interpreted war trauma through their own disciplinary lens. In the United States, Salmon refused to admit shell-shock victims to psychiatric hospitals—no matter their socioeconomic background—where they might be labeled insane or feebleminded. They were war casualties, he said, and should be treated either in specialized hospitals for veterans or as outpatients, typically with rest but occasionally with hypnosis. But others, including Charles Myers in England, were convinced that many of the bodily symptoms were the result of the repression of trauma from consciousness.[54] Clinicians also disagreed about whether shell shock had to be defined in terms of immediate symptoms following a traumatic event or could have a delayed onset. And no one knew how to distinguish between someone with genuine shell shock and someone just pretending to have it. Were they sick or did they have what the British doctors—a much less sympathetic crew than the Americans—had begun to call LMF: a "lack of moral fibre"?[55]

At war's end, Lord Moran tamped down his previous class bias to argue, in capitalist terms, that a soldier's mental health was a limited good. "A man's willpower was his capital and he was always spending. Wise and thrifty company officers watched the expenditure of every penny lest their men went bankrupt. When their capital was done, they were finished."[56] Government leaders were more sympathetic to people with major physical injuries, such as someone with an amputated limb, than to people with psychological issues. For the soldiers, the emotional effects of war were a darkness—Barbusse called it "an internal shadow"—that disfigured a person from within. Traumatic memory was a continuous agony, with no end in sight, a wound branded not into flesh but into one's faculties.

For the British government, the war was over. Ongoing suffering was either weakness or deception. Lord Southborough, who headed the 1920 Government Committee of Enquiry into Shell Shock to resolve debates over the diagnosis of shell shock, affirmed that shell shock now bore the stigma of malingering. Noting that veterans were slothful and living off the government, he said, "In quasi-mental cases I can imagine no more miserable fate for a patient than a continued source of absolute idleness."[57] Add to this debate the anticipated long-term financial costs of caring for people with shell shock after the war, and it's no surprise that shell shock was unsustainable as a diagnosis. However, given the number of people receiving financial compensation for shell shock, and the public sympathy for those with the diagnosis, it wouldn't be easy to eliminate.[58]

The British military issued an order in 1918 stating that in the absence of proof that a weapon had physically damaged a soldier, the symptoms of shell shock could no longer constitute a "wound." Historian Ben Shephard noted how much changed in just one year. "What was once a disease had in 1917 become a stigma, and by 1918 a forbidden term."[59] For all but officers, fictional characters in postwar literature whose quirky personalities were shaped by war trauma, and dead soldiers who had been unjustly executed as malingerers, shell shock would become firmly linked to cowardice.[60]

Once the category of shell shock was invalidated, and the symptoms stigmatized, shell-shock symptoms nearly disappeared. There was no benefit to expressing one's emotional pain through the now-shameful disorder. Over time, new symptoms of war trauma replaced those of shell shock. The loss of speech, inability to walk, and contorted body postures, so frequent during WWI, would be relatively rare in WWII among combatants of every nation, and would mostly disappear by the mid-1950s. By the beginning of WWII, British clinicians spoke instead of a post-concussion syndrome characterized by headaches, vertigo, fatigue, poor concentration, and nervousness.

Symptoms of war trauma would continue to change throughout the twentieth century. For example, in neither WWI nor WWII were flashbacks, now a hallmark of PTSD, a common symptom; in fact, they are seldom mentioned in American and British military records until the Persian Gulf War (1990–91).[61] And whereas in WWI and WWII the symptoms of stress were apparent during or just after combat, and were treated using frontline clinical care (sometimes called "forward psychiatry"), combat stress during the brutal Vietnam War was rare.[62] The spike in the prevalence of combat-related trauma among veterans of the Vietnam War only occurred well after the United States left Vietnam—hence the postwar development of the apt term "*post*-traumatic stress disorder."[63]

How can the symptoms and the stigma of emotional distress change so much, and in so little time? One possible answer is that the combat environments are different. Different weapons and exposures have different consequences, and we know that the industrial violence of WWI was unprecedented. But there is little evidence to suggest that unexplained paralyses and loss of sensations were the result of actual brain injuries or toxicity, especially among soldiers with shell shock who had never been in combat or even close to an explosion.

A more likely answer is that the idioms of distress vary according to culture and history. One feeling, like anxiety, can at a certain place or time manifest itself through emotions like anger, fear, and sadness; in other contexts, anxiety presents as physical symptoms, such as a fast heart rate, shortness of breath, and dizziness. Not everyone in the world expresses emotions or pain through words, or even associates those feelings with the event(s) that might have precipitated them. This would be especially true for soldiers who developed symptoms months or years after any exposure to violence.

War, as Stephen Crane suggested in his 1896 poem "War is Kind," has its pleasures. It can be a form of patriotism, a means to individual and collective glory, an act of right, religion, and morality. People come together for a common purpose; a government flexes its power; an economy mobilizes and flourishes; a nation reaffirms its reason for being and articulates its vision for the future. War can even redefine the stigma of illness. Crane was disgusted by war and thought that whatever goodness seemed to emerge from it merely helped justify bloodshed. Yet he also recognized that wars reflect a society's values and produce change.

It's discomforting to say that wars are kind—even ironically. But wars are productive in the sense that they build on existing values, change how we think about human differences, and motivate growth in knowledge. Even if just for a moment, WWI generated new empathy for mental suffering, and it necessitated medical advances that are still with us today. Though the compassion quickly receded during peacetime, the nations at war had trained doctors to do things they could never have imagined before, such as providing short-term therapies to people other than the insane or developing surgical methods to repair the genitals of men wounded in combat—the same methods that would make possible the first gender-affirming surgeries. Many of the most important medical advances in anesthesiology, surgery, emergency medicine, prosthetics, immunization, and occupational therapy, among other areas, came from—and still do come from—military medicine.[64] The majority of Americans will at some point in their lives receive a medical treatment that can be traced directly to the advances in medicine made during wartime. The whole field of psychological testing arguably derives from the screening of recruits in the world wars.

Nonetheless, this history remains largely untold, perhaps because it seems so objectionable to say that anything useful can come from war or because we tend to think of wars as aberrations in history, as chaos rather than a reorganization of society. We remember mostly what benefits the political and economic goals of a nation and forget much of the rest—like the fact that WWI also produced new genres in the visual arts, poetry, and fiction. It has been said that the Great War was the war of a thousand legacies.

CHAPTER 6

FINDING FREUD

*Dear Roy, I have received your communication
regarding your interest in psychoanalysis and request
for permission to stay in Zurich and be analyzed. I
can only say briefly, and to the point, if you have no
better way to spend my money, come home at once.*

Your loving father, Julius Grinker
April 5, 1924

The Great War motivated a change in psychiatric thought, away from a purely biological model of mental illness and toward a more psychological one. But that transformation would not be complete until the Freudian intellectual revolution took hold—the revolution that shaped the psychoanalytic careers of most mid-twentieth-century psychiatrists, including my grandfather, Roy R. Grinker Sr., and my father, Roy R. Grinker Jr.

Recall that one reason why doctors and patients latched onto biological models of psychological distress was that psychiatry was long considered administrative work. It was carried out in large mental institutions (journalists often called them "snake pits"), some of which housed thousands of men and women, many of them impoverished, intellectually disabled, or elderly, abandoned by their families.[1] But psychoanalysis was different from psychiatry. First, it was a scholarly endeavor to study the mind. Second, it was more comfortable and lucrative for the doctor. Most patients in psychoanalytic treatment were neither seriously ill nor poor; they had to be wealthy enough to afford expensive and multiple sessions per week.

In 1911, even Julius briefly practiced psychoanalysis. He was simply following the pattern of neurologists in Paris and Vienna who were trying to find a way to study the brain, and to treat psychosomatic disorders like hysteria, without having to suffer the indignity of being a psychiatrist.[2] But Julius couldn't stomach the intimacy of the sessions.[3] He told his son Roy that he felt his patients either wanted to marry him or kill him, and that there were only a few, and unremarkable, emotions in between love and hate. In 1912, Julius published one article on the topic, calling Freud's theories plausible, but it would be more than twenty years before another Chicago doctor published anything about psychoanalysis.[4]

I remember that my grandfather did not like to talk about Julius, and when he did, he had only negative things to say. He once wrote to Dr. Walter Freeman, the man responsible for developing the lobotomy in America, "As a boy I needed him, yet was afraid of his strictness, violent tempers, and severe punishments."[5] For the rest of my grandfather's life, a photograph of the burly Julius, with a square-shaped head and thick moustache, stood on his desk in his home office alongside other family photos, as a sign of respect to his father. My grandfather looked at that photograph often when he was young. He'd stare at Julius and conjure up different ways to win his praise. In one recurring fantasy, he authored a giant medical textbook, lifted it over his head with two hands, and threw it down on the picture, smashing it to bits.

Julius was dictatorial, made his son's educational and professional decisions for him, and consistently told him that "he would never be good enough." So it was predictable that Roy became a neurologist after medical school and, in 1922, joined his father's practice. He quickly realized that he was dissatisfied in the field of neurology, in part because he felt insignificant in comparison to his father. As a constant reminder of his supposed inferiority, medical professionals in Chicago seldom referred to Roy by name, instead calling him "Julius's boy."

My grandfather was also dissatisfied with neurology because most of his patients believed that they suffered from neurological diseases when they were actually suffering from psychological distress, even if they were not conscious of the distress. It seemed to him that there was far too much untreated mental suffering in the world because the focus of psychiatry was always on the severely and chronically ill rather than on the broader spectrum of mental illnesses. He was intrigued by the coming wave of psychoanalysis, and by the Freudian proposition that we are all in some way mentally ill. He was just naive enough to believe that, if this were true, people might not be ashamed to seek psychiatric care for problems, maybe even minor problems, that they thought were medical rather than psychological. And perhaps more medical students would decide to become psychiatrists. It was at least worth exploring these ideas, especially if you had become a neurologist only in a vain attempt to please your unpleasable father.

Unfortunately, both psychoanalysis and psychiatry were mainly European professions, so my grandfather would have to go to Germany or Austria for legitimate training. Even decades later, in 1969, when a national poll was conducted among mental health professionals to identify the "most outstanding living psychiatrists in America," only three of the top eight (Karl Menninger, Lawrence Kubie, and Roy Grinker) were American-born.[6] Of course, Julius wouldn't let him go. Roy knew it would take no less a figure than the great Sigmund Freud to pull him away from Julius's shadow. That, and his father's death.

On January 11, 1928, Julius died at the age of sixty, of pancreatic cancer, and Roy's mother, Minnie, died just a few months later. The Chicago Neurological Society held a memorial for Julius, and the president, Peter Bassoe, gave the eulogy. He said that Julius had been unpopular due to his tendency for "acrimonious discussion" and "display of asperities rather than amenities." He was an authoritarian, Bassoe said, and independent to a fault—refusing, even in his early days of poverty in New York, any financial help from relatives. Bassoe implored the audience to remember Julius for his positive qualities: his "iron will" and "dogged determination."[7]

My grandfather now felt free to pursue his own academic research and writing interests at home and abroad. He left the Grinker practice, became an instructor of neurology at the University of Chicago, and made plans to spend two years in Europe. In 1933, just a few months before he left for Austria, he finished writing a massive neurology textbook entitled *Grinker's Neurology*—well over 1,000 pages long. He lifted the thick pile of papers above his head and dropped it on his desk in front of the framed photograph of Julius. But he didn't break the glass, as he had once fantasized. He asked his father's image, "Now are you happy?" He already knew the answer.

My grandfather's efforts to eradicate the shame and stigma of mental illness wouldn't really begin in earnest until World War II, in the deserts of North Africa. So I'll take this opportunity to tell you how he got there—not surprisingly, by way of Vienna and a complete psychoanalysis. What we'll find is that his therapy was more than a treatment, an education, an internship, or an indulgence. It was a lesson about the deep divide between psychiatry and psychoanalysis, between a profession that all too often confined and punished patients and one that tried to normalize them. It was an experience that, however personal, would also change the field of American civilian and military psychiatry. During and after WWII, the mental health professional would learn to deal not only with severe and chronic mental illnesses but also with the more minor problems of anxiety, mild depression, and what Freud called "normal unhappiness."

It was September 1, 1933, just after his thirty-third birthday. My grandfather found the double apartment over a butcher shop at 19 Bergasse, a five-story building on a middle-class street in Vienna, just a short walk from the Danube Canal. Inside Apartment no. 6, the waiting room smelled of cigars and wet dogs, and it was littered with old magazines. He waited for the last patient to leave, but no one did. He would soon learn that patients walked through one door to enter the office and exited through a different door. This was by design, so that patients would never meet, and he found it curious. Patients in, say, a neurologist's or urologist's office would sit in the same waiting room together. Why not in a psychiatrist's office? The question was partly resolved some weeks later when a distraught woman opened the wrong door and ran through the waiting room, crying. The doctor, Sigmund Freud, apologized to Roy for the scene with a joke. "You should have seen her *before* she started therapy." The other explanation for the two doors, the shame of seeing a psychiatrist, would dawn on him later.

At this first of many future sessions in his psychoanalysis with Freud, my grandfather was met with what he remembered as long, cold fingers that pulled him into the office in the home Freud had occupied for forty years. Freud said, "Shall we use English or German?" "English," Roy said, though his first language was German. The room was dark and cluttered with curios, maps, and framed images of European Jews. There were antiquities from Europe, Asia, and the Middle East, and Freud seemed eager to show off his extensive collection. They were extraordinary artifacts— several hundred first-, second-, and third-century AD Roman figurines and flasks, nineteenth-century Chinese jade, and fourth-century BC Greek terra-cotta, strewn throughout his home and office. It looked less like a doctor's office than the office of a museum curator. He found this curious too, but the more he learned about Freud, the more he saw that psychoanalysis and archaeology were related. After a vacation in Rome, Freud noted that the ancient city, like a psychoanalytic patient, still contained within it the traces of the earliest stages of its development.[8]

On the desk was an audience of warriors. The historian Peter Gay suggests that Freud identified with them as he fought his own battles for the acceptance of psychoanalysis: a small bronze Athena, and next to it a series of small figurines of helmeted ancient soldiers.[9] The office's eclectic array of furniture was worn, much of it draped in velvet, and rested on Turkish rugs. Everything he owned spoke of the past. Many years later, my grandfather and his colleagues in the Chicago psychoanalytic community would buy replicas of Freud's collection, as if the art forged an ancestral link.

Roy had previously traveled to Vienna in 1924 to visit cutting-edge neurology labs, and he met there a host of students enthusiastic about psychiatry and its offshoot, psychoanalysis. Yet, from the time he was born until the day in 1933 when he left Chicago for his second trip to Vienna, there was little growth in academic psychiatry in the United States, even as the asylum population grew.[10] Scientists were passionate about the brain but hostile to the mind, despite the high prevalence of mental illness among soldiers in WWI. There was no psychiatry unit at the University of Chicago, and patients at the university hospital who needed psychiatric care had to be referred to the handful of psychiatrists who saw outpatients in offices downtown. In 1933, in the entire state of Illinois, there were thirty-five psychiatrists for a population of nearly eight million, three million of whom lived in Chicago. Patients too ill to live at home were sent to rural sanatoriums outside Chicago and Milwaukee.[11] Lifelong luxury care was available for the rich, and some wealthy families built separate homes for their relatives on sanatorium grounds.

As a Jew, my grandfather already felt alienated from the medical establishment, even if, by objective measures, he was successful.[12] As Europe became increasingly dangerous for Jews due to the rise of Nazism, doctors throughout the United States continued to be anti-Semitic, preferentially arranging for non-Jewish doctors from eastern and central Europe to immigrate because they were easier to place in jobs in the United States. Many hospitals and universities simply refused to hire Jews desperate to flee Nazi Europe, and many college and university departments that did employ Jews had a "one-Jew rule" to prevent their schools from becoming too Jewish.[13] To address the potential for anti-Semitism, my grandfather legally changed his name from Roy Reuben Grinker to Roy Richard Grinker in 1925, just before his first publication. He thought Richard sounded less Jewish, and he was determined that if he had a son he would be Roy Richard Jr., and if he had a grandson he would be Roy Richard Grinker III. Since Jewish custom discouraged naming a son after a living father, fewer people would suspect that he and his descendants were Jews.

As for psychiatry and psychoanalysis, it wasn't easy to learn. As a neurologist, he was well versed in Freud's neurological research on cerebral palsy, but when he first decided he wanted to read Freud's psychoanalytic work, a librarian told him "the dirty books" were in a back room, locked in a case, and that they had to be read under a librarian's supervision. Psychiatry was so marginalized that when the University of Chicago invited the famous Hungarian-American psychiatrist Franz Alexander to become a visiting professor for a year, he agreed only if he was given the title professor of medicine. He knew what people would think of a psychiatrist. My grandfather recalled that the psychiatrists were hopeful that Alexander would encourage the university to take their field seriously. But Alexander was a comical disappointment. In his first lecture, he described how he cured a chronically constipated female patient by having her husband give her a dozen roses. The scientists at the medical school thought he was a quack, and most never returned to hear him lecture again.[14]

Alexander would eventually establish the Chicago Institute for Psychoanalysis. An exciting import from Europe, psychoanalysis promised to bring psychiatry out of the asylum. But American doctors, while praising psychoanalysis as a highly intellectual field, resisted thinking about it as medicine because it wasn't based in laboratory science. Nonetheless, my grandfather persisted, and the Rockefeller Foundation eventually awarded him a two-year fellowship to support a psychoanalytic education, which meant undergoing a complete psychoanalysis.

My grandfather was certainly ambivalent about psychoanalysis. Like his father, he disliked the lack of a scientific method in psychoanalysis. He disliked the elitism even more. Freud had originally envisioned analysis as a treatment for people with paralysis, catatonia, and the other acute symptoms he had seen in his neurology clinic. But psychoanalysis was becoming a highbrow therapy for the worried well—introspective intellectuals and intellectually ambitious women who had been denied academic opportunities—while the seriously mentally ill rotted in deplorable institutions. New students at the Chicago Institute for Psychoanalysis were told to turn away patients with severe mental illnesses because they were unsuitable for the method of psychoanalysis. My father recalled that when he was in training during the 1960s, the supervisors at the institute told the students, without any hint of humor, "Don't treat any sick patients." The result was that the best-trained doctors treated the healthiest patients, while the worst-trained treated the sickest.

Working-class Americans were seldom candidates for psychoanalytic psychotherapy because of the cost and time involved, and because analysts also believed that poor and uneducated people were actually incapable of being analyzed. As late as 1970, one psychoanalyst wrote that "many psychiatrists and analysts assume that the poor, and especially Negroes, are essentially unreachable by psychotherapy because of limited verbal facility, suspicion of doctors in general, and a tendency to believe that pills and pills alone can work miracles."[15] Others argued that poor and uneducated patients were only interested in alleviating their symptoms, and not in identifying the unconscious processes that caused them. When, in 1970, 184 psychiatrists responded to a survey about the characteristics of their caseload, only three of the clinicians who practiced psychoanalysis said they had one or more African American patients, and 45 percent said the vast majority of their patients were Jewish. None reported a single patient who was Mexican, American Indian, or Puerto Rican.[16]

A few progressive therapists felt the need to publish reports of success in treating blue-collar workers, but even those efforts came off as condescending. In one case, a senior psychiatrist at Bellevue Hospital in New York noted that, although the patients he treated under a contract with the United Auto Workers union were not immediately able to have the kind of insight or introspection characteristic of middle- or upper-class patients, they were open to receiving emotional support from a caring, listening analyst. "The blue collar worker," he wrote, "with his perhaps more limited aspirations than the striving-to-better-himself, middle-class individual, still suffers as much psychic pain from symptoms and impaired functioning due to neurotic mechanisms."[17]

Such were the contradictions of psychoanalysis. Despite Freud's early interest in debilitating neurological and psychiatric disorders, most of the patients Freud and other analysts treated were ordinary sufferers, not people with severe mental illnesses. Freud also wanted psychoanalysis to be biologically based, but it ended up separating psychiatry from the rest of medicine. He wanted psychoanalysis to be available to everyone, but it ended up as a luxury few could afford. Psychoanalysis proved to be less of a therapeutic answer than an orthodox belief system, and to the extent that it was isolated from advances in other disciplines, it remained frozen in scientific time. My grandfather did not want a career indulging elites to talk about their problems: he saw himself as a scientist who treated sickness. He also believed he had a strong enough ego to manage the smug analysts and find a way to put Freud to use in mainstream psychiatry.

The relationship between a doctor and a patient can be powerful, but the relationship between a psychotherapist and a patient has a special potency. Though the revelations are one-sided, it is ideally one of the most intimate and honest of relationships. Still more powerful is the unusual circumstance when the patient doesn't even think he's a patient. From Roy's perspective, his sessions with Freud were supposed to be didactic, not therapeutic, intended to teach him about the techniques and theory of psychoanalysis, not help him address his own pathology. He naively thought of himself as a happy, stable, well-balanced student.

And so that first meeting was surprisingly difficult. Freud acknowledged the high cost of the analysis ($25 a session, equivalent to $300 today) and then quickly shifted the topic to my grandfather's childhood. In recounting his father's cruelty and his unfulfilled wish for his father's affections, he recalled that he cried, "perhaps as I never cried before." Being in the very presence of Freud was an unforgivable act of rebellion against his father. He retreated to a local coffeehouse stunned and ashamed by how vulnerable he was—how psychologically prepared he had been for analysis, though he had been unaware of it. The next day he was disappointed to find only Freud's daughter, Anna, there to meet him in the waiting room. Her father had suddenly become ill with pneumonia, she said, and would likely not return for two weeks. My grandfather sent him a get-well-soon card, and Freud later interpreted this concern for his health as an unconscious death wish—Roy's vengeance for having been inconvenienced.[18]

In the third session, after Freud had recuperated, Roy met Anna's wolfhound. Earlier in the week, at a nearby pub, another American doctor studying in Vienna warned him that it was vicious, known to escape into the countryside, where it had eviscerated livestock. Because the dog liked to jump up, to be stroked and nuzzled between a visitor's legs, Roy felt physically threatened. After first meeting the dog, my grandfather lay on the couch and closed his eyes. Freud asked him to say the first thing that came to mind. Surprising himself, Roy blurted out "castration." It was a joke, but the kind of joke that reveals what one has repressed. Everything about these sessions seemed to point to his unconscious. He started to realize that if a highly functional professional like him could have such primitive anxieties, then anyone could. Maybe psychoanalysis really did hold the key to moving psychiatry out of the asylum and into everyday life.

Freud believed that all human beings were fundamentally primitive, driven by animalistic impulses that modern societies struggled to suppress. These impulses would always find a way to escape a society's constraints, through the complex symbolism of dreams, and by distorting themselves into the bodily and psychological symptoms of mental illness. Psychoanalysis was supposed to show the world that what it believed was progress—systems of law and order, morality, social and economic structures—was, actually, a sickness and the source of civilization's discontent.

In the fourth week of his analysis, after having completed fifteen sessions with Freud, Roy went to a dinner party where curious guests peppered him with questions about the famous doctor. The next day Freud seemed angry. He opened the session by scolding him. "One of Anna's patients was at a dinner party last night and she says that you were talking about me. I remind you that these sessions are confidential!" "I was very upset," my grandfather told me. "I was disappointing my father all over again." Of course, the patient didn't need to keep the *doctor's* behavior confidential! The real breach of confidentiality was when Anna told her father what her own patient had said, and when Freud then disclosed this to my grandfather. It took him a few days to realize the hypocrisy of Freud's warped idea of confidentiality, and it infuriated him. But he couldn't bring himself to criticize Freud. This was no ordinary conflict. Though I find it hard to believe that my grandfather was oblivious to it, his emerging relationship with Freud was imperceptibly becoming like his relationship with his own father. Freud had transformed himself into the object of Roy's ambivalence. With this admonition, Freud established the father transference that would become so important to Roy's ability to work through the emotional conflicts he had about his father.

And as he narrated his life to Freud over the next year, Roy's relationship with Freud began to change. He became possessive of Freud and competitive with Freud's other patients, though he didn't know any of them. He now understood another reason Freud's clients left the office through the back door. They wanted to be Freud's only patient.

Transference is a crucial part of any analysis. It is the unconscious attachment and pattern of expectation a patient develops in relationship to the therapist who, as a somewhat blank slate, can become symbolically like someone else in the patient's life—a father, for example. Freud was a good model for Julius if only on objective grounds: Freud and Julius were both older, male, neurologists whose first language was German. But the analyst's greatest power is symbolic. If all goes well, the transference can help a patient correct the problems of early emotional experiences by reliving them in the therapeutic situation. The doctor can manipulate the relationship into a certain kind of transference (sometimes the doctor does this without being aware of it), as can the patient: my grandfather never knew whether Freud consciously intended to become the symbol of the tyrannical father, or whether he unconsciously pushed Freud in that direction.

Freud would embody Julius's star power as well as his stern and ungenerous personality. Roy would in turn become frustrated by his desire for Freud's approval and his inability to express that frustration to Freud. This sense of impotence in the sessions was patterned on my grandfather's passivity toward his own father, the primary source of his anger. What was unattainable through Julius—love and praise—would, at least for the moment, also be unattainable through Freud. But that was the point. He soon realized that Freud was a safe stand-in for Julius. My grandmother, Mildred, on the other hand, was less satisfied with the analysis, and soon wrote to Freud about problems in their marriage: "A couple of months of analysis have now passed and I see no changes in him."[19]

The transference was enhanced by Freud's depressive moods. Freud didn't smile often, and when he told a joke it was sometimes hard to tell it was a joke. He said that he hated old age and welcomed death. "Sometimes I thought Freud didn't give a damn about people," my grandfather once told me. "I don't know if he had a therapeutic urge." When challenged on this, Freud said that if psychoanalysis was only a therapy, he would have abandoned it long ago. It was really a science of the mind, and patients were samples to be investigated for the general principles they revealed. Nevertheless, Freud worked hard at the analyses. As other former patients recounted, he was not the silent thinker, listening to the patient, and responding only with "I see" or "Tell me more," as cinematic depictions of psychoanalysts suggest. Freud actually did much of the talking.[20] He also tried to make his patients feel anxious, because he believed anxiety would stimulate the patient to express his or her unconscious desires. My grandfather would understand this some years later when treating WWII pilots who were too frightened to fly.

The interpersonal dynamic between Freud and my grandfather was, intended or not, the secret to the success of the analysis. Talk therapy worked. Because the analyst didn't give you what you wanted, you needed to develop a language of your own to make sense of the conflicts in your life. It was *your* past, once lived and now reexperienced, even if the memories of that past were imperfect, distorted by time and the shape of one's personality. Roy was determined to offer something similar to other patients back home, and to show his colleagues that psychiatry did not have to be associated with asylum management. Psychoanalysis could help the profession free itself from its own stigma.

When he returned to Chicago he was no longer just the resentful son of an implacable father, for Freud had liberated him. What he really wanted to do—treat the sickest and neediest patients, and advance psychiatry as a science—was now more feasible since he had more prestige among his peers. The most famous analyst in the world had analyzed him. Doctors now referred to him not as "Julius's boy" but as "one of Freud's last patients."

Roy never thought about Freud uncritically, and he implored others not to as well. In 1956, in an event to honor the one-hundredth anniversary of Freud's birth, he said that psychiatry and psychoanalysis will go further "if we do not deify Freud and deny him the privilege of human error."[21] Nonetheless, what he had done with Freud was life-changing. Roy was now known in every corner of the Chicago medical community, and he would repeat, to anyone who asked him about his time in Vienna, the parting sentiment Freud conveyed at the end of his final analytic session: "Your analysis was one of my last few remaining pleasures."

My grandfather held on to that sentence like a talisman.

On July 1, 1935, at the beginning of the new academic year, my grandfather set up a small psychiatric unit at Billings Hospital at the University of Chicago and focused his attention on developing a lab to study schizophrenia, just the kind of serious illness the psychoanalytic community warned him away from.[22] The best doctors were uninterested in schizophrenia because, it was assumed, people with schizophrenia lacked the rationality and insight required for a successful psychoanalysis. As my father told me, "Psychoanalysis was the Grade A level of psychiatry—everyone wanted to do it. All the really smart people from the best universities, those with the best chance of actually advancing psychiatry as a science, became analysts." Psychoanalytic training was not only elitist and potentially irrelevant to my grandfather's interest in the most serious mental illnesses; it would also entail going through another analysis—it was the Chicago institute's firm rule that to be a member you had to be analyzed there—and Freud's potential disapproval weighed on his mind.[23]

Finally, in late 1938, Roy began an analysis with Franz Alexander, but he didn't tell Freud until January 19, 1939, after Freud and his family had fled to London to escape the Nazi annexation of Austria. He wrote, "Although it has been a long time since I finished with you, my analysis has started just as if I left off last week. It is incredible the way the unconscious ignores time. I fully realize that writing this letter is symbolic of expiating guilt for going to another analyst and in an unconscious way asking permission. Consciously, however, I know that you will be pleased to learn that my career is marching along according to plan."[24] As far as I know, Freud never responded directly to my grandfather's request for approval. Freud died that September. His last letter to my grandfather was dated July 19, 1938. He said simply that he was happy to be in London, far from the Nazis, and wrote, in English, "I hope you are allright [sic]."[25]

Just a few years later, my grandfather would confront the war as well, as one of just a handful of psychiatrists working near the front lines in WWII. Looking up from the U.S. Air Force command in Algiers where he was stationed, one would have been impressed by the skies, busy with pilots and bombardiers on their missions. But on the ground, men slept, tried to sleep, and walked aimlessly. Depression and anxiety flourished in the desert. By the time Roy arrived, more than 1,700 men had been sent to the 95th General Hospital in Algiers for psychiatric treatment. He would try to figure out if psychoanalysis offered them anything at all.

CHAPTER 7

WAR IS KIND

Mother whose heart hung humble as a button
On the bright splendid shroud of your son,
Do not weep.
War is kind.

Stephen Crane (1896)

During World War I, 25 percent of all "casualties"—the term the military uses to describe soldiers who cannot fulfill their duties—were psychiatric.[1] Yet the military did little after the war to prepare for future mental health treatment. Between 1920 and 1930, members of the US military were hospitalized for mental disorders at a rate of a little more than one percent per year. This low rate was not because of a lack of mental illnesses. Mental illnesses as a whole were the leading cause of medical discharge and medical evacuation from overseas, and schizophrenia (then still called dementia praecox) was the largest cause of discharge among all listed diagnoses.[2] In the absence of war, the military had no reason to care for these men; they could simply be kicked out of the service. And given that psychiatry was still an uncommon profession, and that the medical community still had little respect for psychiatry, the military was hard-pressed to find anyone to do psychiatric work.

Between the wars, the US military did employ a large number of psychologists to screen for potential soldiers who might have mental illnesses or be at risk of developing them. But a 1927 handbook for military medical workers described a need for beds only for the physically sick and wounded, and none for psychiatric patients, perhaps because the authors assumed new screening measures would identify and exclude them during recruitment.[3] A 685-page military medicine manual published in 1937 had only one page devoted to mental health.[4] And by the time the United States entered World War II, there were only 100 psychiatrists active in the armed forces. Many of these doctors were just *called* psychiatrists since they had actually received their medical education in other, unrelated fields. In the interwar period, the British military had maintained only six so-called psychiatrists, and most of them had no training in psychiatry.[5]

The late Gerald Grob, probably the most celebrated historian of American mental health care, once told me, "Little was learned in WWII that hadn't been learned in WWI—it's just that everyone forgot about it." This neglect of military psychiatry during peacetime would become a tradition. It would happen after WWII and again after the Korean War. Stigma followed the same pattern. Soldiers and their families who suffered from psychological trauma during the war would be hailed as courageous and patriotic, but mental illnesses after the war would signify weakness.

Few Americans—even experts in psychology and psychiatry—know that the classification and description of most of the mental illnesses we are familiar with today were first produced by the army in WWII. During that time, psychiatry emerged as a more respected discipline largely by treating the one million members of the military who were diagnosed with mental illnesses. It was in WWII that scientists for the first time realized how common mental illnesses were in American society, that stress in times of combat could cause or exacerbate emotional problems, that many more doctors needed to be trained as psychiatrists, and that mental illnesses were treatable outside of asylums and other institutions. Just as importantly, doctors would more fully appreciate that the future of psychiatry might involve a combination of drugs and psychotherapy. The first could save your career, or even your life; the second could give it strength and meaning.

The United States was involved in WWI for only about eighteen months, and in only one theater of combat. WWII was lengthier, and far more complicated geographically. For the United States, the war would last more than three and a half years and was conducted in Europe, North Africa, and the Pacific. American military personnel were distributed in the Middle East (Palestine, Syria, and Lebanon), in West Africa (Liberia and Senegal), and in China (the China-Burma-India theater). Despite the size of this undertaking—or perhaps because of it—military psychiatry had been better organized at the beginning of WWI than WWII.[6] It took more than two years after the start of WWII for the United States to reach the level of psychiatric services achieved at the height of WWI.[7]

At the onset of WWII, screening—not treatment or research—seemed to be all that mattered to the US military. The vast majority of mental health professionals involved in the first months of the war spent their days administering surveys and questionnaires in an attempt to remove unfit recruits. I remember my grandfather telling me that these psychiatrists were not the cream of the crop. By and large, the best and the brightest psychiatrists—in those days, the psychoanalysts—heeded the words of the president of the American Psychoanalytic Association, Karl Menninger, to keep their distance from the war effort. Just a few months after Pearl Harbor, Menninger told an audience in Boston: "The Army, Navy, and the Public Health Service, recognize psychiatry; they do not recognize psycho-analysis. . . . It behooves us to pay prime attention to our patients and not attempt to get a foothold in political or governmental activities."[8] Those few well-known doctors who volunteered for military service, like my grandfather and his protégé Dr. John Spiegel, often complained that they spent more time identifying malingerers and diagnosing criminals (for assault, homosexuality, and drug use) than they did treating war trauma. The military would be compelled to quickly train civilian doctors (obstetricians, surgeons, ophthalmologists, for example) in psychiatry. They were known as "90-day wonders," because they had just three months of psychiatric training before beginning their work. Many of them permanently abandoned their previous specializations and went on to become leaders in modern psychiatry.

Why was the military so preoccupied with screening in WWII? In WWI, the American military developed and administered psychological tests for both literate and illiterate young men—more than 1,500,000 examinations in all—in an effort to identify "unfit" recruits.[9] They ended up turning away only about two percent of them. In fact, about half of all soldiers accepted into the US armed forces during WWI had a "mental age" of thirteen or younger (likely because so many soldiers were uneducated and illiterate). Many of these men left mental institutions or residential schools to fight. There was even a specific regulation permitting "feebleminded" men with the intelligence "of a child of eight years" to be inducted if they could comprehend simple commands.[10] However, these men were not the biggest problem for military psychiatry; reports suggest that the "feeble-minded" were actually successful soldiers.[11] It was the people with neurasthenia, hysteria, manic-depressive illness, psychosis, or alcoholism who formed the bulk of the neuropsychiatric discharges.

By the end of WWI, so many soldiers had been discharged for neuropsychiatric reasons that the military was eager not to repeat the same mistakes. The sheer financial cost of providing care for these men during and after the war was enough to frighten any government. British and American military officials were determined that if there was another war in the future, they would have rigorous psychiatric screening procedures to weed out the mentally impaired recruits before they entered combat. As one American psychiatrist put it in 1940, "If we thus set up filters against the defective, the unstable and potentially neurotic . . . we'll go far towards drying up our post-war neurotics at the source and so lighten the load of the Veterans bureau."[12]

In England, at the start of WWII, a more progressive mental health system focused on ending the discriminatory practice of rejecting recruits of low socioeconomic status as inherently inferior. The British tried to use psychological screening not to turn away willing soldiers but to place them in jobs suited to their intellect and personalities. As a result, the British military rejected only 1.4 percent of all WWII recruits while the Americans ended up rejecting 7.2 percent. After the war, General William Menninger, the chief of all psychiatry for WWII, and the brother of psychoanalyst Karl Menninger, put the rate of rejection at induction centers at 12 percent.[13] During WWII the American military rejected nearly six times the number of recruits they rejected in WWI.[14] So many men were excluded at induction who might have contributed to the war effort that they would later be called the "lost divisions."[15] What most of the WWII leaders in the United States had forgotten was that screening didn't work. Despite the intensive screening, the incidence of psychiatric disorders in WWII would be about three times greater than in WWI.[16] And those who did remember argued that the WWI screeners had just been bad screeners who had looked only for the most obvious mental defects and problems. They said they would do better in this war. They would look for covert, potential problems rooted in ingrained personality defects.

The American screening methods in WWII were an utter failure, unless you were in the field of psychology. The academic discipline of psychology arguably owes its present-day strength to the massive growth in psychological testing during the war. Tests for cognitive ability and personality traits became the bread and butter of psychology. There was so much emphasis on screening "at-risk" recruits, rather than mobilizing clinicians to provide care, that once the war began the military was unprepared for the consequences of combat. Over the course of the war, nearly 550,000 soldiers were discharged for "neuropsychiatric reasons" (abbreviated as NP)—386,600 honorably and 163,000 dishonorably (many as the result of criminal infractions).[17]

In retrospect, it was clear that the psychological tests had little predictive value.[18] Some of the best soldiers had been deemed "mentally defective" at the time of enlistment. One report on recruits who came from the Elwyn State School in Pennsylvania for "mental defectives" indicated that four men with below-average IQ scores, ranging from fifty-nine to ninety-one, became sergeants. One man with an IQ of sixty (which qualifies as an intellectual disability, or what used to be called "mental retardation") became an air force instructor. A corporal with an IQ of eighty-one became a mechanic.[19] Many of these "mentally retarded" soldiers, though integrated into the military during the war, returned to their previous residential institutions after the war.[20]

In contrast, some of the most problematic soldiers had passed the screening with flying colors. The testing didn't work because no one could know, prior to induction for active duty, who would or would not experience significant psychological distress. Furthermore, studies conducted during and after WWII showed that a substantial percentage of soldiers hospitalized for mental disorders had symptoms that had originated before entering the service but that were unknown to the recruiter, or unrecognized by the soldier himself, at the time of enlistment.[21]

In a memoir of his father's career as a military psychiatrist, the writer Eric Jaffe notes that some screeners interviewed so many soldiers—sometimes more than a hundred a day—that they had time to ask only the most superficial questions, informed by stereotypes: "Do you like girls?" "Do you wet your bed?" Eleanor Roosevelt herself was concerned that too many good men were being eliminated. Twenty-four men who played football for the Tulsa Golden Hurricanes in the 1943 Sugar Bowl were deemed unfit for military service.[22] The military psychologist's questionnaire I located at the National Archives in Washington, DC, lists sixty-four questions, several of which concern bed-wetting. Others included: "Have you ever had a headache?" and "Have you been arrested more than three times?"

Early in WWII, American psychiatric patients who had somehow escaped diagnosis before enlisting were at first identified by the label NP—although in the navy that classification was quickly replaced by the letters A (patients under locked care), B (patients under unlocked care in a hospital but not a ship's setting), and C (patients in unlocked care). For the most seriously ill patients, those under lock and key, the navy initially used cages—six feet long by three feet wide and three feet high—constructed out of wire mesh. The patients could not even sit up inside them, and there was a significant risk of death for patients with psychosis. In one six-month period in the navy, out of 2,980 psychiatric patients there were nineteen deaths (nine by drowning, one by hanging, and the others by cardiac events, malnourishment, and unknown reasons).[23]

In September 1943, the U.S. Air Force published a lengthy classified document entitled *War Neuroses in North Africa*. It was the first publication by American psychiatrists in WWII.[24] *War Neuroses* conveyed the military psychiatrist's sense of horror at the psychological problems that emerged from the battlefield, and it provided unparalleled details about soldiers' ongoing terror. The military historian Ben Shephard called it "a descriptive masterpiece,"[25] and Eric Jaffe says that during WWII it was known as the "bible of military psychiatry."[26] The document changed the way the military looked at mental illnesses in war. And after the war, when it was declassified and published under the title *Men Under Stress*, it changed public perspectives on mental illness as well.

The authors of this "bible" were Lt. Colonel Roy R. Grinker and his former student Captain John P. Spiegel, both of whom volunteered for service in WWII, unlike most of their counterparts in the psychiatric and psychoanalytic community. Writing just nine months after beginning their work in Algiers, they made several arguments. First, they said that anyone, anywhere, could develop a mental illness under conditions of great stress—whether in combat or not. Indeed, nearly two-thirds of all "nervous breakdowns" in the army were among nondeployed soldiers, most still in training, in the United States.[27] Second, they said that mental illnesses were treatable and often required only short-term therapies. Third, mental illness in war was not a sign of weakness but was a normal reaction to stress. They said the men they treated were not abnormal; they were normal men in abnormal circumstances.[28] Fourth, reflecting my grandfather's training with Freud, they argued that the men were not usually aware of the cause of their suffering because their trauma was unconscious. The most useful therapeutic action, therefore, was to relive those repressed memories, and by reliving them to release them from the unconscious. That release could be achieved through a combination of talk therapy and intravenous injections of Sodium Pentothal, a chemical compound otherwise known as "truth serum."

Beginning in January 1943, Grinker and Spiegel together managed the psychiatric operations in the North African theater of WWII. Working at the Twelfth Air Force Base in Algiers, they were among only a few psychiatrists posted overseas to treat soldiers close to combat, predominantly from the 1943 Tunisian campaign. The allies in North Africa were losing to stronger and more experienced German forces, and so there was no shortage of physically and psychologically wounded men to treat. But most psychiatrists and psychologists, both in the United States and in England, were still preoccupied with screening. Another reason few psychiatrists were near combat was that the military leadership didn't trust them. One U.S. Marine Corps war hero, General John Lucien Smith, angry at even the suggestion of bringing psychiatrists near front lines, said, "We don't want any damned psychiatrists making our boys sick."[29]

Like the doctors in WWI, my grandfather and Spiegel were astounded by the number of soldiers whose bodies appeared unscathed but who suffered debilitating mental and physical pain. They had never seen such men before, and did not even expect to see them, given that they knew little about WWI shell shock and had previously treated soldiers only months or years after any traumatic event. Here they were able to examine soldiers within two to five days of their "breakdowns." In doing so they were following the advice of more experienced military doctors who emphasized that effective medical treatments required proximity and promptness, the strategy the US military called PIE: *proximity* of the treatment to the site of combat, *immediacy* of treatment, and *expectation* of recovery. The acronym remains in use today with an additional word, "simplicity," added at the end, hence PIES. What's more, because they were close to combat, but not so close that they were on the front lines providing triage, they were able to simultaneously treat patients in residence at their hospital and conduct systematic research.

Although military physicians observed and treated patients quickly after combat, some doctors argued that psychiatric care needed to be provided within combat itself, where there was no opportunity to take refuge in a hospital and where war neuroses could not be rewarded with "a one-way ticket home."[30] William Menninger wrote that there should be no middle ground for the psychiatrist: either the soldier is put back "on the line" or he should be discharged.[31] In fact, my grandfather and Spiegel gained a measure of fame in the American press for returning anxious and emotionally stressed soldiers to combat (at least that's what the media thought). On the NBC radio series *The Doctor Fights*, the actor Vincent Price portrayed my grandfather as a hero of the war effort who helped "broken" pilots get back in their planes.

But that was far from the reality. While Grinker and Spiegel were able to return the majority of their patients to active duty, almost all of these soldiers were assigned desk jobs. They authorized the return to combat for only about two percent of their patients. Military leaders were unhappy about this practice and came up with their own psychological theory to explain Grinker and Spiegel's tendency to relieve the traumatized soldier from combat duty. After the war, Albert Glass, the chief of neuropsychiatry at Fort Sam Houston, would write that therapists like Grinker and Spiegel were overly sympathetic and kind. Because their method involved reliving the trauma with the patient, the therapist "invariably identified with the distress and needs of the patients and was therefore impelled to promise relief from future battle trauma."[32] One can understand Glass's and Menninger's concerns. About a third of all soldiers who received medical care during the Tunisian campaign were psychiatric casualties.[33]

Like the psychiatric casualties of WWI, many of the soldiers Grinker and Spiegel treated—pilots and infantrymen, artillerymen and radio operators—had no discernible physical wounds or diseases, but they had plenty of psychiatric symptoms. Given the growing popularity of psychoanalysis in the mid-twentieth century, WWII military psychiatrists and their patients were more willing to think about trauma in emotional rather than only biological terms. Most likely for this reason, the prevalence of bodily symptoms of war trauma, so common in WWI, declined. "Hysteria" had been largely replaced by "anxiety." The term "shell shock" was replaced by "combat fatigue," "battle exhaustion," and "war neurosis." In a report prepared by the eldest generation of British psychiatrists for the year 1940–41, the authors noted: "Those of us who treated the psychoneuroses during the last war have been struck by the difference in the picture presented of the neuroses in hospitals in this war. . . . The most striking change is the far greater proportion of anxiety states in this war, as against conversion hysteria (blindness, paralysis, etc.) in the last war . . . 64 percent were anxiety states and only 29 percent hysteria."[34]

Grinker and Spiegel wrote: "Terror-stricken, mute, and tremulous, the patients closely resemble those suffering from an acute psychosis."[35] They saw men shaking, with vacuous or fearful facial expressions, some of them unable to speak. But WWI symptoms like paralysis and awkward gait were much less common. They saw sudden and inexplicable fits of crying and laughing. Some had amnesia, and others could remember the recent past only in nightmares, sometimes waking up in the middle of the night attempting to dig through their mattresses, as if to find safety from enemy fire.

They saw men who startled at the slightest stimulus, who had chronic headaches, nausea, and ulcers. Others wet their beds, drooled, and sweated excessively. They saw nearly every symptom any psychiatrist ever imagined seeing in his career. Still, most patients had two things in common: they had regressed to the point of being childlike, and they had lost the ability to talk about how they felt or even about what had happened to them. "The patient," Grinker and Spiegel wrote, "resembles a frightened inarticulate child, with only a few persistent 'islands' of his past well organized behavior." The patient's lack of language with which to describe his experiences was a challenge to these psychoanalysts since their treatments relied on patients' ability to talk about their problems. Perhaps, they wondered, a truth serum like a barbiturate or anesthetic could help the patient relax and become aware of the reasons behind the anxiety, reasons that had been repressed into the unconscious.

One of the treatments Grinker and Spiegel offered these anxious men is described in the psychiatric literature under the terms "narcosynthesis" and "narcotherapy," but it was more akin to a short-term psychoanalysis than a drug therapy. The method, illustrated in the 1945 NBC radio show *The Doctor Fights*, involved the administration of a truth serum the soldiers called "flak juice"; flak was the word soldiers used for the antiaircraft bullets aimed at American planes. The episode, "Mission in the Dark," adapted from Case 40 of *Men Under Stress* ("Depression and Anxiety of One Year's Duration Due to Loss of a Buddy in Combat"), dramatically shows how a psychoanalytic understanding of repressed hostility combined with injections of a barbiturate facilitated the return of a pilot to active duty. Once the soldier reexperienced the source of his anxiety—releasing his emotions in a powerful catharsis—the symptoms of his war neurosis began to disappear.[36]

The episode begins as the narrator describes two decorated air force pilots who are incapable of flying any more missions. They reside, stateside, at the Don CeSar hotel, a luxury beach resort near St. Petersburg, Florida, that had been converted into a 900-bed convalescent hospital exclusively for the treatment of war neuroses. After returning from Algiers, Grinker and his colleagues had fought hard to convince the army to buy it. They feared that if the men were in a general hospital they would be stigmatized.

"They come, brave young men, depressed, frightened, not knowing what has happened to them under the terrible stress of combat." A young pilot named Eddie Rohmer cannot use his right arm. An older pilot, Captain Steve Woodard, angry and sullen, refuses to fly again. Inexplicably, Steve has turned down a prized promotion from flight leader to squadron leader, saying simply, "I've had enough." He cannot describe why he is so depressed, and he doesn't want to try.

My grandfather wrote about Steve in the hospital's case files. He described him as having an expressionless face. Steve spoke slowly, couldn't smile, reported insomnia and nightmares, and tried unsuccessfully to forget his experiences by getting drunk. In the episode, Eddie encourages Steve to accept psychiatric treatment. Eddie says, "They say this Colonel Grinker really knows his stuff. He's the guy who started using that flak juice. Just a couple of drops and you'll start remembering." Steve replies, "I'm not interested. . . . My nightmares will stop. . . . I'll take care of myself. Just let me alone so I can forget." Only after a violent confrontation with a friend does Steve realize that he needs counseling, at least to help him manage his anger. Steve consents to Dr. Grinker's treatment with Pentothal, and when Steve is in a drug-induced semi-unconscious state, Grinker, played by Price, begins the hypnosis.

"You are inside the plane. You are the lead pilot on a mission!" He tells Steve he is at the front of a V formation, with several other planes on his wing. Steve begins to relive the traumatic event that caused his depression. With antiaircraft fire ahead, Steve notices that one of the pilots, his best friend Joe, has broken from his wing position to take the lead, putting himself in the most vulnerable position. Steve yells out, "Joe is my best friend, the greatest guy in the world," "the sweetest guy in the world." "Look at Joe!" Steve yells. "He's taking the lead! Bail out! Why doesn't he bail out? Why doesn't he stay in formation?" Joe's plane is then hit by antiaircraft fire and he descends, out of control, to his death. "It's all my fault!"

"That was the start of the cure," the narrator says. "Steve's inner wound had to be located. Now it had to be probed."

During his second Pentothal injection, Steve describes how he became a better pilot than Joe and was promoted to flight leader, even though they had trained together.

> "Poor Joe, my best friend. The greatest guy in the world."
> "What didn't you like about him?" Grinker asks.
> "He was always jealous of me. . . . He's trying to take the lead, trying to crowd me out, but I'm going to win!"

In the actual case files, Steve talked about how he had been ambitious and competitive since early childhood, always wanting to be "top man" even though winning gave him more guilt than pleasure. Given this tendency, my grandfather reasoned that if someone with whom Steve was in competition died, he might then blame himself, as if he had actually killed him. In the radio show, Dr. Grinker says to the now-awakened pilot, "When Joe went down, in your subconscious mind it was *as if* you killed him." The episode then ends as Steve, Eddie, and other pilots board their planes on an airstrip, saluting Grinker. Grinker says, "It was more than a salute. It was a gesture of friendship—thanks from the young soldiers whose inner wounds were at last healed."

The listening audience likely interpreted Sodium Pentothal as a wonder drug and Dr. Grinker as a miracle worker. The *New York Times* hailed the procedure as a "mental X-ray" and said Grinker had "exploded as a myth" the idea that mental illnesses are a sign of weakness.[37] But the novelty of the mental X-ray was mostly spin, since my grandfather didn't actually invent the use of Sodium Pentothal or hypnosis. Hypnosis had been a common therapy for decades, and Eli Lilly had manufactured barbiturates during the late 1920s to help psychiatrists communicate with severely ill psychiatric patients in asylums. The police used barbiturates to elicit confessions. Even the ancient Romans knew *in vino veritas* (in wine there is truth).

My grandfather also garnered far more glory than Spiegel, due to his seniority. In truth, my grandfather actually got the idea to use Sodium Pentothal from Spiegel. Spiegel got the idea from a 1940 paper in the *Lancet* in which William Sargant and Eliot Slater reported the emergence of suppressed memories in soldiers who had survived the Dunkirk campaign.[38] And Sargant and Slater got the idea from an earlier paper in the *Lancet*, in 1936, by British psychiatrist J. S. Horsley, who called the treatment "narcoanalysis."[39] In fact, in February 1943, before my grandfather ever administered Pentothal to a patient, he observed British psychiatrists use Pentothal at the British 95th General Hospital.[40] In addition, despite the hype and headlines, narcosynthesis was an impractical treatment outside of research protocols. Because each procedure took between ninety minutes and three hours to administer, it never became routine.[41]

The *New York Times* also suggested that Grinker and Spiegel's work had eliminated the shame of mental illness in the military. The pilots they treated, men who had flown dozens of missions, were actually the very strongest of soldiers, the paper wrote. The weak soldiers could never have made it through combat. Grinker and Spiegel had, in effect, normalized mental illness in the war. For them, the more interesting question was not why these soldiers became sick, but why so many *didn't* become sick. Stigma, they said, should be reserved for those who avoided service or had committed serious crimes.

In 1945, in a joint civilian and military book on military medicine, the authors wrote of the soldiers suffering from psychological problems: "They are normal human beings." Furthermore, they wrote, the soldiers resemble people everywhere since their symptoms, which lie on the spectrum of human behavior, "are manifested by people in civilian life to a greater or less degree.... Some of our most successful business and political leaders were psychoneurotic."[42] And in 1946, a year after *The Doctor Fights*, my grandfather restated the claim made by the *Times* and prematurely announced an end to the stigma of mental illnesses. Speaking about the high prevalence of psychiatric conditions within and outside of the military, he said, "Such ailments are now rightfully considered neither shameful nor the source of inferiority feelings."[43]

Despite the many psychiatric successes in WWII, war did practically nothing to change the stigma of homosexuality. Unlike Grinker and Spiegel's "normal" patients whose sicknesses were considered temporary and caused by extraordinarily stressful situations over which the sufferer had no control, homosexuality was deemed a permanent and defining feature of one's character. Toward the end of his life, Freud argued, in vain, that homosexuality was not a mental disorder. Yet military leaders during every modern American war have supported research to identify homosexuals and remove them from their ranks. At the same time, leaders also denied that homosexuality was common in the military. However, the fact that virtually every publication on sex published by the US military during WWII concerned male homosexuality suggests otherwise.[44]

Throughout WWII, doctors studied homosexuals' urine, hormones, and IQs, and carried out detailed genealogies to explore hereditary causes and biological differences associated with this "psychopathology." Curious about why a man might want to give another man oral sex, doctors measured the sensitivity of homosexuals' lips, mouths, and throats. They tested homosexuals' gag reflexes, and even questioned them about whether they ever wanted to eat feces or drink urine.[45] With the exception of a few doctors who described the rare soldier who faked being a homosexual in order to get discharged from the military[46] (rare because the stigma of being discharged for homosexuality was so great), no one was interested in studying heterosexual men. Doctors assumed that they all tacitly understood the difference between sickness and health and that anyone who wanted homosexual sex was sick. Within and outside the military, homosexuality was widely regarded as a form of sexual deviance caused by a child's failure to grow out of his infantile narcissism—a condition in which the homosexual desired a version of himself.

I have no record of how many homosexuals my grandfather and Spiegel were responsible for releasing from the military with a dishonorable discharge, branding those men with a diagnosis of sexual pathology. It is possible they may have refused to act as informants and harm the lives of good soldiers. But it was the psychiatrists' duty as medical officers to assist military prosecutions. Soldiers discharged for homosexuality were subsequently unable to obtain military or government employment, and potential civilian employers could legally require an applicant to supply military separation documents, which would show not only a dishonorable discharge but also the reason for the discharge: "sexual pathology."

When a society wants to suppress something, it has to talk about it. Otherwise there is no way to justify the suppression. So, if you want to control homosexuality, you need to classify it, write articles and books about it, train experts, amass case files. The homosexual had to become a legitimate object of scientific inquiry, and then institutions such as the military and the disciplines of psychology and psychiatry had to create the practices—

like diagnoses, treatments, and court-martials—to justify the homosexual as a distinct kind of person. The German physician Magnus Hirschfeld counted more than 1,000 articles on homosexuality published in Germany between 1898 and 1908, 320 of them in just one year, 1905. This is the process by which knowledge becomes a form of social control.

Many of the hundreds of articles written about sexuality during and after WWII sought to describe homosexuality not as a behavior but as a personality type. In a 1945 paper, for example, two psychiatrists in the U.S. Navy, Herbert Greenspan and John D. Campbell, wrote that the major signs of a homosexual character were feminine interests, high intelligence, high socioeconomic status, and an interest in socializing with the opposite sex. Their description of homosexual traits also included "pseudointellectual" speech and writing, and the use of phrases like "Dear me!" and "Oh my goodness!"[47]

Other doctors created typologies of homosexuals. The "*true* homosexual" was someone whose interest in or sexual behavior with someone of the same sex was long-standing, exclusive, and not fabricated in order to be discharged from the military. In the army, male nurses were particularly susceptible to accusations of true homosexuality since they occupied a traditionally feminine role.[48] The "*incidental* homosexual" was someone who, though perhaps not otherwise inclined, engaged in same-sex sex due to context, such as living for months in combat or in barracks at a military base. The "*accidental* homosexual," as the term suggests, was someone who might have been duped into a homosexual act or had homosexual sex while incapacitated by alcohol or drugs and was unable to comprehend or resist what the partner or perpetrator was doing. Nonetheless, there were gay soldiers in noncombat arenas who, though not openly gay, acted as female impersonators in popular drag shows.[49] One of the more well-known groups was the Amputettes, a drag troupe created by the US military to entertain veterans being rehabilitated at the Walter Reed Memorial Hospital and other convalescent centers.[50]

The U.S. Air Force Regulation (AFR) 35-66 that Grinker and Spiegel were required to follow was entitled "Discharge of Homosexuals" and stated: "Homosexuality will not be permitted in the Air Force and prompt separation of true, confirmed, or habitual homosexuals is mandatory." If someone in the military, including a psychologist, psychiatrist, or chaplain knew of homosexual desires or behaviors, they were obliged to report them to the commanding officers. Chaplains had to make sure that the people they spoke with were aware of the limits of confidentiality. Unless someone was confessing homosexuality in the confession booth itself—as a specifically religious act—the chaplain was duty bound to report it.

Officers who were homosexuals could resign "for the good of the service," but enlisted men, the lowest-ranking soldiers, would be given what was called a "blue discharge."[51] A blue discharge, whether for homosexuality or for some other reason to declare a soldier "unfit," denied the enlisted man any benefits from the G.I. Bill (financial assistance for service members' education). The blue discharge was a big obstacle for employment and was disproportionately given to African Americans. Though they constituted less than 7 percent of the army's soldiers, 24 percent of all blue discharges were for African American soldiers.[52]

Servicemen who were merely suspected of being homosexuals because their behavior was interpreted as effeminate, or because a rumor about their sexuality reached a commander, were often discharged. Air force psychiatrists described a case in which one pilot accused another of being a homosexual. An investigation followed, during which the accuser realized that he had mistaken the man for someone else. He withdrew the accusation and gave investigators the name of the correct "homosexual." Although the charges against the innocent man were dropped, the soldier's fiancée, and others in her community, found out about the charge, and she broke off the engagement. In a discussion of this case, the clinicians wrote that the wrongly accused man "felt that he would never be able to go home again and that he was stigmatized for life."[53]

Other unjust cases involved the prosecution of men who expressed their feelings to a counselor in an attempt to find emotional support, and under the assumption that they had done nothing in violation of any military policy. Soldiers who told counselors they had had a homosexual experience in their early teens were discharged as having homosexual tendencies. And they were sometimes prosecuted for fraud as well, because they should have told the recruiter this information before enlisting. Commanders applied a double standard. Any hint of homosexuality could lead to prosecution and discharge, but heterosexuals were given greater latitude and were seldom investigated for sexual irregularities. In one research study of active duty men, 25 percent of "confirmed heterosexuals" reported some kind of unusual sexual history, including sex with a close relative, farm animals, and watermelons.[54]

Although I do not know exactly what my grandfather and Spiegel believed about homosexuality and mental illness, I hope they sided with Freud—especially Spiegel, since he was compelled to uphold the view that homosexuality was a mental illness even as he kept his own secret.

In 1981, Spiegel celebrated his seventieth birthday with his children and grandchildren at a beachfront resort. During that vacation, he revealed the secret he had kept for fifty years from everyone in the family except his wife, Babette, who had died a few years earlier. On the first morning, he introduced his children and grandchildren to his lover, David, and told them of his other male lovers in the past. He told them that Babette had known, that he had confessed to her that he was a homosexual before WWII, and just weeks before their wedding.[55]

In the early 1970s, Spiegel and other like-minded psychiatrists met often at his kitchen table in Cambridge, Massachusetts, to develop strategies to reform the stodgy, conservative American Psychiatric Association and to remove homosexuality from its list of mental disorders. Their group, dubbed the "Young Turks" by the Spiegel family, helped to elect younger and more liberal members to leadership positions in the association. And in 1973, when the association's members voted to remove homosexuality from the DSM, Spiegel was the APA's president-elect.

Mixed among the hundreds of letters, articles, and patient files Spiegel saved from his time in WWII is a set of precise instructions for how to discharge homosexuals from service—perhaps a clue to his own camouflage.

In the end, WWII produced an entire generation of psychiatrists. Erik Erikson developed his theory of ego identity during WWII after working with men who had "broken down" due to combat.[56] Psychiatric epidemiology emerged out of the war as a bona fide specialization. The war gave birth to American psychology and convinced many people that the mental health professions, especially psychoanalysis, offered something useful and socially acceptable to the "everyman," not just the insane. As evidence of how mainstream psychoanalysis had become, the 1945 Alfred Hitchcock hit movie, *Spellbound*, begins with these lines: "Our story deals with psychoanalysis, the method by which modern science treats the emotional problems of the sane." The greatest psychiatric achievement of WWII was arguably the diagnosis, treatment, and destigmatization of common mental conditions, such as depression and anxiety, both within and outside the military. In fact, the military produced the classification of mental illnesses that became the DSM-I.[57] Universities founded new residency training programs in psychiatry. And just after the war, President Truman, recognizing the value of psychiatry, created NIMH.

Given that the war was such a triumph for American psychiatry, and that it launched so many psychiatric careers, it's surprising that military histories and military medical documents during most of the twentieth century pay little attention to psychiatry. This "professional amnesia"[58] explains why in each new war medical personnel complain that they never learned the lessons of the previous one and why, between the wars, the military devoted few resources to developing a robust system of psychiatric care. The neglect was mutual. There is little mention of military psychiatry in most histories of psychiatry, as if wars didn't produce knowledge. Yet Grinker and Spiegel's account of WWII psychiatry, *Men Under Stress*, sold tens of thousands of copies and played an important role in transforming psychiatry from asylum administration to short-term therapy for a more diverse and less acutely ill patient population.[59] They had also proven that the presence or absence of stigma did not depend on how one defined mental illnesses scientifically, but on how one valued them morally. Despite the fact that my grandfather's war experience established his reputation in psychiatry, in his own autobiographical account of his psychiatric career he mentions WWII only briefly.[60] Such contempt for military psychiatry is echoed in the saying that military psychiatry is to psychiatry as military music is to music.[61]

CHAPTER 8

NORMA AND NORMMAN

*What immortality was to the Greeks, what virtù
was to Machiavelli's prince, what faith was to the
martyrs, what honor was to the slave owner, what
glamour is to drag queens, normalcy is to the contemporary American.*

Michael Warner, *The Trouble with Normal* (1999)

The end of World War II is often remembered as a heroic return: ticker-tape parades and Alfred Eisenstaedt's iconic photo for *Life* magazine of a sailor kissing a woman in Times Square after Japan's surrender. The horror and moral complexity of the war was reduced to what Studs Terkel called "the good war."[1] But the abruptness of war and demobilization, and the sharp contrast between wartime and civilian life, was cataclysmic, especially for people who came home physically or mentally disabled. The homecoming was also a shock to civilians who, during the war, had access only to information and images censored and sanitized by the government. "The war-time government..." historian Hans Pols writes, "provided a fictive account of the war in which no mistakes were made, soldiers fought heroically, good and evil were clearly demarcated, and no bodies were ripped apart."[2]

Celebratory war narratives mask or at best postpone trauma.[3] This whitewashing was an additional stressor for veterans, who suffered silently, concealing their pain, amid the celebrations of their patriotic service. Men who lost limbs, or who were wheelchair-bound, were also burdened as people sought to resuscitate prewar American gender roles. How could the disabled veteran be the autonomous head of household he was supposed to be? How could such men represent the self-sufficient masculinity of the idealized soldier when they returned home more passive and dependent than before, as incomplete men, less as victors than as victims?[4]

Grinker and Spiegel's answer was that only some of these men would adapt to their new situations. In *War Neuroses*, they had convincingly argued that psychiatric problems among soldiers were not the result of poor or defective character, but were the expected consequences of war among normal, well-adjusted men. But in their 1945 version of that report, released as a commercial book entitled *Men Under Stress*, they turned to the increasingly popular concept of "adaptation," a mental process they believed was fundamental to all psychological functioning in all contexts. Grinker and Spiegel said that everyone in combat had pretty much the same stressors, and so the question for the mental health professional was why one person's adaptation to the stress of war was to continue fighting, while another's adaptation was to avoid the risks of combat by becoming sick. It was a short step to a conclusion that unintentionally resuscitated the stigma of postwar mental illness: the men who adapted to stress by becoming sick must have been psychologically impaired to begin with. By neutralizing combat stress as something everyone experienced—what Grinker and Spiegel called a "universalizing context"—they actually pushed clinicians to pay less attention to the specific contexts of war trauma and to focus instead on the unique, noncombat history of the individual that predisposed him to have a maladaptive reaction.

A second answer lay in another concept related to adaptation: "normality." Often called the Age of Conformity, post-WWII America was defined by a desire to follow traditional patterns of social life—including the division of labor between the female homemaker and the male breadwinner. As David Riesman warned in 1950 in his best-selling book, *The Lonely Crowd*, the American people were becoming what he called "outer-directed" rather than "inner-directed," motivated to be as much as possible like everyone else—as "normal" as everyone else—even at the risk of losing their individuality. In this context, the traumatized soldier could only be "normal" if he conformed to his community's ideals. Normal became a powerful ideological tool with which to stigmatize people whose adaptive capacities kept them from "fitting in."

Like Riesman, my grandfather was also vexed by the vague concept of "normal," so much so that I have no memory of him ever saying the word without putting another word—"approximately"—in front of it. In 1953, he told a journalist that the desire for "normalcy" in American society was "the essence of neurosis."[5] As he explained it, Americans were increasingly neurotic because they were unable to accommodate change and diversity.

For soldiers, the order and social stability of military life contrasted sharply with the relative chaos of everyday civilian life. There were tensions between those men who spent their formative years fighting and those who had been able to stay home and advance their careers. Suspicions about infidelity, and other latent hostilities, damaged marriages. Survivors felt enormous guilt and missed the comradeship of the war. Much of that comradeship was interethnic and interracial, despite the fact that Black and white soldiers were segregated. Military doctors worried that minority soldiers would be traumatized by their reintegration into communities that were far more racist than the military. They also worried that minority soldiers would receive substandard health care. In statements that would sound strange to the many critics of veterans' hospitals today, Menninger and my grandfather both thought it would be wonderful if all hospitals could be as well run as the VAs.

In the lead article of the January 1945 volume of the prestigious *Ameri-*

can Journal of Sociology, five months before V-E (Victory in Europe) Day, the conservative sociologist Robert Nisbet warned that the return to civilian life would be a "profound psychological experience," and he called for the creation of psychiatric clinics to help with the inevitable problems of assimilation. Nisbet said that the soldier at home "will find himself a marginal figure, no longer a part of military society, not yet a member of civilian society."[6] Others warned that the disabled veteran was a threat to the nation because he had nothing to lose and could easily become an antisocial, violent criminal.[7] These experts also worried that disabled and disfigured men would be looked on with repulsion, or ignored out of discomfort and disgust.

Pols writes, "After the war, the mental condition of soldiers *before* they were drafted came to be seen as the most important factor in causing breakdowns."[8] This post-WWII attitude echoed Lord Sutherland's comment three decades earlier that the soldiers who continued to suffer after WWI had been susceptible to mental illness. And as my grandfather put it after the war, "There is one thing of which we can be sure: that most of the people who broke down early in the war were prepared to be sick before they went into the army."[9] A colleague of my grandfather's, Henry Brosin, agreed, saying that "those men who now come to us with problems show the clear outlines of difficulties which accrue through their early development."[10] The same argument would reappear at the beginning of the twenty-first century when clinicians questioned whether the original trauma behind a large number of PTSD cases in the military occurred long before the soldiers enlisted, perhaps in difficult childhood circumstances.

The general problem of adaptation also helped to shape the first DSM. After the war, Captain George Neely Raines of the U.S. Navy, a career military physician, served as the chairman of the Committee on Nomenclature of the APA.[11] In this position, Raines was in charge of adapting Medical 203, the army classification of mental disorders, into a manual for civilian use. The surgeon general's office had released Medical 203 to the public in 1948, but it wouldn't become the DSM until 1952. Published during the Korean War, DSM-I was a marriage of military experience and psychoanalytical theory. Psychiatric symptoms were no longer expected responses to external stressors. Now they were maladaptive neurotic reactions. To reflect the problem of adaptation, the new term of art for combat stress was "gross stress reaction." Other illness names in the DSM-I also included "reaction" in the name because the DSM defined mental illnesses as pathological reactions or failed adaptations to stress (depressive reactions, anxious reactions, paranoid reactions, and so on). Clinicians believed that these reactions were largely the result of a person's inability to control the world, a sense of helplessness that began in infancy, was shaped during childhood, and persisted into adulthood.

For decades, American clinicians, such as the distinguished pediatrician L. Emmett Holt (1855–1924) and the behavioral psychologist John Watson (1878–1958), had written that American parents were to blame for most forms of psychopathology, including homosexuality—especially strong mothers and weak fathers. According to them, American mothers were so involved with their children, and fathers so absent, that they prevented their children from developing the adaptive skills they needed as adults. Holt discouraged breastfeeding and suggested that, like the Puritans, parents tie metal rods to their children's arms to prevent thumb-sucking. Watson told mothers not to kiss their children (especially boys) or even bandage their wounds if the children were old enough to do it themselves. He sarcastically dedicated his 1934 book, *The Psychological Care of Infants and Children*, "To the first mother who brings up a happy child."

Philip Wylie and Edward Strecker—other well-respected experts— also wrote of the dangers that affectionate, overprotective mothers posed, specifically to men. In his 1944 book, *Generation of Vipers*, Wylie coined the term "momism" to refer to the willful efforts of a mother to make her son worship her. Mothers, he said, robbed their sons, and the nation as a whole, of masculinity. Two years later, after interviewing traumatized soldiers from WWII, Strecker went further to say that momism threatened national security. He divided the dangerous American mother into several types, including the Pollyanna mom, the self-sacrificing mom, the protective mom, and the pseudointellectual mom—all of which have their parallels in contemporary mother blame, in terms such as the helicopter mom, the stage mom, the tiger mom, and the Jewish mother. There is little that Strecker didn't blame on mothers.

In 1947, a year after Strecker's book was published, journalist Ferdinand Lundberg and New York psychiatrist Marynia Farnham wrote: "Women are one of modern civilization's major unsolved problems . . . at least on par with crime, vice, poverty, epidemic disease, juvenile delinquency, group intolerance, racial hatred, divorce, neurosis, and even periodic unemployment, and inadequate housing."[12] To be sure, there were scientists, like psychologist Harry Harlow, who would argue the opposite position. Harlow's controversial and often cruel studies proved that maternal deprivation, rather than too much affection, led to behavioral disturbances in rhesus monkeys.[13] But whatever position researchers took, they still held women responsible for both normality and abnormality in children and set the stage for the blame that would devastate a generation of mothers of autistic children, as well as the mothers of gay men and women.

Mental health professionals attributed homosexuality to a defect caused by overinvolved, hyperprotective mothers and distant fathers. In 1973, psychiatrist Irving Bieber from New York Medical College said, "Every male homosexual goes through an initial stage of heterosexual development, and in all homosexuals, there has been a disturbance of normal heterosexual development." Bieber continued, "What you have in a homosexual adult is a person whose heterosexual function is crippled like the legs of a polio victim."[14]

American children are still exposed to such views, but they increasingly resist them. In 2016, when my younger daughter Olivia was in college, she took a class with the preeminent historian of gay America, George Chauncey. He asked the students to interview someone elderly about homosexuality, and she chose her grandfather, psychiatrist Roy R. Grinker Jr. He told her that every homosexual he had ever encountered in his office was unhappy, and that many were marginalized from their families or living a partly secret life. Most gay men, he said, had strong mothers, and weak or distant fathers they longed for in childhood, and so they identified with women and desired men. Olivia countered, "But how do you know there aren't happy gay people? You are talking about people who come to your office because they are unhappy. Why would anyone who was happy come to a psychiatrist?" He answered that he simply believed all homosexuals would be happier if they were heterosexual. In her report to Professor Chauncey, Olivia wondered why a doctor would think a gay person's emotional distress was caused by something in early childhood, rather than by the bigotry and bias in the society in which the patient lived. She wrote: "If the pain of being gay is caused by a community's moral system, is that pain still a mental illness?" For my father, the answer was yes, since the individual was unhappy and had failed to conform to society.

My father said that, during the 1970s, any gay psychiatrist who applied to be trained as a psychoanalyst at the Chicago Institute for Psychoanalysis would be turned away. He told me, "We'd be very nice and interview the person, but if we thought he was gay, and certainly if he told us he was gay, we'd just say thank you and goodbye. He had enough psychological problems of his own without having to deal with the emotional intensity of being a psychoanalyst." Even female analysts, who had experienced stereotyping and sexism within the medical profession and in society at large, adhered to the views of their pale, male, frail, and homophobic colleagues. Many psychoanalysts also tried to cure homosexuality. One of the most vocal advocates for cure was Columbia University psychiatrist Charles Socarides. My father described his speeches on the abnormality of homosexuality as persuasive and compelling. As it happened, Socarides was unable to cure his own son, Richard, who in 1993, as special assistant to President Bill Clinton, became the highest-ranking, openly gay federal government employee.[15]

Scientists had been interested in "normality" since the word entered the English language in 1849, but it remained an academic concern until the mid-twentieth century, mostly in controversial studies of criminality, intelligence, and forced sterilization. Normal was a mathematical term that meant average, and where it was used in everyday life, as in the phrase "Normal School" (for the training of K–12 teachers), it meant the beliefs and knowledge shared by the average members of society. When the nineteenth-century mathematician Francis Galton described the features of a person at the median in a normal curve, he called him "mediocre." But not until WWII and the decade that followed did normality became an ideal, with scores of lay and expert pundits offering Americans their advice on how to be normal. Their opinions were motivated by an effort to understand mental illnesses after war, an unabashed contempt for American mothers, and a preoccupation with conformity.

After WWII, three developments propelled the concept of the "normal" out of mathematics and medicine and into American popular culture. One was the production and public display of two his-and-her white alabaster statues to represent the average American man and woman. Another was a landmark study, sponsored by the William T. Grant Foundation, to fully describe the physical characteristics and personality of the normal American man. The third was the publication of scientist Alfred Kinsey's bestselling book, *Sexual Behavior in the Human Male*.

In 1945, the team of Dr. Robert Latou Dickinson and artist Abram Belskie compiled the statistical average measurements of the anatomy of 15,000 white men and women between the ages of twenty-one and twenty-five to create two composites. They called the statues "Norma" and "Normman," and arranged for them to be exhibited first at the famous American Museum of Natural History in New York City and then at the Cleveland Museum of Health. If you look up the pictures on the Internet, the first thing you will notice is that they look ill-proportioned. Both have unusually big hands and long limbs, especially the length between the elbow and the wrist. This is because the statistical average of arm length and hand size does not necessarily fit with the statistical average for height, or for any other part of the body for that matter. There is likely no one in existence whose limbs, head circumference, waist size, nose length, and so on, all represent the statistical average of a large population. As it turned out, however, the *Cleveland Plain Dealer* newspaper ran a national contest in search of the American woman who looked most like Norma. They found one—a twenty-three-year-old theater cashier named Martha Skidmore—and gave her a $100 U.S. War Bond. It might have been the first time someone got an award for being average.

With the exception of Norma, normality in the mid-twentieth century was defined by white men, about white men, and for white men. The same year Norma and Normman were displayed, Harvard professors published the results of a costly research project called the Grant Study of Normal Young Men. They sought to determine the typical characteristics of the average American man, and naturally they decided their study population would be composed entirely of 268 Harvard male undergraduates. Over a period of four years, the investigators studied the students' physique, temperament, health, and social background in order to figure out their typical balance of features. They carefully measured all of these characteristics so that they could produce statistical averages. In 1945, the eugenicist Earnest A. Hooton described the unremarkable results in his book, *Young Man, You Are Normal*. To no one's surprise, the normal man, Hooton wrote, was young, white, native-born, intelligent, and physically fit, just as one might have expected of the male Harvard student in 1945.[16] These men embodied normality because the investigators had decided ahead of time that the elite group to which they belonged would represent the normal.

Hooton interpreted the results of the Grant Study through his own eugenic lens to argue that one's body and one's mind were inseparable. The study, he said, had to focus on precise measurements of men's physique because "your carcass is the clue to your character."[17] It was important to make sure that scientists and doctors could identify people who were fit and unfit, if only to withhold care from the unfit; he had long argued that public charity and institutionalization would ruin humanity by preserving rather than eradicating defectives. Hooton observed, "There can be little doubt of the increase during the past fifty years of mental defectives, psychopaths, criminals, economic incompetents and the chronically diseased. We owe this to the intervention of charity, 'welfare' and medical science, and to the reckless breeding of the unfit."[18] He said that if nothing was done to rid the world of the unfit, by the year 2000 women and men would have numerous malformations, such as tiny hands and feet. For Hooton, the masculine body with hands as large as Normman's was essential to the strong worker.

This new definition of normality as a physical adaptation fitted neatly within capitalist concerns about efficient mass production and consumption. Industries wanted to standardize their products, but they certainly couldn't do something as absurd as make all shoes or hats the same size. They could, however, produce goods that would accommodate most people. Manufacturers used statistical averages of bodily dimensions to design everything from car seats to park benches, buses, and office desks. Even psychologists framed normality in capitalist terms. Reflecting the sexism of the time, the challenge for the psychological professions was how to manufacture psychologically normal children—boys who would grow into independent American workers and girls who would become housewives and mothers devoted to raising such boys.

Some doctors fought against normality. As early as 1941, the American psychiatrist Nathaniel Cantor said that modern civilization was by definition neurotic. He asked, "Who of us, then is normal?" and replied, "None of us."[19] But the major challenge to the concept of the normal came from Kinsey's famous book, *Sexual Behavior in the Human Male*. Published in 1948, it was a stunning declaration. It was a blockbuster hit on the *New York Times* Best Seller list for more than six months. *Time* magazine said booksellers could compare its success only to *Gone With the Wind*.[20] Kinsey's name became so well known that it was included in the chorus of Cole Porter's popular "Too Darn Hot," a song featured in the musical *Kiss Me, Kate*, about the difficulty of making love in very hot weather ("According to the Kinsey Report / Ev'ry average man you know . . ."). Kinsey provided the remarkable statistic that 37 percent of the thousands of men he surveyed had at least once in their lives reached orgasm while in physical contact with another man.[21] He said that homosexual sex was actually a statistical norm, yet in this case the "normal" was still a mark of shame. What we "think" is normal, Kinsey remarked, is often not what we actually do.

The word "normal" was new to most readers, and so Kinsey tried hard to impress his own perspective, cautioning the reader against using "normal" and "abnormal" loosely in everyday language. He argued that normal and abnormal were simply poles on a continuum of culturally variable attitudes, and that they didn't belong in science. Yet by writing so much about normality, his argument backfired. Intellectual historians Peter Cryle and Elizabeth Stephens write that Kinsey's works "were one of the main conduits by which the term 'normal' moved into widespread circulation."[22] The word became more popular than ever. For the first time, "normal" was a word used by ordinary people, not just statisticians, and gradually normal came to mean more than just average. It became something for Americans to aspire to.

One reason Kinsey's critique failed to stop "normal" from becoming a household word was that his argument was based on statistics rather than sentiment. Sometimes the statistically normal fits the social expectations of what is normal, but sometimes—as with homosexuality—the two diverge. "Even if you prove something is statistically normal, like homosexual sex," Stephens told me, "what ends up being more important is what people already *believe* to be normal." She added, "Even the best and most heroic critiques of the normal don't bring that concept crumbling down, and to think that will happen is a mistake."

In 1961, the year I was born, my grandfather and my father (then a newly minted psychoanalyst) coauthored a long and remarkable article in the *Archives of General Psychiatry* entitled "Mentally Healthy Young Males (Homoclites)."[23] They described a group of students at the now-defunct George Williams College, in Chicago, who were "healthy," meaning that they had no diagnosable mental illnesses. Their research was distinctive because so few psychiatrists were interested in healthy people. Ten years earlier, the prominent psychologist Henry Murray had written, "Were [a psychoanalyst] to be confronted by that much-heralded but still missing specimen—the normal man—he would be struck dumb, for once, through lack of appropriate ideas."[24] Typically, doctors studied only those with sicknesses, pushing the rest aside as "screen negative." But Grinker and Grinker wondered what such people would look like to a psychiatrist. After all, the only definitions of "mental health" in the scholarly literature at the time were of little help. The World Health Organization said mental health was the control of one's instincts, and scientists offered equally imprecise definitions like "feeling good to be oneself" and "having a clear grasp of reality."

After giving half of the student body a battery of psychological tests, including a 700-question survey, they identified a few dozen men who did not qualify for any psychiatric diagnosis and interviewed them. They found that these "healthy" men were not necessarily happy. All had some problems—they were upset about something, had phobias, anxieties, etc.—but they showed few signs of any severe disturbance, disability, or potentially disabling personality traits. My grandfather called these men "homoclites." There is no such word in the English language, but there is a word, "heteroclite," which means people or things that deviate from a common rule. *Homo*clites seemed suitable because these "normal" men were so ordinary and unspectacular; it was perhaps a nicer and more technical way of saying they were boring.

Homoclites had average grades and average intelligence scores. They had friends and girlfriends, enjoyed athletics, and had hobbies, although their interests were narrowly defined. They reported little fantasy life, were not introspective or creative, and when encountering problems, emotional or practical, they addressed them compulsively with quick action. They preferred to always "do something" rather than to reflect on a range of possible responses. They were unambitious, with modest goals—to get decent jobs that would provide them enough food and housing to live in a safe neighborhood without too much anxiety. In short, they were interesting only for being so uninteresting. However, when these ostensibly healthy students were allowed to take some courses at the University of Chicago, they stood out as deviant. Faculty members at the university criticized them for the qualities we usually value, deriding them as "upright," "virtuous," "goal-directed," "muscular Christians." In contrast, the professors idealized the risk-taking, eccentric individualists who were their usual students.

Noting how often mental health professionals talked about the costs of mental illness to society at large, my grandfather and father asked: But what are the costs of mental *health*? It was such an unusual question that, two sentences later, they felt the need to tell the reader that the question was not a joke. They wrote of the men at George Williams: "Are the compulsive character and rigidity, the sharply focused and limited interests, the use of activity to maintain comfort, the absence of creativity, fantasies and introspection, the costs we have to pay for stability and mental health?" What an amazing thing to say in 1961! This was many decades before neurodiversity advocates urged us to appreciate the value of different kinds of cognitions, intelligences, and personalities, and before my students began wearing T-shirts that read "I hate normal people." My grandfather and father were suggesting that normality was crippling, and that some degree of mental difference might be necessary for humanity to remain vibrant, creative, and diverse.

In this Age of Conformity, where everyone wanted to be "normal," being diagnosed with a mental illness once again became a source of shame. Even though psychoanalysis was gaining traction in American society, there was a difference between talk therapy for someone dealing with the ordinary stressors of daily life and treatment for a serious condition like major depression, schizophrenia, or substance abuse. One of the advantages of psychoanalysis compared with psychiatry was that its practitioners had little interest in diagnosis beyond the catch-all "neurosis." What's more, even though almost all psychoanalysts in the mid-twentieth century were also psychiatrists, psychoanalysts seldom used medications or shock therapies since those treatments, they believed, masked the neurosis they needed to identify. So, if political figures or celebrities experienced severe mental illnesses and sought care, they went to psychoanalysts or general practitioners, avoided physicians trained only in psychiatry, and seldom went to psychiatric hospitals. Doctors would give them the dubious and vague diagnoses reserved for the rich and famous, "fatigue" or "exhaustion"—euphemisms for the privileged, like the old adage that if you are poor you are crazy but if you are wealthy you're eccentric.

Of course, being tired is a valid complaint that can have myriad causes and meanings. But unless exhaustion is associated with a serious medical or psychiatric condition, sleep will take care of it, and you do not need to sleep in a hospital. Physicians don't diagnose exhaustion, and insurance companies don't reimburse for it. Yet celebrities Mariah Carey, Lindsay Lohan, Selena Gomez, Justin Bieber, Demi Moore—and the list goes on—have been admitted to hospitals for "exhaustion."

In April and May 1949, James Forrestal, who served as secretary of the navy during World War II and was the United States's first secretary of defense, was admitted to Bethesda Naval Hospital in suburban Washington, DC, sick from "exhaustion." Press releases said his fatigue was due to his heavy workload. A *New York Times* article described the condition in military terms as "operational fatigue," a condition that afflicted many soldiers "fighting too long without respite."[25] After seven weeks of rest, restrictions to Forrestal's movements were loosened in an attempt to give him a sense of "normalcy" and facilitate his recovery.

On Sunday morning, May 21, at 1:50 a.m., after reading and transcribing a poem from book to paper in a room on the sixteenth floor of the hospital, Forrestal tied his bathrobe sash around his neck and attempted to hang himself from the window. The cord broke, and he fell to his death on a third-floor landing made of asphalt and cinder rocks. Despite the obvious evidence of suicide, conspiracy theories abounded that Communists or American Zionists killed him. The navy launched an investigation into Forrestal's death and concluded that he had received appropriate and humane medical and psychiatric care.

How had it come to this?

Forrestal had been psychologically troubled since childhood. He was homeschooled, and his mother withheld affection, routinely beating him with a strap.[26] He was shorter, less handsome, and more frail than his two brothers, and as a child he was often physically ill. All of these factors, Forrestal's biographers agree, led him to become insecure about his masculinity. As an adult, and at the pinnacle of his political career, he was harassed by two journalists, the muckraking Drew Pearson and the syndicated columnist Walter Winchell. Pearson and Winchell both launched personal attacks on Forrestal, motivated largely by their strong opposition to Forrestal's conservative political views as well as his links to Wall Street, Big Oil, and the military. Unlike Pearson and Winchell, Forrestal did not favor a speedy withdrawal of troops from Europe, was strongly anti-Communist, supported large increases in the defense budget, and did not believe that a Jewish state was in the US national interest. Pearson and Winchell called him "the most dangerous man in America." They also directly challenged his masculinity.

In an account of a 1937 crime in which Forrestal's wife was robbed of her jewelry at gunpoint outside their home, they alleged that Forrestal had witnessed the event from an upstairs window and fled out a back door "trembling" with fear. Though most accounts indicate that Forrestal was asleep at the time, and knew nothing of the robbery until his wife entered the house, the reports broadcast widely in both the US and the Russian media made him look like a coward. President Truman, troubled by the gossip about Forrestal's mental state as well as by Forrestal's continued opposition to additional cuts in defense spending, asked him to resign.

In public, Forrestal looked anxious and weak. He told colleagues he was being followed by foreign agents and that his phone had been tapped. In one radio report, Pearson claimed that Forrestal had responded in panic to the sound of planes overhead, screaming, "The Russians are attacking us!" Radio Moscow aired Pearson's report three times in one night.

Concerned about his mood, Forrestal's friend, the investment banker Ferdinand Eberstadt, arranged for him to fly to Florida to stay with friends at a seaside home near Palm Beach. Meanwhile, Eberstadt also arranged for William Menninger, the most recognized name in American mental health, to come too. Menninger diagnosed him with a severe "reactive depression" that he compared to "combat fatigue" in WWII. Noting that Forrestal was paranoid, saw himself as a failure, and was contemplating suicide by hanging, Menninger promptly took Forrestal back to Washington and admitted him to the Bethesda Naval Hospital for what he told the media was "a routine checkup." Menninger believed that Forrestal would feel less stigmatized, and would be better protected from the media, in a general rather than a psychiatric military hospital. Forrestal's wife, Jo, was also concerned that any admission to a psychiatric hospital would damage the reputation of her family.[27]

Forrestal's psychiatrist at the hospital, George Raines—the navy captain who was adapting the army's manual of mental disorders into the DSM-I—diagnosed him with "involutional melancholia psychosis,"[28] a term obsolete today but which midcentury clinicians used to describe a form of paranoid and agitated depression with psychosis. Unlike Menninger, Raines did not think Forrestal would try to kill himself. Perhaps intimidated by Forrestal's fame, Raines admitted him to a room, with windows, on the sixteenth floor, and without placing him on a suicide watch.

Forrestal must have understood much of what was happening to him. Although it was reported that he didn't leave a suicide note, he had in fact written something just before he fell to his death and, given the content, it's hard to imagine it as anything but a suicide note. A few minutes before Forrestal leaped out of the window, an attendant noticed that he was carefully copying the ancient Greek poem "Chorus from Ajax" by Sophocles.[29] He stopped writing after completing the fragment "night" in "nightingale," placed the papers in the book, and rested the book on his nightstand. In that chorus, soldiers from the Greek island of Salamina mourn the madness of their insane friend Ajax and wonder what misery his insanity will bring to their people, and especially to Ajax's mother. The text suggests it is better to die than to live with the disgrace of madness: "Woe to the mother in her close of day, / Woe to her desolate heart and temples gray, / When she shall hear / Her loved one's story whispered in her ear! . . . The deepest, bitterest curse thine ancient house hath borne!"

Many blamed Pearson for Forrestal's death. After all, Pearson had tormented Forrestal, attacking him where it hurt most—his mental state and his masculinity. Some journalists stressed the political consequences of Forrestal's illness, especially Truman's appointment of Louis Johnson to succeed Forrestal as secretary of defense. "Johnson, for whose accommodation Forrestal was destroyed," one critic wrote, could have prevented US involvement in the Korean War had he followed Forrestal's policies.[30]

But Pearson shot back at his critics, not using the word stigma, but clearly implying that it had played a role in Forrestal's tragedy. He wrote, "In the end, it may be found that Mr. Forrestal's friends had more to do with his death than his critics. For those close to him now admit privately that he had been sick for some time, suffered embarrassing lapses too painful to be mentioned here. . . ." He added that navy doctors "minimize psychiatric treatment, which may have been why they called Mr. Forrestal's illness 'nervous exhaustion' and that illnesses like severe depression do not come all of a sudden like a fall from a horse. It begins months in advance. And such an illness cannot be pushed aside or overlooked. It must be treated."[31] The *Washington Post* editorial page also wrote: "There has been something wicked . . . about the disingenuousness with which the illness of Mr. Forrestal has been handled. The authorities lied when they said he entered Bethesda Naval Hospital for a routine checkup."[32]

The fact that Forrestal is today remembered largely for having committed suicide rather than for his political contributions is part of the stigma of mental illness. In addition to delaying treatment, the diagnosis of exhaustion probably only exacerbated his shame, since he must have known it was just a genteel substitute for depression. It took another two decades for the psychiatric community to take seriously the special plight of the celebrity with a mental illness. In 1972, a leading mental health think tank, the Group for the Advancement of Psychiatry, published a short book entitled *The VIP with Psychiatric Impairment*, noting that for an individual in the public view, "his bias against psychiatric consultation, evaluation and treatment, therefore, has a realistic as well as an emotional basis."[33] The report further noted that psychiatrists themselves may be to blame for stigma, as even they hesitate to seek treatment for themselves. And when they do seek treatment, they justify it as part of their professional training (as my grandfather did with Freud) and not for any real therapy. But the authors placed the bulk of the blame on society at large: "Since mental illness is stigmatizing, it must be concealed."[34] Sadly, even today, we too often indulge the rich and famous, with appalling consequences.

CHAPTER 9

FROM THE FORGOTTEN WAR
TO VIETNAM

"A psychiatrist is the God of our age."

Sylvia Plath, *Journals* (1950–53)

In 1948, a few months before NIMH first opened, President Truman said, "In this World War Number Two, one of the most disgraceful things that came to light was the fact that nearly 33 1/3 percent of all the young men who came up for physical examination for the purpose of serving their country . . . were not fit for service, due to either some mental defect or some physical defect."[1] Dr. Harry Holloway, former chair of psychiatry at Walter Reed, told me, "World War II is the reason why NIMH was founded—to figure out what the heck went wrong."

Knowing that the Mental Health Act of 1946 that launched NIMH would be remembered as the greatest advance in psychiatry in the twentieth century, Truman tried to leverage the law by pleading with Congress to increase funding for research on prevention and treatment. He said that 10 million Americans would be hospitalized for a mental illness during their lifetime and that psychiatric patients occupied half of all hospital beds in the country. At the time, the total amount of state and federal money spent on mental health research was just $28 million. To put that figure in context, it was 1/300th of the amount Americans spent on alcohol every year. Americans spent more than that—$36 million—on pets and veterinary care. Just after the war, psychologist Henry Brosin noted that all the money spent for all medical research in the United States in 1944 would have paid for only eight hours and twenty minutes of American military activities during WWII.[2] William Menninger complained that half the number of people who saw a doctor in any given year had a mental illness and yet psychiatry made up no more than five percent of any medical school's curriculum.[3]

Despite Truman's complaint about the high prevalence of psychiatric casualties in the war, WWII was for many mental health professionals an unqualified success. War neuroses during WWII were relatively free from stigma, and the general concept of neurosis became part of the American vernacular. This is not to suggest that everyone wanted to disclose their psychological difficulties, but soldiers were more open about their feelings, and clinicians more empathic. For some, war trauma was almost a badge of honor. In 1945, Jon Rawlings Rees, the British psychiatrist who supervised Hitler's deputy Rudolph Hess in prison after the war, wrote of the paradoxes of WWII, its destructiveness and intellectual and scientific productivity: "There is no time and no experience in our whole social life in which psychological principles are so challenged as in war, and psychiatry has perhaps matured more as a result of the war experience than it could have done in five years of peace."[4]

Whereas psychiatrists during WWI treated soldiers with demonstrable functional impairments—like people unable to speak or walk—the bread and butter of the WWII psychiatrist was the more minor problem, such as the anxious or depressed soldier, and this clinical emphasis on what became known as the common mental disorders generalized to the public at large. As William Menninger reported, only about seven percent of the one million psychiatric admissions to army hospitals during WWII were people with severe mental illnesses.[5] The influence of this war experience was to make American psychiatry a profession for what was called "ambulatory care": the ordinary person living his or her life in the community, not just in the asylum.

There were, of course, criticisms to this change in American psychiatry. One was to blame the military doctors for creating mental illnesses where there were none, treating typical emotional problems as if they were pathological. Another was to argue that there was an actual increase in the incidence of mental illnesses and that the United States was becoming a sick society. Still, the psychological problems of functional persons—people employed and married, for example—couldn't be completely ignored or hidden. Civilians, especially educated professionals, began to embrace psychoanalytic therapy as a socially acceptable course of action, even as something fashionable, for treating the expected stresses and strains of life in rapidly changing postwar America. This was what Freud had hoped for.

For the soldier, however, the absence of stigma didn't last long, much to my grandfather's dismay. In wartime, the soldier had been separated out from everyday life, his individuality transferred into a serial number, objectified and absorbed into the military body as a collection of parts that worked together efficiently—arms (armies), hands (. . . on deck), and boots (. . . on the ground). In peacetime, the veteran was a unique and whole individual whose personality was shaped by the entirety of his life—not just his military service. Mental illness became a sign of personal weakness, as well as being a financial liability. If the war helped to establish psychoanalysis as a method to return brave soldiers to duty, the war's end helped to make psychoanalysis a method to blame the veteran's emotional problems on his childhood and family. Physical disabilities were, of course, a different matter, and less susceptible to the stigma that comes from the separation of body and mind in Western philosophy. As Descartes put it centuries ago, "If a foot, or an arm, or any other part, is separated from my body, it is certain that, on that account, nothing has been taken away from my mind."[6]

By the onset of the Korean War in 1950, military health care had retreated into the civilian world. Despite everything learned during WWII, many military doctors thought the United States could carry on its operations in Korea without any psychiatrists at all. Military medical staff in general, not only psychiatrists, were once again unprepared for the war. In just a few years after WWII, the U.S. Navy had shut down more than half of its hospitals and reduced the medical staff from 170,000 to 21,000. When the Korean War began, the US military had to enact a Doctor-Draft Law, compelling into service physicians whose education had been paid for by the military but who had never served.[7]

At the start of WWII, the army employed only thirty-five doctors in the role of psychiatrist, and only four of them had actually received any psychiatric certification in the United States. Now, at the start of the Korean conflict, Col. Albert Glass, the psychiatrist who accused my grandfather of being too kind to soldiers, became the director of all psychiatric services in the Far East Command, with a grand total of nine "psychiatrists," only one of whom had actually completed a residency training in psychiatry.

More than 33,000 Americans, and millions of Koreans, died during the Korean War (1950–53). The war is known as "the Forgotten War," but not only because we've failed to remember it today or because its influence on American history pales in comparison to other wars. *U.S. News & World Report* called it the forgotten war in 1951, just a year after the conflict had begun, because the media seemed uninterested in it. When it comes to US military psychiatry, all wars seem to be forgotten, but the Korean War is a special case. It is missing almost entirely from most histories of military psychiatry, even though the rate of psychiatric casualties was higher in Korea than in Vietnam (3.7 percent of soldiers in Korea versus 1.2 percent in Vietnam).

As soon as American boots hit the ground in Korea, psychiatric casualties started to accrue. Within three months, 25 percent of the American soldiers removed from combat were removed for psychiatric reasons. Glass now begged for psychiatrists, and they trickled in over the coming months. He decided to place them at the front. He thought that if psychiatrists truly understood what combat was like, and the importance to the soldier's morale and mental health of staying with his buddies, they wouldn't evacuate as many men from the battlefield as doctors like Grinker and Spiegel did. This innovation paralleled the general trend to lodge doctors as close to combat as possible. It is for this reason that mobile army surgical hospitals (MASH) were first employed during the Korean War.

Glass wrote that if the doctor was in a combat zone, he would be freed of his own anxiety and guilt and would appreciate that "it is in the best interest of the individual to rejoin his combat unit."[8] Other experts agreed with Glass that evacuating a traumatized soldier could be psychologically damaging. Evacuation prevented the soldier from doing what both he and the community at large valued the most: fighting for his country. Psychiatric treatments included good food and a bed ("three hots and a cot"), barbiturates for sleep, and nonconvulsive shock therapy (an amount of electricity below the seizure threshold).[9] But even more importantly, talk therapy, the staple of psychoanalysis, became routine as soldiers learned how to have conversations about their feelings. There was a sense among many doctors that psychiatrists were carrying out both humanitarian and patriotic work, caring for the suffering while also preserving the fighting force.

In the end, the Korean War would be remembered as a crucial building block for what became the golden era of psychiatry and psychoanalysis. During the war, writer Sylvia Plath wrote: "A psychiatrist is the God of our age."[10] By 1961, psychiatric thought would be so powerful and pervasive that *The Atlantic* magazine ran a special issue on the centrality of psychiatry, Freud, and psychoanalysis to nearly every aspect of American science and letters, from the study of the brain to music criticism. By 1965, more than 10 percent of American medical school graduates chose to become psychiatrists, a much higher proportion than among today's students, and there was still more consumer demand for psychiatry than there was supply.[11] Although psychiatry is becoming a more popular medical specialty, only 3.9 percent of medical students applied to psychiatry residency training programs in 2012, and about 6 percent in 2019. For some groups, like professors and well-heeled east coast urbanites, it had become almost chic to have a therapist, and psychoanalysis became the dominant form of therapy in much of South America and western Europe as well.[12] Buoyed by an influx of money from NIMH, in 1965 there were more teaching positions in psychiatry departments than in any medical specialization other than internal medicine.[13] Psychiatry, and psychoanalysis in particular, were now more than therapies; they were tools for social and intellectual progress— in my grandfather's sarcastic words, "the answer to all the problems of mankind."[14] He warned psychiatrists that the profession had overreached by making "extravagant promises" without humility or scientific rigor, and he predicted a fall from grace.[15]

The early stages of this psychoanalytic awakening were visible among Korean doctors during the war. With little knowledge about mental health care, Korean doctors floundered as they sought to help their own. Before the war, Korea's main access to psychiatric ideas had been through Japan. Not only were Koreans unenthusiastic about anything their colonizers had taught them, but the Japanese word for mental illness (*seisinbyo*), and the Korean word that is a direct translation of it (*chŏngsinbyŏng*), was frightening, suggesting brain disease, mental derangement, and a propensity for violence. In addition, Koreans associated psychiatry with the Japanese practice of giving electric shocks to political dissidents as punishment.[16] Koreans did follow the Japanese pattern of institutionalizing criminals and people with what were believed to be contagious diseases (like leprosy), but they had not generally confined people suffering from mental illnesses without any associated violence (or suicide attempts).[17] For the most part, these people remained in their communities without psychiatric diagnoses (and of course without psychiatrists) and therefore without the stigma of a brain disease. Until the outbreak of the Korean War in 1950, there were only a handful of psychiatrists in Korea, mostly Japanese, in universities established by Japan, and in some American Protestant missions.

During the war, however, the American military trained approximately forty-five Korean doctors using, as a guideline, Medical 203, soon to become the DSM-I. Because about ten percent of the total South Korean population served in the war, many Koreans with mental illnesses received psychiatric care for the first time. With the help of their teachers, these new and quickly trained Korean clinicians sought to minimize stigma by distinguishing between mentally ill soldiers and "non-effective soldiers"—a phrase that would later become "personality disorders." Soldiers with mental illnesses stayed in the military; non-effective soldiers were discharged without a pension or other compensation. The goal was to convey to soldiers that as long as they were still in the military, they were within the range of "normal."

This was an ingenious strategy. It eased emotionally distressed soldiers' worries about stigma because they compared themselves favorably to those who were discharged. It also encouraged soldiers to remain in the fighting force. Instead of using frightening illness labels, doctors talked about stress and fatigue. When soldiers showed signs of psychiatric illness near the end of their deployment, they were often given the label "short-termer's syndrome" or "rotation anxiety" to avoid a medical discharge.[18] The soldier would be retained and comforted until the rotation officially ended. This method protected the soldier from the stigma of a medical expulsion, and because fewer soldiers were discharged for psychiatric reasons, it made the psychiatrists look like better doctors.

But at the same time that these newly trained Korean doctors disarmed the stigma of the mentally ill soldier who stayed in the force, they devastated the non-effective soldier. The soldier discharged from the army for being "non-effective" left in disgrace, his character and masculinity tarnished. To add insult to injury, the Korean army developed the diagnosis of "eunuchoidism" for many of these men. The word already existed in the medical literature as a syndrome caused by insufficient male hormones and manifested by the persistence of prepubertal features, like a high voice, lack of facial hair, and small genitals. But the South Korean army turned eunuchoidism into a diagnosis of emotional immaturity, explained in Freudian terms.

It's now clear from medical documents recently unearthed by the historian Jennifer Yum that Korean doctors believed many people with mental illnesses had inadequate or absent mothers. Dr. Yu Sŏk-jin, for example, described the case of Private First Class Shin Yu Hui. Military doctors attributed his back pain and other symptoms, including cognitive impairments, to the fact that his mother died when he was an infant. Shin was raised by his father, only occasionally seeing an older sister who did not live at home. When he was seven, Shin's father remarried, but his stepmother sent him to live with his sister, thus creating, in Yu's view, an emotional void. Yu said Shin was obese and had small genitals and insufficient pubic hair for his age. Though married, Shin was sexually "inexperienced," had "repressed hostility" toward women, and little insight or "ability to relate to others." He was also dull, apathetic, and unable to complete simple arithmetic. Yu recorded a primary diagnosis of oligophrenia, a term that was once something of a catchall for "mental retardation," and a secondary diagnosis of eunuchoidism.[19]

Once again, a war had ushered in a new language with which to understand mental suffering. Within just a few years after the fighting stopped, the South Korean government would launch its first-ever national mental health awareness campaign. New mental hospitals opened, and a substantial portion of the patients treated there had been first diagnosed with a mental illness as soldiers. Responding to popular concern about an increase in violence among poor and disaffected youth, officials came to rely on psychiatrists to shape policies for discipline and rehabilitation. In the legal system, mental health professionals administered personality assessments, like questionnaires and Rorschach tests; in the academic community, they attributed problems among Korean youth to the instability of the family, and produced new guidelines for child-rearing. This is almost exactly what happened in the United States as well. For both Korea and the United States in the decades of the 1950s and 1960s, Yum writes, "Though it may sound ironic, the decade of total war followed by a grueling decade of national reconstruction gave rise to a 'renaissance of psychiatry' in South Korea that would not be seen again."[20]

The Korean War did not dramatically transform everyday American life in the way WWII had. Nor did it elicit the same level of public support for the military. After WWII, politicians, journalists, and medical professionals openly discussed their concerns about how soldiers, especially those with chronic disabilities, would reintegrate into American life. Films explicitly but compassionately portrayed those anxieties, as in the highly popular 1946 movie *The Best Years of Our Lives*.[21] One of the first films to feature an actor who was actually disabled (Harold Russell, who lost both hands during WWII), the film won seven Academy Awards. In contrast, the veterans of the Korean War tried to return to life as usual, with relatively little public discussion about the potential problems of military demobilization. There was one major exception to this silence: rumors that the North Koreans, the Chinese, or the Soviets had been able to brainwash American prisoners of war into collaborating with the Communists.[22]

This conspiratorial belief was an unintended consequence of the psychoanalytic revolution. If doctors had the power to change minds through hypnosis and Sodium Pentothal as Grinker and Spiegel had done in WWII, then perhaps America's enemies could do the same to prisoners of war, and even to the American people as a whole. The terms "head-shrinking" and "brain-washing" first appeared in English around 1950, and quickly entered into common usage. "Brain-wash" was the literal translation of the Chinese term *xĭnăo*, the process by which Maoists sought to eradicate and then replace a person's ideas and values.

The soldiers who arguably suffered the most from this paranoia were the former prisoners of war. They had survived during captivity in miserable conditions with little food and without medicine or blankets. Many of them had lasting cognitive impairments as the result of malnutrition and vitamin deficiencies.[23] They were also subjected to repeated efforts to indoctrinate them into Communism. When the more than 4,000 Korean War POWs eventually returned home after 1953, many were greeted with hostility and suspicion. Their poor reception was not just the result of a war that lacked the clarity, patriotic fervor, and triumphalism of WWII,[24] but of something more insidious.

After the military reported that twenty-three American POWs defected to China, the media quickly became preoccupied with the question of whether the several thousand prisoners who didn't defect, but returned home to the United States, might still have been subjected to brainwashing. A *New York Times* editorial noted that the twenty-three defectors were "living proof that Communist brain-washing does work on some persons."[25] Columbia University psychiatrist Joost Meerloo said that former prisoners who returned home to their American communities might only "appear" to be the same people who left. The Chinese had been capable of "menticide," killing the soldiers' minds and replacing them with Communist ideology. One American admiral said that the captors were capable of planting the seeds of treason in all the prisoners' minds so that at some later date the Chinese could activate them.[26]

Remember that, after WWII, the realities of the soldiers' trauma faded quickly into the background as Americans shifted their attention from what was wrong overseas to what was wrong at home. That process now repeated itself. Fueled by sporadic sightings of soldiers wearing women's clothing, there were rumors that the POWs had become homosexuals. The US government claimed that two-thirds of the medically ill POWs who returned home in the first round of repatriation were a "red-tinged" risk to national security.[27] Psychiatrists reinforced these fears—and provided support for the anti-Communist frenzy of the McCarthy era (from the late 1940s through the 1950s)—when they counseled Americans not to be hostile toward returning POWs lest they provoke them to betray the United States. "Menticide" was the premise for Richard Condon's best-selling novel (and, later, two successful films) *The Manchurian Candidate* (1959), about a decorated Korean War veteran, connected to the highest levels of the US government, who is brainwashed to become an assassin for the KGB. Was American patriotism really that weak? One historian noted: "An increasingly affluent society was excoriated as soft, degenerate and vulnerable.... The enemy without was recast as an enemy within."[28] Unfortunately, conspiracy theories, and the climate of fear surrounding these POWs, persisted for many years, even after McCarthy's humiliation and death.

During the mid-1960s, there were more psychiatrists in the US military than ever before—at least two hundred at any given time—but there were only a few psychiatrists overseas. Even at the height of the Vietnam War, in 1968, there were never more than twenty-three stationed in Vietnam.[29] By all accounts, this small number didn't matter much since Americans had fewer psychiatric casualties during the Vietnam War—at that point, America's longest war—than in any war for which we have medical records. Whatever category one looks for in medical records—combat stress, battle fatigue, anxiety, etc.—the estimated total prevalence of psychiatric diagnoses during the Vietnam War was between 2 percent and 5 percent.[30] Glass commented on the results of the remarkably low rate of psychiatric problems in Vietnam: "Military psychiatry in the Vietnam conflict achieved its most impressive record in conserving the fighting strength."[31] Those words would soon be used against him by critics of the war who argued that Vietnam War psychiatrists simply didn't make diagnoses because they were more concerned about returning soldiers to combat than about any individual soldier's welfare.

It is clear that the tool kit of the Vietnam War psychiatrist was deficient. Compiled during the beginning stages of the war, and published the same year that the number of US troops reached its peak in Vietnam, the new diagnostic manual, the DSM-II (1968), no longer focused so heavily on reactions to stress. In fact, the category of "gross stress reaction" that had proven useful for diagnoses of war trauma during the Korean War was removed. There is no clear answer among historians of psychiatry as to why it was removed, but historians propose three possibilities: the authors of the manual had little or no war experience; the early reports from Vietnam indicated that psychiatric casualties were low; and doctors believed the existing nomenclature was sufficient to characterize whatever psychiatric conditions did afflict soldiers in combat.[32] All that remained for diagnosing psychiatric casualties of war in the new DSM was "adjustment reaction of adult life" under the category of "transient situational personality disorders." In other words, the only available diagnosis was for temporary illnesses. There was now no category to denote psychological impairments that emerged during military service and endured. There was no diagnosis that could help the veteran who had longer-term psychiatric needs to receive ongoing care from the Veterans Administration.

Despite the fact that more than 58,000 Americans died in Vietnam (58,193 men and 8 women), the war was, from the psychiatrist's perspective, an outlier. According to David H. Marlowe, former chief of the Department of Military Psychiatry at Walter Reed Army Institute of Research:

> *Vietnam produced an extremely low proportion of proximate combat stress casualties.... Therefore, Vietnam breaks with the past normative pattern of combat and war zone stress casualty production. A claim of those espousing the singularity of the Vietnam War is that it was designed, by its horrifying nature, to produce masses of posttraumatic stress casualties; however, this claim was a postwar development.*[33]

Throughout the military, psychiatrists congratulated themselves but could only offer a few vague explanations for their apparent success, all of which make it difficult to accept the Vietnam medical reports as an accurate assessment of the rate of psychiatric casualties, or to compare the reports from Vietnam to those from other wars.[34]

First, some doctors reasoned, because most of the small number of American psychiatrists in Vietnam worked in combat settings rather than in hospitals, there may have been little need to record a diagnosis, especially if the goal was to treat soldiers quickly and return them to the front lines. In previous wars, casualties were admitted to treatment centers where they were given specific disease classifications. Second, once gross stress reaction was removed from the DSM, clinicians didn't have diagnostic terms available to specify combat-related conditions. Simply put, no doctor could make a psychiatric diagnosis without an appropriate diagnostic language. Of the psychiatric casualties that were recorded, 3.5 percent were listed as "combat exhaustion," and everything else (personality disorders, anxiety neuroses, substance abuse, etc.) was classified as unrelated to combat or trauma.[35] Third, the incidence of psychiatric conditions was mitigated by deployments that were shorter (typically twelve months) than in previous wars; shorter periods of combat might explain why most psychiatric problems emerged or became apparent to clinicians only after the soldier returned home.

Fourth, some historians term the Vietnam War "low intensity" in comparison to previous American wars. Doctors attributed war trauma in WWI, WWII, and, to a lesser extent, the Korean War to the incessant and agonizing fear created by prolonged bombardments. In Vietnam, however, even at the peak of fighting, the war involved brief skirmishes in which small and mobile tactical units conducted search-and-destroy operations from secure bases. Moreover, the vast majority of personnel in Vietnam were support staff rather than combat soldiers. Historians are certainly not suggesting the war wasn't brutal—tens of thousands of Americans, and countless Vietnamese, died—but rather that psychiatric casualties *during* combat may have been minimized by the war's particular kind of combat. In fact, the highest prevalence of psychiatric problems was among those soldiers who served during the period of lowest combat intensity.[36]

A fifth possible explanation is that the doctors who went to Vietnam were unfamiliar with military psychiatry, and inexperienced in general, unless they were old enough to have participated in the Korean War. According to one psychiatrist who treated hundreds of soldiers in Vietnam, "the man least trained and most junior in rank became [for some months] the sole representative of Army psychiatry in the only combat zone of the United States Army."[37] Most psychiatrists who went to Vietnam had been trained in a community of clinicians that didn't care much about military mental health.

As a sign of how disaffected civilian psychiatry was with the war, in 1973, the year the last of the American troops came home, there were only three papers delivered at the annual meeting of the American Psychiatric Association on Vietnam: one on men addicted to heroin, one on marijuana use, and one paper questioning the validity of military psychiatry as a branch of study, entitled "Military Psychiatry: Fact or Fiction?" There were more papers on the psychology of diarrhea than on Vietnam, and even the panels on violence did not include the topic of war. In 1975, when the meetings were in Boston, and where all the important lectures took place in the Boston Sheraton's War Memorial Auditorium, there was ironically only one paper on veteran readjustment to civilian life, and none on war.

CHAPTER 10

POST-TRAUMATIC
STRESS DISORDER

There is no agony like bearing an untold story
inside of you.

Maya Angelou (1970)

On May 8, 1945, Robert Jay Lifton, an eighteen-year-old student from Brooklyn, New York, went to Times Square to rejoice. It was V-E Day, and hundreds of thousands of people crowded the streets of New York to celebrate the surrender of Nazi Germany to the Allied forces. Film clips and photographs show soldiers and civilians smiling, embracing, kissing, and holding newspapers above their heads with headlines in all caps: "V-E DAY IT'S ALL OVER" and "THE WAR IN EUROPE IS ENDED."

On Sunday, January 28, 1973, the day the Vietnam War ended, Lifton, now a forty-six-year-old psychiatrist and writer, and a fierce opponent of the war, turned on his TV and saw images of the same place where he'd exulted twenty-eight years earlier. It was forty degrees outside—not a particularly cold day for January in New York—but it was rainy. On TV,

Times Square looked rundown and gray. There were no crowds, perhaps because it wasn't a workday but also perhaps because it wasn't an unequivocally happy occasion. Although a ten-story bank of windows on the Allied Chemical Building lighted the word "Peace," it was more a day of mourning than celebration. There were a few war veterans screaming at the TV camera that the war had been unjust, a deception perpetrated by a corrupt government. One angry veteran yelled, "The war isn't over!"[1] The Associated Press reported that many churches decided not to hold any special services to mark the day. In Washington, DC, one minister said, "The reason many of us are not throwing our hats in the air is that we are just so stunned and ashamed because the war went on so long."[2]

Six months later, Lifton made it clear how angry he was at both the military and his own profession. Though he had once been an air force psychiatrist in Korea, he was now an intellectual, working with his mentor Erik Erikson to develop the new field of psychohistory and publishing books and articles on brainwashing and nuclear weapons. He believed the relationship between the military and psychiatry was "an unholy alliance," and he began to work on how to help the Vietnam soldier. In the short term, his efforts would have serious consequences for veterans. He alternately vilified Vietnam veterans as war criminals and exonerated them as innocent pawns of a US war machine, a contradiction conveyed by the subtitle of his 1973 book, *Home from the War: Vietnam Veterans—Neither Victims nor Executioners*. The American public couldn't figure out whether to fear or feel sympathy for the Vietnam veteran. In the long term, Lifton helped give us one of the least-stigmatized mental illnesses today: post-traumatic stress disorder (PTSD).

The early 1970s was a difficult time in the history of American psychiatry. The field had become so popular, and in its embrace of psychoanalysis so separate from the other areas of medicine, that it had nowhere to go but down. During World War II, my grandfather had called psychiatry "a crumbling stockade of proprietary dogmatism."[3] Psychiatry was now facing a backlash from self-described "anti-psychiatrists," such as Lifton and

Thomas Szasz, who argued that psychiatry was as much a form of discipline and punishment, alchemy, and pseudo-science as it was a therapy.

In a 1972 exposé of the New York mental health system, civil liberties attorney Bruce J. Ennis found that judges too hastily decided that certain defendants were mentally ill and couldn't stand trial, depriving them of due process.[4] And once they were committed to hospitals for the criminally insane, they were given harsher forms of treatment than were necessary. Hospitals administered medicines to patients against their will and exploited them in menial jobs in the name of "therapy." Former inmates had little or no opportunity to find employment or admission to colleges.[5] Ennis concluded that no expert really knew what a mental illness was. It was simply whatever a psychiatrist said it was.

The next year, 1973, one of the most-prestigious scientific journals in the world, *Science*, published an article by Stanford University psychologist David Rosenhan about his adventures in California mental hospitals: "On Being Sane in Insane Places." In an effort to discredit psychiatry, Rosenhan reported that "eight sane people gained secret admission to 12 different hospitals." His partners in crime included one of his graduate students, a few colleagues, a painter, and a "housewife." Each visited a hospital, provided a false name, vocation, and place of employment, and reported hearing unfamiliar voices saying words like "empty," "hollow," and "thud." He also told them to report no other symptoms and that, if they were admitted to the hospital, to report no additional auditory hallucinations or other abnormalities.[6] According to Rosenhan, psychiatrists diagnosed all but one with schizophrenia (the exception was one diagnosis of manic-depressive disorder), based solely on their reports of auditory hallucinations, admitted them into mental hospitals, treated them with psychotropic drugs, and kept them there against their will. The "patients" described their time in the hospital as frightening and stigmatizing. Rosenhan concluded that psychiatrists were unable to distinguish between the mentally ill and the healthy. Only in 2019, through dogged sleuthing, was the writer Susannah Cahalan able to provide good evidence that Rosenhan distorted and likely fabricated much of his data.[7]

The so-called "Rosenhan hoax" was a public relations disaster for American psychiatry—despite the fact that the experiment wasn't really believable. It was more a test to see whether a "sane" person could fool a hospital than a study of the characteristics that influence psychiatric diagnosis. Psychiatrist Seymour S. Kety compared Rosenhan's use of pseudo-patients to a person who secretly drinks a quart of blood, goes to an emergency room, vomits blood, is given immediate treatment for an internal bleed, and then criticizes the doctors for misdiagnosing the cause of the bleeding.[8]

Others joined the disbelieving chorus, but they could do little to control the emerging popular consensus in America that psychiatry was a sham. Insurance companies responded by reducing coverage of psychiatric services, since they saw little reason to pay for medical care that lacked scientific credence. By their own admission, psychiatrists, still largely dominated by psychoanalytic thought, did not distinguish the sick from the healthy since the goal of psychoanalytic therapy was to treat symptoms, not discrete diseases.[9] My father used to say, "We psychiatrists diagnose someone's character, not mental disorders." But in this new climate, fueled by the antiestablishment sentiments of the late 1960s, patients began to look for help outside of psychiatry. Other mental health professions, like social work and clinical psychology, quickly expanded in the United States, especially in the Northeast, the northern Midwest, and California.[10]

Also in 1973, Americans were reminded of the persistent stigma of mental illness after President Richard M. Nixon's vice president, Spiro Agnew, resigned. Nixon nominated Gerald Ford to replace him, and because the appointment of a vice president during a president's term requires confirmation by the Senate, Ford had to testify. Linda Charlton, in the *New York Times*, wrote of the first day of testimony: "If one thing was made perfectly clear in this first slow, polite day of Senate committee hearings on the nomination of Representative Gerald R. Ford to be Vice President, it is that consulting a psychiatrist or psychotherapist is still an unforgivable sin for an American politician."[11]

Five years earlier, Drew Pearson, the same journalist who harassed Secretary Forrestal after WWII, had charged that Nixon, while Eisenhower's vice president, was treated by Dr. Arnold A. Hutschnecker, an anti-Semitic New York psychiatrist and personal friend of Nixon's.[12] Nixon and Hutschnecker both denied that they had a therapeutic relationship, saying that Nixon had sought expert help only for "internal medicine," since Hutschnecker was both a medical doctor and a friend. Once Nixon was elected, the issue became irrelevant to the electorate, but now the question was whether Gerald Ford had also been in treatment with Hutschnecker.

Republican senator Robert Griffin asked Ford directly if he had ever seen any psychiatrist. Equating psychiatric care with insanity, Ford replied, "I am disgustingly sane."[13] Although he admitted going to Hutschnecker's office once, he told the Senate: "Under no circumstances have I ever been treated by any person in the medical profession for psychiatry."[14] Hutschnecker was then asked to testify before the committee, where he confirmed that Ford had never been a patient but had come to his office only for a "social visit."[15]

But 1973 wasn't over yet. That same year, Lifton, Canadian psychiatrist Chaim Shatan, and groups of Vietnam veterans who opposed the war began to lobby the APA and the American Orthopsychiatric Association (AOA) to pay attention to the psychological needs of veterans. Lifton had previously succeeded only in providing stories to the newspapers about veterans who were homeless, drug users, suicidal, and violent. There were few scientific data to support the epidemic of maladjustment he claimed existed, or the creation of a new mental illness term to characterize it. Even so, the *New York Times* published an article on a violent Vietnam veteran afflicted with a new disease called "post-Vietnam syndrome," to which the psychiatric profession had turned a blind eye. The author used statistics gathered almost entirely from a series of articles in *Penthouse* magazine.[16]

Lifton and Shatan established close connections with the increasingly popular "rap groups," confessionals in which veterans discussed their war experiences. Many of these groups were organized by the Vietnam Veterans Against the War (VVAW). In 1971, Lifton and the VVAW participated in a nongovernmental event launched by the Citizens Commission of Inquiry, an activist organization that conducted research on US war crimes in Vietnam. At that event, he instructed veterans to focus their remarks on atrocities because, he said, being open about the violent acts they committed would inspire other veterans to talk. The participants Lifton recruited said that the killing of civilians, women, and children was not an anomaly, the actions of a few men like Lt. William Calley, who had murdered dozens of people at My Lai; it was "standard operating procedure" for American servicemen in Vietnam.[17] Lifton was creating the very stereotype that would stigmatize veterans as mentally unstable, if not murderers and rapists. "Post-Vietnam syndrome," the condition that would eventually be renamed "post-traumatic stress disorder," and be included in the DSM-III (1980), was beginning to define the veteran's personality.

Throughout the 1970s, stories of atrocities committed during the war filtered into Hollywood. Just as *One Flew Over the Cuckoo's Nest* (1975) validated public antipsychiatry sentiment, frightening films like *Taxi Driver* (1976) and *Apocalypse Now* (1979), and even empathic films like *Coming Home* (1978) and *The Deer Hunter* (1978), confirmed public perceptions of the Vietnam veteran as morally and psychologically damaged.

Some journalists and researchers argued against the stereotype of the mentally disabled and dangerous veteran.[18] The media reported, for example, that Vietnam veterans were using the G.I. Bill at a higher percentage than soldiers did after WWII or the Korean War, that only 2 percent of veterans used narcotics after returning home, and that the hospitalization rate for mental illnesses was 50 percent lower than that for the WWII soldier. The *New York Times* wrote that military veterans were finding jobs faster than at any time in the previous ten years,[19] and the *Los Angeles Times* concluded that "the American soldier in Vietnam was psychologically healthier than his counterpart in previous wars."[20]

In 1974, military psychiatrist Jonathan Borus presented data showing little difference between the behavioral, emotional, or disciplinary problems of soldiers who served in Vietnam and those who did not.[21] Borus's work was then validated six years later in a powerful longitudinal study of 92,000 navy servicemen who had enlisted in 1966. That study, conducted by navy researchers, found low rates of psychiatric problems in veterans, with rates falling as time went on. Contrary to expectations, "it was the non-combatant Vietnam veterans who had the highest hospitalization rates for stress-related disorders both during and after the Vietnam War."[22] And Marlowe noted: "The high proportion of Vietnam veterans reporting the syndrome (about one-third) might make sense if the level of combat for all involved had been parallel to that of the heavy fighting of World War II. But it was not, and many of those reporting PTSD symptoms were support personnel who were far removed from the fighting."[23] Advocates for veterans fiercely criticized Borus and others who challenged the stereotype of the psychologically unbalanced veteran, even though Borus didn't argue against the potential utility of PTSD as a diagnostic term. And those who had the gall to suggest that a person who fought in Vietnam might have actually become more mentally healthy during the war were vilified. Yet in past wars, experts had recognized some positive effects of war experience, such as the benefits of comradeship, or the development of empathy, coping skills, and an appreciation for the value of life.[24]

The proponents of the new post-Vietnam diagnosis relied on Freud—ironically, since they were simultaneously rejecting the psychoanalytic theory of homosexuality. In 1973, when the APA eliminated homosexuality from the DSM, the association argued that psychoanalysis was a soft science that couldn't be used to claim that homosexuality was a mental disorder. Yet the APA rejected or accepted psychoanalytic theory depending on whether it served their purposes. Advocates for a post-trauma disorder drew on the concept of repression—one of the hallmarks of psychoanalytic theory—to make their case. As Shatan wrote in the *New York Times*: "During World War I, Freud elucidated the role grief plays in helping the mourner let go of a missing part of life, and acknowledging that it exists only in the memory." Vietnam veterans, in this view, had repressed their feelings and were numbed to the world. They were filled with rage and resentment, but with no way to express it. He added, "the sorrow is unspent, the grief of their wounds is untold, their guilt is unexpiated."[25] Just as in psychoanalysis the patient must chronicle his past, a past that he remembers only in the process of narrating it, so does the trauma victim have to narrate his memories. A post-Vietnam syndrome was that narrative form. And despite the APA's antipsychoanalytic bias, it would ultimately accept the proposition that people who suffered from a post-traumatic condition had repressed their memories.

The APA also had to figure out a way to protect a post-Vietnam syndrome from the antiwar bias in its membership. In previous wars, doctors had accepted with little debate that they could not work in war in the same manner as in civilian life, that in war one had different goals and techniques. For a war as unpopular as the Vietnam War, however, they were not willing or able to reconcile their conflicts of interest. Many in the association argued that military psychiatrists were committed to the war and not to the patient.[26] There was also too little coverage of veterans' problems in psychiatric journals and professional conferences to pique their interest in veterans' mental health. In 1969, during the height of the violence, the only paper on Vietnam listed in the annual weeklong meeting of the APA, out of hundreds of papers, was on the topic of GI-Vietnamese marriages. Moreover, civilian psychiatrists saw the treatment of soldiers and veterans as the government's responsibility, not theirs.[27] Psychiatrist Thomas Maier wrote in 1970, "Whatever else Army psychiatry may be, I see neither moral nor scientific justification for the dignity of its definition as clinical psychiatry."[28]

Another challenge was finding a rationale for creating a new disorder. For both homosexuality and PTSD, there were virtually no data to justify either exclusion or inclusion, but the APA could defend its decision to remove homosexuality from the DSM in terms of civil rights. Advocates for inclusion of PTSD relied mostly on anecdotes about troubled Vietnam veterans, but they couldn't claim a moral high ground since there was so little public compassion for people who had participated in an immoral war— even if against their will, as draftees. But advocates were able to argue that the new diagnosis would not overlap with any others. They rejected outright the assertion that existing diagnoses—such as depression, anxiety, and brief reactive psychosis—were adequate for their needs,[29] and pointed out that the APA had no category at all for trauma since "gross stress reaction" had been eliminated in the DSM-II.[30] All that the DSM-II offered was the category "adjustment reaction to adult life," a diagnosis advocates for PTSD dismissed as vague and irrelevant to Vietnam War trauma because it was defined as temporary (a "transient situational personality disorder"). Adjustment reaction was also thought to appear soon after the person experienced stress, not years later as happened with the Vietnam veterans with PTSD. The DSM-III was in the works, and recognizing that the main goal of the new edition was to provide data-driven diagnoses, the APA leadership looked for scientific evidence that might validate PTSD and help them develop strict diagnostic criteria.

Why did they need scientific evidence? Because the APA wanted to reject both psychoanalysis and the idea that mental illnesses were features of normal psychological variation on a spectrum. The new criteria, they argued, would establish "real" diseases, and would improve reliability in research and clinical care by making sure that researchers and providers everywhere in the world used the same diagnoses with the same criteria. Without standardization, there was little hope for a scientific psychiatry: patients with the same symptoms easily received different diagnoses depending on the whims of a doctor; epidemiological rates varied widely depending on what criteria the researchers used to decide what constituted a "case" or not; and two researchers conducting a drug trial weren't sure they were studying similar populations. What better way, the authors of the DSM-III asked, to make psychiatry more objective and less susceptible to variations in clinical and research practice than to create universally agreed-upon categories and symptom checklists? And what better way to make sure insurance companies paid for mental health treatments than to provide them with specific diagnostic labels that clinicians would apply with scientific rigor?

Scientific support for a post-trauma condition came partly from Grinker and Spiegel's WWII studies, in which they had suggested that pathological responses to traumatic experiences could occur many years after the event, or even become chronic.[31] My grandfather said, in 1945, that he was astonished that "the majority of the neuroses that are hospitalized today . . . developed the first signs of their neurosis on return to this country or have become worse after landing on these shores."[32] But validation for PTSD came mostly not from the military. It came from the work of doctors who had gathered data on the victims of fires, car accidents, sexual violence, and other kinds of trauma.

In tracing the APA's acceptance of PTSD, historians of psychiatry often give much of the credit to Nancy Andreasen, a highly respected psychiatrist at the University of Iowa, who had published articles on the victims of severe burns. In one article, Andreasen wrote that half the survivors of the 1945 Cocoanut Grove nightclub fire in Boston (which killed 492 people) had been diagnosed with what was then called "post-traumatic neuroses,"[33] and that their emotional pain endured for decades. Additional validation came from data gathered on the long-term psychological problems of Holocaust survivors. But such chronic emotional suffering is only treatable, Andreasen said, if the clinician has a framework—a diagnosis like PTSD— with which to comprehend the distinctive psychological ramifications of tragic events.[34]

There was another, albeit relatively invisible, contributor to the social history of PTSD: feminism. By the early 1970s, feminist groups had directed public attention to the psychological consequences of domestic abuse and child abuse (especially sexual abuse of children). At the same time, feminist therapy emerged in the United States as a distinct method of treatment, addressing issues such as sexual violence, domestic abuse, the failure of women to enjoy economic gains in a growing economy, and the objectification of women as sexual and reproductive bodies to be evaluated and used by men. In academic articles, feminist clinicians proposed new illness names like battered women's syndrome, rape trauma syndrome, and child abuse syndrome, and the symptoms they described sounded very similar to those proposed for PTSD, thus providing additional data to the APA in support of adding a PTSD category to the new DSM.[35]

Feminist clinicians objected to a diagnosis with the word "Vietnam" in the name but viewed PTSD as potentially empowering.[36] They asked: Why shouldn't battered women get the same benefits as soldiers?[37] If the soldier can describe the atrocities of Vietnam, why shouldn't people be able to talk more openly about rape and incest? And if a Vietnam veteran can repress a traumatic event, only to rediscover it months or years later in therapy, why can't the same thing happen to victims of sexual violence? In 1973, the American Psychological Association founded the Committee on Women in Psychology and the Society for the Psychology of Women to support female researchers and clinicians and bring attention to the way a wide range of social factors influence women's psychology, including their internalization of sexist norms as a kind of self-stigma.

PTSD formally entered the DSM-III when it was published in 1980, although clinicians had been using synonyms like "Vietnam syndrome" and "post-Vietnam disorder" for nearly a decade. Veterans advocacy groups favored, first, "post-Vietnam disorder," and then proposed as a compromise, "catastrophic stress disorder." The final name of PTSD made certain that the diagnosis would be relevant not only for active-duty military and veterans but for anyone who had been subject to severe stress, including victims of sexual violence. The APA defined it as either chronic or delayed, and caused by a "psychologically traumatic event that is generally outside the range of usual human experience."[38]

Over the next two decades, the diagnosis gained traction because of its relative absence of stigma, and researchers were steadily accumulating data on psychological trauma. For example, scientists studied the child survivors of the 1972 Buffalo Creek dam collapse in West Virginia, in which 125 residents died and more than a thousand were injured from the flood of millions of gallons of black wastewater from a coal mine. As adults, seventeen years after the flood, 7 percent of these individuals met the criteria for PTSD.[39] Similarly, a retrospective analysis of Israeli teenagers who had been kidnapped by Palestinian guerrillas in 1974—an abduction in which twenty-two children were killed—showed persistent symptoms of PTSD seventeen years later, often triggered by news of a terrorist attack.[40] One study of Holocaust survivors found that about half of the sample met the criteria for PTSD—with symptoms like hypervigilance, amnesia, and emotional detachment—fifty years after the end of WWII, and that the symptoms did not vary based on whether one had been in a concentration camp or survived in hiding.[41]

In 1988, the National Vietnam Veterans Readjustment Study (NVVRS) reported that 15.2 percent (479,000 men) of all male Vietnam veterans in its sample met the criteria for PTSD, as did 8 percent (160 women) of female Vietnam veterans. Although the study found that most veterans had successfully readjusted to life postwar, the researchers also found that "over the course of their lifetimes through 1988, 30.9 percent of men in the study and 26.9 percent of the women had developed PTSD." An additional 22.5 percent of men and 21.2 percent of women had developed what the researchers called "partial PTSD," because they met most but not all of the DSM criteria.[42] In a follow-up analysis, 78 percent of Vietnam veterans with full or partial PTSD were still suffering from the symptoms of PTSD twenty to twenty-five years later.[43] By 2012, the U.S. Army called PTSD an "epidemic."

PTSD remained a contradictory diagnosis. Was the person with PTSD a harmless victim to be cared for, or a perpetrator to be feared? A resilient survivor or an unbalanced ticking time bomb? Those contradictions vexed the clinician, and the American public too, because the cause of this signature wound was an unresolved and politically divisive war. By reducing psychiatric symptoms to the effects of the war, soldiers were entitled to mental health care, but also vulnerable to the stereotypes shaped by the war and public opinion.

As an illness supposedly caused by the specific events during one's military service, PTSD also affected soldiers' treatment. Veterans could receive care for the effects of war, but not for the impact of a longer and unique life history that preceded the war. Even today, soldiers have little incentive to disclose psychological problems separate from or predating combat or interpersonal trauma (such as sexual assault) during their service. Soldiers who reveal preexisting conditions can be discharged without benefits since the military can argue that their illnesses were not caused during military service. To ensure benefits, a clinician may interpret other mental illnesses as PTSD or as comorbid with a primary PTSD diagnosis. The policy of providing psychiatric care only for conditions incurred during service is grounded in the illusion that our military personnel enter the armed forces emotionally intact; and even if they are not intact, the military ideology is that boot camp breaks down soldiers and remakes them into new beings.

If clinicians or patients imagine PTSD as something that occurs only as the result of particular, discrete events that transpired after enlistment, the military might actually impede effective treatment, such as psychotherapeutic interventions tailored to someone's particular life history. We do not know how many military men and women with PTSD come into their service having already experienced or witnessed various forms of violence, but it's likely that a substantial portion do. In an all-volunteer army, large numbers of enlistees come from disadvantaged backgrounds in which they experienced poverty, discrimination, and violence.[44] Early conditions of vulnerability—what mental health professionals refer to as "adverse childhood experiences" (or ACEs)—are major risk factors for adult health, and mental health, problems, including suicide.[45] Omitting more complete histories and privileging experiences only on active duty also masks diversity among service members. Poverty and hunger are not the same as child abuse or sexual violence, and growing up an American Indian on a reservation is not the same as growing up Hispanic in the Bronx.

PTSD has, to a large extent, become an all-purpose diagnosis, an equalizer of sorts that mutes biographical and cultural differences, and offers a relatively nonstigmatized diagnosis by blaming an environmental stressor rather than an individual's distinctive personality and history. It has become a kind of scientific currency circulated throughout the world by relief organizations as they provide care for the victims of tragedies such as political violence in the former Yugoslavia, the 1995 Kobe earthquake in Japan, the 2004 tsunami in the Indian Ocean, and the 2010 earthquake in Haiti. Originally intended as a diagnosis for US war veterans, PTSD, in the words of anthropologist Josh Breslau, "has become a taken-for-granted dimension of humanitarian assistance on a global level."[46] Writer Ethan Watters calls PTSD the "international lingua franca of human suffering," and anthropologist Kimberly Theidon writes of the "trauma industry" in global mental health.[47]

Critics of the global expansion of mental health care warn that PTSD turns expected reactions to stress into a psychiatric diagnosis; anxiety and hyperalertness, for example, are symptoms of PTSD but they are also rational reactions to trauma. Today, whenever there is a natural disaster, public health officials warn of a new wave of PTSD among survivors. But not everyone in the world reacts to traumatic events in the same way. Remember that traumatized soldiers during WWI and WWII rarely mentioned anything resembling flashbacks, now a key symptom of PTSD. In fact, reports of dissociative flashbacks, in which the person feels as if he is reexperiencing the actual traumatic event, were uncommon until the Gulf War (1990–91).[48] In some parts of Latin America, emotional numbing and avoidance, also central features of PTSD, are uncommon reactions to trauma. In sub-Saharan Africa today, as we'll soon see, reactions to trauma include fears of genital loss; in South Asia, war trauma frequently leads to paranoia and "thinking too much."[49] None of these symptoms are part of the DSM criteria for PTSD.

Of course, not every reaction to a traumatic event is pathological, even if it transforms someone's life. In the United States, anthropologist Zoë Wool writes that "homecoming trouble and postcombat transformations have become tethered to, if not enveloped by PTSD."[50] It is such a dominant condition among veterans that it continues to draw clinicians' attention only to those symptoms that are part of the PTSD symptom checklist, concealing the other effects of war that psychiatry doesn't define as pathological, like the numerous disruptive and disorienting professional and personal changes that take place in a soldier's everyday life after war.[51]

PTSD also reminds us of how doctors and patients collaborate to shape particular symptoms and their description, a process that is made explicit when doctor and patient do *not* share the same culture or language. Refugees from Cambodia, for example, receiving care for psychological trauma in the United States, described the horrors of mass killings and torture under the Khmer Rouge regime, but they tended not to report the flashbacks, nightmares, and intrusive traumatic memories that are so common in PTSD, as we think of it today.[52] American doctors were at first surprised by this. But these refugees actually did have flashbacks and hyperarousal. They didn't tell their psychiatrists because they saw these symptoms as spiritual rather than psychiatric. Refugees examined by psychiatrist Devon E. Hinton at Harvard University attributed startling and arousal not to a psychological condition but to weakness of the heart or a *khyâl* attack, in which khyâl, a windlike substance that flows through the bloodstream, becomes dysregulated and surges in the body.[53] A man might tell a shaman about a nightmare, because dreams are spiritual. But it might not occur to him to mention it to a doctor, unless a doctor (trained in the twenty-first century to associate nightmares with historical trauma) asked him about it. After their meetings with the American clinicians, however, they reframed their suffering in terms of PTSD.

PTSD is also an illness of the individual, a model best suited for the person who suffers in cultures of individualism and interprets trauma as an affront to self-reliance and self-control. In many parts of sub-Saharan Africa, people narrate their trauma as familial or spiritual, political or economic, and describe their pain not as the result of insults to them as autonomous actors but as insults to a social group. For some American Indian communities living in Northwest coast reservations, "historical trauma" is more appropriate than "PTSD," since the former affects everyone in their society while the latter affects only the individual. Although the concept of stress was first developed by social scientists to take account of how social context impinges on mental health, it became a context-free affliction that a person experienced internally—as his own memories, his own knowledge—and ended up obscuring the social factors that shape different kinds of trauma, and different perceptions, experiences, and treatments of trauma.[54]

Some communities in the war-torn regions of the former Yugoslavia interpret PTSD negatively, as a disease of passivity. Someone with PTSD is, in that view, a victim rather than a resilient fighter. They also reject the assumption, implied in the diagnostic criteria of PTSD, that people who experience suffering are "traumatized" by an external force. They reject the implication that PTSD is chronic, incurable, and that even when absent might be ready to emerge in years to come. In Kosovo, international aid organizations have employed PTSD as a way to help patients understand that they are the victims, and to channel their feelings of anger and resentment toward the perpetrators.[55] But in the process, they have unwittingly fueled interethnic hatred and desires for revenge.

These cross-cultural examples suggest that PTSD is to some extent a privileged diagnosis. When patients or clinicians explain symptoms as the result of a traumatic event, they are thinking of that event as out of the ordinary. But what about people for whom trauma defines everyday existence, such as chronic domestic abuse, malnutrition, or unpredictable violence? What about people who have been discriminated against all their lives, or who have been incarcerated for years on end? In these cases, it doesn't make sense to talk about a small number of discrete traumatic events.

As a diagnostic term, PTSD certainly can be useful; even unreliable or invalid diagnoses can motivate beneficial treatments. PTSD helps victims explain and legitimate their symptoms, and helps providers understand and address mental health problems. But while trauma causes great suffering, it does not necessarily cause "PTSD." PTSD is our own construction, and it might not be valuable everywhere. We created it as a way to comprehend a particular kind of pain in a manner that is culturally acceptable and does not blame the afflicted. PTSD, our face-saving diagnosis, is one of the only diagnoses people with psychological problems might actually want to have. Were he alive today, Thomas Salmon, the WWI psychiatrist who once said that patients clung to the diagnosis of shell shock like a lifeline, would recognize PTSD as its offspring.

CHAPTER 11

EXPECTATIONS OF SICKNESS

*A cultural system commonly thought to serve a heal-
ing function may also have a contrary outcome, fos-
tering the same pathologies intended to be healed.*

Robert A. Hahn,
"The Nocebo Phenomenon" (1997)

When I met with Thomas Insel in 2014, he was still director of the National Institute of Mental Health and had been lecturing widely about efforts to reduce barriers to mental health care. A neuroscientist and psychiatrist in his late sixties, Insel looks and acts much younger. He is at once serious and affable, voicing strong opinions with boyish enthusiasm. He told me, "'Stigma' is one of the biggest problems in mental health care, and you should look at the military, and what's happening with soldiers deployed to Afghanistan and Iraq. I think the military is doing more to address stigma than any other sector of American society." I didn't believe him at first. Now I do.

No American war has lasted as long as our conflicts in Afghanistan and Iraq. Depending on how one marks the end of the Vietnam War, that war lasted either eleven or thirteen years. But a young person entering the armed forces today might not even have been born when the current conflicts began. All told, there have been nearly 7,000 military deaths, and tens of thousands wounded or psychologically traumatized, since troop deployments were initiated after September 11, 2001. Many of these wounded are women. In Afghanistan and Iraq, where there are ill-defined boundaries between combat and noncombat roles, and no front lines, women are just as likely to be exposed to combat as men, and to develop combat-related PTSD. Women are also likely to develop PTSD as the result of sexual assault; as many as 36 percent of female veterans have experienced what the US military calls "military sexual trauma" (MST).[1]

Given their duration, these wars have broken the cycle of building capacity for mental health care and then forgetting about all that was achieved. Because there is no peacetime, there is no chance to forget. Enmeshed in these conflicts, the military has been able to sustain its focus on mental illness, stigma, and barriers to care. Doctors conduct extensive surveys and lengthy interviews with soldiers through the entire deployment cycle; the annual Mental Health Advisory Team (MHAT) reports real-time health assessments on the battlefield in Iraq and Afghanistan; and military researchers publish their results in mainstream journals, like the *New England Journal of Medicine*. In a conversation I had with several staff at the Walter Reed Army Institute of Research, Dr. Debra Yourick said, "Sometimes you think that the civilian world doesn't know what we do, and that in medicine we're second class citizens." Dr. Jeffrey L. Thomas responded to her: "Yes, but things are different now. We'll write a paper and the media will pick it up. I think we've never been more appreciated."

The diagnosis of PTSD, popularized by the military, has now become a colloquialism. When a student of mine talked about getting a poor grade in an economics class, she said, "I can't take another econ class. It gave me PTSD." I cannot judge what actually transpired in her class, or how her performance in the course resonated with past histories of failure. But in answer to my follow-up questions, she did not indicate that the course, or even the contemplation of another one, caused any problems with her other work or her social relationships. She did not have nightmares, physical symptoms of distress or hyperarousal, and had not lost interest in any of her hobbies. It's thus unlikely that she actually met the criteria for PTSD. Still, a group of psychologists from San Francisco State University showed that in a sample of 769 college students, about 25 percent met the criteria for clinically significant PTSD symptoms two to three months after the 2016 US presidential election. The symptoms, attributable to their shock and dismay at the outcome of the election, included intrusive thoughts, avoidance, and alterations in close social relationships.[2]

Experts bristle at such liberal usage of the term because, they say, it trivializes a serious condition. Dr. Rachel Yehuda, a neuroscientist and director of the Traumatic Stress Studies Division at the Mount Sinai School of Medicine, is gratified that stigma has been reduced for mental illness in general, but when I met her at her office at the Bronx VA Medical Center, she expressed some misgivings. The suicides of designer Kate Spade and celebrity chef Anthony Bourdain were still in the headlines, and she was conflicted about all the media attention to their deaths. She mentioned them as she said, "Sometimes I wonder if we have swung the pendulum too far in reducing stigma, making some diagnoses far too broad and also glamorizing some mental illnesses, and perhaps even suicide." PTSD has become so common, she suggested, that anyone who experiences a traumatic event might now expect to get sick. But trauma, she said, is by definition emotionally difficult. "Distress after trauma is not only OK, but it's what's supposed to happen. The sickness is when that distress goes on for a long time and interferes with the rest of your life."

Her concern, it seemed to me, was not that there are real or fictive illnesses—as if the economics student and the students upset by the election of Donald Trump didn't really feel traumatized—but that PTSD, and other illness terms as well, have become a way of claiming a right to legitimate pain and misfortune. It is as if, without the illness label, their anguish wouldn't be valid, and they wouldn't be granted a passport to what Susan Sontag once called citizenship in "the kingdom of the sick."[3] What Yehuda did not point out, however, was that only some realms in that kingdom offer a refuge from the stigma of mental illnesses: the diseases that come to us from the outside, apparently through no fault of our own, like PTSD and the enigmatic Gulf War syndrome (GWS).

In 2008, six years before Insel recommended I learn more about military psychiatry, Pete Geren, the secretary of the army, phoned Insel at NIMH to discuss the increased suicide rate in the military. Geren had been secretary of the army for less than a year, and from the moment the U.S. Senate confirmed him, suicide and stigma were his top priority. There were plenty of survey data showing that soldiers feared that if they sought mental health care, their fellow soldiers would have less confidence in them and they would be seen as weak, would not be promoted, and might even be discharged. In a major study conducted in 2004, fewer than half of the soldiers and marines who were symptomatic for PTSD and depression sought mental health care from anyone, even a chaplain. The lead investigator, Charles Hoge, who directs US military research on mental health, says that "stigma was the main reason they avoided getting help."[4]

Others place the blame for stigma on military commanders. As many as 190,000 new soldiers enter the U.S. Army, the U.S. Army Reserve, or the U.S. Army National Guard (USANG) each year, and according to Dr. Paul Kim of the Walter Reed Army Institute of Research, "from the moment those new soldiers arrive—whether from ROTC, West Point, or basic training—the commander can be an agent of change or an impediment." Col. Robert Certain, a retired air force pilot and military chaplain, told me that some commanders also dismiss mental health concerns for those who were not directly exposed to violence in combat. He said, "The reality is that very few people in combat are actually shot at or shoot their weapons. But this doesn't mean they're not incredibly frightened and anxious." One veteran with PTSD had another theory for the persistence of stigma. He told me that the military thinks there is more stigma than there really is and that "the military uses stigma as an excuse so they don't get blamed for having too few mental health care services."

By the turn of the twenty-first century, the suicide rate in the military, which had for many years been lower than in other sectors of society, was steadily inching upward. And by 2008, when Geren took over, it exceeded the rate of suicide in the civilian population (20.2/100,000 versus 19.2/100,000 among civilians). Most people who committed suicide, within and outside the military, did so successfully in their first attempt, having never been treated by a mental health professional. Just four years later, in 2012, the rate of suicides in the military would exceed 30 per 100,000 soldiers.[5] As one result of the high suicide rate, and in an attempt to decrease the prevalence of mental illnesses in the military, the army decided to end a waiver program that allowed some soldiers with preexisting conditions like bipolar disorder and substance abuse to enlist.

Geren and Insel agreed to join forces and conduct the largest-ever study of military mental health, at an initial cost of $65 million, $50 million from the U.S. Army and $15 million from NIMH. Insel likened it to the longitudinal Framingham Heart Study, so named because it investigated the cardiac health of the people who live in Framingham, Massachusetts. The Framingham study began in 1948 with more than 5,000 research subjects and is still active. Geren and Insel wanted the same kind of surveillance of mental health among soldiers—especially for PTSD—and they called the project the Army Study to Assess Risk and Resilience in Servicemembers (Army STARRS).

STARRS researchers gathered historical data on the 1.3 million active-duty soldiers who served between 2004 and 2009, and followed the mental health of more than 100,000 soldiers, young and old, pre- and post-deployment, in the theater of military operations, and in hospitals between 2009 and 2014. Since 2014, the new STARRS Longitudinal Study (STARRS-LS) has continued to focus on mental health outcomes over time, administering lengthy surveys to soldiers with the promise of confidentiality. Most of the results have been unremarkable. For example, more men commit suicide than women; soldiers who deploy soon after enlisting, and before they have time to acclimate to the military, are at higher risk of suicide than those who deploy later; soldiers who have been demoted in the past two years also have a higher risk of suicide.

The STARRS survey results, while not surprising, were still concerning. Twenty-five percent of nondeployed U.S. Army personnel met criteria for anxiety, mood, disruptive behavior, or substance disorder, and 11.1 percent had multiple disorders. Seventy-five percent of these disorders had their onset pre-enlistment.[6] In another study, intermittent explosive disorder (IED), a condition characterized by impulsive anger and aggression, was the most common pre-enlistment condition, appearing at nearly six times the civilian rate.[7] In other words, thousands of soldiers were passing their enlistment screening with their preexisting mental illnesses hidden or overlooked. And as the Iraq and Afghanistan Veterans of America association points out, once they enlist, the burden "is on the service member or veteran to self-diagnose and seek out care."[8] Even if a soldier seeks care, it may not be available quickly; currently in Afghanistan, American soldiers with acute mental health needs often wait on average 40 hours to be seen by a psychologist or psychiatrist.[9]

Many soldiers who receive a diagnosis of PTSD in the military might have other mental illnesses, or they might have experienced other trauma during their lives—perhaps in a violent upbringing. Yet, in their mental health assessments those traumas tend to be superseded by whatever trauma occurred during service. Moreover, when there were multiple possible diagnoses, PTSD became the primary one. PTSD has the triple allure of facilitating benefits, reducing stigma as a barrier to care, and conferring some degree of honor at the same time.

It is not uncommon for people to embrace new and relatively less-stigmatizing diagnoses if they confer a benefit. Anthropologist Adriana Petryna uses the term "biological citizenship" to explain how survivors of the Chernobyl nuclear disaster in Ukraine struggled to receive diagnoses linked to exposure to radioactivity in order to qualify for health and financial benefits reserved for Chernobyl victims. Like other identity-based illness movements—for example, Gulf War syndrome in the United States—Ukrainians merged identity and biology in order to be visible, and to receive financial compensation, at a time of economic insecurity. There were both psychological and material benefits to being "publicly ill."[10] Like Chernobyl-related contamination claims, a new diagnosis of PTSD suggests that the recipient of the diagnosis was healthy before the event.

PTSD thus creates a false biographic boundary.[11] Taken in isolation from the rest of a soldier's life, the treatment of PTSD typically involves addressing the symptoms but not the longer-term developmental reasons behind them. And without a more historical perspective, it becomes difficult to address the question of why one person and not another, exposed to the same trauma, develops PTSD symptoms. Former military psychiatrist Lance Clawson told me that a diagnosis of PTSD might help a soldier get over the barrier of stigma and get into treatment, "but it doesn't necessarily help the clinician figure out *how* to treat him."

Imagine, for example, there is a service member who has a desk job and has never been deployed. After one of his friends dies in combat in Iraq, he suffers not only from the loss of his friend but also from the disturbing details he learns about his friend's death. He has sleep disturbances, anxiety, and sometimes shortness of breath. He is referred to a psychiatrist for treatment of PTSD, but the psychiatrist knows that if he digs into the soldier's background there is a risk of uncovering evidence prior to service that might have facilitated the onset of symptoms—perhaps the soldier's own history of maltreatment in childhood, or history of depression and anxiety disorder.

In the absence of a history that informs the patient's mental health, PTSD may justify coverage for some treatment, but then the patient has a diagnosis that might not actually meet the generally accepted criteria and might not be as therapeutically useful as other diagnoses. The value of any diagnosis is what it has to offer the sufferer. Although the APA long ago specified that PTSD was not a condition to be diagnosed only in previously "normal" individuals, many illnesses in the military continue to be reduced to PTSD. Equally problematic, if PTSD is so broad a category that one can fit a multitude of psychological symptoms within it, then what happens when someone has features that cannot fit into PTSD, like autism, obsessive-compulsive behaviors, or gender dysphoria? Do those conditions then warrant a denial of care or discharge from the military?

PTSD is not the most common psychiatric condition among active military. Substance abuse is the most common, followed by depression. Depression is also the most commonly reported condition among veterans.[12] PTSD is just the one most frequently recorded in a soldier's medical files, and the one most often discussed in the media. In addition, the more elite the soldier, the more influence that soldier has on what is recorded. A military psychiatrist said, on condition of anonymity, that soldiers in the U.S. Army Special Forces, hospitalized at Walter Reed, the army hospital outside Washington, DC, have been able to review and edit their medical records, and sometimes substitute PTSD for other diagnoses. Soldiers who are financially able will often seek mental health care in the private sector, and pay out of pocket in order to avoid a military record of mental illness. The Department of Defense also runs Military OneSource, which has been advertised to soldiers who cannot afford private sector care as a way to get free short-term mental health care off base.

There is clearly a conflict between the ideal of military medicine—to treat men and women for conditions they acquired during their military service—and the reality of an all-volunteer army that struggles to recruit enough soldiers, especially in a strong economy that offers other kinds of employment. In September 2017, faced with a severe shortage of soldiers, the U.S. Army resuscitated the waiver program, allowing men and women who had a history of self-injury, mood disorders, and drug and alcohol abuse/dependence to apply for a waiver for enlistment. The army did not justify the waiver program as a method for reducing the stigma of mental illness, but it could certainly have that result. Relaxing the ban on enlisting someone who many years earlier struggled with and overcame a substance-abuse problem suggests that one's prior mental illness is not a permanent brand. It also suggests that the military is relaxing its ideology of death and rebirth at enlistment. Time will tell if having admitted to such mental health conditions prior to enlisting will affect their access to psychiatric care if they develop PTSD symptoms later on.

The US military employs several strategies to reduce barriers to mental health care. In 2007, the U.S. Navy, for example, established thirteen deployment health clinics that sailors are required to visit for annual and post-deployment health assessments. Previously, mental and physical health facilities were in separate locations. The navy reasoned that if they incorporated psychological services in the same location, it might facilitate mental health treatment, since the soldier would not fear the stigma of being seen entering a psychiatric clinic. One benefit of this practice is to avoid the body-mind separation that has so often negatively affected treatment. Soldiers with PTSD may experience emotional difficulties, but they also experience myriad physical symptoms, including shortness of breath, a racing heartbeat, and abdominal pain. Moreover, in studies in the civilian population, PTSD—like other mental illnesses—is associated with smoking, substance abuse, sexual risk-taking, and other behaviors that increase the chances of acquiring serious medical problems.

Another governmental strategy to reduce barriers to care was to revise the United States Office of Personnel Management Standard Form 86. This form, completed by anyone seeking a security clearance, includes a question about whether the applicant has sought care for "an emotional or mental condition" in the past seven years. Although an answer of yes does not necessarily doom an application, the question certainly implies that psychological treatment is a demerit. But since 2008, applicants can answer no on this question if they sought mental health care for "adjustments from service in a military combat environment" or for nonviolent marital, family, or grief-related issues. In other words, most soldiers do not have to worry that receiving mental health care will jeopardize a security clearance. Charles Hoge hopes the takeaway message will be that "there are life situations, particularly involving combat and relationships, where counseling is expected."[13]

In 2011, General Peter Chiarelli, the army vice Chief of staff, began to argue that one of the best ways to reduce stigma was to drop the "D" from PTSD. Chiarelli said of "disorder": "that word is a dirty word"[14] and "it seems clear to me that we should get rid of the 'D' if that is in any way inhibiting people from getting the help they need."[15] Advocates in the civilian and nonprofit sectors agreed that the word "disorder" connoted weakness: "PTSD is a wound you suffer in combat, just like a bullet wound."[16] Still, PTSD does not earn a soldier a Purple Heart. General Eric Schoomaker, the army surgeon general, said that PTSD is a normal reaction and asked, "Well, if it's *normal*, why is it called a *disorder*?"[17] The APA, however, retained the name PTSD in its 2013 revision of the DSM, the DSM-5, because the editors feared that removing the word "disorder" might restrict insurance coverage for sufferers, and because "stress," while contributing to mental illnesses, does not by itself constitute a diagnosable or treatable condition.

Other leaders focus on developing pre-deployment resilience programs, at great financial cost, though critics argue that when soldiers return from combat and nonetheless have PTSD, their stigma increases.[18] If they failed to be resilient despite having completed the program, some soldiers reason, they must be truly deficient.

It's not clear that any of these efforts are affecting barriers to care, or the suicide rate. Beginning in 2004, the military's Mental Health Advisory Team (MHAT) published annual assessments of the efforts to promote early intervention for mental illnesses and reduce stigma, and they show little change in perceptions about mental health care since that time. The degree of stigma, measured by surveys to ascertain soldiers' willingness to seek counseling, was stable across all of the MHAT assessments, with the exception of a slight drop in 2008, which then leveled off. Dr. Paul Kim at Walter Reed said, "We were disappointed. We had such massive anti-stigma campaigns." Robert Certain also expressed frustration at the inability to curb the suicide rate. He told me, "You look at the trainings, the way doctors communicate with the leadership, and the way commanders are communicating with soldiers, following up with soldiers who had problems, keeping in contact with them, and literally you'll see they're doing all the right things. But have we made a real impact?"

In his account of combat in eastern Afghanistan, writer Sebastian Junger remarked on how deeply affected the soldiers were despite what he called "an enormous amount of psychiatry oversight from the battalion shrink." One counselor, helping a soldier who described himself as "messed up," suggested that the soldier start smoking to deal with his nerves. Most men, Junger says, will do whatever it takes to defer mental health care until after deployment. But one of the units Junger describes, Battle Company, experienced such intense combat that "by the time the tour was over, half of Battle Company was supposedly on psychiatric meds."[19]

Junger doesn't mention the several reasons why the soldiers he followed might have been especially prone to developing and reporting mental illnesses. First, they were young. Most mental illnesses are developmental, meaning that the seeds of the illnesses exist well before any obvious clinical presentation, but they have their onset in late adolescence—which is why military psychiatrists tell me that the best practitioners in their field are those trained in child psychiatry; eighteen- and nineteen-year-old men are, in the clinician's view, still children. Second, many soldiers grew up in difficult circumstances and may have experienced any number of psychological hardships that predispose them to develop common mental illnesses. Third, the more psychological infrastructure that is in place, the more likely the soldier is to take advantage of it. In Battle Company, it seems, seeking mental health care was to some extent normalized.

I'm not surprised that so many soldiers in Battle Company sought psychiatric care. If a psychiatrist is available, more soldiers are likely to be sensitized to their psychiatric issues and seek help—especially for milder conditions that might have gone untreated under less oversight—and then, of course, it will look as if more people are actually sick. At the same time, the psychiatrist will also actively look for conditions to treat. Psychologists sometimes call such cognitive bias the "law of the instrument," popularly known by the phrase "if one only has a hammer everything looks like a nail." If the available doctor making a concerted effort to monitor the health of Battle Company had been a gastrointestinal or headache specialist, it is possible that more gastrointestinal and headache symptoms would have been reported as well. What changes from war to war is less the prevalence of particular symptoms than, in the words of military psychiatrist Charles Engel, the conditions under which "soldiers and veterans report the symptoms and how physicians and other health care providers interpret them."[20]

The murky relationship between a soldier's past and present was brought into relief in Gulf War syndrome, a condition acquired during Operation Desert Storm (1991) and marked by fatigue, headaches, and gastrointestinal, respiratory, and skin diseases. The soldiers first afflicted with GWS were mainly those associated with the 700,000 US and 50,000 British troops deployed in the Persian Gulf. After months of aerial bombing in Kuwait there was a brief ground war, in February 1991, lasting four days.

Like PTSD, GWS became a relatively nonstigmatized diagnosis for sick soldiers who had no direct combat experience. Though many advocates still publicly state that GWS was the result of experimental vaccines and exposure to toxins during those four days in Kuwait, the military clinicians I've interviewed for this book tell me that soldiers returning from the Middle East in the late 1980s, before the first Gulf War, reported similar symptoms, only there wasn't a name for it back then. Many of those soldiers, like the soldiers who developed GWS, had a history of psychological impairments, often beginning in childhood. Many female soldiers who reported painful intercourse as the result of their deployment in the Middle East also disclosed histories of being sexually abused both before and after they entered the service.

An extensive report ordered by President Bill Clinton concluded that the symptoms of GWS were real—the soldiers were indeed suffering—but that they were, most likely, caused by stress. The researchers did not find evidence that the soldiers could have developed their symptoms from nerve gas, biological weapons, pesticides, vaccines, depleted uranium, or smoke from burning oil wells.[21] But despite being caused by stress, the symptoms of GWS were physical rather than emotional and therefore did not meet the criteria for PTSD.

Why did these soldiers experience GWS? Before and after the ground offensive, they were frequently warned about chemical exposure and its bodily symptoms. They were afraid that Saddam Hussein was employing chemical weapons, and they looked for the symptoms they were told to anticipate. Public health specialists sometimes use the word "nocebo," the opposite of the word "placebo," to describe this process. A placebo is a fake medicine—a pill, a shot, or ointment, for example—that makes someone feel better. A nocebo, in contrast, is a fake medicine that makes someone feel sick. Suppose I lied to a group of people by telling them that a small gas leak had been detected in their office building earlier in the day and that they should report any shortness of breath, dizziness, headache, or nausea. In all likelihood, some people would soon experience these symptoms because they would be attuned to their bodies, actively looking for them, monitoring their breathing and balance. You, the reader, might have even begun to think about your breathing while reading the previous two sentences, or realized you have a headache. Such attention bias, as psychologists call it, helps explain shared symptoms without medical findings.

According to the Department of Veterans Affairs Health Registry, about 15,000 of the nearly 700,000 Operation Desert Storm military personnel developed persistent physical problems that could not be explained medically.[22] In a separate study in the Comprehensive Clinical Evaluation Program, the U.S. Department of Defense found 13,000 such cases.[23] Soldiers who were in the war zone suffered from these unexplained symptoms at a rate far higher than those who were in the Gulf but not near the war zone. However, repeated scientific studies have failed to identify a biological basis for the symptoms of GWS.

GWS would appear in England too (where it became known as Gulf Related Illness), but not until the summer of 1993 after the BBC aired two reports on GWS among American troops from the Gulf War.[24] At that point, the British government had no records of anyone from the first Gulf

War complaining of the symptoms of GWS. But immediately following the airing of the second program, the government appointed a physician, Commander Bill Coker, as the contact for referrals. By 2001, there were approximately 3,000 British Gulf War veterans registered with his medical assessment team, and it looked as if GWS was reaching epidemic proportions.[25] And the longer an epidemic continues, scholar Elaine Showalter writes, "the greater the participants' need to believe it is genuine. In a sense, they feel their honor and integrity are at stake ... each wave of publicity recruits new patients who feel more and more invested in the search for an external cause and a 'magic bullet' cure."[26]

Lance Clawson was one of the doctors ordered to perform the multi-hour standardized tests called SCID (Structured Clinical Interview for the DSM) on all the men (and a small number of women) suspected of having GWS, or when lab tests were unable to identify any organic cause for a soldier's physical complaints. "These men were truly suffering," he told me. "But we could never figure out what they were suffering from." He and his colleagues did dozens of SCIDs on men they'd never met before and would likely never see again. Clawson said, "The SCIDs were pretty good at helping us separate the psychological symptoms from the physical ones, but they were not well suited to helping us figure out the psychological *meaning* of the physical symptoms. For that, you need time, therapy, talk, and the patients often thought we'd think they were 'crazy'—their word, not mine—if we asked them to tell us their life stories."

One combat veteran at Walter Reed had a urological and radiological exam after complaining of a painful, migrating lump in his penis. The urologist and radiologist, after finding nothing, referred him to psychiatry. Clawson said, "The patient was convinced there was a lump but no one could find it. He was so angry about it. So what do we do? He's pretty sure he got this lump from something he inhaled in the desert and refuses to think of his problem as psychiatric. Do we say that he has a physical disability caused by something in the desert? If we do, are we being completely honest? If we don't, he might not be eligible for any care for his problem, psychiatric or otherwise, and he deserves to get treated."

Many Gulf War veterans resent the experts' conclusion that GWS is "unexplained," as if that word was "code for psychiatric."[27] They also resent the fact that there is little epidemiological evidence to suggest that veterans with GWS were exposed to anything different from veterans without GWS. Therein lies one of the sources of stigma: the assumption that a psychological explanation is a denial of illness. As one group of researchers noted, "Veterans and their healthcare providers do not want Persian Gulf War Veterans' physical symptoms to be mistakenly attributed to psychogenic causes because this could lead to the stigmatizing of ill veterans as 'psychiatric somatizers' who react poorly to stress."[28] They also warn that to focus solely on the psychological component could result in a failure to detect the effects of real toxic exposures.

Dr. Charles Engel remembers that in the summer of 1996, five years after the Persian Gulf War ended, the Pentagon sent a letter to tens of thousands of soldiers, including him (since he had served in the Persian Gulf), telling them that they might have been exposed to deadly chemicals in 1991. These included the deadly nerve agents sarin and cyclosarin, possibly released into the air after the US military demolished an ammunition storage facility in southern Iraq called Kamisiyah. Investigators had only just concluded, after months of plume and rocket destruction modeling in Nevada, that the plumes from Kamisiyah had probably traveled farther than they previously thought. No soldiers died during the time the depot was burning, but doctors didn't want to rule out the possibility of long-term health consequences. In a careful study of "any cause" hospitalizations between the time of exposure, March 10, 1991, and September 30, 1995, researchers found no difference in hospitalizations between the Gulf veterans who were exposed and those who were not. Nonetheless, Engel said, after that letter went out in 1996, "we saw a massive spike in reported symptoms to the registry." By "registry" Engel is referring to the Comprehensive Clinical Evaluation Program (CCEP). A more recent study also showed no difference in the mortality rate of veterans exposed and not exposed to the plumes.[29]

Many veterans continue to oppose the idea that GWS is a psychiatric condition. Not only are the symptoms different from PTSD, but GWS involves skin lesions, incontinence, respiratory disorders, neuropathy, and other symptoms that, many GWS sufferers believe, could not possibly be of psychological origin. However, psychological distress is often associated with rashes, hives, psoriasis, acne, impotence, coughing, as well as diarrhea, constipation, stomach pain, and low and high blood pressure. Gastrointestinal symptoms are so common in mental illnesses that some doctors call the intestines a "second brain." Stress can also lead to nonepileptic seizures, tremor, visual impairment, back pain, and gait abnormalities. In fact, the majority of people in the United States and the UK with common mental illnesses, such as anxiety disorder and depression, do not present with psychological complaints.[30] They go to their primary care physicians who attempt to treat bodily symptoms and likely never find out if the patient is anxious or depressed unless the patient describes his problems as at least partially psychological.[31]

All symptoms, including psychological ones, have a biological component, even if they originate from environmental stressors; and, conversely, many biological phenomena have a psychological component. We need only think about something as simple as blushing, which most people will agree is caused by an uncomfortable social interaction, or sometimes just the fantasy about such an interaction. Embarrassment triggers a reaction in which chemicals and hormones come into play to dilate our veins, bring blood to the surface of the skin, and cool the body. Our heart rate increases too. Moreover, scientists have repeatedly demonstrated that psychiatric conditions, and stressors in general, are a significant risk factor for a variety of different medical illnesses.[32]

And if military psychiatry has taught us anything—from the deaths due to nostalgia and soldier's heart in the Civil War, to shell shock in WWI, war neuroses in WWII, GWS in the Middle East, and now PTSD—it is that illnesses that derive from the stresses of war come in many different forms. Every war has its own syndromes.

PART THREE

BODY AND MIND

CHAPTER 12

TELLING SECRETS

Perseus wore a magic cap so that the monsters he
hunted down might not see him. We draw the magic
cap down over our own eyes so as to deny that there
are any monsters.

Karl Marx, *Capital*, Volume 1 (1867)

In perhaps his most famous allegory, Plato conceived of a cave in which prisoners have been chained and in the dark since their birth. Because the chains are arranged so the prisoners must face forward, they can see only the shadows made by people walking in front of a fire behind them. And so, Plato tells us, these people would think that the shadows themselves—not the people who cast them—were real objects.[1] The cruel allegory is meant to humble us, to help us see the tenuous border between what is real and what is a representation.

The stigma of mental illness, like a shadow, also tells us about the importance of vision to perception and knowledge. Because everything we see is affected by how we see it, pure vision is an illusion. Like Plato's imagined prisoners, we always look at something *from* somewhere else—whether a front or back, a cardinal direction, the cultural categories we've learned over time and take for granted, or in the manner someone or some institution has designed for us. I'm often reminded of this fact when I travel by car and see an amorphous landscape dotted with placards reading "scenic view," telling tourists where, in an expansive vista bordered only by the horizon, they should look, and what they should see.

For decades, people with serious mental illnesses and developmental disorders were, in effect, invisible. We sent them to asylums or state hospitals so we wouldn't have to see or interact with them, and we visualized them mostly as symptoms and categories rather than as actual persons—as the "schizophrenic" or the "idiot," for example. The rest of us were like Plato's prisoners, seeing only the shadows that doctors and scientists cast on the sick and suffering.

During the late nineteenth and early twentieth centuries, people with mental and physical disabilities in the United States were largely hidden from public view, unless they were displayed as curiosities or "nature's mistakes" in circuses. The so-called ugly laws helped enforce their invisibility. People concealed their illnesses, and even war wounds, from friends and relatives, and doctors often lied to patients to spare them from confronting the reality of their condition. In the 1970s, Susan Sontag reported that a leading oncologist told her that less than 10 percent of his cancer patients knew they had cancer. They knew only that they were dying.[2] Actors, athletes, and politicians did their best to hide the extent of their diseases or disabilities. Only the rare celebrity could use fame as a platform from which to project an image of strength, grace, or dignity, as Lou Gehrig did when, in uniform in 1939, he told a packed Yankee Stadium that, despite his degenerative neurological condition, he was "the luckiest man on the face of the earth." And even that performance was filtered through the media. As experts on disability among war veterans have noted, "most Americans' primary encounters with disabled soldiers do not come face-to-face."[3]

The American family was sanitized during the first decade after WWII to fit the postwar ideal of the middle-class housewife and the working husband who centered their lives around their several "normal" children playing behind white picket fences.[4] Growing up in downtown Chicago during the 1960s and early 1970s, I seldom saw children with obvious intellectual disabilities, despite the fact that there was a school for children with what was then called "mental retardation," the Bateman School, near where I lived. I often walked by the school, but I don't remember ever seeing any of the children on the school grounds, through the windows (which were shuttered), or at the park nearby. My friends and I would hold our breath and run past, so we didn't inhale the air around it.

Children with disabilities sometimes spent years, if not their entire lives, in residential institutions, often because their families had no other choice. Until 1974, school systems throughout the United States could refuse to provide an education to any student the school deemed uneducable. The District of Columbia Public Schools, in its projection of educational services for the 1971–72 school year, said that "an estimated 12,340 handicapped children were not to be served."[5] The tendency to deny education for children with disabilities was especially biased against African American students.

By that time, it had been a decade since President John F. Kennedy had signed the 1963 Community Mental Health Act—the last law he would ever sign.[6] Kennedy argued that the new law would free people with disabilities from their "custodial isolation." The process he initiated, today called "deinstitutionalization," shut down large and often abusive government mental hospitals and returned to the community the thousands of patients who had lived there, sometimes for decades. In his 1961 study, based on a year's fieldwork at the US government's St. Elizabeth's Hospital in Washington, DC, Erving Goffman described the repeated assaults on human dignity in asylums, and concluded that "mental patients can find themselves crushed by the weight of a service ideal that eases life for the rest of us."[7]

Kennedy was emotionally invested in the legislation because he had experienced intellectual disability in his own family. His sister, Rosemary, had a learning disability and as a young adult was highly anxious and irritable. Throughout her childhood, the family doctors all agreed she was "retarded," but they could identify no cause and had no treatment plan to recommend.[8] In 1941, when she was twenty-three, Rosemary's parents decided to send her to George Washington University psychiatrist Walter Freeman for a lobotomy. The surgery was a disaster, leaving her severely brain damaged. Her younger siblings would later recall that one day Rosemary just disappeared from their lives. She spent the rest of her life in an institution in Wisconsin.[9] Photos taken there show her in a wheelchair, her chin down, her head cocked to her left. Rosemary's tragedy motivated another of her siblings, Eunice Kennedy Shriver, to found the Special Olympics.

During the 1960s, advocates began to argue that the free labor the mentally ill provided in state institutions was exploitative. Depictions of mental hospitals in the media, and in Hollywood films in particular, increased popular and academic support for radical changes in public policy. The push to deinstitutionalize was distinctively American. In France, Germany, the Netherlands, and other European countries, governments reformed rather than dismantled their institutions, and built extramural mental health care facilities that were linked directly to state-run hospitals.[10] Through deinstitutionalization, the US government was actually abandoning the mentally ill. Cities became dumping grounds for discharged residents of asylums. They ended up sleeping in municipal shelters, or on the street atop heating vents, begging for money and scavenging for food. Deinstitutionalization was a modern-day ship of fools.[11]

By the mid-1970s, when I was a teenager, I started to see an increasing number of homeless people in my neighborhood in Chicago, many of whom talked to themselves and appeared to be hallucinating. My father and his colleagues called them "ambulatory schizophrenics" or "sidewalk psychotics." In 2002, the number of psychiatric inpatients in the United States had fallen sharply from 559,000 in 1955 to 80,000 in 2002[12]—and this was during a time when the population of the United States had increased by 75 percent (from 166 million in 1955 to 288 million in 2002).

Deinstitutionalization was facilitated not only by a humanitarian imperative but also by the development of the antipsychotic medicines that dramatically reduced agitation and the severity of psychosis. These medicines made it possible for many sufferers to leave institutions and hopefully become outpatients. There was also a capitalist motive—to reduce the government's health-care budget. Policy makers argued that shifting psychiatric treatment from the hospital to the community would at once save the government from the high costs of institutionalization and provide more humane and effective care.

The promise of deinstitutionalization was never realized. First, the medicines didn't always work well, and many patients stopped taking them in order to end the uncomfortable side effects, like tardive dyskinesia, a movement disorder associated with antipsychotic medicines. It involves involuntary muscle contractions of the jaw, lips, and tongue, and is itself stigmatizing. People stared or looked away, and it marked the person as "schizophrenic." What's more, although the medicines curtailed psychosis, they were less helpful against the negative symptoms of schizophrenia (inexpressive faces, low energy, monotonic and monosyllabic speech, and social withdrawal). Second, policy makers made insufficient plans for community-based treatment. Community, for-profit, and nonprofit organizations delivering mental health care depended on poorly funded federal and local government agencies. Third, policy makers did not address the scarcity of housing and shelters,[13] and many Americans resisted the construction of affordable housing in their communities. The result was that more people became homeless, or ended up being incarcerated for petty crimes.[14] Over time, jails replaced state psychiatric hospitals as the largest providers of mental health care.[15] Although the proportion of Americans who were homeless declined by 15 percent between 2007 and 2018, on any given night in the United States today, more than half a million people are homeless, most of them in unsheltered locations.

Some people who once advocated for deinstitutionalization are having second thoughts. In a phone interview, Emory University scholar Sander Gilman reflected, "If I knew back then what I know now, I'm not sure I'd have been such a staunch supporter." Indeed, many of the people who are homeless today would likely not have been homeless in previous decades, but would have been either taken care of by family or lodged for years or decades in state residential institutions. The late neurologist Oliver Sacks even wrote an essay called "The Lost Virtues of the Asylum."[16] He acknowledged that, in many state hospitals, people had been physically abused in a state of desolation. However, he also recalled that in the early twentieth century, a state mental hospital called Creedmoor, in Queens, New York, had a swimming pool, ping-pong tables, and music rooms, and by the mid-twentieth century it had its own television studio where the patients wrote, produced, and directed their own plays. Sacks said that "there were often, even in the worst hospitals, pockets of human decency, of real life and kindness." Hospitals provided safety from weather, violence, and hunger, he said—"in a word, asylum."

Yet deinstitutionalization also transformed our understandings and experiences of mental illnesses for the better. The process compelled the public to see people who were formerly concealed, and to reflect on how American society contributed to their plight—not just the soldiers who were physically and emotionally scarred in the Vietnam War but also people who had languished in isolation in dilapidated hospitals. Soldiers and state hospital residents had both come home, and at least now communities were aware of them.

Increased visibility set the stage for an explosion of diagnoses (including new ones like ADHD, PTSD, autism, and eating disorders), necessitated a robust special education system, and spawned a range of new therapies. Deinstitutionalization also led to the reduction of the stigma of many, though not all, mental illnesses. The more people talked about mental illnesses, and saw them as part of any average human life, the more ordinary and less frightening they seemed, and the more likely it was that people would accept psychiatric care. It's possible that without deinstitutionalization we would not speak as openly today about mental illnesses, and that more people would suffer in silence and shame.

In 1944, in the fourteenth year of their marriage, Erik and Joan Erikson had their fourth child, Neil. Joan was forty-one, and Erik was forty-two. Erik, a German-American professor at the University of California, Berkeley, was poised to become one of the most illustrious psychologists and psycho-analysts of the twentieth century. Among his many achievements, he and Joan collaborated on a classic framework for understanding child develop-ment, known as Erikson's stages of psychosocial development, and when he became a professor at Harvard University, he won the Pulitzer Prize for a psychological history of Mahatma Gandhi. He was *the* expert on child and personality development. Biographers have noted that Erikson was insecure, and he carefully developed a public image of himself as confident, empathic, and a master interpreter of children's health, development, and play. Even his own children thought he had a godlike aura. A champion of honesty and transparency, he told the parents of his child patients that they should never keep secrets. But Erikson was a different person in his office than in his home.

Neil was born with Down syndrome, though at that time the hospital staff used the current terminology and told the Eriksons that their son was a "Mongolian idiot." At a loss for what to do, Erik telephoned two friends, the anthropologist Margaret Mead and the psychoanalyst Joseph Wheel-wright. Both recommended he and Joan send Neil to an institution imme-diately, and that to fail to do so would hurt Erik's career and public image. Erikson's whole life was devoted to describing normal development, and now he had a child who was physically deformed and would be intellectu-ally disabled.

On Mead's advice, Erik didn't even let Joan see the baby, and made the decision to institutionalize Neil without ever consulting her. Mead was con-cerned that Joan might become attached to Neil and prevent Erik from send-ing him away. And when Joan found out, she made no effort to change things. Her sense of paralysis and guilt remained with her for the rest of her life.[17] Erik told her that Neil had already been taken to a facility where he would likely die before he was two years old. Within weeks, however, she decided to see Neil, and devastated by his appearance and lack of responsiveness she resigned herself to the institutionalization. Erikson's biographer Lawrence Friedman wrote that Joan "recognized that Neil's presence would damage the romantic image that she, even more than Erik, liked to invoke of a healthy, attractive, and vibrant family headed by a young child analyst."[18] Over the years, Joan did visit Neil occasionally, typically without Erik, but none of the children, except for the eldest, Kai, who discovered the truth when he was in high school, knew that they had another brother. The Eriksons had lied to their children and to their friends, telling them that the baby died at birth. There was no ceremony or funeral, and Kai was sworn to secrecy.

The siblings eventually found out about Neil, but only a few years before he died from cardiac complications associated with Down syndrome. Erik and Joan were in Italy when it happened, since Erik was on sabbatical. They told their children Jon and Sue to arrange for the cremation of the brother they had never met. Erik and Joan, the authors of the eight-stage theory of child development that stressed the importance of parents and family to normal health, didn't even come back for the burial of Neil's ashes. The secrecy and disclosure damaged all of the relationships in the family, and almost led the Eriksons to divorce. The children never trusted their parents fully again, as if they feared they too could be abandoned. Ironically, Erik's own mother had lied to him about his illegitimate birth in Germany, and he never discovered the identity of his father. And, in yet another irony, Neil's birth led Erik and Joan to an epiphany that stimulated them to develop their now-famous stages of the normal human life cycle, a model that shaped the way psychologists would understand human development for decades to come.[19] Neil was, for Erik and Joan, the opposite of normality, what Friedman calls the "negative background" to the Eriksons' framework.

Reflecting on her parents in 2005, the Eriksons' daughter, Sue Erikson Bloland, wrote, "In truth, both of my parents were profoundly dependent on the achievement of fame and an idealized public image of themselves as a couple. It was the overwhelming need to feel admired by others that left them so vulnerable to the crisis posed by Neil's birth."[20] But the Eriksons' feelings about Neil cannot be explained just by their narcissism. Erik and

Joan "simply followed the pervasive response of parents of Down Syndrome children during those years—silence, shame, and profound sorrow."[21] And because they did what was expected, they never had to take personal or emotional responsibility for institutionalizing Neil.

Neil was twenty-one when he died. There are no photographs of him.

In 1954, when Harry Holloway was twenty-two, he joined the staff at Griffin State Memorial Hospital in Norman, Oklahoma. The director told him that the capacity of the hospital was 2,000 patients, yet there were nearly 4,000 living there. The staff members were overwhelmed as they tried to manage overcrowded wards, and most were given responsibilities far beyond their training and capabilities. On some nights in Harry's unit, he worked alone with a hundred residents and a security guard. He was simply a caretaker and an orderly, with no clinical experience. But Griffin was such an undesirable place to work that they were understaffed, and Harry was given the title "nurse." On Harry's 3 p.m. to 11 p.m. shift, only one person other than Harry knew how to read and write.

Founded in 1907 as the Oklahoma Sanatorium, Griffin was called a hospital, but it looked more like an experimental farm, since the patients grew their own food and managed their own livestock. It was also called an asylum for the "insane," yet only a small number of patients had a psychotic disorder. Harry told me, "Most of them were cognitively disabled—what we used to call mentally retarded." Some had severe psychiatric problems, including paranoia, loss of speech, and other cognitive impairments as the result of advanced, untreated syphilis. Others were elderly people abandoned by their families.

Harry dreamed of becoming a psychiatrist. Years later he would be the chief of psychiatry at the US military's medical school, the Uniformed Services University of the Health Sciences. So he was drawn to one of the few patients with a diagnosed mental illness, a forty-four-year-old man with schizophrenia named Enoch. To Harry, Enoch seemed sadder than the others, more vulnerable, or perhaps just more beaten down from the years. At forty-four, Enoch had been at Griffin for almost as long as Harry had been alive. "At some level," Harry said, "the minute I saw Enoch, I felt I knew him." At the hospital, Enoch lived in a building called Hope Hall, and Harry said the name was a lie. Renée Mixon, a former administrator at the hospital, said that in the early days the hospital director would tell people there was no hope. "Pretend you've been to a funeral," they used to say, "because your family member will never leave."[22] Many patients were buried in a mass, unmarked grave next to the hospital.

Harry combed through Enoch's files and discovered that in his twenty-two years at Griffin, "Enoch had had nearly every bone in his body broken. He had been beaten and isolated. He had been horribly mistreated. It was awful." He also discovered that he and Enoch had once been neighbors.

In 1932, the year Harry was born, his father decided something needed to be done about the young man who lived with his parents on the adjacent farm. Enoch, at the age of twenty-two, was psychotic and there were rumors that he had once thrown a butcher knife at his mother "so hard that it almost disappeared into the wall." Harry told me, "My father had a baby now and he was afraid Enoch would come on to our farm and hurt me." Harry's father convinced the police to order a psychiatric evaluation. "They took one look at Enoch," Harry said, "they said he's a danger to our community, and they shipped him off."

The guilt was awful for Harry, and still palpable when we spoke decades later. Harry had tried to befriend Enoch. He told him that he remembered his brothers and sisters well, that he grew up on the farm next to theirs. But Enoch never seemed to understand that Harry had known his parents, and never responded to his questions. Harry began to cry when he told me, "Enoch rotted in this place for twenty-two years, and he rotted here because I was born."

By the end of Harry's first year at Griffin, there would be a revolution in psychiatry that would help make deinstitutionalization possible. Antipsychotic medicine had become available earlier that year, when the Smith, Kline & French company introduced chlorpromazine (marketed as Thorazine), an antipsychotic medicine originally designed in the 1940s as a potential anti-malaria drug and battlefield anesthetic. In her Pulitzer Prize–winning account of Creedmoor hospital, Susan Sheehan writes that Thorazine was so effective that violent patients quickly became calm; those who screamed incessantly at others now talked to themselves quietly; chairs were permitted and curtains were hung; patients were allowed razors and matches, unthinkable before antipsychotic medicines.[23] In just one year, from 1955 to 1956, the state of New York reported, the frequency of restraint and seclusion as mechanisms of discipline and care dropped by 50 percent.[24]

Before Thorazine, doctors had grasped at whatever treatments might help reduce a patient's pain, self-harm, or violence—even the rough-hewn methods of lobotomy and insulin-induced comas. They used mechanical restraints and administered a range of drugs, such as sulphonal to induce drowsiness, and arsphenamine, an anti-syphilis medication, to treat paralysis. Other drugs included hypnotics like chloral hydrate and paraldehyde, which when mixed together became a green liquid concoction my grandfather called the "Green River," a term that may have been unique to the Chicago psychiatric lexicon. The liver didn't metabolize it well, he told me, so the patients exhaled it, and because it had a fruity odor, it attracted insects. "You would always know the patients with psychosis," my grandfather said, "because they'd be the ones with flies buzzing around their faces."

By July 1955, Thorazine was made available to the patients at Griffin. Harry remembers that the university experts weren't impressed at first. "They were using Thorazine at low doses like seventy milligrams because they were scared of it, and sometimes it didn't make a difference. But at Griffin we gave seven thousand milligrams sometimes, and our average dose was probably three thousand." There were side effects from these large doses, of course, but the medicine alleviated the so-called positive symptoms of schizophrenia (hallucinations and delusions) and made it possible for some patients to leave the hospital.

At roughly the same time, a series of federal court rulings prohibited governments from confining against their will people who had committed no crime. The courts noted that there were still instances in which commitment of someone was warranted, such as to protect the safety of that person or others. But states were now required to seek the least restrictive way of achieving that goal.[25] In August, Harry encouraged the doctors to give Thorazine to Enoch. The next month, Enoch left the hospital and never returned. His family welcomed him home.

Harry remembers that by the mid-1970s, nearly every building at Griffin had been razed, and the number of patients had dropped to 200 or fewer. "Pretty soon," Harry said, as he reflected on his age, "no one will be alive who can remember that experience of seeing what the world looked like before and after those medicines were developed." Indeed, given the availability of antipsychotic medicines today, few clinicians in North America and Europe have ever seen schizophrenia untreated over an extended period of time. "No one's going to see that again," he said. "No one in this country is going to see that transformation. It was amazing."

Recall that the institutionalization of an undifferentiated mass of unemployed people during the Enlightenment led to the creation of the first mental illness categories. The deinstitutionalization of another mass of people during the 1970s did the same. Patients who had previously been given vague diagnoses like idiocy and feeblemindedness within institutions were now, on the outside, supposed to become members of their communities, and they faced the prospect of getting a diagnosis better tailored to the services they needed.

Within institutions, it had mattered little whether someone was diagnosed as schizophrenic, autistic, or mentally retarded since they were all treated in roughly the same manner. People were not committed to asylums because they had this or that diagnosis or IQ measure, but because they were deemed incapable of functioning independently in the community.[26] Crowded and understaffed institutions were incapable of providing individualized therapies or carefully monitoring someone over time. But after deinstitutionalization, new mental illness categories would proliferate.

In the new twentieth-century world of medications, patented therapies, and special education programs, diagnostic classification became crucial. "Mental retardation," the all-purpose term for anyone with pronounced cognitive deficits who resided in an institution, was soon refashioned into other conditions like learning disabilities, developmental disabilities, and autism. A diverse group of actors worked in concert to identify psychiatric conditions and introduce them as topics for public discussion. This network included parents, school psychologists, doctors, insurance adjusters, research foundations, advertisers, lobbyists, philanthropists, and advocates. It also included epidemiologists, the researchers who estimate the distribution of a condition in a given population. Clinicians provided the labels, schools provided individualized education plans, and epidemiologists provided the statistics.

The first publications from large epidemiological projects, like the Midtown Manhattan Study (1962)[27] and the Stirling County Study (1963),[28] revealed a greater prevalence of mental illnesses outside of mental institutions than the experts anticipated. Both of these studies used the Neuropsychiatric Screening Adjunct (NSA), the mental health scale that the army developed during World War II to screen recruits. The Manhattan study showed that 80 percent of the 1,911 adult residents (ages twenty through fifty-nine) sampled in midtown had symptoms of a psychiatric disorder. In Stirling county, in eastern Canada, 83 percent of adults had clinically significant symptoms of psychiatric illness. And in the 1980s, the Epidemiologic Catchment Area Study (ECA) concluded that "one of every five persons in the United States suffers from a mental disorder in any 6-month period, and half of Americans will suffer from a mental disorder in his or her lifetime."[29] More recent national prevalence studies of mental illnesses estimate that between 26.2 percent and 32.4 percent of adults in the United States have a diagnosable mental illness within any twelve-month period.[30]

Together these actors represented a far more complex assemblage than existed within institutions. In the community there was now competition in a therapeutic marketplace.[31] And not surprisingly, the number and range of diagnoses steadily increased. The 1968 DSM-II had 193 diagnostic categories; in 1980, the DSM-III had 292; in 1994, the DSM-IV had 383; and since 2013, the DSM-5 has 541.[32] During the 1980s, some of these diagnoses were not well known outside of medicine, such as trichotillomania (the uncontrollable impulse to pull out one's hair) and factitious disorder (the intentional faking of psychological or physical symptoms). But even the more prevalent conditions, such as obsessive-compulsive disorder, autism, and anorexia nervosa were still relatively new and esoteric.

Illness categories became increasingly important because medicines had been developed for specific diagnoses. In addition to Thorazine, by the mid-twentieth century there were tricyclic antidepressants for depression, lithium for mania, and stimulants for lethargic geriatric patients. The pharmaceutical company Ciba initially marketed methylphenidate, the stimulant now used for the treatment of ADHD, as a "pep pill" for the elderly under the name Ritalin (named after Marguerite Panizzon, wife of the lead chemist Leandro Panizzon, who went by the nickname Rita). But in 1937, a pediatrician named Charles Bradley noticed that at low doses some people became calm rather than excited, and that it improved school performance in children of "normal" intelligence who had been hospitalized for "behavioral problems."[33]

If Thorazine made it possible to treat people with the most serious and debilitating conditions, Ritalin helped to make psychotropic medicines more acceptable for the treatment of less severe illnesses in everyday life. In 1961, the year the Food and Drug Administration (FDA) approved Ritalin for the treatment of children with behavior disorders, advertising expenditures for psychotropic drugs, much of it for Ritalin, soared.[34] Ads in women's magazines included images of children working quietly at their desks and quotations by mothers and teachers describing Ritalin as a miracle drug. One ad in the early 1970s depicted a handsome boy before and after medication. The first image showed a posed family of four with a young boy in casual attire struggling as his mother tried to hold him for the picture. The caption read, "1971: A difficult child, a distraught mother." The second photo showed the same boy, after taking his medicine, smiling in a school photo, wearing a crisp shirt and tie with the caption, "A regular 4th grader, accepted at home." Today, about 15 percent of boys and more than 10 percent of girls in the United States have at some point been diagnosed with ADHD.[35]

In the decades that followed, mental health professionals became ever more optimistic that psychopharmacology could turn psychiatry from a soft, subjective science to a hard, objective one. If a drug like Ritalin, for example, helped correct abnormal activity in the areas of the brain responsible for attention and activity, then this must mean that hyperactivity is a brain disorder. Researchers also hoped that by making psychiatry more biological, it would reduce the stigma of mental illness, that mental illnesses would become illnesses like any other kind. In 1990, psychiatrist Alan Zametkin, who had published papers on the neurobiology of ADHD, said that brain-based studies proved ADHD is not a psychological problem caused by poor parenting. He told the *New York Times*, "There are people who say you should not use medications, that it's a matter of upbringing. . . . We're hoping that this will put an end to that kind of thinking."[36] Neuroscientists now felt pressure to develop quantitative measures of abnormal metabolic activity and chemical imbalances, to show that mental illnesses were "beyond the patient's control."[37]

The reported prevalence and range of different mental illnesses lessened opposition to psychotropic medication and bolstered public awareness and prevention efforts. By the 1980s, the media seemed particularly concerned with eating disorders, especially because of the high mortality rate. One review of forty-two major studies published between 1935 and 1995 showed an average mortality rate of 5.9 percent among people with anorexia nervosa, the majority of whom died directly from the disease, while about one quarter committed suicide.[38] Mental health care advocates argued that if more people knew the signs and symptoms, more people would be treated and fewer would die.

In 1981, ABC aired a made-for-television movie called *The Best Little Girl in the World*, based on the novel by Stephen Levenkron about a dejected teenage girl who becomes acutely ill with an eating disorder. That same year, researchers founded the first academic journal devoted exclusively to the topic, called the *International Journal of Eating Disorders*. The next year, two successful memoirs on anorexia were published—Sheila MacLeod's

The Art of Starvation and Cherry Boone O'Neill's *Starving for Attention*—and in 1983, actress Jane Fonda revealed that she had suffered from an eating disorder, bulimia, for more than twenty years, beginning in 1954. In 1984, the singer Karen Carpenter—at the time, one of the most famous musical artists in the United States—died of heart complications related to anorexia and bulimia. Eating disorders were now suddenly a part of the national consciousness, in magazines and on talk shows, and were widely assumed to be a new group of conditions linked to modern ideals of feminine beauty.

There appeared to be an explosion of new diagnoses of eating disorders. No one knew if there were really more cases, or if celebrities had made the disorders more acceptable to the broader public. It was clear to the experts, however, that images of skinny fashion models could not, by themselves, make people sick enough to die. Rather, the images gave girls at risk for mental illness with an idiom with which to articulate emotional distress. The control of appetite and body mass, some psychologists think, is a way for girls to exert some mastery over themselves and their environment at a time of great change and uncertainty in their lives, perhaps not unlike the women with mandike in colonial Zululand. And because thinness in women has been idealized and complimented, society endorses many of the behaviors that facilitate it, like intensive exercise and dieting.

Anorexia nervosa was not new. It was described independently in 1873 by Sir William Gull in London and Charles Lasegue in Paris. No one knows if this synchronicity had anything to do with a sudden increase of the disorder. But Gull's and Lasegue's writings offer solid historical evidence that the condition has existed for centuries and thus cannot be attributed solely to body images and preoccupations with weight in modern societies. Prevalence studies from Korea, Iran, Hong Kong, Japan, and Norway, among other countries, show rates in line with those in the United States, and most of the first reports suggesting that anorexia was anything more than a rare curiosity came from Italy, Germany, central Europe, and Japan. However, the symptoms of anorexia vary across cultures, significantly enough that in some places they may not even meet the DSM criteria. In Hong Kong, for example, anorexia tends not to include a distorted view of one's body, and sufferers often attribute their limited food consumption to a lack of appetite or the sensation of being bloated.[39]

Reflecting on his training in psychiatry in New York, Dr. Timothy Walsh of Columbia University, and the chair of the DSM-5 working group on eating disorders, told me, "In the late 1960s and early 1970s, I never saw anorexia at the city hospital in the Bronx where I worked, or at least nothing that was described that way." Walsh's wife, who was an undergraduate at Wellesley College in the late 1960s, also recalled that there were students who, in retrospect, must have had anorexia, but at the time she and her classmates had no vocabulary with which to understand it as a discrete disorder.

Bulimia nervosa is a much more recently named condition than anorexia, despite documentation of patterns of binging and purging for centuries. It was first described and named in 1979 by British psychiatrist Gerald Russell after he saw patients diagnosed with anorexia but who had a distinctive symptom profile. These patients were not underweight, and they binged and purged. Some had yellowing and chipped teeth, ulcers, and brittle hair and nails, the consequence of stomach acid and malnutrition. Looking back, Russell wonders if by making bulimia visible he inadvertently encouraged people to become bulimic. In 2017, he told a journalist, "Once it was described, and I take full responsibility for that with my paper, there was a common language for it. And knowledge spreads very quickly."[40] Indeed, visibility cannot be underestimated as a factor in the increase of a diagnosis, as one study of an eating disorders prevention program at Stanford University suggested.[41]

Because high school and college-age females are the population at greatest risk for developing eating disorders, responsible educational institutions often arrange public presentations or informational sessions on how to identify and treat them. The goal of these programs is to prevent the disorders, encourage those with symptoms to seek treatment, and decrease stigma. But greater awareness can actually cause greater reported prevalence. Among a group of 509 female Stanford freshmen, the researchers invited half to attend a small discussion group (ten to twenty women in each) and a panel presentation by two women. The panelists were a high-profile staff member in the university and an upperclassman who had been successfully treated for bulimia. The two women, the researchers noted, were "poised, self-assured, attractive, and personable."

All the women in the study, including those who did not attend the presentation, were administered a survey designed to elicit ideas and behaviors associated with eating disorders. As expected, prior to the presentation there were no differences between the two groups, since the subjects had been divided randomly. After the program, the researchers conducted two follow-up surveys with all of the women (those who attended as well as those who did not), once after four weeks and again after twelve weeks. Because there had previously been no variation between the control and experimental groups, any variation now reported could be attributed to the effects of the program.

The researchers found that the women who attended the prevention program reported more symptoms of anorexia and bulimia than the control group. In other words, the program seemed to have the paradoxical effect of facilitating the onset of eating disorders. The researchers were baffled. Perhaps the students who attended the presentation learned more than prevention. Perhaps they identified with the charismatic panelists. Perhaps they learned new behaviors, new ways of losing weight. Or perhaps they learned how to recognize and report preexisting symptoms.

The Stanford researchers concluded that their prevention strategy had been, at best, ineffective. As to the question of why the program increased symptoms, the authors suggested that they had "inadvertently reduced the stigma of eating disorders to such an extent that they were normalized."[42] It was as if they were saying stigma had a protective effect. But an equally plausible conclusion is that the students came to recognize that certain symptoms formed a pattern, symptoms that had previously been just an unorganized group of thoughts and behaviors. Perhaps the program had indeed decreased stigma, and thereby increased the possibility for diagnosis and treatment. In other words, contrary to the authors' view, the prevention programs might have actually been effective.

By the end of the twentieth century, eating disorders had become what some mental health experts call a "hidden epidemic." A "hidden epidemic," scholar Lennard J. Davis writes, "is virtually a code phrase used to launch public relations campaigns for new disorders."[43] We've seen dramatic increases in the popularity of other diagnoses as well, such as ADHD, autism, bipolar disorder, and PTSD. The more a particular disorder is diagnosed, the more it becomes visible, and the more it looks as if the condition is both new and authentic. Messages about illnesses become contagious when they are communicated under just the right cultural and historical conditions and reach a kind of tipping point.

For example, autism emerged as a common diagnosis in tandem with the growth of child psychiatry, psychiatric epidemiology, psychopharmacology, and the special education industry. Autism then looked like a new and more prevalent condition. But just because more people were diagnosed and enrolled in special education programs didn't mean that autism had increased in incidence, any more than the big increase in the number of people who go to coffeehouses in the United States today is by itself proof of an increase in coffee drinkers in the United States. According to researchers Stephen Hinshaw and Richard Scheffler, the same process happened with ADHD. "The message," they say, "is that once a diagnostic category generates medical and educational services, its use tends to soar."[44] It also happened back in 1845 when the rates of lunacy skyrocketed after the British built new asylums: build it and they will come. The point is that sometimes more diagnosis is actually a good thing. It might mean that more people are actually getting treatment or that psychiatric conditions are no longer concealed, as when the prevalence of autism increases in rural and minority communities that have less access to early intervention, therapeutic, and educational services.[45]

If a diagnosis is uncommon, the symptoms may not even be visible, as my wife, Joyce, and I learned when we looked back at our old home videos of Isabel. On one tape, Isabel, fourteen months old, is sitting on her bedroom floor carefully putting dozens of pennies into a piggy bank, one at a time. We call out to her, "Isabel! Look at us! What are you doing?" Her eyes don't move; she just continues inserting the coins. On tape, I say, "Wow, what focus she has." And Joyce says, "She's got the mind of a scientist; this is incredible." Isabel pays no attention to us. And we weren't concerned. We are only able to read in the languages that we know.

It was December 1992, and it never occurred to us to think that this repetitive behavior, her lack of desire to interact with us, and the inability to shift her attention, were signs that she was at risk for autism. Autism was not a household word, and was then considered to be rare enough that most parents (even parents who, like Joyce, were psychiatrists) didn't look for autism in their children, especially in babies and toddlers. Parents of school-aged children often conversed about ADHD and anxiety, but not autism, and in 1992 we didn't often use phrases like "restricted interests" and "repetitive and stereotyped behaviors." Pediatricians did not routinely screen for autism, and most didn't even believe it could be identified before the age of two or three. Asperger's wasn't a legitimate diagnosis until 1994. Today, many parents and most pediatricians know the signs of autism and would spot the symptoms Isabel exhibited easily. Clinicians increasingly feel comfortable making a diagnosis, or at least recommending some form of intervention for children fourteen months old, and even younger in many cases. The media now represent autism as an epidemic in search of a cause and cure.

Once a diagnosis becomes popular, the rate of other diagnostic classifications can plummet. And so, over the last two decades, though autism classifications in the American public school system tripled, the proportion of children in special education programs in the public schools remained the same.[46] There is only one way that can happen. A static special education rate and a huge increase in autism can only occur together if other classifications decline. In fact, numerous classifications that parents have found uncomfortable if not stigmatizing, such as intellectual disability and specific learning disability, declined precipitously as autism became a more unexceptional and less frightening and shameful diagnosis. The expansion of autism from a narrowly defined disorder into a broad spectrum, the decline of the mother blame popularized by psychoanalysts, and the temporary inclusion in the DSM of Asperger's disorder as a way to describe people with autism who were highly verbal, all reduced stigma and made autism more valuable as a replacement for other diagnoses.

Despite the fact that the DSM still considers autism idiopathic (of unknown cause), in actual practice autism has become a primary diagnosis for many people whose symptoms have a known etiology, like children with identifiable genetic syndromes in which autistic features are one part of their syndromes.[47] The parent of a child with a rare, complex genetic disorder may prefer "autism" to "intellectual disability" because, through that parsimonious category, the child joins an ever-widening group of peers and their families, and perhaps fits more neatly into preestablished or new programs.

The best clinicians know that they have a multitude of diagnoses at their disposal and can select the one most likely to benefit a given patient at a given time. In other words, when someone makes a diagnosis it doesn't always mean there is a discrete disorder that is completely separate from all others. As Dr. Judith L. Rapoport, former chief of child psychiatry at NIMH, once told me, "I'll call a kid a zebra if it will get him the educational services I think he needs." What's more, as a diagnosis becomes increasingly useful for a more diverse group of individuals, the differences between people with and without the diagnosis can decrease. In a 2019 analysis of the symptoms of autism, comprising historical data on 27,723 individuals described in hundreds of published studies, the authors found that over the past two decades people with a diagnosis of autism have steadily become less distinct from their nonautistic counterparts.[48] If that trend continues at the same rate, it won't be long before everyone is autistic.

The case of schizophrenia in Japan illustrates how a change in diagnostic language can facilitate visibility and treatment and can reduce stigma. In Japan, schizophrenia used to be so closeted, so stigmatizing, that doctors seldom disclosed the diagnosis to their patients with schizophrenia, or even to their patients' families. Many people who suspected they or a family member might have schizophrenia studiously avoided mental health professionals. In an effort to decrease that stigma, Japanese clinicians experimented with new psychiatric language. One project began in 1993 when the Japanese National Federation of Families with the Mentally Ill asked the Japanese Society of Psychiatry and Neurology (JSPN, the Japanese equivalent of the APA) to find a new word for schizophrenia. The term that had been used for decades, *seishin bunretsu byo*, meant more than just a "split mind." It connoted a mind torn asunder, permanently ruptured, but in which the rupture would continue to widen over time with no chance of recovery. Moreover, when Japanese heard the term it evoked images of straitjackets.

The JSPN looked into the clinical use of the diagnosis and reported in 1999 that 52 percent of its members said they only occasionally informed patients and families of the diagnosis. Just 7 percent of members said they told all their patients with schizophrenia the name of their disorder, and 37 percent informed only the patients' families. According to psychiatrist Mitsumoto Sato, 167,000 patients with schizophrenia in Japan, who had spent on average one year in a psychiatric hospital, never knew their diagnosis.[49]

In 2002, after deliberating on the terminology in conferences, symposia, and academic papers, the JSPN voted to replace the old term with *togo shitcho sho*, literally "integration disorder." Clinicians rapidly embraced the new diagnosis. In 2002, 36.7 percent of clinicians disclosed the diagnosis to all their patients with schizophrenia, and that number continued to climb to 65 percent in 2003 and to 70 percent in 2004.[50] As the years have passed, younger people in Japan have grown up exposed to the new diagnosis, and are not even learning the old one. Recent surveys indicate that young adults in Japan view *togo shitcho sho* as a serious but treatable condition that can improve over time.[51] Changing the name clearly had a big impact.[52] As a result, many European and American doctors recommended that the English word "schizophrenia" be changed as well.[53] But a new name couldn't change the condition itself. Schizophrenia is chronic, severe, and difficult to treat. It is also perhaps the most isolating of all mental illnesses. The symptoms themselves—delusions, anhedonia, lack of interest in being with others—not to mention the apprehension that psychosis elicits in the public, produce what sociologists have sometimes called social death and psychologists call social defeat. People with schizophrenia also learn not to tell others about what they are thinking, for fear they will be isolated further.

But in a remote region of Japan there is a place called Bethel House, a nonprofit founded in 1984 to help people with schizophrenia. The people who live in or around Bethel House manufacture and ship seaweed, noodles, and other local products, and run a café and gift shop. Once a year the residents hold a festival called the Hallucinations and Delusions Grand Prix. Several thousand tourists come every year to the two-day event. What could be more visible?

With the help of a local Christian church, and a dedicated psychiatrist named Dr. Toshiaki Kawamura, a community of people with schizophrenia formed Bethel in a small fishing village, Urakawa (pop. 13,000), on the island of Hokkaido in northeast Japan. The residents had all been patients in the sixty-bed psychiatric unit at the Urakawa Red Cross Hospital. At Bethel, they talk about schizophrenia (using the old name for it), sing songs about schizophrenia, write stories and poems and make films about schizophrenia. Karen Nakamura, an anthropologist who has studied this community intensively for many years, told me that "the idea Dr. Kawamura had was that you listen to what people say they are thinking and feeling rather than silence them because it makes you feel uncomfortable."

Nakamura notes that, unlike in the United States, in Japan antipsychotic medicines did not result in deinstitutionalization or the development of a community mental health system. In fact, between 1956 and 1966, when the medicines were widely available, the number of hospital beds for psychiatric patients increased fourfold. Institutionalization of people with serious mental illnesses continues today, which is one reason why Japanese don't assume that people who are homeless have severe and chronic mental illness. If they did, they'd likely be in a hospital somewhere. Instead, the typical person thinks first that the homeless person has suffered terrible financial losses, has trauma from the brutal university exam system, or has been abandoned due to their old age.[54]

Bethel House is thus unusual. Instead of hiding their conditions, the members talk about and even celebrate them. During the annual festival, the members perform skits, sell their products, present the results of their self-directed research on disabilities, and allow tourists to observe their social skills workshops. In doing so, they control the narrative of their existence and do not allow themselves to be reduced to a disease. Indeed, Nakamura says that though the festival sometimes seems like "psycho-tourism," she sees these activities as empowering. Many of the residents, she told me, could easily feel abandoned by their families "in the middle of nowhere," and "in any other world they would be there to die, or spend their lives without leaving a legacy. Most don't have kids." Nakamura recognizes that serious mental illnesses too often take away a person's belief that they are important, that they can make a difference for the future. She says, "Bethel becomes a way of making a mark in the world, of being remembered. I think we all want to be remembered."

The Grand Prix is the signature event of the festival. The award goes to that person whose delusion or hallucination contributed the most to the social cohesion and social supports of Bethel House. In 2002, for example, the award went to a former engineer named Kohei Yamane. He was convinced that a UFO was coming to pick him up, and he made plans to meet it. All the members talked with him about the UFO, asked him what it looked like, how many people could fit inside, and so on. After Kohei felt comfortable with the discussion, the members told him that he couldn't go meet the UFO without a UFO license, and that this license could be obtained from Dr. Kawamura, their psychiatrist, who they said was moonlighting at the Kawamura Space Research Center. This is how they were able to take Kohei to see Dr. Kawamura and prevent him from taking a potentially dangerous trip into the countryside. In 2007, the award went to all four residents of one particular apartment at Bethel House because all four had the same delusion—that there was an invisible man in the house—and this shared symptom led them to discuss their concerns openly and support each other. The awards, and the experiences that merited them, also create a memory, a perpetual bond, among the members.

Their celebration is the opposite of social defeat.

CHAPTER 13

AN ILLNESS LIKE ANY OTHER?

"Depression is a cold of the heart" ("Kokoro no kaze").

PsychoDoctor, Japanese television drama (2002)

Beginning in the 1980s, pharmaceutical companies, mental health advocates, the US government's National Institutes of Health, and researchers and clinicians throughout the world formed what the writer Robert Whitaker calls a four-part harmony, a "powerful quartet of voices" to convince the public of the biological nature of mental disorders.[1] They all agreed that stigma could be reduced only if people understood that mental illnesses were diseases of the brain, not of character.

Yet biological models of mental illness have been central to the stigmatization of mental illnesses. Whereas the DSM-I and DSM-II conceptualized mental illnesses as emotional reactions to one's environment—often quite appropriate reactions, like having anxiety in combat or grief after the death of a loved one—in 1980 the DSM-III redefined mental illnesses in more scientific terms. In the DSM-III, mental illnesses were distinct clinical conditions essential to a particular kind of person, disorders that doctors could measure, reliably diagnose, associate with certain demographic groups, and attempt to treat with medications. Someone with a psychosis was now "a schizophrenic"; someone with depression was "a depressive." And that's exactly what stigma is about: when a diagnosis comes to represent a person as a whole.[2] To counter the risk of stigma, most of the clinicians I know thus tend to say that someone *has* schizophrenia or depression, not that they *are* a schizophrenic or a depressive. But the rest of society doesn't necessarily heed this linguistic detail.

Many experts reasoned that if mental illnesses could be conceived of as medical conditions they would be less likely to define one's personhood. This is why British doctors rejoiced when, in the 1960s, they discovered that the confusion and hallucinations of the mad king, King George III, had been caused not by a mental illness of unknown cause but by the metabolic disorder called porphyria. They declared: "Finally, by implication this diagnosis clears the House of Hanover of an hereditary taint of madness."[3] In 1984, in an attempt to reduce stigma, psychiatrist Nancy Andreasen called mental illness a "broken brain." Someone with a broken arm or leg wouldn't think of staying away from a doctor, but someone with a serious mental illness does. Andreasen argued that prejudice and discrimination of people with mental illnesses derived from ignorance, "from a failure to realize that mental illness is a physical illness, an illness caused by biological forces and not by moral turpitude."[4]

Social scientists often call this desire to comprehend humanity in medical terms *medicalization*. Medicalization has its roots in the Enlightenment, in secularism, science, and the drive to make material those aspects of human experience—like the spirit, the mind, and the personality—that used to be immaterial. Medicalization is the process of turning previously nonmedical problems into medical ones, as when people think about childbirth as a sickness that requires admission to the maternity ward of a hospital or when they take medicines for menopause. Privileging the body over the mind, medicalization in the mental health professions, like the broken-brain model, tends to minimize the fact that in many cultures, including our own, character, beliefs, and morals derive from the mind, not from our bones.

Medicalization is also an integral component of capitalism. In capitalism, societies organize and make use of—capitalize on—human bodies for political and economic purposes, like voting, paying taxes, working in factories, and fighting wars. If society as a whole is ideally an efficient mechanical organization, like a factory, then it makes sense that the human body itself can be explained in mechanical and utilitarian terms. Medicalization thus reduces the body to those aspects that can be observed and measured in biomedical terms. And when bodies become sick in capitalism, they become vulnerable to technologies like pharmaceuticals and reimbursable diagnoses that shape them for the medical marketplace. Such technologies govern the healing process in order to help bodies return quickly to the labor force and limit the loss of production.

It's no wonder, then, that in 1996 the World Bank adopted a measure of the burden of diseases defined in terms of the impact of disease on a country's economic productivity. This metric, the disability-adjusted life year (DALY), measures the number of years that are lost due to early death, disability, or disease.[5] While DALYs are not strictly an economic metric, since they are not expressed in currency values, they implicitly value human lives in economic and material terms. DALYs thus cannot capture the immaterial aspects of illness experience in individuals or populations.

The broken-brain model is a reincarnation of the centuries-old effort to give mental illnesses an objective reality apart from culture. Many of the first doctors who studied insanity in the early nineteenth century were phrenologists, scientists who tried to explain and predict mental illnesses, personality, and the propensity for criminal behavior by measuring the gross anatomy of the cranium, the nose, the jaw, or the ears. The scientists called these various measurements *stigmata*. They were the legible evidence of pathology.[6] The broken-brain model is, in one important sense, a modern version of phrenology. Phrenologists studied the cranium to understand personality as innate, so that culture couldn't be held responsible for it, and now we're studying the brain for the same reason. Today's stigmata are brain images.

For the past two decades, Thomas Insel, a former director of NIMH, has attributed stigma, underdiagnosis, and undertreatment to the public's inability to recognize the biological foundations of mental illness. Insel lectures widely, showing his audiences brain images, vibrant with color, to demonstrate that brains with distinct disorders are different from one another. For example, children with ADHD have less cortical surface area than their non-ADHD peers, and people with schizophrenia have reduced thickness of the cerebral cortex in comparison to controls.[7] Audiences typically find these facts unsurprising, but they are intended less to educate than to push the mental and behavioral aspects of psychiatry into the background and to bring the brain into relief. Why the brain? Because, Insel says, the neurobiological abnormalities associated with mental illnesses often occur in the brain long before they become visible in behavior. It is imperative, he says, for us to look for and potentially treat brain changes *before* behavior symptoms appear. To do otherwise would be like not examining or treating people for heart disease or high blood pressure until after they have a heart attack or a stroke. In his plea for progress in neuroscience, the brain holds the key to helping people with the one kind of disease—mental illness— that we have been the least successful treating.

Some of the images Insel uses in his presentations come from the brain scans of children, such as those who participated in Judith L. Rapoport's longitudinal studies of childhood-onset schizophrenia, an extremely rare condition.[8] Her images show that structural differences, as well as the pattern of structural change over time, are visible before behavioral symptoms become severe. When I met Rapoport in her office several years ago, she showed me how her team splices together, like an animated film, multiple structural MRI scans taken at different intervals over a period of eight to ten years. These time-lapse "movies" show the process by which children's brains lose the excess neurons and synapses that develop in utero and through about age two. This process, called pruning, continues until about the age of ten, but the pattern of pruning is distinct for different conditions. Rapoport can look at that pattern in the movies of children who have been diagnosed with mental illnesses and make educated guesses about which of them is from a child with early-onset schizophrenia, autism, or ADHD. These are important neuroscientific findings because more than half of all cases of mental illness have their onset by age fourteen.[9]

Similarly, autism researchers are using computerized vision analysis to detect and quantify variations in motor behavior, such as eye movements and head turns in toddlers at ages previously considered too young for standard clinical evaluations—a method often called digital phenotyping.[10] For PTSD, researchers are using computerized speech analysis to identify auditory markers of the condition's core features in tone, variation, pacing, and enunciation.[11] And schizophrenia researchers have been working hard since the 1980s to identify patients with what is called the prodrome (from the Latin *prodromos*, "running before"), the early stages before schizophrenia actually declares itself through a first psychosis. Pharmaceutical companies are eager for these studies to pan out since they could sell drugs for people who have yet to even exhibit the disorder the drugs were developed to treat. Although the stated goal of such research is to improve diagnostic precision, and remove subjectivity from clinical assessments, the underlying project is to ground psychiatric diagnosis in the hard facts of science.

Scanners and computers help researchers learn more about the brain, but they tell us practically nothing about the experiences and needs of people with psychiatric or neurological diseases, persons enmeshed in their lives, in their societies. People caring for a loved one with advanced Alzheimer's, for example, have little need for a clinical description of the brain; they want the doctor to look not at the brain image but at them, the patient and the caregiver, to recognize and appreciate their experience.[12] Brain scans have also done nothing to aid in psychiatric diagnosis and treatment. Just because an image shows an apparent abnormality does not mean that the abnormality was originally caused by a brain-based problem, and it certainly does not provide a road map for any particular kind of therapy.[13] In fact, the neuroscience literature has amply demonstrated that experience itself—for example, trauma, chronic physical pain, malnutrition, education, and even meditation—produces observable anatomical changes in the brain. If the structure of the brain is so plastic, and so susceptible to such environmental factors, isn't it too simplistic to say that a mental illness is a disease of the brain?

In 2005, Insel wrote, "Psychiatry's impact on public health will require that mental disorders be understood and treated as brain disorders."[14] His agenda parallels the international efforts of many public health workers to diagnose and treat mental illnesses, conceptualized in Western, DSM terms, everywhere in the world, often at the risk of seeing the individual in isolation from culture. The APA's website, for example, lists readings in global mental health, such as "Personality Disorders in Basque, Spain," "Trauma and Depression in Ethiopian Women," "Post-partum Mood Disorder in Iran," and so on. The World Health Organization's Mental Health Gap Action Programme (mhGAP) recognizes that the use of such labels across the globe is problematic. In an admirable effort to mitigate wholesale exports of Western psychiatry, the mhGAP seeks to balance the use of Western models of care with those that are culturally appropriate, as well as balance the use of pharmaceuticals and local, indigenous systems of healing. Nonetheless, they tip the balance toward the science of the brain. In a 2011 issue of the *Lancet*, the mhGAP leaders wrote that "irrational and inappropriate interventions should be discouraged and weeded out."[15] They added: "The absence of cures, and the dearth of preventive interventions for [mental, neurological, and substance-abuse] disorders, in part reflects a limited understanding of the brain and its molecular and cellular mechanisms."

In another article, published the same year, this time in *Nature*, a large consortium of mental health experts laid out the priorities for global research and treatment over the next ten years. Although the consortium called for an understanding of how both biology and culture affect mental health, the article reaffirmed the individualism of Western medicine. The article featured a photograph of a Somali girl, perhaps five or six years old, presumably with a developmental disorder or intellectual disability, chained to a tree.[16] The editors probably selected the image of a lone child because it resonated with humanitarian discourses about human rights, namely the proposition that each individual has the right to life, liberty, and dignity. She is the quintessential mentally disabled child in a low-income country, just as other images that nongovernmental organizations circulate depict other quintessential objects for saving, such as the refugee, the trafficked woman, and other victims.[17] In the picture of the Somali girl, the viewer sees no evidence of family, politics, or religion, only an individual. The image conceals the content of her life.

Anthropologist Dominique Béhague says that, where she works in southern Brazil, mental illness terminology "takes the politics out of suffering, like discussing depression or suicidality instead of the impoverishment of a community due to government policy." Indeed, Brazilian psychiatric reformers argue that the concept of stigma itself can also efface politics since "stigma" can be a sanitized word for discrimination.[18] "The stigma of class and race for the low-income people of Afro-Brazilian descent where I do research," Béhague says, "is so strong, and so strongly connected to suffering, that it makes little sense to talk about any kind of illness or stigma apart from social conditions." In that community, teenagers might seek or accept counseling for an inability to pay attention at school, but not under the banner of a biological or brain-based attention deficit disorder. It is more likely that they, and their counselors too, will think about their attention issues in relation to poverty, hunger, and prejudice.

Nowhere is this problem of reducing the person to a medical label, and rendering apolitical the misery of a discriminated group, as clear as in France, where illegal immigrants are allowed to remain in the country if they obtain an "illness visa." The government grants the visa as a humanitarian gesture for people with a serious, life-threatening disease who would likely receive inadequate treatment in their home country. But for this reason, some people refuse medical treatments in order to remain sick, while others seek ways to infect themselves with HIV—a disturbing twist on Sontag's notion of the bad passport that grants entry into the kingdom of the sick. Scholar Miriam Ticktin, who has documented this phenomenon, says that the illness visa offers no rights for employment or other benefits or participation in French society. Moreover, visas are not offered to people who are impoverished or seriously mentally ill. Ticktin writes, "With humanitarianism as the driving logic, only the suffering or sick body is seen as a legitimate manifestation of a common humanity, worthy of recognition in the form of rights; this view is based on the legitimacy, fixity, and universality of biology."[19]

The story of William, recounted by Columbia University psychiatrist Myrna Weissman, shows how in the United States clinicians differently value "biological" and "psychiatric" conditions. Born in the mid-1980s, William had numerous psychiatric diagnoses throughout his childhood—attention deficit disorder, obsessive-compulsive disorder, autism, and paranoid schizophrenia, among others—and had no friends. Psychiatrists blamed William's mother for being too attentive to William, too lenient and unstructured. He was bullied and suspended from school, and when he was hospitalized in a psychiatric unit for being physically combative, the staff discouraged family members from visiting. In 1999, William developed leukemia. Unlike the psychiatrists, William's oncologists praised his mother for how attentive she was, and encouraged relatives to visit him at the hospital. College student volunteers came to his bedside to play games with him or just keep him company. Weissman thinks that "by authoritatively labeling this boy as having a particular type of brain disease, the mental health workers might have been less likely to blame the mother for a child whose behavior was out of control."[20]

I understand the desire for a biological model of mental illnesses in a society in which people think about and act toward medical and psychiatric conditions so differently. I understand the seductiveness of simplicity; that explaining one's illness to others in scientific terms can sometimes be easier than explaining it in psychological or emotional terms; and that many people are hopeful that a broken-brain model will shift responsibility from the person to the organ—as if to say "it's not *me*, it's my brain."[21] But, as we'll see, there is little evidence that "illness like any other" models have ever succeeded in reducing stigma.

One problem with trying to make mental illness more like medical illness is that much medical care is actually concerned not with identifiable biological phenomena, like bacteria, viruses, or cancers, but with unexplained symptoms like fatigue and bodily pain. A headache, for example, is one of most common "medical" symptoms, but the causes are mostly unknown, as is the mechanism through which painkillers reduce headache pain. Europeans and North Americans experience many more headaches than people in sub-Saharan Africa and the Middle East, and they also experience and explain them differently. In some societies in Africa, a so-called tension headache is a sensation of ants or worms crawling in one's head; in the United States it is often a throbbing pain; some Southeast Asians describe headaches as a feeling of acid on the scalp. Many people with headaches seek medical help, and are probably treated in some manner, but rarely with the assistance of brain imaging or other laboratory tests, and almost always without a diagnosis other than "headache."

Doctors also frequently prescribe treatments for all sorts of diseases, including viral, bacterial, or parasitological infections, without even knowing what virus, bacterium, or parasite might be causing them. The aisles of grocery stores are stocked with gluten-free foods, yet there is no medical test for gluten sensitivity, with the exception of the test for celiac disease, which has a prevalence of between 0.5 percent and 1.0 percent in the United States. People also seek treatments for the often debilitating neurological and rheumatologic symptoms of Lyme disease long after treatment, but scientists have yet to find any underlying medical reason for what has become known as chronic Lyme disease (CLD).[22]

Many scientists still hope that mental illnesses will one day be medical conditions as "real" as, say, diabetes or heart disease. But this is an intellectually faulty comparison. First, comparing mental illnesses to such diseases sets up false expectations. Mental illnesses are hard to treat—and are still diagnosed clinically, on the basis of behavior—but not because of bad science. The brain is far more complex than the heart or the pancreas, so complex that the future that Insel and others imagine may never materialize. Mental illnesses cannot be reduced to a bacterium, a virus, or a blockage of an artery, and their incredibly complicated genetics is only one aspect of their etiology. Second, it's problematic even to juxtapose "physical" and "psychological" conditions since scientists have repeatedly shown that psychology plays a vital role in worsening or improving outcomes of people with heart disease, cancer, and other medical illnesses. For example, depression, anxiety, and stress are all major risk factors for morbidity and mortality in patients with coronary artery disease.[23]

Third, many people often seek treatments to stave off certain medical conditions if laboratory tests suggest a clear risk, but there is no test that can predict an impending mental illness. We can treat heart disease, for example, long before someone has a heart attack because certain findings—like high cholesterol or a blockage of an artery—are predictive. Clinicians can certainly be on the lookout for psychiatric symptoms—as when a patient has a sibling or parent with a highly heritable condition like schizophrenia, autism, or bipolar disorder—but there is no way to treat patients before they become ill. There are some behaviors that might seem predictive, but only in retrospect. Relatives of people with schizophrenia may say in hindsight that the person was aloof as a child, had few friends, and exhibited behaviors that didn't fit social expectations. Parents of people with anorexia nervosa may recall that their children were picky eaters many years before they became seriously ill. But whereas we can treat the person with hypertension before he has a stroke, we can't treat the aloof teenager for schizophrenia or the picky eater for anorexia. How many mentally healthy adults were aloof and disaffected as teenagers? How many adults without eating disorders were, or still are, picky eaters?

Fourth, unlike other organs, the human brain cannot be easily biopsied for study. Animal models are, of course, highly useful for developing treatments for everything from vision impairment to cancers. Mouse brains, for example, are widely available for study. But while mice can get cancer, no one knows if the mice in, say, a federal research study can hallucinate or have paranoid delusions that they are the object of government surveillance (which in this case would actually be true). Given these challenges, I think psychiatry is actually doing pretty well.

Fifth, it's as simplistic, and dehumanizing, to reduce a person to his or her brain as it would be to reduce someone to their genes, their ethnicity, religion, sex, or sexual orientation. Given how much we know about the role of social factors in shaping mental illnesses, how could we ever remove culture and experience from the brain? If we did, we'd risk overlooking how poverty, trauma, and other kinds of adversities affect us. Although some clinicians claim that a brain-based model of mental illness would minimize the tendency to see mental illnesses as a reflection of a weakness of character, that claim may now be out of date. Increasingly, we have few expectations that someone can experience the traumas of war or a violent childhood without being profoundly affected, and we more often view someone tackling those effects as resilient.

If we describe someone with a mental illness as having a chemical imbalance or abnormal brain circuitry, we risk providing reasons to fear that person, to see them as permanently damaged; it is the person's brain, and not the social context, that needs to be fixed. And if doctors treat the brain with medicines and the medicines don't work, or the patient doesn't tolerate them, then the person may be labeled as a troublesome or non-compliant patient who is causing their own suffering, or they may feel like a failure.

And what about the possibility that brain scans might someday help clinicians diagnose and treat mental illnesses? Today, of course, a brain scan of a person with pronounced personality changes might reveal that their psychiatric symptoms are caused by a brain tumor, but that biological finding is beyond the purview of the DSM. Remember that mental health professionals aren't even supposed to diagnose something as a mental illness unless they've ruled out an organic cause. At the moment, far too little is known to support using brain scans as the basis for diagnosis and treatment of mental illnesses. But if it does become possible, could those tests potentially be abused? Might a person with an abnormal brain scan, but who has no behavioral symptoms, be fired or turned away from a job, or denied medical or life insurance?

During the 1982 trial of John W. Hinckley Jr., who was acquitted by reason of insanity for an attempted assassination of President Ronald Reagan, defense attorneys introduced scans of Hinckley's apparently smaller-than-average brain into evidence. They suggested that Hinckley's brain had "shrunk." Although there were no data to suggest a relationship between criminality and brain size, his lawyers' goal was simply to introduce to the jury the possibility that something was wrong with his brain, something over which he had no control. If that was the case, the judge and jury did not need to worry that an acquittal was based on a subjective judgment colored by bias. Hinckley's brain, the radiologists said, was smaller than a "normal" brain, and that simple fact, the lawyers argued, couldn't be fabricated.[24] Never mind that no one knows exactly what a normal brain looks like, or that mental illnesses cannot be diagnosed by a brain scan.

Scientific efforts to characterize the normal brain through imaging have failed because there are too many confounding variables: the genetics of the scanned subject, the time of day of the scan, what the subject ate that day, whether he is right- or left-handed, among many others. In studies of schizophrenia, some researchers have tried to eliminate population differences by scanning only white people,[25] but this is a strategy that would risk making the normal brain the white brain, and the white brain then the ideal brain. That approach is as misguided as the mid-twentieth-century attempt to define normality by studying only Harvard male undergraduates.

Several studies suggest that the brain-based model of mental illness is mostly popular in scientific and medical circles. In a large Italian survey, for instance, only 21 percent of relatives of someone with schizophrenia cited "heredity" as a cause, as opposed to 74 percent of nurses and 75 percent of psychiatrists.[26] Relatives place less blame on individuals since they see their suffering as the outcome of participation in a world larger than the person—whether the trauma of war, environmental catastrophe, or social and economic crisis within the family. When people in England, Ethiopia, Germany, Greece, Japan, Russia, and South Africa, among other places, contemplate the causes of schizophrenia, depression, PTSD, and other conditions, they privilege social stressors, especially family conflicts, over biological factors.

In Germany, in 1990, a sample of mental health professionals and non-professionals ranked the causes of schizophrenia. Professionals ranked biological factors and genetics at the top, and ranked stress, broken homes, and lack of willpower at the bottom. Nonprofessionals listed the causes in the opposite way. In 2001, the authors repeated the survey and showed that public beliefs were moving closer to those of the professionals. But rather than decreasing stigma, nonprofessionals reported an increased desire for social distance from people with schizophrenia. Whereas in 1990 19 percent of the respondents said they would not want to live next door to someone with schizophrenia, in 2001 that percentage had risen to 35 percent.[27] A brain-based model thus appeared to increase stigma.

Another study showed that from 1996 to 2006 the American public increasingly saw mental illnesses in general, and depression and schizophrenia in particular, as neurobiological. And the more neurobiological they saw the condition, the more they endorsed treatment for it. But, the authors wrote, "in no instance was a neurobiological conception associated with significantly lower odds of stigma."[28] Understanding the neurobiology of mental illness actually *heightened* the belief that people with schizophrenia and depression are dangerous and unpredictable. Similarly, critics of autism research argue that the millions of dollars being funneled into research to develop diagnostic and genetic tests for autism spectrum disorder (ASD) risks stigmatizing autistic people and their families as "genetically unfit."[29]

Genetics now forms a crucial part of the effort to locate causes and diagnostic biomarkers and put an end to parent and family blame. Genetics might also hold the key for developing new treatments, cures, or even the eradication of an illness. Down syndrome (also known as trisomy 21), for example, is not difficult to identify in utero. A person with Down syndrome has a duplication—three rather than two copies of chromosome 21—that can be detected through a prenatal genetic test toward the end of the first trimester. Down syndrome has virtually disappeared among newborns in Iceland because nearly 100 percent of unborn babies receive prenatal genetic testing and any child found with trisomy is aborted. The selective eradication of Down syndrome through abortion is one of the most hotly contested debates in bioethics, including among autism advocates.

In contrast to Down syndrome, scientists have located more than one hundred risk genes implicated in autism, commonly referred to as "candidate genes," and predict there may be 1,000 more. They are called candidates either because variants of those genes are known to be associated with autism as we define it today or because the genes lie in a region suspected to be involved in autism. In addition, more than 2,000 copy number variants—deletions or duplications in a person's genome—have been identified for individuals with autism. And this is what frightens many autistic self-advocates. Autism, for many advocates, is a kind of human diversity, not a disease. If there was a prenatal genetic test for autism, would all people with a high risk of being born autistic be aborted?

There are many medical conditions that we know are associated with a specific genetic mutation. For example, Huntington's disease is linked directly to a mutation in one of the two copies of the huntingtin gene. Early-onset Alzheimer's is associated with a variant of ApoE (coding for apolipoprotein E) on chromosome 19. But there is no single gene that produces autism. Indeed, there are probably thousands of different ways that thousands of different genes can cause the observable characteristics (or phenotype) we call autism. And autism is itself a condition of multiple phenotypes. As science writer Steve Silberman notes, it's possible that if you randomly selected one hundred children with autism for study, each child would have his/her own, unique genetic causes.[30] In fact, only 3 percent to 5 percent of autistic children in the samples of large research studies share the most common genetic factors for autism. This means that we shouldn't think of autism as a genetic mistake. There are just so many ways to produce the phenotype—so many pathways, combinations of genes and regulators of genes—that reducing autism to a malfunction in our genes makes no sense scientifically.

The theory of natural selection can help us understand the proposition that autism is not a genetic mistake, and can also go further to suggest that autism is part of normal human variation. We know that, due to their relative social isolation, people with autism, and schizophrenia too, tend to have fewer children than people without those conditions. So why, over the last many thousands of years, didn't natural selection eliminate variants of genes associated with them? One possibility is that the effect of these genes is so small that they don't influence reproduction, but that seems unlikely since the symptoms of autism often inhibit a person's ability to form relationships, marry, and reproduce. Another, more compelling possibility is that the genetic variants implicated in autism are "bystanders," meaning that they are linked to or coevolved with other gene variants that are under positive selective pressure. In other words, if the evolutionary process of natural selection has preserved the risk for autism, then the common genetic variation that puts us at risk for autism probably serves a positive function for humans.

The claim that there is a meaningful relationship between aspects of human variation we value (like linguistic and social skills) and those we have tended not to value (like autism) is supported by recent genetic studies. Scientists have found that genes associated with autism are adjacent to areas of the genome that are distinctly human, the areas called HARs (human accelerated regions). HARs consist of enhancers and regulators that influence whether or not a gene will be expressed. They are not genes, and they don't code for proteins, but they lie adjacent to genes and regulate their expression. To locate the HARs, scientists looked at the full genome of a large number of different species of mammals and located the areas that were completely conserved over the 65 million years of mammalian evolution. These areas generally contain a very small number of base pairs (approximately one hundred). Evolutionary conservation is one reason the genetics of all living things are actually quite similar: humans and bananas, for example, are genetically about 50 percent the same, and humans and daffodils are about 35 percent the same.

Next they looked for the segments within these conserved areas that exist only in humans. Scientists have identified about fifty HARs to date, and they provide a kind of signature of acceleration in the relatively short history of human evolution. Some scientists argue that HARs are associated with genes for cognition, intelligence, and learning, as well as for autism and schizophrenia. UCLA scientist Daniel Geschwind, one of the pioneers in the genetics of autism, is especially interested in what conserved regions of the genome have to tell us about normal human variation. When I spoke with Geschwind, he said, "Genetic variation that increases risk for autism has a 0.3 correlation with educational attainment," meaning that there is a positive relationship, albeit weak, between the two. If this is the case, then autism is inextricably linked to the same genetic pathways that make us such extraordinary mammals, capable of education, creativity, and high intelligence. And if these genes were somehow eradicated, it is possible these human capacities might be at risk.

In a recent lecture at NIMH, Geschwind described a study conducted many years ago by the psychologist Laurence Binder, and in doing so it seemed to me that Geschwind was suggesting that intellectual disabilities, like those in people with autism and other developmental disorders, might actually be a part of "normality." Binder wondered how adults with above-average intelligence performed on the different subtests in the fourteen-part Wechsler Adult Intelligence Scale-III, a common and well-validated psychological test. Binder found that 28 percent of adults in his sample received abnormal scores on at least two parts of the test. More than 19 percent performed in the abnormal range on three or more parts, and 14 percent received abnormal scores in four or more parts. A quarter of the adults scored three standard deviations below normal on at least one part of the test—borderline intellectual functioning indicative of a pronounced intellectual disability.[31] Yet these were highly intelligent adults! Binder's finding, Geschwind said, demonstrates that "there is no such thing as an average human being, because everyone is good at some things and not at others."

My daughter Isabel, for example, has some extraordinary skills. She can draw magnificent cartoons, has perfect pitch, and can tell you all the individual notes within any chord she hears on a piano or guitar. She also has a memory like no one else I know. In July 2019, Isabel, Joyce, and I were listening to the radio in our car when Stevie Wonder's "Superstition" came on. Joyce asked Isabel if she'd ever heard the song before. Isabel said, "Yes, it was playing on the radio in the taxi in San Francisco on Saturday, October 31, 2015, when we went to dinner on our vacation." Her memory makes it possible for her to precisely manage the animals she takes care of in her work, remembering the details of each animal's vital signs and medications. She also remembers the birthdays of most people she meets, and this skill helps her to maintain social relationships, one of the greatest challenges of someone with autism. In contrast, I have a terrible memory, cannot complete simple jigsaw puzzles, and have no artistic skills.

Experts in psychiatric genetics don't deny that many variables—environmental and biological—shape our lives. Schizophrenia, for example, is arguably one of the most genetically determined of all mental conditions. Yet studies of identical twins, people who started off with the same genetic code and who were raised together in the same family, show that when one twin develops schizophrenia the other develops it as infrequently as 30 percent of the time.[32] Two people can also be genetically predisposed to depression and yet only one of them develops the illness due to different life experiences—if, for example, one of these two people becomes depressed after the loss of their loved one. The depression cannot be said to be entirely genetic since the death precipitated the symptoms. Neither can it be said to be entirely due to experience (or what scientists would call environment) since genetics did play a role.

Even an entirely genetic condition is not beyond environmental control. Phenylketonuria (PKU) is a clearly identifiable, inherited defect in the PAH gene, the gene that regulates the production of the enzyme that breaks down the amino acid phenylalanine. Because people with PKU don't produce enough of the enzyme, phenylalanine builds up in the body and can cause a range of symptoms including seizures and intellectual disability. But a special diet low in phenylalanine can drastically limit the effects of the genetic defect. PKU can be said to be entirely genetic, but it does not exist independent of environment and experience (diet).[33]

The complexity of gene-environment interaction is hard enough for scientists to comprehend, let alone nonscientists. In South Korea, where I have conducted research, the stigma of autism is often related to beliefs about the primacy of genetics and its social implications. The many Korean parents I've interviewed tend to understand that autism has a significant genetic basis—that it can be highly heritable—but a person with only a passing knowledge of genetics often assumes that heritable means inherited. "Heritability" is not the same as "inherited" (despite the fact that the two words sound so similar) or familial. Measures of heritability tell us only the degree to which a certain trait can be attributed to genetic differences, and say nothing about how inheritable it might be. Heritability also includes de novo mutations, the countless mutations that occur for the very first time in a person, which is one reason why none of us are exactly a combination of our parents' genes. A substantial portion of cases of autism are caused by de novo mutations—which is likely what happened with Isabel, since Joyce and I have no family history of autism—while in other cases it runs in families. But the parents I interviewed in Korea viewed any genetic disorder as a blight on the genetic integrity of the family and on the lineage as a whole.

A mother may thus react to her child's autism diagnosis with fear, not just because she is worried about her child but because she is worried about her other children, and their marriage prospects. If "genetic" is presumed to be that which is inherited, mothers ask, who would want to marry into a family with a genetic disorder? As one result, parents sometimes reject the diagnosis of autism and instead seek a different diagnosis that has no hereditary burden, namely reactive attachment disorder (RAD).[34]

RAD first appeared in the DSM-III in 1980 but gained traction in clinical circles much earlier, even in the era of the DSM-I (first published in 1952), due to the dominance of the psychoanalytic paradigm that considered mental illnesses to be an unhealthy reaction to one's family environment. Following WWI and WWII, and an increase in detailed documentation of abusive institutions in which young children were born or spent their early years—such as prisoner-of-war camps and large orphanages—psychologists posited that certain environmental conditions could explain the lack of social responsiveness and failure to thrive among some children, symptoms observable even in infancy.[35] Clinicians thus tended to diagnose RAD in children with a history of "a pattern of extremes of insufficient care," such as neglect, deprivation, or lack of any continuous caretaker.[36] But, as happened in Korea, some clinicians also made the diagnosis in children with symptoms of RAD without any evidence of abuse. They presumed that the children must have been abused.

When my colleagues and I conducted a large-scale epidemiological study in South Korea between 2006 and 2011, we found that autism was seldom mentioned in school and clinic records, and most clinicians said it was a rare disorder in Korea. This isn't because autism, as the DSM defines it, didn't exist. When the clinicians in our study evaluated more than 50,000 children, ages eight through twelve, in a midsized city—a complicated process that took five years—they found a prevalence rate of more than 2.6 percent, just a little higher than the estimated prevalence of autism in New Jersey.[37] We were surprised to find that two-thirds of the students in mainstream schools who qualified for a diagnosis of autism had never received any special education or clinical diagnosis for any developmental issue. Some were miserable; others had just muddled through their education, daunted by the academics and the increasing social demands in each new year.

The stigma of diagnosing and recording a condition that people define as genetic may be one of the legacies of the matchmaker system in Korea. Matchmakers, even today, serve an important role in Korea, not to arrange marriages but to facilitate introductions to potential spouses, partners who are compatible in terms of their economic and educational status, genetics and bloodlines. When a mother seeks and accepts a diagnosis of RAD for her autistic child, she takes the blame—as if she is saying, "Our family does not have bad genes; I was just a bad mother to this child." By taking on the social stigma of poor parenting for herself, she protects the rest of the family from the biological stigma of a genetic abnormality.

If it is just the mother and not the child who is truly ill, then there is also an assumption of a greater chance for recovery. In fact, over the last ten to fifteen years, in large part as the result of a group of Korean clinicians who have popularized RAD in Korea, programs began to appear in Seoul to help mothers learn how to become more emotionally attached to their children. Mental health experts sometimes encourage mothers of children with RAD to quit their jobs. If the child gets better, the diagnosis and the treatment are validated. If the mother refuses to quit but the child improves nonetheless, the diagnosis is validated by an argument that the therapeutic relationship between mother and doctor helped the child. The case of Korea shows us the limits of both biomedical and psychoanalytic models. Both can increase stigma, but each increases a different kind of stigma.

In Japan, genetic and biological explanations of illness are just as stigmatizing as they are in Korea. Whole families can be impugned because of a single individual's illness, making it challenging for matchmakers to locate willing marriage partners for their clientele. Anthropologist George Vickery writes that by the turn of the twenty-first century, Japanese rarely wanted to speak about the brain or chemical imbalances in relation to mental illnesses. "Instead," he says, "mental illness is couched in terms of stress," and they use the English word "stress" rather than a Japanese one. Japanese also began to use a range of different English words to refer to mental illness and mental health care providers because the foreign words soften the emotional power of the equivalent terms in Japanese. People receiving mental health care might say they go to a *"mentaru kurinikku"* (mental clinic) or see a *"kaunseraa"* (counselor), just as in the United States many people prefer to say they are seeing their "therapist" instead of their psychologist, social worker, or psychiatrist.[38] Similarly, because the Japanese words for specific mental illnesses, and even the word "psychiatrist," still connoted severe disability and reminded people of institutionalization, in the early 2000s mental health advocates began translating the Japanese word for mental illness, *seishin shōgai*, as a "disability of the soul," in part to locate distress more in the heart than in the mind or brain. Hence, for marketing purposes, pharmaceutical companies appealed to consumers by glossing depression as "a cold of the heart."

However, with the inexplicable increase in rates of depression and suicide over the last two decades, it became much more difficult to speak of mental illnesses in such a mild manner, as it seemed to minimize their severity. Japanese thus sought an answer not in mental illness terms but in work stress, embracing new words like *karo jisatsu* (overwork suicide), *karoshi* (death from overwork), and *hikikomori* (social withdrawal). Such external causation limits stigma because stress is something that everyone deals with, and because stress can be ameliorated by changing one's environment. In many societies, physicians say that mental illness words get in the way of treatment. Doctors in Calcutta, for example, describe talking to patients about "tension" rather than "depression" or "anxiety" because tension is, in their view, "something somebody else has done to you."[39]

The history of depression in Japan shows how the popularity and usefulness of a mental illness name can fluctuate depending on whether one explains the cause as internal (biological) or external (environmental) to the person. Over the course of the last century, rates of diagnosis and treatment of depression in Japan increased when depression was removed from the domains of neurology and psychiatry and explained by social and historical factors. For a time, in the late nineteenth century, for example, depression was common and could even reflect positively on someone's character. According to anthropologist Junko Kitanaka, being depressed, like having neurasthenia in the United States and the UK in the late nineteenth century, "evoked images of accumulated sorrow, excessive contemplation, or silent endurance." Depression, she says, was "an extension of normality."[40] But by the early 1900s, Japanese doctors, heavily influenced by American and British psychiatry, came to define depression as a hidden, dangerous, unpredictable, and irreversible brain disease. With that definition, no one wanted to be associated with depression, or for that matter with any mental illness. Kitanaka writes that "disconnected from psychological, social meanings . . . [depression] became an illness that was so experience-distant, so stigmatizing, that Japanese could no longer afford to suffer from it."[41] Diagnoses of depression nearly disappeared from Japan.

But depression is once again common. Why? Because it has been reconnected with social meanings. Like neurasthenia, Japanese now think about depression as a symptom of exhaustion from work and the great stresses of modern life, such as caring for aging parents and competing in the marketplace. The male worker in the starched white shirt, suit, and tie is becoming the symbol of stress-induced depression, and people are said to die from karōshi, literally "overwork." Whereas in the United States, depression is often associated with women (the prevalence of depression among women in the United States is twice the rate as men), in Japan depression is increasingly masculinized, embodied by the struggling salaryman. There is a growing concern in the United States about overmedication with psychotropic drugs, while in Japan there are concerns about underuse, especially given the high prevalence of suicide.

I'm not suggesting that brain-based and genetic models are unhelpful to research and treatment. The more we know about how the brain works, the more likely we will be to discover effective therapies. But neurobiological and genetic knowledge form just one piece of a larger system of which the brain is a part. There is no "either-or," as in the stale nature-nurture debate. Biology and culture work together, and to assume otherwise is to risk a return to the past when people used the concept of "biology is destiny" to justify institutionalization, lobotomies, sterilization, racism, and even extermination. I'm saying, rather, that biological models are firmly rooted in the individualism of capitalist societies and that even when they lead to beneficial treatments they may not lessen stigma, and might even make it worse. They also mask our complex political, economic, and social lives. Just as workers under capitalism are alienated from the products of their labor, so too does the "illness like any other" model alienate us from the products of our emotional and social lives—the good and the bad, the successes and the failures, all the circumstances and all the people other than ourselves that make us who we are.

In her poems about illness, Anne Sexton thus rejected the supposed truth and objectivity of medical science. Arithmetic could not explain the progression of cancer; no clinical checklist could capture what it meant to be an absent mother while hospitalized with manic depression. In "The Double Image" Sexton watches yellow leaves fall in a hard autumn rain and says to her four-year old daughter:[42]

I tell you what you'll never really know:
all the medical hypothesis
that explained my brain will never be as true as these
struck leaves letting go.

CHAPTER 14

"LIKE A MAGIC WAND"

And so we came forth, and once again beheld
the stars.

Dante's *Inferno* (1472)

The directors of NIMH, chairs of psychiatry departments, and other mental health leaders often argue that the best way to treat mental illnesses is by understanding them as disorders of the brain, and that by treating the brain rather than the self we will also reduce stigma. But what about electroconvulsive therapy (ECT), which acts directly on the brain? ECT is a safe and highly effective therapy for treatment-resistant depression, and yet it is arguably among the most feared of all treatments, so much so that patients and their families are reluctant to accept it even when a life is at risk.

Many authors who disclose the most personal details about their social and sexual lives in their memoirs of mental illness still will not disclose that they had ECT. One writer, who claims ECT helped her enormously, and has written widely about her depression without mentioning the treatment, told me recently, "Depression is one thing. Shock is another. Telling people about it won't win you any points, and it might mean an employer won't hire you because they'll think you're really sick, really not right in the head." In contrast, psychotropic medicines are much less stigmatizing, perhaps because their action on the brain seems so indirect and mysterious. Few people who take psychotropic medicines actually know how they work in the brain. The pills we take, despite also acting on the brain, do their job only after being swallowed, absorbed, metabolized, and sent through the bloodstream, almost like magic potions.

Many doctors, complicit in the stigma associated with ECT, don't even contemplate the treatment for their patients. When I interviewed clinicians at George Washington University's department of psychiatry, they didn't even know where in the city a patient could get ECT. Arguably, any psychiatry service that presents itself as comprehensive should offer the treatment as part of the continuum of care. This isn't because ECT is better than medicines or psychotherapy but because clinicians should be able to use whatever the best treatment is for particular symptoms at particular times in the course of a patient's illness.

The remission rates for both psychotic and nonpsychotic depression after ECT treatments are as high as 90–95 percent in some studies. As early as 1985, the NIH issued a consensus report about ECT that stated, "Not a single controlled study has shown another form of treatment to be superior . . . in the short-term management of severe depressions."[1] Given that suicide is increasingly common—there were nearly 45,000 suicides in the United States in 2016, and suicide is the second leading cause of death for ten- through thirty-four-year-olds[2]—we may need to be using more of this therapy. It has side effects, to be sure. But imagine the lives that could be saved.

Given this evidence, why is ECT still so stigmatized? The answer begins with another form of intervention: the lobotomy, a brutal and imprecise neurosurgical procedure that my grandfather fiercely fought against. In the mid-twentieth century, insulin, Metrazol, and electrical stimulus were used together with lobotomies, and so they were associated with each other, not only by stigma but also by the fact that scientists often described lobotomy itself as a form of shock to the brain.[3] No one misses the lobotomy. It had tragic consequences for thousands of people who suffered brain damage from it.[4] But when lobotomy fell out of favor, so too did ECT.

In 2007, Howard Dully, a bus driver from California, published an account of his shame and silence after undergoing a lobotomy in 1960 when he was twelve years old. At that time, doctors reached the brain by hammering an ice pick through the orbital bone behind the eye. Dully has no memory of the procedure, probably because of the amnesia associated with the electroshock that preceded it. His father and stepmother didn't discuss it with him (Dully's biological mother had died seven years earlier), and he was too scared to ask about it. Until he wrote his book, he kept it a secret from everyone but a few close friends and his wife. He was simply too ashamed to tell anyone his brain had been damaged.

Dully said, "I've always felt different, wondered if something's missing from my soul." So he dug up his medical records, which led him to the George Washington University (GWU) and a neurologist named Walter Freeman. Now he knew. Freeman was renowned for only one thing: the hundreds of lobotomies he performed at GWU. The details of Dully's case were in the Freeman archives at the university library, in notes that described him, prelobotomy, as a violent, emotionless "misfit."

In 1949, the Portuguese neurologist Egas Moniz, who invented the lobotomy (first called leucotomy), was awarded the Nobel Prize in Medicine. Moniz was applauded for "his discovery of the therapeutic value of leucotomy in certain psychoses" and for devising a method that had improved the lives of the more than 10,000 patients who had undergone the operation.[5] The word derived from the Greek *leuko* ("white") and *tome* ("knife"), to denote the cutting of the brain's white matter. Moniz himself never performed an operation; his hands were too deformed from the effects of radioactive substances he used in his research.

It was Freeman who would rename the procedure "lobotomy" and create the famous method in which he used an actual ice pick from his kitchen on which was written the name of a Washington, DC, ice plant, "Uline Ice

Company." An ambitious doctor with the energy of a salesman and the the-atrical flair of a showman, Freeman created a niche for himself as America's first lobotomist. He performed lobotomies on camera, wearing a sleeveless gown to show his muscles, and touted the benefits of the operation in popu-lar magazines. He was balding, with a neatly trimmed goatee and round wire-rimmed glasses, and outside of the operating room he wore expensive three-piece suits with pocket squares. He was also known for his quirky and sometimes disturbing personality. Early in his career, he had a patient who couldn't remove a metal ring he had put around his penis. Freeman removed it, but the patient wanted it back. He told the patient that it had to be retained at the hospital like all surgical specimens; he took the ring to a jeweler, had it engraved with the Freeman family crest, and wore it around his neck for years.[6]

Like Pinel centuries before him, Freeman promised to liberate the severely mentally ill from state institutions. Between 1936 and 1970 about 50,000 Americans were lobotomized, many of them by Freeman and his partner, neurosurgeon James Watts, just a hundred yards from where I am writing these words. Lobotomy was imprecise, not that different from what the serial murderer Jeffrey Dahmer tried to do to his victims when he drilled holes through their skulls and injected acid—a method Dahmer believed would turn them into zombies.[7]

Here's how an actual lobotomy worked in Freeman's day. Electroshock would render the patient unconscious. Then the doctor would place an ice pick above the eyeball, hammer it through the orbital plate, and move it around to sever parts of the prefrontal cortex from the rest of the brain, especially from the thalamus, the part of the brain that sends sensory infor-mation to the cerebral cortex. The doctor would repeat the action on both orbits. The patient would recover from the surgery within a day, though with bruised eyes.

Lobotomy, Freeman thought, eliminated the circuit of communication in which sensations were turned into excessive or imbalanced emotions. As he put it, the procedure disconnected the emotional brain from the think-ing brain. One historian compared the lobotomist to an electrician: "If a light bulb burnt at too high a wattage and it risked catching fire, the solution was not to change the light bulb but to cut the power cord."[8]

In the prestigious *Journal of Nervous and Mental Diseases*, Freeman wrote that "H.D." (Howard Dully's initials) was a bully who lied, stole, cheated, and smeared feces and urine. His stepmother, Lou, told Freeman, "He doesn't react either to love or to punishment. . . . He objects to going to bed but then sleeps well. He does a good deal of daydreaming and when asked about it he says, 'I don't know.' He turns the room's lights on when there is broad sunlight outside." Many years later, Howard's father, Rodney, admitted that Lou had fabricated the behavioral problems because she disliked her stepson so much and wanted him out of the house; after the lobotomy, Lou and Rodney arranged for Howard to go into foster care.

Freeman performed lobotomies on many such children: children who were unruly, inattentive, hyperactive, had what we would today call autism, had learning or cognitive disabilities, were deemed unemotional or too emotional—anyone who did not fit his definition of "normal" behavior. He also performed them on adults: men who were impotent; women with postpartum depression, or who were "frigid" or promiscuous, or did not pay enough attention to their appearance. One of the main functions of the lobotomy was to enforce existing gender norms in women. "If she could cook, clean, care for the children, and provide sex," one scholar noted of female lobotomy patients, "her recovery was considered complete."[9]

In reality, postoperative clinical descriptions portrayed many of the thousands of people who received lobotomies as dull, calm, lethargic, and apathetic. Like Dully, relatives of people who had received lobotomies commonly talked about the procedure as if it affected the soul. "His soul appears to be destroyed," one British woman said of her husband; another woman in Sweden said of her daughter, "She is my daughter but her soul is in some way lost."[10] Freeman himself described the lobotomized patient as pliable, a "wax dummy."[11]

However, many parents and spouses were apparently happy with that result, as a dull and calm personality was preferable to the one that motivated them to seek the treatment in the first place. Freeman was convinced that lobotomies would help people become employed in low-paying, low-status positions as janitors, or in the service sector, but without the shame that might normally accompany those jobs. This effort to use surgery to "normalize" or "fix" people would be mirrored in the medical treatment of physical differences as well, such as the forced separation of conjoined twins and "genital normalization surgeries" for children who were born with ambiguous genitalia—approximately 3 percent of all live births—and thus did not conform to the dimorphic ideal at birth.[12]

My grandfather had a hard time containing his outrage. Lobotomy was a drastic, imprecise, and irreversible procedure to damage the brain that, despite resistance from many in the medical community, was being accepted as a useful procedure. In 1941, Freeman arranged for the journalist Waldemar Kaempffert to publish an article in what was then one of the highest-circulation magazines in America, the *Saturday Evening Post*, lauding the lobotomy. Kaempffert wrote: "On the whole, this sensational procedure justified itself. Long-standing cases of dementia praecox were not helped, but the hypochondriacs no longer thought they had cancer or that they were losing their minds; the would-be suicides ceased to yearn for death and to attempt self-destruction; the sufferers from persecution complexes forgot the machinations of imaginary conspirators. . . . In the whole history of mental therapy there was no success just like this."[13]

Grinker and Freeman, once friends, now became adversaries. My grandfather leveled a number of criticisms. First, he challenged the assumption that mental illness is wholly organic, and so could be fixed through brain surgery. Second, he criticized the subjective nature of the decisions to perform lobotomy. How much anxiety was so much that one needed to have his brain severed? How could the clinician make such a determination since anxiety is not easily measured? My grandfather knew from World War II how important anxiety could be to healthy psychological functioning, to make us alert to danger and motivate us to survive under difficult circumstances. Anxiety itself, he said, "is not pathological," only its degree.

Third, he argued that doctors were rushing to lobotomy. He thought many of the patients who received lobotomies could have been treated with other methods, including talk therapy.[14] My grandfather said, "It is obvious that even the natural process of recovery has not been allowed to take its task of cure."[15] Fourth, he noted that even if the lobotomy reduced anxiety or hyperactivity, it might also take away initiative, ambition, creativity, and spontaneity. And, given that the surgery traumatized brain tissue and blood vessels, and produced scarring, who knows what the long-term effects might be. He said of lobotomy, "One of the great dangers that may occur is a spurious kind of normality, a kind of normality that may permit the patient to return to situations or responsibilities with disastrous results." Finally, and perhaps most jarring to Freeman and his followers, whose patient pool included so many children, my grandfather objected to the use of such a radical method on young people since their brains were still developing.

None of these arguments sat well with the many doctors who performed lobotomies. They firmly believed that all mental illnesses were organic in origin and that lobotomies were the solution. In a panel in Cleveland on lobotomies, my grandfather was the only voice of opposition. Freeman responded, "I always take issue with Dr. Grinker and he knows it." In her book *American Lobotomy*, disability studies scholar Jenell Johnson chronicled just how Grinker taunted Freeman, telling him that he had read all of the medical literature on lobotomy, "including the *Saturday Evening Post*." Freeman, in turn, criticized Grinker's emotional reaction to lobotomy. On his own copy of the transcript from Cleveland, lodged at the GWU library, Freeman underlined every use of the word "feel" or "think" in my grandfather's statements, as in "I feel that one cannot lightly dismiss" or "I think there is a danger," and in his rebuttal Freeman pointed out that medicine should be practiced not by feeling but by reason. Freeman accused Grinker of "thinking with his thalamus." Grinker replied that he used phrases like "I feel" or "I believe" because neither he nor anyone else knows what lobotomies do, in the short or the long term.[16] In response to the accusation that he was thinking with his thalamus, my grandfather asked Freeman if he was recommending he should get a lobotomy when he returned to Chicago. After all, Grinker said, he was "extremely anxious" about so many people with mental illnesses being mutilated.

My grandfather would be vindicated, of course, but only after the media started to pay attention to celebrities who suffered from its horrible consequences, such as Eva Perón, Rose Williams (the sister of Tennessee Williams), and Rosemary Kennedy. Freeman, who was responsible for Rosemary's brain damage, went from being celebrated to scorned. In 1954, GWU denied him emeritus status, and in 1967 he lost his medical license, for malpractice. By that time, he had conducted nearly 3,000 lobotomies.

Lobotomies are still carried out today, but only occasionally for psychiatric conditions, such as severe and treatment-resistant obsessive-compulsive disorder. Though rare, some people with untreatable epilepsy can be helped by removing some brain tissue. The procedure is carried out like any other kind of neurosurgery—not with an ice pick through the eye socket but with high-resolution imaging, and carefully monitored by EEGs.

Whispers are the sound of stigma. And when I was young, I heard my parents' friends whisper about people who had been admitted to a psychiatric hospital and received what they called "shock therapy," like they were serving a prison sentence. They talked more about the treatment than the person's depression, as if the treatment itself was a discrediting transgression. My grandfather was less judgmental. Throughout the 1940s and 1950s, he continually warned against lobotomies. But he never dismissed ECT, which he once let me witness, in 1977, when I was in high school and he was trying to get me interested in psychiatry.

The patient I observed was being treated at Michael Reese Hospital, on the south side of Chicago. She was elderly, perhaps in her mid-seventies, and though she was of average height she probably weighed less than ninety pounds. She had been depressed and was now catatonic. I remember the acrid body odor in the room where the procedure was done, because she had poor hygiene. My grandfather told me her immobility had also caused her to have life-threatening blood clots. None of the available medicines in the hospital's tool kit had worked and, wasting away, she likely had only a few days to live.

One of the staff, probably an anesthesiologist, gave her two shots, the first a general intravenous anesthetic to make her unconscious, and the second a muscle relaxant. Next, they placed electrodes on her scalp and put a bite block in her mouth to minimize the risk that she might bite her tongue. They initiated a brief delivery of electricity—a little less voltage than comes from an electrical outlet, I was told—just enough to produce a short seizure. There was a slight tremor in her toes that lasted about ten seconds.

I remember feeling disappointed. I had expected something more theatrical. My father had told me that when he was a resident in psychiatry in 1954, two of his ECT patients suffered broken bones during the procedure—one had a cervical fracture and another a broken wrist—because they didn't use a muscle relaxant back then. But this patient barely moved. Anyone who watches a video on the Internet of an actual ECT treatment today will see that it doesn't look anything like shock therapy in the Hollywood movies.

I do not remember if this was the patient's first round of ECT, but I do remember seeing her a couple of weeks later sitting on a couch watching television with a bowl of popcorn in her lap. Without ECT, she would not have survived. So I understand why, despite never having received ECT himself, writer Andrew Solomon uses words like "miraculously effective," "wondrous," "boon," and "the most successful physical treatment for depression" to describe it.[17] I understand why talk-show host Dick Cavett said ECT was "like a magic wand," and why Kitty Dukakis, the wife of former Democratic presidential candidate Michael Dukakis, decided to write an entire book on the stigma associated with ECT. She wrote:

> *The mentally ill have enough to worry about, and shouldn't decide on a therapy based on what other people will think. That isn't fair. I know about the stigma because I was caught up in it. For the first year or two that I was getting ECT, I didn't tell anyone but my immediate family and closest friends, and I swore all of them to secrecy.*

Given the public perception that ECT is a drastic measure, patients also internalize that stigma, seeing themselves as "crazy" if they agree to undergo the treatment.

Jenell Johnson remembers battling with her own bias against ECT in 1995, when she was nineteen and a sophomore in college. Her seventy-year-old grandfather had a psychotic depression, meaning that he was depressed *and* had hallucinations and delusions. He refused to eat and didn't respond to any of the medications he had been prescribed. Treatment options for severe mental illnesses were poor in his rural hometown in North Dakota where he had spent most of his life as a farmer. So his family sent him to the psychiatrists in Fargo, more than a hundred miles away. When the doctors recommended ECT, Johnson strongly protested. She said it was inhumane and barbaric. The next day, she paused to think about her resistance. Referring to the film *One Flew Over the Cuckoo's Nest*, she told me, "I had this moment where I just thought: here I am literally making a life and death decision about someone I love, based on little more than a Jack Nicholson movie." She ended up supporting the doctors' recommendation. Her grandfather had the treatments, and continued to get ECT on occasion, as a form of maintenance therapy, for the rest of his life.

Nonetheless, when Johnson began writing a book on the history of the lobotomy, she made a conscious decision not to disclose her own depression. "At first," Johnson told me, "I didn't want to write about it because I was on my first year of a tenure-track job and I was afraid people would see me as diverging from their ideal of rationality. I was performing the same stigma I deplored; I was devaluing the insider perspective in disability studies that I advocate—nothing about us without us." She asked herself, "Who else's stories haven't been told?" Johnson ultimately decided to disclose her relationship to the topic in her book on lobotomies, but those untold stories of others still haunt her, shadows of people who were never allowed to disrupt the status quo.

Given the ongoing stigma of depression and ECT, many readers of the *New York Times* were surprised when in 1988 Pulitzer Prize–winning novelist William Styron published an op-ed in the paper revealing that he had suffered from severe depression and had spent seven weeks in a psychiatric hospital.[18] He would later write that he also received ECT. During the summer and fall of 1985, he had become morose, lost twenty-five pounds in just six weeks, and looked for ways to kill himself. He knew he needed urgent care. For far too long his doctors had advised him against hospital-ization because of the stigma. "The stigma meant nothing to him," his biog-rapher wrote, but Styron was simply too depressed to put up a fight.[19] In 1992, he published a concise memoir of his depression, *Darkness Visible: A Memoir of Madness*, and gave hope to countless sufferers. He ended the book with the last line of Dante's *Inferno*, "And so we came forth, and once again beheld the stars."[20] "To end on a note of such beauty," Mary Cregan wrote nearly two decades later in her own moving memoir of depression, "was Styron's gift to the many readers who had no words to describe what they had been through."[21]

The writer Pagan Kennedy credits Styron for bringing depression out of the shadows and showing the world that fabulous professional success and a loving family cannot immunize someone from mental illness. Styron's daughter, Alexandra, told Kennedy that her father's disclosure empowered readers to talk about their mental illnesses. "It was like the #MeToo move-ment," she said. "Somebody comes out and says: 'This happened. This is real. This is what it feels like.' And it just unleashed the floodgates."[22]

Disclosure of ECT treatment ended the vice-presidential candidacy of Thomas Eagleton. In the 1972 presidential election, George McGovern and Eagleton represented the democratic party against Richard M. Nixon and his running mate, Spiro Agnew. Chosen for his good reputation and his appeal to working-class Catholics, Senator Eagleton, a Democrat from Mis-souri, was widely considered an excellent choice. Yet he would be McGov-ern's running mate for only eighteen days. As a senator, Eagleton was remarkably productive and served until his retirement in 1987. He was one of the central proponents of the Education for All Handicapped Children Act (1975), the precursor to the later Individuals with Disabilities Educa-tion Act; he authored the bill that effectively ended US military involve-ment in Vietnam; he was a key proponent of the Clean Water Acts of 1970 and 1972, arguably the most important pieces of legislation in the twentieth century to protect the environment. But most people remember him only for his illness. Eagleton himself predicted this legacy, telling a journalist in 2003 that his obituary would probably read: "Tom Eagleton, for a short time the vice-presidential candidate on the McGovern ticket."[23] This is exactly what stigma is about: defining a person solely in terms of their disability.

When Eagleton accepted the offer, he said nothing about having received three treatments of ECT in 1960 for what was then called manic-depressive illness. This was before lithium and Wellbutrin, the medicines that would eventually help Eagleton, became available. But the truth came out quickly in the media, and in a news conference Eagleton said, "On three occasions in my life I have voluntarily gone into hospitals as a result of nervous exhaustion." After the press conference, a journalist wrote that Eagleton "is going to be one of the most visible vice-presidential candidates in history . . . he will be campaigning in the full knowledge that his audiences will note every tic, twitch, or quaver for signs that the doctors fell short of their goal."[24] Indeed, when interviewed on CBS's *Face the Nation* after the nomination, the moderator, George Herman, said to Eagleton, "I notice that right now you're perspiring and your hands are shaking."[25]

Once he was seen as mentally ill, Eagleton's relationship with the public permanently changed. In effect, he lost his ability to speak for himself; he became the patient, the passive object of others' eyes that would stare at him to make sense of this new person.[26] People with a serious mental illness often lose both voice and volition. They try to keep their condition and their treatments a secret. And if they do speak or write—in memoir, fiction, and poetry, for example, or in a television interview like Eagleton—what they say is often valued only as evidence of the illness, as when scholars analyze the writings of someone with schizophrenia, looking only for examples of irrationality and disorder. What's more, because doctors and politicians often assume that people with disabilities lack the ability to capably represent themselves, they question whether the most outspoken and articulate advocates for disability rights are "truly" disabled.[27] "To be disabled mentally," scholar Catherine Prendergast writes, "is to be disabled rhetorically," not because one inherently lacks the ability due to the disease but because it has been taken away by society.[28] It is as if when you are ill you can no longer mean what you say. One wonders if it is for this reason that Susan Sontag, in her famous essay on the stigma of cancer and tuberculosis, made no mention that she was undergoing treatment for breast cancer at the time she was writing it.

As a politician, Eagleton knew there was nothing politically dangerous about many physical illnesses. Dwight D. Eisenhower was reelected president even after he had suffered a heart attack in office. But leaders of the McGovern campaign, including its director, Gary Hart, as well as numerous major newspapers, encouraged Eagleton to withdraw quickly for the sake of McGovern's candidacy. At the height of the Cold War, according to Hart, the voters would reject a candidate who had both a history of mental illness and access to the nuclear arsenal. McGovern and Eagleton quickly came to the conclusion that a history of mental illness would be fatal to the campaign, and McGovern replaced him with John F. Kennedy's brother-in-law, Sargent Shriver.

Some blamed Eagleton for McGovern's landslide loss to Nixon, but McGovern probably never had a chance. It's even possible that McGovern underestimated the American public. Polls showed that a majority of Americans were sympathetic to Eagleton and critical that McGovern "dumped" Eagleton for reasons of politics and fundraising. Journalists reported that many Americans believed McGovern had been cruel, and that Eagleton had, in contrast, shown strength and integrity and had opened many eyes to the prevalence of depression. Eagleton said, "I've come out of it stronger than I went in. I'm at peace with myself. . . . This may be the most important week of my life. I did the job. I took the heat and I endured."[29] And when McGovern went to a preseason exhibition Washington Redskins football game soon after Eagleton's departure from the ticket, he was booed and jeered. Just a few days later, Eagleton attended a St. Louis Cardinals baseball game and received a standing ovation. A thousand people had been at the airport to greet his plane. In an interview a few days later, Eagleton remembered being depressed when he twelve years old, looking in the mirror every day and asking himself, "Will someone find out today?" He said, "So now it's out. And the wonderful thing is how good almost everyone has been. I mean the man in the street. The kind of person I was afraid would not understand."[30]

One can only wonder how a politician with a psychiatric history like Eagleton's would fare today on a presidential ticket. No president has yet admitted to receiving specialized mental health care. When a reporter asked Nancy Reagan about psychiatry, she said "getting psychiatric treatment means that you are not really trying to get hold of yourself. It's sloughing off your own responsibilities."[31] And when Bill Clinton and other American political leaders have reached out for emotional support, they turned only to Christian ministers.

Describing what actually happens when someone has ECT in the twenty-first century might help make it less frightening. A course of ECT is usually between eight and twelve individual treatments, typically given two to three times per week for three to four weeks. Each treatment session takes place in a procedure room with several staff, including a psychiatrist, and an anesthesiologist who makes sure that the patient is asleep for the entire five- to ten-minute session and that the patient's muscles are completely relaxed. A nurse places an intravenous plastic catheter into a vein in the patient's arm to deliver an anesthetic, usually methohexital, a short-acting drug that surgeons and dentists often use. The unfortunate word "convulsive" makes people think patients are moving during ECT but they actually don't move at all. They lie still, and the muscle relaxant, succinylcholine—called "sux" for short—is fast-acting and of short duration. The nurse also puts a blood-pressure cuff just above one of the patients' feet and pumps it up a bit. The cuff acts as a tourniquet so that very little of the muscle relaxant goes into the foot. That allows the doctors to see a very slight movement in the foot during the seizure, just so they know the seizure is happening. The seizure produced through ECT lasts only about a minute, during which time much of the electricity is absorbed by the skin and the cranium, with only a small amount actually reaching the brain.

There are four electrodes placed on the patient's head: two that lead to the EEG (the electroencephalogram that records brain waves) and two that lead to the ECT device. While the physicians monitor the EEG, blood pressure, heart rate, and respiration, the psychiatrist sends a dosage of electricity to the patient that is calibrated to the individual patient's needs. Dosage involves both placement of the electrodes and the pulse width of the electricity. Almost two decades ago doctors found that placing the electrodes only on the right side of the head seemed to minimize memory loss, and that it was just as effective as bilateral placement, so doctors now almost always start with a unilateral placement.[32] The standard of care today for the delivery of the electricity itself is called "ultra-brief," meaning that the pulse widths last only about half of 1/1000 of a second, and this duration also minimizes memory loss.

Doctors start a course of ECT treatments by giving the smallest amount of electricity possible to induce a seizure. They give a brief period of stimulation, then a little bit longer, and longer, until the patient has a seizure. The measure at which the seizure begins is that person's seizure threshold—their individualized dosage—and the most effective dose, doctors have found, is just one interval above it. From that point on, and for every session that follows, the doctor adjusts the dosage based on the patient's response, and any side effects, after each treatment.

Why is ECT so effective at treating severe depression? As with most medical interventions, it's probably better not to ask the question "why does the treatment work?" but rather "what does the treatment *do*?" We all know that antibiotics, for instance, kill bacteria and that aspirin can alleviate a headache, but few of us (including me) know exactly how they are able to do it. About ten percent of Americans take antidepressant medications, the same percentage of Americans who take statins, the medicines that lower cholesterol. I doubt most people who take either antidepressants or statins know how they work, but they certainly know what they do. Kitty Dukakis once wrote, "I don't know how ECT works. I don't really care ... ECT works for me. It makes me better."[33]

There is now a large literature on the physiology, prediction of response, technique, dosage, and efficacy of ECT. As with any complex scientific topic, there are multiple perspectives and debates. But the received view is that ECT works because it induces a seizure that, in turn, stimulates the brain to stop the seizure.[34] In the process, brain cells quickly release neurotransmitters and change the metabolism and blood flow of the brain. It's as if the brain's effort to stop the seizure is itself an internally produced, natural antidepressant. ECT increases blood flow to the areas of heightened electrical activity[35] and influences nearly every kind of neurotransmitter in the brain, including serotonin, dopamine, acetylcholine, and the innate pain-relieving system of naturally occurring opioids (e.g., endorphins).[36]

ECT is actually one therapeutic intervention that doctors can be proud of, even though a person's first thought might be to shudder. It's the fastest-acting treatment for patients with severe depression and suicidal thoughts, and it's the most effective treatment for catatonia, the life-threatening condition associated with affective disorders and schizophrenia. Someone who is catatonic may no longer eat, move, speak, or even make a facial expression. The symptoms—dehydration, malnutrition, incontinence, immobility, and even staring without blinking—can affect every organ system and lead to death.[37] But ECT can reduce suicidal thoughts and catatonia after only one or two treatments.

ECT is a medically approved therapy that falls under the larger category of "neuromodulation," which the International Neuromodulation Society defines as "the alteration of nerve activity through the targeted delivery of a stimulus." The mere mention of ECT raises eyebrows since it is still closely tied to the brutal images of electric shock from decades ago—images so stubborn it's as if, with ECT, time has stood still. ECT today bears little resemblance to the "shock therapy" of the past. Even in 1975, when *One Flew over the Cuckoo's Nest* was released, with its fictional scene of electric shock as punishment and torture, ECT was already a useful and relatively safe intervention for depression when nothing else worked. Ken Kesey, the author of the book on which the film was based, admitted that he wrote the scene from his imagination without firsthand knowledge of the therapy.

Psychotherapy and medications are vital to the long-term treatment of serious mental illnesses, but they may be of little use in the short term for someone at risk of dying and who has not responded to antidepressant medicines. Antidepressant medications can take six weeks or more to show any therapeutic results. And if one medicine doesn't work, and the patient needs to try another, they've lost precious time. One rigorous study conducted by NIMH, called the STAR*D trial, demonstrated that if someone with major depression didn't respond to a first medicine, there was a smaller likelihood they'd benefit from a second, and even a smaller likelihood they'd benefit from a third, or fourth, and so on, even if the new drugs came from a different class of medicines. The law of diminishing returns applies here because every time someone doesn't respond to a new medicine, it gets more and more unlikely that they will respond to any of them.[38]

That's why ECT becomes so important. Most patients see positive results almost immediately. It is arguably the least toxic of any medical intervention for mental illness, and though there are potential side effects—like short-term and long-term memory loss—the list of side effects is much smaller than that for psychotropic medications (side effects that include sexual dysfunction, weight gain, dry mouth, and constipation). Moreover, because ECT does not negatively interact with any medications, it's safe for elderly people who may be taking multiple drugs. The therapy has also been used safely for children and for pregnant women. Short-term memory loss is usually temporary, and some of that loss is related not to ECT but to the anesthesia itself, which disrupts the memory of any patient anesthetized for any medical procedure. Still, because some patients have experienced permanent long-term memory loss, people have to be prepared for the side effects.

To be fair, however, it's not easy to tease out which side effects are caused by the depression and which are caused by the treatment. Depression itself often involves cognitive problems, including deficits in verbal memory, decision speed, and information processing. Patients sometime attribute these problems to ECT when they are actually evidence of residual depression—cognitive deficits that can persist even when other symptoms of depression have been relieved.

Rebecca is a fifty-year-old mother of three who lives near Boston and who asked me not to use her real name. She writes about mental illness and has even published a book about her own depression. Despite her openness, she does not want anyone to know that a decade ago, after years of unsuccessful psychotherapy and treatments with a range of different medicines, she had twenty sessions of ECT. When I asked her why she didn't want me to use her real name in my book, she replied, "For exactly the reason you are writing this book, because it's just so stigmatizing."

Rebecca experienced her first bout of depression in college. She went to an internist at the university health service who said she probably didn't need a psychiatrist and that he'd be happy to talk to her "three or four times to get me through it." She remembers, "I don't think people really saw me as sick. And I didn't see myself as sick either. I just thought I had some kind of personality defect that made it harder for me to deal with life than other people. When I finally admitted to myself that this was a real sickness, I had to fight to be heard." Her internist eventually realized she needed expert help and encouraged her to see a psychiatrist.

Medicines alleviated her bouts of depression for more than a decade. But she stopped taking medicines when she was pregnant and then, after her first child was born, she became seriously depressed. At home, she'd leave her husband at the dinner table and sit alone in the dark. She didn't understand why she wasn't fired from her job for poor performance. "I was barely a mother or a wife and I didn't know how long this was going to last." Wanting her depression to end, she consulted a doctor trained in ECT. He promised to help her depression and assured her that while memory loss was possible, it would probably come back over time.

After ten sessions, Rebecca felt as if she was losing part of her memory and decided to stop the treatment. But her depression got worse. "I had to go back for the rest of the treatment," she said. "I was moving backward, and going back to treatment was the hardest thing I've ever done. Even now, when I drive anywhere near that place I start to hyperventilate." Within a few weeks, she felt like she was waking up, "enjoying colors and music, getting up in the morning, brushing my hair and putting on makeup. And for my husband it must have been like he'd been married to a person with Alzheimer's, a person a shell of their former self, gone away, but who had suddenly come back."

As time went by, however, Rebecca realized she'd lost big chunks of memory, and the discovery of each loss was traumatic. The most painful was not remembering experiences her children spoke about, the spontaneous recollections that affirm our relationships, like "Mom, remember that time when we . . . ?" A couple of years after her treatment, Rebecca attended a symposium on ECT where one of the speakers, a clinician and researcher, insisted that the memory loss due to the treatment was always minimal or temporary. "I was incandescent with anger," she recalls, "and I followed him out of the conference hall and told him about my own memory loss. He was dismissive and patronizing, didn't take me seriously, maybe because I was a woman, maybe because I was a former psychiatric patient—I don't know why—and he just kept saying that 'they' had the data."

I asked Rebecca what she would advise for someone who was considering ECT but was frightened. She said, "I hated it. But it worked. I lost so many memories. But I got better." She compared ECT to getting a gangrenous body part amputated. "You may have to lose some part of yourself permanently to survive." The analogy sounded to me like an overstatement, but the more I thought about it, the more apt it seemed. In this era of precision medicine, ECT is still a blunt instrument—in the words of one clinician, "like trying to right a watch with a hammer."[39] ECT does not appear to have a negative or lasting effect on cognition and intelligence. But while many patients recover all their memories, some people, like Rebecca, do have permanent loss of memory about events that occurred before the therapy—what is called permanent retrograde amnesia. And, unfortunately, because such memory loss is always anecdotal, doctors have been slow to appreciate it when it does occur, leaving many patients feeling as though no one believes them.[40]

In recent years, the barbaric images of ECT have faded from memory. And in both the United States and the UK the number of patients receiving the treatment has increased.[41] In 2015, *The Atlantic* magazine ran a story entitled "The Return of Electroshock Therapy," and in 2018 Anderson Cooper hosted a television segment on CBS's *Sixty Minutes* entitled "Is Shock Therapy Making a Comeback?" Both the article and the *Sixty Minutes* segment referred to the many celebrities who have described their own ECT experiences as miraculous, such as Dukakis and Cavett. Other outspoken advocates for ECT include Roland Kohloff with the New York Philharmonic and the pianist Vladimir Horowitz, neither of whom forgot any of the notes in their expansive musical repertoires, despite some short-term memory loss. Actresses Carrie Fisher and Patty Duke also wrote about their positive experiences with ECT. Dr. Leon Rosenberg, who was dean of Yale University medical school, wrote that ECT saved his life.

The two television reports also featured Dr. Sarah Lisanby. ECT saved her grandfather's life before she was born. Lisanby is striking. Tall, serious, elegantly dressed, and a deliberative speaker with an authoritative air, she is one of the leading figures in the science of ECT and the more general field of neuromodulation. On television, she made a persuasive case for the efficacy of ECT, though it was unfortunate that the journalists in both shows used the word "shock," a word mental health professionals eschew but that the media still can't seem to do without. Dukakis herself titled her book *Shock*, but only because, as an advocate, she wanted to take ownership of the word rather than leave it to the journalists to characterize what was for her a lifesaver.

When I met with Lisanby at her office at the National Institute of Mental Health, she said, "Imagine you have depression and you are terrified of ECT because of those ideas and images you've seen in the movies, and you and your family prolong your suffering to avoid ECT, even putting your life at risk. Or you have a psychotic depression and you hear voices saying terrible things, tormenting you, telling you that you did something horrible for which you need to be punished, telling you to commit suicide.

That anguish, the depth of that despair . . . it doesn't have to be there. It's treatable. But, tragically, people do commit suicide before they get ECT." It remains difficult for her to understand how the medically inaccurate image of ECT has endured.

When we spoke, Lisanby had just read a CDC report, released in the summer of 2018, showing a disturbing trend in the suicide rate in the United States and Canada. Since 1999, the rate of suicide has increased by 30 percent in half of American states. "The population in North America has grown," Lisanby said, "but the utilization of ECT has not. The mismatch between the number of people who could benefit from ECT and the number who receive it is a gap that continues to widen. If we could close that gap, if we could bring effective antisuicidal treatment to people wherever they are, when they need it, we could have a chance of reducing the suicide rate."

Even if people wanted ECT, there is still the problem of availability. In Washington, DC, neither my university nor Georgetown University has an ECT service, and ECT services are even harder to come by in poorer communities in the United States. Medical insurance can also be a barrier to ECT treatment. Indeed, the major predictor of whether someone with serious depression can get ECT or not is having Medicare or private insurance. A full treatment with ECT, which typically involves several sessions over a period of many weeks, can cost as much as $40,000. Whereas, in the past, ECT was used in state institutions (less as a treatment than as a punishment for misbehavior)[42] where many of the residents were poor, the situation has now reversed. Today, the typical recipient of ECT is a middle-class, or wealthier, white person over the age of forty with good insurance.

Due in large part to the antipsychiatry advocates (like Scientologists, for example) who have been successful in perpetuating the stereotypes of ECT, some states have actually passed laws to regulate it and make it less accessible. With the exception of abortion, I'm not aware of any other attempts on the part of state legislators to regulate medical procedures that are approved by the federal government and the medical profession as a whole. Although there is no evidence that ECT negatively affects children and adolescents who are at risk of death from depression, in Colorado and Texas no one under the age of sixteen is permitted to have ECT. Legislators in those states insisted that they needed to protect children—though it's not clear why regulating ECT is protective, especially when less than one percent of all people receiving ECT in the United States are under eighteen[43] and ECT has been considered safe for children since the 1940s.[44] One wonders why protection does not also include protecting youth from depression and suicide.

In Florida, the written opinions of two doctors not affiliated with the ECT facility are required in order to treat a child or adolescent, but there is no such requirement for any other medically approved procedure in the state. And in Missouri, a person under sixteen can have ECT but only by court order. According to the historian Edward Shorter, ECT is allowed in Tennessee, but only for depression and mania, a dispensation permitted solely because a legislator read an article from the 1960s in the *Saturday Evening Post* indicating that ECT for children was preferable to child-suicide.[45] Laws in California, a state subject to greater influence by Scientology than any other, require that no fewer than three physicians concur and that the patient be provided with written information indicating that "there is a difference of opinion within the medical profession on the use of [ECT]."[46] In Europe, ECT has faced fewer obstacles, but its use still declined during the antipsychiatry movement of the 1970s and the expansion of Scientology into Europe.

For her part, Lisanby continues to work on refining ECT and developing new methods of neuromodulation that will have fewer cognitive side effects. She's doing this not only because she wants to make therapy as safe as possible but also to diversify the psychiatrist's tool kit. And since many patients decline ECT because they are afraid of amnesia, Lisanby also wants to remove memory loss as a barrier to care. To minimize memory loss, one of the methods she is testing involves magnetic stimulation of the brain to produce electrical currents. Doctors can focus magnetic pulses more precisely, targeting regions of the brain that are important for antidepressant response and avoiding parts of the brain that are important for memory, like the hippocampus. One of the strategies Lisanby has helped pioneer is called magnetic seizure therapy or MST. It produces a seizure without the cognitive side effects and is currently being tested internationally. "People should not have to choose between their memory and their mood," Lisanby told me. "We can do better."

We are doing better. In March 2019, the FDA approved a nasal spray, administered only in a doctor's office, called esketamine, and marketed as Spravato, for adults with treatment-resistant depression. It is a novel reformulation and application of its close cousin, ketamine, a chemical used for several decades for anesthesia in surgery, but also widely abused as a recreational drug. Esketamine works even faster than ECT. The positive effects of ECT last longer, but this new treatment at least gives doctors a chance to salvage the patient's life and try new combinations of therapy.

Despite what we now know about ECT, and about neuromodulation in general, doctors still face an uphill climb. The battle against ECT has been championed by the Citizens Commission on Human Rights International (CCHRI), a branch of the Church of Scientology that has offices throughout the world. When I visited the organization's Los Angeles museum, I couldn't wait to leave. It's designed to be like a torture chamber, with chains and instruments of torture on display, and a giant prison door that closes behind you when you enter to induce a sense of horror. According to Jan Eastgate, who runs the CCHRI, psychiatry "is the greatest fraud of all time," and psychiatrists are driven by greed to destroy people's lives under the banner of science and medicine.

CCHRI shouldn't be underestimated. In 1999, just before the United States Office of the Surgeon General issued its first report dedicated to mental health, the CCHRI got wind of one line of text in which the federal government described ECT as a "safe and effective treatment for depression." CCHRI and its allies acted quickly and exerted enough political pressure to have the sentence changed to stress that ECT is a last resort. In published form, it read: "First-line treatment for most people with depression today consists of antidepressant medication, psychotherapy, or the combination. . . . In situations where these options are not effective or too slow . . . electroconvulsive therapy (ECT) may be considered."[47]

———

To the best of my knowledge, ECT is not dangerous. But even if it were, I would still recommend it for my loved ones if they were suffering and nothing had helped alleviate their pain. Yet ECT continues to be associated with violence on the body while the side effects of radiation therapy and chemotherapy for cancer—and major operations like heart surgery, in which the surgeon makes an eight- to ten-inch cut through the sternum—are associated with recovery. Nor are the range of electrical implants doctors now use considered torture, like pacemakers and the nerve-stimulating implants that comprise the new "electroceutical" industry. In her discussion of ECT, Mary Cregan reminds us that the hero of many television dramas is the defibrillator, which delivers a powerful electric shock to the heart to save lives—but that generates no stigma.[48]

The scientists who study ECT, and the doctors who provide it, continue to be harassed and threatened for what critics think of as brutality. In fact, some doctors who are well trained in ECT stopped doing it because they didn't want the fight. Not long ago, when experts on ECT arrived at the U.S. Food and Drug Administration to speak about the approval of a new ECT device, antipsychiatry and anti-ECT activists lined the hallway, forming a gauntlet. As the experts passed, some protestors hurled insults, addressing each of them as "Dr. Shock." Others, mimicking the sound of a jolt of electricity, spit out the sound "*bzzzzt.*"

CHAPTER 15

WHEN THE BODY SPEAKS

"The sorrow that has no vent in tears makes other organs weep."

Henry Maudsley (1867)

In 1975, three men showed up at the office of Sunny Ilechukwu, a young doctor stationed in northwestern Nigeria, with a story that was, at the time, so preposterous he initially refused to see them. A policeman stood between two men and said that one of the men had accused the other of stealing his penis.

In order to charge the thief with a crime, the policeman needed a medical report verifying the theft. The policeman was so persistent that Ilechukwu eventually examined the victim. As he anticipated, he found a fully attached, complete, and apparently functional organ. The victim wasn't so sure. Yes, it appeared intact, but was it really there, and would it still work? For his part, the policemen, happy to have cleared things up, charged the victim for falsely accusing the other man.[1]

Penis theft was now on Ilechukwu's radar, and he started noticing more cases, almost all of which followed the same pattern. In a crowded marketplace or bus stop, a stranger dressed unlike the locals (usually wearing the clothes of someone from far away, or even from another country) approached the victim, asked for the time or directions, and touched him or his clothing. The typical victim soon developed what Ilechukwu called a "chill" through the groin or "a sickening and sinking feeling," and grabbed for his genitals to check that they were still there. Realizing they were gone, the victim would scream, "My genitals have been stolen!" and try to mobilize people in the crowd to chase after the thief, and beat, club, burn, or even lynch him. The more pain and fear the crowd could inflict on the thief, short of death, the more likely he was to return the penis. By the late 1980s, Ilechukwu wrote, "men could be seen in the streets of Lagos holding their genitalia either openly or discretely with their hands in their pockets."[2] This is an example of how the body speaks for the mind.

Anthropologists argue that genital theft is an understandable response to the anxieties about anonymity in rapidly changing and urbanizing communities where previously most social interactions were limited to people one already knew. The stresses of population growth, border crossings, and regional trade and travel, according to Yale anthropologist Louisa Lombard, have provided fertile ground for occult fears: "The 'Other,'" she told me, "threatens a person's individual and social identity, much of which is centered on the ability to reproduce." After one theft in Central African Republic, Lombard recalled, the victim she interviewed spent several days lounging in his courtyard on a mat, surrounded by friends and family. He was being treated like any sick person or victim of a crime. The village came to support him in his time of need. Many said they had seen him naked, absent his genitals, but with no visible wound.

The important question is not whether organ theft, or any other symptom of pain or peril, is "real," but rather why certain bodily symptoms become culturally appropriate languages with which to articulate distress at certain times and places. The question is about what Freud once called "the sense of symptoms." When symptoms make sense, they are not only more common but less often stigmatized. Stigma may not disappear, but it increases when the individual rather than the society is held responsible for their illness, when psychological pain comes from within the person rather than from some external agent, and when their symptoms are idiosyncratic and baffling rather than common and expected. Stigma decreases when the form the illness takes is understandable and acceptable as a vehicle to express shared pain and sacrifice, when the sufferer is innocent, a victim of circumstance. When a victim of genital theft cries out for help in a busy marketplace, he isn't worried that people will think he is crazy. He knows the crowd will believe it to be true. And he isn't embarrassed to draw public attention to his genitals, or lack thereof. They understand his distress as a rational response to a crisis. And because it makes sense, there is no pressing desire to look for physical proof. Even if a missing body part appears to be there, its presence is probably an illusion since the theft itself was an act of magic.

Most societies prefer to externalize blame. The cause of an ailment in the United States may not be a malevolent stranger in a market, but rather a virus or bacterium. We tend to explain our physical suffering through medical frameworks and seek medical solutions to our problems, in large part because we have so much faith in science and the impersonal, seemingly objective, mechanisms of genetics and physiology that lie outside of any individual's control. When a doctor tells us we have an infection, we trust that these microbes exist in our bodies, even if we don't see them ourselves. Come to think of it, I've never heard of patients receiving treatment for an infection demanding that their doctors show them the actual viruses or bacteria under a microscope.

This process of medicalization has strengthened over time as the result of scientific progress and increased optimism in the benefits of public participation in American medicine.[3] Throughout the world, biomedical knowledge is distributed across the Internet, celebrities start foundations for particular illnesses, and researchers more often call their studies "partnerships," "collaborations," and "coalitions" of scientists and the public.[4] In fact, because of better enforcement of informed consent in research studies, research subjects are now supposed to learn about the science behind the projects—the background, purposes, risks, and benefits, for example. But the reality is that, with increased public access to scientific knowledge, and public confidence in the lay person's ability to comprehend it, new and sometimes bitter conflicts have arisen between the public and scientists, especially when the experts are unable to explain a sickness.

Nowhere have these conflicts been more obvious than in the debates about autism and vaccines. Televised panels on CNN, MSNBC, and Fox have included celebrities like Jenny McCarthy and Don Imus, as if their voices had the same import as those of the scientists. When the disgraced doctor Andrew Wakefield was on trial in England for fabricating data claiming a link between autism and the measles vaccine, one of his supporters carried a sign that read, "We want bad science!" Jenny McCarthy insisted that the many studies showing that autism was not caused by vaccines were flawed because the scientists had studied the wrong population; they had failed to study the children whose autism was caused by vaccines. McCarthy's followers refused to see autism as a developmental disorder or a mental illness and maintained that it was a bodily disease with an external cause.

It's ironic that the democratization of science, built on faith in knowledge, led to so much mistrust. If, for example, a doctor cannot confirm what a person believes to be true or cannot find the cause of a condition they are certain they have, the patient might presume the doctor is incompetent. If the doctor finds nothing wrong other than the symptoms the patient reports, the person "doctor-shops," looking for someone who will find the cause and treat them. In the case of autism, some parents who believe that their children's symptoms were caused by vaccines, mercury, or other toxins search until they find doctors willing to use unconventional and often dangerous treatments. These include chelation, hyperbaric oxygen chambers, nutritional therapies, and other treatments based on unproven ideas, such as the hypothesis that autism is caused by chronic bacterial or viral infections, yeast infections, and mercury poisoning.[5]

My grandfather was strongly opposed to both medicalization and the overemphasis on the psychological origins of suffering. As early as 1945, he began developing plans for a research institute to study how biological, psychological, and social systems interacted with one another. The Institute for Psychosomatic and Psychiatric Research opened in 1951, at a cost of $2 million, as part of Michael Reese Hospital in Chicago, and he served as the director until 1976. The institute supported a staff of ninety-five researchers to study the relationship between the body and the mind, and to treat patients for the psychological aspects of cancers, heart disease, hyperthyroidism, migraine headaches, and ulcerative colitis, among others. As my grandfather put it, "There is no single cause for any disease. There is no single reason for health."[6] But, he told the *New York Times*, "there is still strong resistance, on the part of many patients and doctors, to treating a person with physical illness, such as ulcers or heart disease, for their emotional troubles as well."[7] He insisted that it is impossible to explain health or "unhealth" without also explaining healthy or unhealthy relationships between body and mind. He was summoning up the days before Kraepelin, when all medicine was psychosomatic medicine.

Many patients are wary of getting psychiatric care for what they believe to be a condition only of the body. My wife, Joyce, has spent much of her career as a psychiatrist counseling patients with life-threatening medical conditions—such as rare genetic diseases, advanced cancers, and AIDS—to accept psychiatric care. When someone comes to her for the first time, she told me, "I know it's probably taken a long time for them to get here." They not only have to want care but they have to persevere even to get an appointment, given the shortage of psychiatrists. Joyce doesn't necessarily talk about stigma with her patients but, she says, "it's always a subtext."

Joyce has also found that patients frequently seek nonpsychiatric medical care for psychiatric illnesses. In about one-third of all patient visits to a neurologist today—including people with numbness, vision and speech impairments, seizures, and paralysis—there is no medical finding, no measurable or observable data, no discernible cause for the symptoms. Doctors give some of these patients a diagnosis of "functional neurologic symptom disorder,"[8] yet clinicians are reluctant to tell patients what this actually means: it's the modern term for conversion disorder (physical symptoms that cannot be explained medically), which was once the modern term for psychosomatic disorders, which was once the modern term for hysteria. They know that many patients will react to that diagnosis as if they are being accused of fabricating the symptoms, as if their sickness isn't real. For fear of stigmatizing patients, doctors thus choose their words carefully when referring patients with unexplained somatic complaints to a mental health professional, often telling the patient "a therapist might be able to help you cope with your physical ailments."

Psychiatrists have also largely abandoned the words "conversion," "psychogenic," and "psychosomatic." The DSM-5 includes the awkward mental illness category "somatic symptom disorder," even though a patient who did a simple Google search would quickly learn that this is a fancy term for psychosomatic disorder. To further obfuscate the psychosomatic, a few years ago the American Academy of Psychosomatic Medicine changed its name to the Academy of Consultation-Liaison Psychiatry, the branch of psychiatry concerned with the intersection of medical and psychiatric illness. They made this change precisely because of the stigma associated with the word "psychosomatic," yet many doctors have never even heard of the term "consultation-liaison psychiatry."

Here's the problem. Countless people who suffer terribly from a range of physical conditions could benefit from treatment within the psychological professions. But patients and doctors collude to separate the body from the mind, to see the diseases of the body as "real" and those of the mind as somehow fictive, even though that separation is the source of stigma and a barrier to mental health care. In fact, in the United States, medicalization encourages what doctors call "somatization." Patients comprehend physical complaints, including benign discomforts, as if they were physical diseases or potential physical diseases, and many doctors exploit the financial incentives of the "medical-industrial complex" to treat them.[9]

By 2000, genital theft was an epidemic in sub-Saharan Africa.[10] Newspapers, and government officials as well, helped to circulate the stories by repeatedly addressing them as legitimate concerns. On December 9, 2005,

the Nigerian ambassador to Togo felt compelled to hold a news conference to insist that Nigerians were not stealing Togolese penises. But even
dismissing the cases as false ended up validating them as real possibilities.
Over the past two decades there has been a steady stream of such thefts
in Ghana, Senegal, Nigeria, The Gambia, Democratic Republic of Congo,
and Central African Republic.[11] The episodes have sadly turned violent. In
April 2001, six genital thieves were burned to death in the state of Oyo,
Nigeria.[12] The next month, twelve such thieves were murdered over a two-
week period in the southwestern Nigerian state of Osun. Eight of them, visiting Christian evangelists, were burned to death. The police commissioner
called it "mass hysteria."[13]

Lombard was in Tiringoulou, in northern Central African Republic, in
2010 when, with just a simple handshake, a Sudanese merchant stole two
penises. "I wasn't surprised," she said. "I knew of similar stories in other
African countries." She told me about a Cameroonian woman arrested
in Amsterdam for allegedly attempting to smuggle several penises inside
baguettes—like a fantastical version of the *croque monsieur*. Lombard also
knew about penis loss in Europe during the fifteenth and sixteenth centuries, in China, and in Singapore where, in 1967, there was an epidemic of
the illness called *koro*, the debilitating fear that one's genitals are retracting
into the body and will cause death.[14] Koro (the Malay word for "head of the
turtle" and a slang term for the penis) is still common today. It is believed
to be fatal, and it often happens to people en masse. The symptoms have
been reported in India, Turkey, New Zealand, Korea, the Middle East, and
among West Indian and Greek immigrants to the United Kingdom.[15] Doctors also encounter it in the United States because people from other countries bring their culture with them. In 1989, a doctor acquaintance of mine
was moonlighting at an emergency room in a Boston suburb when a Chinese man and his sister arrived in a panic. She had her hand down his pants,
holding on tightly to his penis to keep it from disappearing.

People do not make such claims because they are uneducated, gull-
ible, or irrational, but because the symptom of loss makes sense to them
and their community. American doctors used to call conditions like koro

"culture-bound" disorders and now call them "cultural idioms of distress." Both terms came to mean "it doesn't happen here in the United States." Yet all illnesses are cultural. When Gulf War veterans believed that their genitals were damaged by toxins and vaccines during the four days of ground combat, we didn't call it koro; nor do Africans call penis theft koro. But all three of these symptom complexes are different endpoints on a similar pathway from anxiety to articulation.

Bodily reactions to stress, scholar Mark Micale writes, are "an alternative physical, verbal, and gestural language, an iconic social communication."[16] The nocebo effect, as we saw with GWS, becomes stronger as more people become sick, and even more so if a society validates or sympathizes with the sickness. When others witness or even hear about the symptoms, they develop them too, as if in a dialogue. In 1962, an epidemic of laughter among schoolchildren in Tanzania (then called Tanganyika) was so debilitating that people experienced intense pain, laughing for hours or even as long as two weeks. Schools closed. Parents panicked. The same year, employees at an American textile mill began reporting a rumor that workers had been bitten by a bug, the size of a gnat, and had become sick within twenty minutes of the bite. Within just a few days in June, sixty-two workers in the same mill developed rashes and nausea. Most of them were women, nonunion, overworked, underpaid, and divorced, and thus especially vulnerable to psychological stress. No doctor, scientist, or epidemiologist ever found any biological basis for the symptoms of what became known as the June Bug epidemic.[17]

In a more recent case of unexplained neurological symptoms, the U.S. State Department reported that twenty-six US diplomats and family members stationed in Cuba between 2016 and 2017 were victims of what Secretary of State Mike Pompeo and his predecessor, Secretary of State Rex Tillerson, both called "health attacks": problems with hearing, vision, balance, sleep, and cognition. Although there had been no reports of a similar illness among Canadian diplomats, the US chargé d'affaires met with the Canadians four months after the first Americans became sick to alert them to the problem. Soon, fifteen Canadian diplomats developed the same symptoms. The afflicted embassy workers remembered "hearing a novel, localized sound at the onset of symptoms in their homes and hotel rooms."[18] For many, the onset was within twenty-four hours of arrival in Cuba, thus ruling out an infectious or chemical agent. The symptoms were consistent with concussions, but the diplomats had no head trauma. Government officials suspected that Cubans had launched a coordinated attack using directional sound waves.

The authors of a scientific article on the illness in Cuba suggested that an "unknown energy source"—perhaps ultrasound, infrasound, or microwaves—was to blame. However, most scientists think the diplomats were suffering from a functional impairment. The affected embassy staff reacted angrily to the suggestion that their condition might be psychiatric. One told Dan Hurley, a writer for the *New York Times Magazine*, "It's a disservice to those of us who were injured to suggest that we were just making it up in our minds."[19] Douglas Smith, one of the authors of the article that suggested the condition represented a new clinical entity worthy of study, said he agrees with the patients: "It's real . . . it's only people outside who think it's psychogenic." But Scottish neurologist Jon Stone told Hurley that "it doesn't help anyone to call what the US and Canadian diplomats in Cuba have a brain injury . . . it can stop them from getting therapy that might help them."[20]

In the winter of 2012, twenty teenage girls from Le Roy, a small town (pop. 7,641) just east of Buffalo in western New York, developed motor and verbal tics—the same symptoms, at roughly the same time, in the same school. The condition resembled Tourette's disorder, in which the person has uncontrollable, sudden, and repetitive motor symptoms, often including stutters, laughs, and cries. But unlike Tourette's, which is a developmental disorder and is not contagious, spontaneous and contagious phenomena like the one in Le Roy are almost always temporary reactions to anxiety or stress, real or imagined, as in the cases of shell shock in soldiers who never saw combat. The children and their parents, as well as a range of different kinds of doctors, went on television shows as news outlets flooded the town. Erin

Brockovich, the protagonist in the eponymous film for which Julia Roberts won an Academy Award, came too, armed with equipment for testing the water and soil for poisons. Segments of television talk shows began with lovely photographs of the girls—happy cheerleaders, artists, excellent students until that one day when they woke up from a nap and began to twitch. "I couldn't stop stuttering," Thera Sanchez said on the television show *Dr. Drew*. The stuttering eventually stopped but gave way to "uncontrollable twitching." Weeks later Thera began to have what her mother called nonepileptic seizures, when she could talk but could not move her body, "almost as if she's a stone statue," her mother said. Another girl, Lydia Parker, appeared with Thera on the show. Lydia's symptoms were so severe that, for a time, she had to use a wheelchair. On the show, viewers could see a large bruise on the right side of her face where she had involuntarily struck herself.

Over the coming weeks, medical tests produced no findings of pathology in the girls. Environmental tests were negative as well. But the parents, children, and residents of the town were outraged. They didn't trust the local government or the doctors who said the condition might be psychological. After all, the parents said, these girls hadn't been emotionally distressed until they developed these symptoms. And when doctor after doctor came on television to say that mass psychogenic illnesses are common all over the world, the parents were insulted. On *Dr. Drew* they said they wanted a *real* diagnosis. Referring to the doctors, Thera's mother said, "Their feeling, their assumption that this is *just* stress and anxiety induced, or a conversion disorder—it's not enough." Lydia's mother told *Newsweek* that it couldn't be psychological: "I just can't make sense of it, it's just so obvious that something is really wrong in her body."

When Dr. Drew asked Thera what she thought about the diagnosis of conversion disorder, she said, "I actually really don't understand what that means, no one has told me what it means." As if to bait Thera, Drew replied, "You don't contemplate something being a psychiatric condition until you have ruled out all potential biological causes." That's a high bar. It leaves open endless possibilities for causation, since it's very hard to prove that you've exhausted every possible explanation. Could it have been the hard rain that fell that month, which could have washed into the water supply the toxins that were allegedly dumped near Le Roy decades ago? Maybe something leached from the stones and gravel that were taken from a quarry near the dump to build the school in 2004. Or maybe it was the gas wells in the town, which had caused some trees to die.

Eventually, the parents found a doctor named Rosario Trifiletti in New Jersey who thought tic disorders could be caused by an autoimmune disease. He suspected they had PANDAS (pediatric autoimmune neuro-psychiatric disorders associated with streptococcal infections), a rare condition associated with streptococcal infections that is not yet universally accepted as a discrete disorder. In 2014, he told *Cosmopolitan* magazine that he had treated more than 3,000 cases of PANDAS and that there is "probably one PANDAS kid in every kindergarten class."[21] The condition was first described by Dr. Susan Swedo and her colleagues at NIMH, who in 1998 reported fifty cases of children who had symptoms of either obsessive-compulsive disorder or Tourette's disorder (forty of the fifty had tics) and who developed the symptoms within a few weeks after being treated for a streptococcal infection.[22] It tends to be reported in young children—the average age of someone diagnosed with PANDAS for the first time is six—and in a study of patients with the diagnosis, only one percent were fourteen or older.[23] Daniel Pine, another child psychiatrist at NIMH, hasn't done research on PANDAS but has seen a range of patients whose parents believe they have it. In only a few cases has he ever thought the diagnosis seemed right. Pine told me, "PANDAS is a real condition, by which I mean that there is a real post-streptococcal entity that has those symptoms." "But," he added, "it's very rare, and you only see it after really severe or recurrent infections. And they also have the tics after each recurrence. You don't see it just once." Indeed, when journalists contacted Swedo to ask her if the Le Roy girls could have PANDAS, she said it was highly unlikely if not impossible. PANDAS, she said, is so uncommon that she couldn't imagine that even two people in the same school could have it.

But the possibility of PANDAS was good enough for the parents and for Trifiletti. He ordered blood tests and found that most of the girls had antibodies for the bacterium. That finding only indicated that the girls had been exposed to streptococcus in the past. It said nothing about how they could develop PANDAS symptoms at such a late age and with no history of recurrent movement disorders. It said nothing about how an entire group of teens could get PANDAS at the same time. And it said nothing about why only girls at the high school got sick—friends and acquaintances who were roughly the same age.

Pulitzer Prize–winning journalist Susan Dominus talked to five of the girls and their families. She found that none of the five had good relationships with their fathers. One girl's father had physically abused her when she was fourteen. Another girl was in foster care; another was in the custody of her sister rather than her parents; and yet another was living in poverty on the brink of homelessness. One girl, Katie, developed the symptoms a week after her mother had undergone brain surgery. When Dominus asked Trifiletti about the possibility that the girls' family lives might have contributed to the onset of the symptoms, he said that "he had not had the time to ask them about those kinds of things."[24] Yet the girls got better while taking antibiotics. Perhaps the medicines had a placebo effect. Or perhaps the girls got better when their fathers reached out to them with sympathy. Or when friends, and the community at large, rallied to support them. Or when, as Laszlo Mechtler, MD, the neurologist in Buffalo who treated fifteen of the girls, believes, the media stopped paying so much attention to them.[25]

The stigma of mental illness has a particular effect on people suffering from such unexplained symptoms. If body and mind are separate, then diseases of the body are diseases *only* of the body. Someone with bodily symptoms may therefore not seek or accept psychiatric care (except as a last resort), and unnecessary medical tests can prolong or exacerbate one's problems, and even cause serious complications, as when a doctor mistakes a panic attack for a cardiac condition. An anxious friend of mine, convinced he was experiencing heart failure, received a cardiac catheterization. He refused to even consider the possibility that the symptoms—shortness of breath, dizziness, chest pain, and a tingling sensation in his fingers—had anything to do with recent and dramatic changes in his family situation. The procedure ended up damaging his otherwise normal arteries. More than a year later, his cardiologist—not his internist or a psychiatrist—prescribed him an antidepressant to help him with the anxiety that had precipitated the cardiac symptoms in the first place.

The initial cardiac symptoms were beneficial to him, however. When he was catheterized, his family and friends came to his bedside in the cardiac care unit. In other words, his symptoms were effective in motivating emotional and social support at a time when the solidarity of his family was at risk. Mental health professionals sometimes refer to such psychological or social benefits of a symptom as secondary gain. The primary gain is the symptom that announces the presence of an emotional issue; the secondary gain, precisely because of whatever benefit it confers, reinforces the primary gain.

Secondary gain can also encourage others who witness those benefits to experience similar symptoms, albeit unconsciously, through what psychologists sometimes call social or behavioral contagion. Such contagion is common enough—we unconsciously smile or yawn when someone else smiles or yawns. But it's even more common to mimic the behaviors of people who belong to a group with which we identify because we understand, intuitively, the bodily language they are using. When my undergraduate research assistant and I watched an interview with the girls from Le Roy jerking their arms and heads in a *Today* show segment from 2012, she suddenly said with surprised concern, "Dr. Grinker, my arm just twitched!"

Doctors tread carefully. An internist in Washington, DC, told me, "Unless I know a patient really well, I find it difficult to tell someone their symptoms could be of psychological origin. It's just too insulting to them, like I'm telling them they are faking their symptoms." She suspects that the dramatic increase in so-called gluten sensitivity is a cultural idiom of distress of psychological origin. "Other than people with celiac disease," she said, "pretty much everyone with gluten sensitivity is just treating their stress or anxiety, but going on a gluten-free diet is harmless, a benign intervention, so who am I to stop them? The placebo effect is just so incredibly powerful." The chair of gastroenterology at a nearby university was more circumspect. He said, "We don't want to get burned and find out one day that there really is a biological basis for widespread gluten sensitivity, so I don't confirm it one way or the other. A lot of times, I say 'go for it!' and 'try going gluten-free!' and then they go home and tell their spouse that I diagnosed them with gluten intolerance!"

In addition to gluten sensitivity and chronic Lyme disease, doctors in the United States also see patients who believe they have chronic fungal infections and who therefore ingest large amounts of antifungal medications. Others who believe they have multiple chemical sensitivity disorder (a diagnosis the American Medical Association does not recognize) severely restrict their behavior because of a fear of chemical sensitivities. Chronic fatigue syndrome/myalgic encephalomyelitis (CFS/ME) is another hotly contested condition. People with CFS/ME have extreme fatigue as well as other symptoms such as headaches and the inability to concentrate. But, like Gulf War syndrome, fibromyalgia, and other multisymptom diseases, there is no lab test for a diagnosis of CFS/ME, no one knows what causes it, and any treatment is directed at ameliorating symptoms, not the syndrome itself. Indeed, in terms of the symptoms, none of these conditions are easily distinguished from the others.[26]

Clinical research has shown that the most effective treatment for chronic multisymptom conditions is a combination of exercise, cognitive behavioral therapy (CBT), and psychotherapy, findings that infuriate many people with CFS/ME.[27] Exercise is crucial because a lack of exercise exacerbates fatigue through deconditioning, and it can lead to a wide range of other medical problems. But doctors who recommend exercise or psychiatric treatment for CFS/ME, and some policy makers who fund psychiatric research on the condition, have received death threats.

A simple Google search with the terms "chronic fatigue death threats" yields dozens of articles on the conflict between the patients who say that CFS/ME is a biological disease (possibly a virus, an immune disorder, or a hormonal imbalance) and the doctors who, the patients believe, dismiss their suffering as psychological. The anger is especially salient in the UK where a writer for the *Guardian* newspaper described the outrage back in 1989: "An infection is respectable. It has none of the stigma of a psychologically induced illness, which implies weakness and lack of moral fibre."[28] My argument is that it doesn't necessarily matter whether CFS/ME is biological or psychological. What matters is that the biological model often impedes potentially beneficial psychological interventions.

In 2001, the hostile climate pushed one of the most vilified researchers, Dr. Simon Wessely from Kings College in London, to shift his focus from CFS/ME to military mental health. He told a journalist, "I now go to Iraq and Afghanistan, where I feel a lot safer."[29]

CHAPTER 16

BRIDGING BODY AND MIND IN NEPAL

"To cure the body you must heal the mind."

Nepali saying

Survivors of war carry with them the weight of trauma and loss, memories of bombings, executions, torture, and sexual violence. Children, in particular, have high rates of mental illnesses in places like Nepal, Sierra Leone, Uganda, and El Salvador, where they have been conscripted into military service. In one study in Nepal, more than half of all former child soldiers experienced significant distress such as anxiety and depression, and the mental health burden for children who were never conscripted, but lived through war, was not far behind.[1] The suffering of these child soldiers is often exacerbated by stigma, as their families may reject them for having carried dead bodies, or eaten or cohabited with other castes or ethnic groups. In Nepal, female soldiers are especially stigmatized because their families and communities suspect they slept near men (a cultural violation) or, worse, had sexual intercourse.

However, a humanitarian worker in Nepal told the psychiatrist and anthropologist Brandon Kohrt, an expert in Nepali culture and mental health, that "PTSD does not exist in Nepal." He didn't mean that the symptoms were absent, but that the disease category is largely unknown, and that if anyone did seek or receive care for psychological trauma it would be highly problematic for them, a sign of bad karma. Karma, in both Hinduism (the dominant religion in Nepal) and Buddhism (the second most common religion in Nepal), refers to the deeds of one's past lives that determine prosperity or suffering in the future.[2] Even experiencing a traumatic event can be a sign of poor karma because it suggests that the individual is vulnerable to misfortune.

During the ten-year Nepalese Civil War, between 1996 and 2006, thousands of people in Nepal went missing, more than 150,000 were displaced, 100,000 were tortured, and 14,000 were killed. Providing medical care for victims of war, such as amputees, was difficult enough for the Nepalese, since their status as victims marked them with bad karma, caused by their sins or their family's sins in past lives. How, then, could one reduce stigma and advocate for and deliver psychological care in Nepal? The answer is not through the science of the brain. In Nepal, clinicians are beginning to have success with a creative reworking of native beliefs, a process that requires anthropological research, the dedication of clinicians with enough force of character to become mental health workers in a country where psychiatry is an unpopular and negatively valued profession, and a lot of optimism.

Brandon Kohrt, M.D., Ph.D., looks equal parts nerd and hipster. He is a goateed bespectacled doctor and researcher who wears a Nepali necklace made from a tulsi plant, one of the holiest plants in Hinduism, and has a tattoo on his right forearm. The tattoo is written in classical Mongolian script and reads: "To cure the body you must heal the mind."

Kohrt has dedicated his career to reducing stigma. As a college student in 1996, he spent a year in Nepal and was struck by the almost complete lack of mental health care resources, despite very high rates of trauma. He saw trauma related to ethnic discrimination, gender-based discrimination, environmental disasters, and motor vehicle accidents. That was also the year the Maoist civil war began. One of the causes of the war was widespread disaffection with social inequality, including access to health care. Ordinary citizens had few options for medical services, and even if they had access, the care wasn't the kind available to elites—members of upper castes, the rich, and those with political power. Women had few opportunities to own property or pursue their lives independently, whether through education or work. Kohrt was interested in how these barriers shaped mental health and whether, given the scarcity of mental health care services, there might be beneficial forms of traditional healing.

He spent two months in southern Nepal at a Hindu healing temple. It was the place people would send relatives who couldn't be cured by a shaman or who could not be cared for at home—for example, those patients with what we would call psychotic and manic episodes. The temple housed them in animal sheds, where they slept on floors covered in hay. New arrivals would typically be chained at first to a post cemented in the ground, so they wouldn't run away and also to indicate to the family that their loved one would stay there. After all, many of the families would bring relatives to the temple precisely because they would flee at night, disappearing for days or weeks—sometimes crossing the border into India. Kohrt saw more severe and intractable psychosis at the temple than he would ever have seen in the United States because the temple patients had gone untreated for so long. In the United States, doctors almost never get a chance to see the natural history of psychosis because, by the time a doctor observes a patient, they have already been given some kind of medicine or, if not, will be given a medicine in short order.

At the temple, there were men and women, old people with dementia, young people who had just had their first psychotic break. There were middle-aged people who had ongoing, untreated psychotic disorders, who heard voices telling them they had done awful things. There were women with psychotic depression who had stopped eating or speaking. Kohrt also saw heavy alcohol drinkers, chained to prevent them from looking for liquor, some of whom died from seizures associated with withdrawal. Every day

the temple held religious ceremonies—a process resembling an exorcism—
to eliminate the spirits that caused the problematic behavior.[3] The twenty
or thirty patients at the temple would gather together, tightly packed and
barefoot, all on their knees next to one another moving rhythmically to
the sounds coming from the megaphone, one person playing a harmonium
and another chanting. There would be one individual, the priest, dressed in
white; he carried a long, thin stick and beat certain individuals whom he felt
were being controlled by a spirit, in order to force the spirit out.

One young man in his early twenties, named Ram Bakas, had suddenly
lost his vision, was speaking in bizarre ways, and kept running away from
home. No one would ever figure out how all of these things occurred simultaneously, if they were related to each other psychologically, or whether he
had some kind of acute infection. Six months after he became blind, his
bewildered and frightened family brought him to the temple where, like
every other new admission, Ram Bakas was chained. As each day passed,
Kohrt recalls, Ram Bakas seemed more interactive, was chained for shorter
periods of time, and then eventually began to take part in the ceremonies.
He even became an assistant at the temple, helping guide others through
their own healing process. In fact, he improved so much that the temple
sent him home to his family.

But his family was afraid he was going to bring bad spirits into the
household or become violent. They made him sleep outside in a goat shed.
Neighbors called him crazy. Eventually the family, seriously concerned that
they were being ostracized from their community, sent Ram Bakas back
to the temple. In Kohrt's words, "They were telling the temple: 'We don't
want him.'"

A year later, Kohrt returned to the temple for a visit and asked about
Ram Bakas. He was dead. His illness hadn't come back, but he had died
accidentally while trying to repair one of the megaphones the shamans
used for the healing ceremonies. Though blind, Ram Bakas was on the roof
of the temple and was either electrocuted, or fell from the roof, or both.
Kohrt found Ram Bakas's death deeply upsetting. "I'm not saying that this
type of injury couldn't happen in the community, but he didn't even have

to be there. He was so much better, and he could have been a productive, functioning part of his own community instead of being ostracized and abandoned." Kohrt learned that Ram Bakas's experience wasn't unusual. No matter where a person went for treatment—a temple, a hospital, an asylum—the same thing would happen when they returned home. In fact, many former patients now live and work at the temple because they have nowhere else to go.

What troubled Kohrt the most was that the patients in the temple were brought in by their families, meaning that they actually did have social supports. The psychiatric patients Kohrt sees in the emergency rooms in American hospitals are typically alone, and are often brought in by the police. "You really get a sense of their abandonment—you're lucky if you get one phone number for a relative, and then no one even picks up the phone." During college, Kohrt also had a part-time job with the University of Southern California School of Social Work assisting men with schizophrenia who were living in group homes; most of them had little or no contact with their families. In Nepal, families typically remain highly invested in relatives with serious mental illnesses and seek treatment outside the family—for themselves or a relative—only as a last resort. They want them to get better and don't abandon them quickly. It was probably hard enough for Ram Bakas's family to take him to the temple in the first place but they must have been absolutely terrified of him to justify sending him back, even after he had gotten so much healthier. This is what made Kohrt so upset and inspired him to ask where that fear came from and whether there was anything anyone could do to reduce it.

When Kohrt finished that first year in Nepal, he spent three months in Japan where he also found a pronounced fear of mental illness and mental health treatment. Seeing a very high-income country and an incredibly low-income country both stigmatize mental illness convinced him to pursue a career in mental health. During graduate school at Emory University in 2006, he returned to Nepal for a period of eighteen months to study former child soldiers who fought for the Maoist People's Liberation Army during the Nepalese Civil War. Called "the People's War" in Nepal, the armed struggle was an agrarian revolt against the Nepali state with the goal of abolishing the monarchy and the social and economic injustice associated with it. Thousands died during the war, the majority at the hands of the government. After the war, survivors were haunted by the atrocities they had witnessed. Some saw friends and relatives die, others were captured and imprisoned.

Surprisingly, Kohrt said, "The story that came up again and again, especially among girls who had been child soldiers for the Maoists, was 'my life was better when I was a soldier than it is now that I'm back home.'" They were not trafficked, nor did they report sexual abuse by their own army; in fact, they told Kohrt that the Maoists protected them from sexual violence, which was one of the benefits of joining up. Kohrt continued, "When they came back home, that's where I really saw stigma."

One woman, whom I will call Asha, was one of two children in a poor, low-caste household. She loved school and studied hard. But when she was twelve, her parents, unable to afford school fees for two children, decided to educate her younger brother and keep her at home, despite the fact that he seemed uninterested in school. A year later, Maoist women came to town looking for recruits. They convinced Asha to flee her family and join the war, assuring her that in the army she would be able to fight for women's freedoms. For one year, she traveled the country, participating in women's rights activities, but also witnessing violence. One day, Asha was accompanying female commanders near her hometown and asked for permission to visit her parents and brother. Her family promptly told her she could not return to the Maoists and that it was imperative she marry someone immediately. Asha refused, but her panicked mother acted quickly and found a twenty-two-year-old man in a nearby village who, for reasons Kohrt does not know, was having difficulty finding a wife.

Asha never went back to the Maoists. She was forced to marry, and her parents hid the fact that she had been a soldier. But it didn't take long for her new husband's family to find out. "And when they did," Kohrt said, "they began to not only disrespect her but to treat her like an animal." She endured the mental torture for months before she attempted suicide. Her father-in-law discovered her hanging by a rope from the ceiling but still alive, gasping for air. He cut her down, handed her the rope, told her she was not welcome in their house, and said, "Go home to your parents' house and kill yourself there."

Asha's parents said she wasn't welcome there either but reluctantly let her occupy a bedroom. They tolerated her presence in a room in the house only as long as she kept her distance, never left the house, and never joined in any household chores. Asha told Kohrt, "They thought I was weak and useless, just a burden; I wasn't even allowed outside to get firewood." Boys would come by her window to mock her, or knock on it in the middle of the night just to disturb her sleep. Her brother ignored her. She had a roof over her head but was, for all intents and purposes, homeless.

Concerned UNICEF staff in the village tried to help. They invited Asha to come to a singing club and to a dancing club, and they offered her training to become a seamstress. But she was in effect a prisoner in the house and could rarely participate. UNICEF also hired a counselor from the organization Kohrt worked with, the Transcultural Psychosocial Organization (TPO Nepal), to go by the house and talk with her for several hours a week. A year or so later, Asha agreed to be recruited, illegally, as a domestic worker in Saudi Arabia. For another year, she suffered abuse there, too, but had an income and sent most of it back for her mother to save for her. When she finally returned home from Saudi Arabia, she discovered that her mother had run away with her boyfriend, along with all the money.

Asha was now more marginalized than ever, accepted by no one, with seemingly no way to become part of society. There were other female child soldiers who had similar experiences, but their suffering was often mitigated by social supports, such as loving parents who didn't steal their money, or even distant relatives who opened their homes to them. But Asha had none of this. She had depression and psychotic symptoms, as well as the symptoms of PTSD. And the sicker she became, the more isolated she was. She told Kohrt, "The only time I was treated as a human being was when I was a soldier in the Maoist army." She may have seen bombs and blood but at least she felt as if she was a part of something. As another young woman put it, "Now we just feel like we're part of nothing."

The last time Kohrt saw Asha she was still living in her old room, though shunned by her father, her brother, and her neighbors.

When he started studying anthropology, Kohrt recognized that there were plenty of global health workers who had devoted their professional lives to researching and treating HIV/AIDS, tuberculosis, and other infectious illnesses. Prominent scholars were examining how culture shapes the experience of mental illness and the construction of psychological knowledge. But Kohrt didn't know anyone who was combining anthropology and psychiatry in order to develop new approaches to reduce the stigma of mental illness. His inspiration came from a small group of Dutch mental health professionals who argued that psychological well-being could not be explained by the presence or absence of a single traumatic event, but had to be understood as part of the total social system in which one lives, including the economy, politics, and gender, among other factors.

The Dutch group's perspective contrasted with that of most of the humanitarian workers Kohrt met. "Again and again," he said, "I encountered this view that everything was great *before* a disaster. It's this romanticizing of populations, often in low- and middle-income countries, and especially in idyllic places like Nepal, where everybody assumes that before this earthquake happened, before that tsunami hit, before that war, everybody was doing just fine." In 2012, Kohrt published the results of a study of depression and anxiety in which he looked at the same individuals before and after the Maoist war. War did increase the prevalence of anxiety, but not depression. In fact, there were high rates of depression *before* people had any exposure to conflict, with little increase in prevalence after exposure. Depression was a product not of war but of multiple preexisting risk factors, such as being a woman in a heavily patriarchal society, being poor, being a member of a low caste, and having little access to education and health care—the connected and cascading effects social scientists sometimes call "intersectionality." Maoists firmly believed that fighting the government in power would be psychologically liberating. But not a single mental illness decreased in prevalence in any demographic group.[4]

Nonetheless, clinicians and policy makers often work as if context is irrelevant to diagnosis, treatment, and treatment outcomes. For if mental illnesses are biologically based, then it is assumed they are universal and can be treated in the same way everywhere. This view, spearheaded by the WHO and publicized by the UK's premier medical journal, the *Lancet*, pits stigma against science. In 160 pages of text, published in 2001, the WHO used the word "stigma" seventy-three times in a document that stated: "As the world's leading public health agency, WHO has one, and only one option—to ensure that ours will be the last generation that allows shame and stigma to rule over science and reason."[5] Despite the fact that the WHO advocates for community participation in mental health care, the organization presents itself as a champion of science over indigenous and superstitious beliefs. With this study, the WHO implied that mental illnesses are biological entities that affect everyone in the same way regardless of class, race, and gender, and as a result, they shrouded the long-term and deeply rooted political reasons for suffering.[6]

Of course, every community has barriers to mental health care. In highly resourced countries with robust medical and scientific infrastructures (such as France, Argentina, the United States, and Japan), less than 25 percent of people with mental illnesses receive "minimally adequate care."[7] Moreover, most mental health care is provided in non–mental health care settings, like primary care. That proportion of people who receive minimally adequate care drops to 11.4 percent in upper-middle-income countries (such as Romania, Mexico, and Lebanon) and 3.7 percent (that's one in twenty-seven people) in lower-middle-income countries (such as Peru, Nigeria, and Iraq).[8] But getting to care won't solve everything. It's not as if someone starts getting treatment and then everything is fine, and stigma is gone. In addition to dealing with the social marginalization, bullying, violence, and discrimination, there is also stigma within the health care system, as clinicians themselves may be frightened by people with mental illnesses, consider them untreatable, and neglect patients' physical health needs as well.

In Chitwan district, a rural area in southwestern Nepal just north of the Indian border, Kohrt and his colleagues carried out a study to see whether scientific education and training about mental health reduced health-care workers' tendency to stigmatize. First, they assembled two groups of primary-care health workers from the same locale and administered standardized surveys that had been used in a number of countries to measure stigma. They included questions about public and clinical views of mental illness, causal explanations, knowledge, and prejudice. The completed surveys indicated high levels of health-care workers' tendency to stigmatize in both groups of primary-care workers. Neither group wanted people with serious mental illnesses to come to their facility for health care. They said there were no treatments they could provide, and they were afraid the patients would be violent. They believed people with serious mental illnesses should be confined in psychiatric institutions.

Kohrt then gave both groups of health care workers the WHO's Mental Health Gap Action Programme (mhGAP) training. This is a straightforward guide to diagnosis and care for health workers who do not have training in psychiatry or psychology. In sum, the two groups had the same knowledge, the same curriculum, and the same backgrounds. But Kohrt then gave only one of these groups an extra training module that involved introducing the health care workers to patients and former patients who had experienced their own mental illnesses. They told the workers their stories of suffering, their resilience, and the degree to which they recovered. Their family members came and spoke too.

Immediately afterward, Kohrt readministered the same surveys he had given before the training and then again eighteen months later. During that time, the group that was exposed to the stories diagnosed a greater proportion of clinic patients with mental illnesses. And when Kohrt looked at the symptoms described in the patient records, he saw that most of the time these primary-care doctors were giving diagnoses and treatments consistent with what the trained Nepali mental health specialists recommended. In the group of primary-care doctors that received just the standard training, but without exposure to the patients' stories, about two-thirds of the diagnoses and treatments were inconsistent with those the specialists recommended because the doctors didn't know what symptoms they were looking for. Reflecting on the efforts of American experts to ameliorate stigma by framing mental illness in terms of biological knowledge, Kohrt said, "We didn't change any of the framing of the illnesses, and we didn't provide them any additional biological knowledge. More people got care, and more people got better, not because the health care workers had more scientific knowledge but because they had a humanistic conversation with people." In fact, he said, in Ethiopia, India, Nepal, and South Africa, the only evidence that the standard WHO trainings had any effect on stigma suggests that they exacerbated it. He said, "Health care workers in India, for example, who learned more about psychosis from the mhGAP trainings were more likely to think people with psychosis were dangerous."

Kohrt attributes the success of his new approach to proximity. This is the same phenomenon that, in the United States, has helped to reduce racial discrimination in schools and the military, and to improve the training of police officers who interact with seriously mentally ill people. "Knowledge alone," he said, "doesn't get us where we need to go. If we spend time with people who are different from ourselves, gradually over time we come to see them as human beings and find similar characteristics." The key is challenging a preconception with a new vision, one shaped by having interacted in the comfortable setting of a training program.

Kohrt is also working on developing treatment strategies that incorporate local beliefs. When he first went to Nepal, Kohrt thought that the Cartesian split between body and mind would be absent, that he'd see the sort of unity of body and mind advocated by so many Asian healing movements. He was already familiar with the work of neuroscientists, like Antonio Damasio, who were dismantling Descartes, showing in biological terms how emotions act on the body and how the body in turn acts on both thought and behavior.[9] Anthropologists had long shown that in most of the world the body and mind are not separate entities, that emotional pain is much more commonly articulated through the body, and that it thus makes little sense to even attempt to distinguish between emotional and bodily symptoms.[10] Health is a problem of the whole, such as the interdependence of all the organs of the body, or the balance of yin and yang. In Nepal, Kohrt discovered that he couldn't pose the simple question of whether body and mind were separate or united. It was more complicated than that.

In medical clinics in Nepal, patients who are depressed don't say "I feel worthless" or "my life has no meaning." They say they have aches and pains, numbing, tingling, and burning sensations in their hands and feet—what doctors call paresthesia and what Nepalese call *jhamjham*. Patients with depression also complain of *gastrik* (dyspepsia or indigestion). Nepali psychiatrist Rishav Koirala told me that most patients with mental illnesses— severe and mild— "ping-pong" from clinic to clinic, and doctor to doctor, in search of a cure for their physical pain, even selling land to pay for it. "They suffer for years sometimes, and end up in psychiatry only at the end."

In southern Nepal, Kohrt found that Nepalese divide the *body* into several parts: the heart-mind (*maan*), the brain-mind (*dimaag*), the physical body (*jiu*), the spirit of a person (*saato*), and social status (*ijjat*). The relationship between the heart-mind (maan) and the brain-mind (dimaag) is perhaps the most important for understanding stigma. Nepalese use the heart-mind as a noun to mean an individual's intentions, feelings, and opinions in both everyday and clinical conversation, as well as one's worries, mood, and memories. Thus it is not you, the reader, who wants to read a book on the history of psychiatry, it is your heart-mind. As a result, a lot of Nepali language is in the passive voice. If someone says they like football, they actually say, "Football is at the top of my heart-mind." If someone feels depressed, he says, "My heart-mind is sad." In Nepali, even saying something as basic as "I want to go" is formulated as "My heart-mind is struck by going." The heart-mind can also result in both physical and emotional illness since long-term hopes and dreams as well as bad memories can be part of it, like a scar or a sore on the heart-mind. Similar words, deriving from the same Sanskrit root (*manas*), are used throughout the world to refer to "thinking" (for example, the Greek *menos*, the Latin *mens*, the Bengali *mon*, and the English *mind*).[11]

Dimaag specifically refers to intentions to behave in ways that conform to social expectations. It represents the thoughts, decision making, and rationality that don't violate the community's rules. If maan represents what you *want* to do, dimaag represents what you *should* do. To some extent, dimaag is like Freud's concepts of the ego and superego condensed into one, while maan resembles the id. Dimaag is the sense of self (the ego) and conscience (the superego) that exercises control over the heart's desires. As Kohrt explained it to me, "The heart-mind is what makes you *you*, but the brain-mind is what allows you to exist in society." An impairment in dimaag is thus evidence of a mental illness, like someone who is addicted to alcohol because his dimaag cannot control the impulse to drink. A broken dimaag is like the Western model of the broken brain, but it is even more stigmatizing because someone with a broken dimaag will not function properly as a social being, and might even be seen as potentially violent.

Kohrt recounts the words of a doctor in Nepal who said that even when he does treat someone for anxiety or depression, he won't call it anxiety or depression. "When the patient hears 'mental disease,' they 'see it as the end of the world.'"[12] Someone with a serious mental illness might be prevented from marrying, be fired from a job, or be banished from the family; spouses will begin to contemplate divorce. Dimaag causes great consternation and shame, including the loss of honor and status—ijjat—that aspect of the social self that is enhanced or damaged by the brain-mind. Kohrt said, "In the US, we've had the decade of the brain, the emergence of genetic thinking about mental illness, we've told everyone that mental illness isn't caused by bad character or failing, but none of this seems to have changed stigma very much." One solution, he says, is to emphasize the role of the heart in improving mental health and social functioning: "In Nepal, when we approach mental illness through the heart-mind rather than just the brain, people are more likely to open up, they want to do the therapy, they are engaged with that process."

Talking about the heart also has the potential to empower patients to actively participate in their own care. For example, Kohrt asks people who are receiving mental health care to take photographs that symbolize recovery from mental illness and then to talk about the photographs with health workers.[13] They tend not to take pictures of people who are smiling, enjoying themselves, or looking healthy. They take pictures of goats, so many pictures of goats that Kohrt and his colleagues call such images "the goat sign." If people take pictures of a goat, it suggests they have recovered to the point of being able to raise goats. The patients are not asking to be respected because they are in treatment, or because they deserve respect as a human being. They are asking to be respected because they are productive and contributing to their families. Stigma declines for such individuals not because they fit into a nonstigmatized disease framework but because they fit into their economy and society.

Because everyone has a heart-mind, the doctor can ask any patient what is going on inside it. Asking a new patient about their brain-mind, however, might end the therapeutic relationship immediately. No one would want to see a doctor about the brain-mind unless their life was in a shambles. After the ten-year civil war, there were clinics to which few people would ever come, because they advertised themselves as clinics for PTSD, which was translated into Nepali as the stigmatized phrase "mental shock," a shock to the brain-mind. Then came the 2015 earthquake, killing thousands and displacing more. Health care workers presumed there would be many cases of PTSD but did not know how to make mental health care more attractive.

Nepali psychiatrist Rishav Koirala had just graduated from medical school and was one of only a few medical students interested in psychiatry, since many viewed it as a low-status specialty. His medical school in Nepal did not even offer a psychiatry rotation. But Koirala is a free spirit, as interested in European philosophy and Jim Morrison and the Doors as he is in science, and he taught himself psychiatry. The World Health Organization heard about this young doctor who was giving patients extended time rather than the few minutes it takes to write a prescription and soon tapped him as a mental health coordinator for the earthquake response.

It quickly became clear to both Kohrt and Koirala that many Nepali counselors believed that people with PTSD were predisposed to commit murder or suicide. So they framed psychological treatment in terms of sores and scars on the heart-mind. It wasn't a stretch for the two psychiatrists to depict PTSD as a problem of the heart-mind rather than the brain-mind since the heart-mind is the locus of memory and feeling. They knew they couldn't ignore the existence of the brain-mind, but they could explain treatment as a method to strengthen it. Kohrt said, "We'd say we want to help you strengthen your body, including your brain-mind, so that when you have distress in your heart-mind you are better able to manage it—in other words, your brain is fine, but we want to train it to have more power of the heart-mind."

Koirala doesn't completely agree with Kohrt's ideas about strengthening the brain. Koirala tends to dispense with the typical heart and brain distinction. Instead, when he sees patients he wants to talk almost entirely about the heart. He tells his patients that their distress has little to do with the brain. "Why should I ever frighten people by talking about the brain and cognitive capacity?" While so many foreign public health workers ask how to translate Nepali concepts into biological or brain-based terms, or how to eliminate Nepali concepts altogether in favor of Western scientific ones, Koirala is interested in refashioning preexisting Nepali illness models. He says that within every person there are two hearts, an inside heart (*bhitri maan*) and an outside heart (*bahiri maan*). We are all aware of our outside heart because it comprises all the emotions and physical symptoms that we feel and that others can observe. There is, however, also an inside heart, a heart that is hidden from our awareness; it is therefore more powerful than the outside heart. It produces bodily symptoms even though the patient is largely unaware of it. When I told Koirala that his idea of an inner and outer heart sounded Freudian to me, he shouted back: "Exactly! One is conscious, and one is unconscious!"

The need to avoid talk of the brain was made clear to Koirala when he set up a temporary "health camp" in a remote area where there were no health-care services. "The first time we set it up," he said, "I relented and let the counselors call it a 'mental' health camp, using the word dimaag. No one came." Some months later, he set it up again and this time the counselors agreed to call it a camp for "chronic headaches." Koirala remembers that "there was a nice queue of patients, and everyone had depression and anxiety! No one thought they had a mental illness. But, you know what? We treated them for depression and anxiety and they got better."

When he spoke to the patients at the temporary clinic, he used long-standing Nepali phrases—"phrases that have been around for centuries, like 'headache due to stress' and 'stomach burn due to stress.'" He also made people feel more comfortable exploring the relation between the heart and their bodily pain by talking to them about the phantom limb, a phenomenon that, unfortunately, too many Nepali citizens know about. "I tell them that their physical symptoms of psychiatric distress are real, even though they come from the heart, just like when someone feels there is a limb there, even though it's been amputated. I also tell them that treatment takes time."

Koirala doesn't seem to mind taking time. He travels to remote villages to see just one or two people if he thinks he can help. In the far western region of Nepal, about a five-hour bus ride from the city of Pyuthan, plus an extra ninety-minute motorcycle ride through makeshift lanes in agricultural fields, there are people tied up or with their feet bound. He showed me a picture of a wooden device into which a person's foot is inserted and then locked with a nail above the ankle so the foot cannot come out. One man I'll call Imay, in his mid-thirties, had been in restraints for eighteen years. Imay had married in his teens, before his psychotic break, and even in restraints had enough of a sexual life with his wife to father two children. His family bathed him, fed him, and provided shelter when the weather was poor. "There were marks on his body, scars from skin infections, and his hair was cut but not like in a proper sense like a gentleman." He had been taken to faith healers, but never to a doctor or a health assistant. That kind of care was simply too far away. The family told Koirala the man was attached to the device for his own safety, that without it he'd run away or jump off a cliff.

The family had not asked for help. A neighbor told Koirala that he thought Imay should see a doctor and brought him to the hillock where he lived. The family welcomed Koirala and gave him some cucumber as a treat.

He started Imay on the antipsychotic medicine risperidone. A few months later, Imay came to Pyuthan. "He was well-dressed and we talked—it was like he was a totally different person—and the idea that someone eighteen years in captivity could recover like this was remarkable. I don't know how things were later, but two years later when I returned to Pyuthan he didn't show up at the clinic."

There have been some notable advances. A girl who used to walk naked in the streets in Pyuthan, wandering aimlessly and surviving only on scraps of food passersby gave her, has become a patient at the hospital, at this point with great success on antipsychotic medicines. The fact that she was so well known in the city heightened awareness of the potential benefits of psychiatric care. Celebrities in Nepal are still reluctant to disclose their struggles, and patients who have been treated successfully seldom recommend a psychiatrist to someone for fear of revealing their own illness or insulting the person they are talking to. But, for Koirala's part, he says he refuses to be discouraged, or to become a part of the brain drain in Nepal, with the best medical students leaving for work in Scandinavia, Australia, or elsewhere. He knows it is an uphill fight, but he is satisfied for now with the short-term results of caring for people who, like Imay, endure their pain for so many years untreated. He hopes to become a pioneer in psychiatry in Nepal and likes to quote Milton's *Paradise Lost* in jest: he'd rather reign in hell than serve in heaven. He said he feels like he could start a psychiatric revolution in Nepal by redefining the symptoms of mental illness in local idioms, and thus reducing stigma. But he's a pragmatist as well as a dreamer. "Nepal is not the kind of place," he said, "where you can survive only on optimism."

CHAPTER 17

THE DIGNITY OF RISK

"You can ask for help here. This isn't a place where we value independence."

Restaurant server to disability rights
activist Sunaura Taylor, Philadelphia

On a hot summer night in January 2013, Australian cybersecurity specialist Michael Fieldhouse was at home in Melbourne entertaining friends. One couple brought along their autistic son, Andrew. A teenager, Andrew is nonspeaking with significant intellectual disabilities, "just the kind of person," Fieldhouse said, "so many people call lower-functioning or, worse, write off from society." Outside of the house, there is a small Japanese pond surrounded by pebbles. Fieldhouse watched Andrew grab a large pile of pebbles and begin to drop them into the pond. "The more I watched, the more it seemed to me that he was dropping the pebbles at a consistent, regular rate." And so, Fieldhouse told me, "I timed him, and he was indeed dropping them at perfect intervals, and continued to do it through the evening."

Fieldhouse said, "It was my epiphany. I thought about how someone who seemed so disabled could do something so precise and repetitive."

Fieldhouse is the director of emerging businesses and cybersecurity at the large IT services company DXC Technology, an offshoot of Hewlett-Packard and the corporate services company CSC. After that evening, he spent the next few months rethinking his definitions of talent and skill, reading everything he could on autism. He learned that many people with autism have profound intellectual disabilities, are nonspeaking, self-injurious, and need lifelong care; that technologies like tablets, computers, and other electronic devices, as well as social media and online chat groups, have made it possible for many autistic people to become more communicative and socially active; and that a segment of the autistic population had talents that some employers were beginning to appreciate, features of autism that were previously disabling but are now enabling, such as extraordinary memory for details about narrow topics, and the ability to detect visual and mathematical patterns.

Such skills are highly advantageous for computer programming, software development, and other areas of basic science. For this reason, the well-known author, autism self-advocate, and animal science expert Temple Grandin once described NASA as the largest sheltered workshop in the country. Climate change activist Greta Thunberg self-identifies as autistic and says that autism is her "superpower." Writer Steve Silberman wonders if autistic people are responsible for more than we ever imagined: "For all we know, the first tools on earth might have been developed by a loner sitting at the back of the cave, chipping at thousands of rocks to find the one that made the sharpest spear, while the neurotypicals chattered away in the firelight."[1]

Fieldhouse had been talking to executives who shared with him the same human resources problem: a shortage of employees capable of working on topics like artificial intelligence, pattern recognition, mechanical reasoning, and the organization of large data sets. Sure, DXC was constantly hiring new employees, but there was high turnover, not only at DXC but also in similar businesses, all competing with one another for the same labor pool. "I spoke with colleagues at places like Marks and Spencer, the food company in England, mining executives from BHK in Canada looking for people with good visualization skills, and the leaders at Freddie Mac, and we all agreed that the demand and supply equations were out of whack in some talent pools, especially those we needed at DXC." Reflecting on Andrew, Fieldhouse asked himself whether people with autism might have those talents but, because of their autism, never apply for jobs or, if they did, never make it past the first round of applications. Why not give people a chance, even the chance to fail?

Then he learned something remarkable from one of his clients, the Israeli Defense Forces (IDF), about its efforts to include people with disabilities. The IDF is the conscript army in which all civilians over the age of eighteen, male and female, must serve for three years. Orthodox Jews and non-Druze Arab citizens are granted exemptions, if they wish, but otherwise the vast majority of exemptions are for young men and women with serious illnesses, autism, intellectual disabilities, and other developmental disorders. Not serving in the military can be very stigmatizing, since it's a rite of passage for Israeli youth. When young people meet, one of the first questions they ask each other is where they completed their service. People who do not complete their service may feel inadequate—as if they are not full citizens—and will be susceptible to negative social judgments. Parents also find it emotionally difficult to deal with a child's military exemption.[2] Just as importantly, the IDF—considered "the people's army"—is one of the only contexts in which people who might rarely interact—members of different ethnic groups or religious backgrounds, for example—work or live together. IDF members also work on numerous civilian projects, further enhancing inclusiveness and public awareness of diversity.

For many decades, the IDF automatically sent all students with a classification of "autism" a letter of exemption. But in 2007, the IDF, in cooperation with a civilian advocacy organization for children with intellectual disabilities, and a branch of the Israeli government that oversees intellectual disabilities and developmental disorders, launched the "Equal in Uniform" program, or EiU. The program trains and then admits young men and women with mild to moderate intellectual disabilities into a host of different roles (although participants in the program do not live on military bases, and they have the right to leave the service at any time if they wish). These roles include cleaning, warehouse stocking, and visual intelligence (such as satellite image analysis and scanning surveillance photos in real time). The military believes, and is supported by the experts, that many people with ASD and other developmental disabilities have useful and untapped skills, and that some have special sensory abilities, including discriminating sounds that others cannot, and detecting visual patterns.

In Unit 9900, the army's visual intelligence unit, for example, dozens of autistic young adults now watch computer screens looking at high-resolution images for anything suspicious. These men (to date only one woman has participated) applied specifically to the program, and those who were admitted received training in satellite-image analysis at Ono Academic College in central Israel while at the same time working with counselors on how to negotiate the social and logistical aspects of the job. If they complete the training successfully, they enlist officially in the military. Parents of children with developmental disabilities are especially eager to have them serve in the military because of the impending loss of special-needs services at the age of twenty-one. In the United States, parents sometimes call this "dropping off the radar" since it's much harder to find supports for adults than for children; in Israel it's called "Bloody 21."[3]

Other similar programs have since been developed for high school graduates, each of which helps the potential conscript to identify his or her comparative advantage. Yossi Kahan, who cofounded the program called "Special in Uniform," says his aim is to challenge overprotection. "Parents of children with special needs," he said, "tend to protect their children so they don't have the same opportunities to do things on their own."[4] Special in Uniform employs therapists, social workers, and special educators to train people with physical and intellectual disabilities, including Down syndrome, to navigate public spaces; they train them first as volunteers and then provide support to them as paid soldiers.

If the Israeli military can find satellite imagery analysts from a pool of people with an autism classification, Michael Fieldhouse asked himself, why couldn't he find good workers too, workers who might be loyal to a company that gave them an opportunity? In January 2014, Fieldhouse started a recruitment program to supplement what he calls their typical "graduate" recruiting. Graduate recruiting targets people who have undergraduate or graduate degrees in computer science, engineering, and related disciplines. The autism program, however, recruits only half of its workers from universities and the other half from Australian "polytechnical" schools (community colleges and vocational schools), and it does not discriminate in hiring based on whether someone has a degree in a computer-related field. "We go to the autism community—to advocacy groups, for example—and say that we are looking for autistic adults who are interested in computers, but not necessarily people with a track record yet, because we can train them ourselves," he said. "We have hired people on our cyber-teams who took courses in nursing, history, psychology, etc." Autistic employees, Fieldhouse says, are particularly good at finding irregularities in data that might indicate fraud, and at detecting computer intrusions by hackers.

Fieldhouse is pleased with the retention of workers. In the last three years, 76 percent of employees hired through graduate recruitment have remained at DXC, but in the last five years, 92 percent of the autistic employees have remained. When I met with Fieldhouse, there were more than one hundred autistic employees, mostly male (which Fieldhouse thinks may be the result of the higher prevalence of autism in boys). Perhaps most rewarding for Fieldhouse, the benefits of the autism program have extended to mental illnesses in general. The major challenge in his workplace, he says, isn't autism per se, or training the managers about autism, but rather mental illnesses that may or may not be associated with autism. "There are so many conditions," he said, "and that's our number-one issue—anxiety, depression, sleep disorders, even suicidal thoughts, but dealing with all these comorbidities in autism has been a great benefit for us, for our company as a whole." The spirit of support for these autistic workers generalized to the rest of the company. For example, managers recently helped a nonautistic transgender employee with PTSD to find a placement that didn't trigger her anxiety; another nonautistic employee was cutting herself and agreed to have her manager at DXC talk to her therapist to find out how he could be supportive to her at work.

"The elephant in the room for us was mental health," Fieldhouse added. Managers at DXC are now more comfortable talking about mental illnesses, which seems appropriate for what Fieldhouse calls a "cognitive-based" company. "If you are in the construction business, it's common for laborers to see chiropractors. If you are in an industry that depends on thinking, reasoning, and learning, it should be common for people to seek mental health care." Mental health is now a regular topic in group meetings for all employees, and just a month before Fieldhouse and I met in Washington, an employee came to see him about difficulties at work related to menopause. She told Fieldhouse she was having trouble sleeping, that she was leaving her workstation frequently to go to the bathroom, and that "she just wasn't herself." Fieldhouse said, "What an amazing thing! Twenty years ago, do you think a woman in business would call attention to herself as a woman, and an aging woman, something that is of course just natural hormonal changes in life, but which used to be unspoken?"

DXC and many other corporations with similar programs do not see this new openness to inclusion and support of workplace diversity as a rejection of the capitalist sink-or-swim ideology. Nor do they see their role as a replacement for government services or interventions. Yet as governments reduce welfare expenditures, we are witnessing increasingly strong advocacy for human rights and equality. For example, courts throughout the world are expanding the rights of people with disabilities, not seeking to advance socialism or state welfare but to eradicate the inequalities and injustices that accompany capitalism—a process that some scholars now call the "third way" between socialism and capitalism.[5] This advocacy includes attention to the concerns raised long ago by Marx and Engels about how capitalist economies insult the bodies of manual laborers and the poor through disease, deformity, and disability. What's more, extended families are becoming more important in capitalism as the institution that not only produces workers but also supports them even after they reach the age of supposed independence.

Inclusive employment, the decline of stigma, mental health awareness, secured maternity and paternity leaves in the United States, and more may be evidence of something the great economic theorist and critic of capitalism Karl Polanyi once predicted. In the 1950s, Polanyi said he was not worried that the growth of capitalism would destroy social supports. He believed that even the most conservative capitalists would always fight against the separation of society and economy. Where there is a desire for government deregulation, he said, there will also be a desire for government to give economies some stability and predictability; where there is a desire for laissez-faire economics—to let the market do whatever it will do—humans will also seek to influence the economy, whether through their governments (like tariffs, monetary policy, or war) or through social movements (like civil, disability, and workers' rights).[6] For example, some kinds of legislation can, paradoxically, empower individuals and individualism while still enforcing the obligations of both the state and the marketplace to take care of people in need—such as the Children Act 1989 in the UK, which gives children rights beyond those conferred on them by their families. In other words, there can be countermeasures against capitalism that still support capitalism's ideological framework.

For autism researcher Bonnie Evans, the dramatic rise in autism diagnoses in the UK occurred, not surprisingly, under the regime of conservative UK prime minister Margaret Thatcher, who supported a retrenchment of government services. "The diagnosis," Evans says, "protected certain people from the mass demolition of social welfare systems in the 1980s."[7] Without the diagnosis, someone might have been simply unemployed; with the diagnosis, a person had rights to services and also the opportunity to establish a new identity as autistic. Capitalism, in her view, thus produced the category of autism as we know it today. In turn, capitalism then also changed autism into a spectrum and a social identity as a defense against capitalism's negative effects.

Similarly, the Independent Living Movement (ILM), begun in California during the 1960s to promote the independence of people with disabilities, was simultaneously a civil rights advance for the disabled and a movement grounded in the rights for autonomy, self-determination, and the free-market ideology of capitalism.[8] The language of the movement directly influenced the United Nations Convention on the Rights of Persons with Disabilities, which states that its goal is "to enable persons with disabilities to live independently." Though motivated by a foundational commitment to self-determination, at times the language of the ILM has been co-opted to also mean economic self-sufficiency. On the one hand, few would argue against expanding opportunities for meaningful work, a sense of purpose, and integration into community life for all people with disabilities. The more people are able to gain access to the same kinds of practices open to people without disabilities, the easier it will be to reduce stigma. On the other hand, this expectation suggests that a meaningful life is impossible for someone who is not economically productive or able to live on their own, a repetition of the capitalist ideals responsible for the stigma of mental illness in the first place, and a far cry from the good intentions of the activists who catalyzed the movement.

If capitalism created new kinds of people to be excluded, like the disabled and the mentally ill, then under new historical conditions capitalism can also facilitate inclusion. Of course, it is true that people with disabilities are more likely to be poor than people without disabilities.[9] It is also true that more people with disabilities are unemployed than those without disabilities.[10] In some US states, the combined unemployment rates for people with serious mental illnesses is as high as 90 percent. But inclusion and exclusion are dynamic processes. Remember that during World War II, nearly 500,000 people with disabilities participated in the British labor force, only to be marginalized after the war.[11] While paid employment for people with disabilities, such as autism, remains a serious challenge, in most countries today people have unprecedented access to education, transportation, the built environment, and information. Companies are initiating novel programs, such as confidential employee assistance with round-the-clock support, and on-site classes such as meditation, yoga, and stress reduction. Recognizing that people with developmental disabilities who have either paid or unpaid work in high school have better employment outcomes, high schools are offering new work programs and facilitating post–high school "supported employment," in which people receive government-funded support on the job so that they can succeed in inclusive work settings.[12]

The vast majority of businesses in the United States do not have disability-targeted recruiting methods or supported employment,[13] but many of the companies that have invested substantial efforts in this direction are large and influential, and include Walgreens, Bank of America, Marriott, and JPMorgan Chase. In these settings, job coaches help the new employee acclimate to the job and check in frequently to troubleshoot. Someone with autism may have difficulty with transitions from one task to another, or understanding how to be flexible, as when a manager requests that the employee arrive earlier or stay later on a particular day. The coach helps the person understand the rules of the workplace, many of which are unstated or become clear only over the course of several weeks or months. For the staff, the coach helps managers and coworkers make accommodations that will facilitate success.

The overall strategy, often called "supported employment," began in the mid-1980s but has only flourished recently. It reverses the long-standing "train and place" process. Instead of first providing general training followed by employment, the new approach, which might be termed "train in place," offers employment first followed by on-the-job training and ongoing support for that particular job.[14] For one autistic woman I know who does the tedious work of counting blood cells in a hematology lab in Washington, DC, one of the accommodations is a greater number of breaks, though of shorter duration, than other workers have. During these breaks, she is allowed to stand in a room by herself and spin. The spinning relieves her stress and makes it possible for her to return to focused work.

In April 2017, fifty large corporations, including JPMorgan, Ford Motor Company, Ernst & Young, and numerous high-tech businesses, met in Silicon Valley to talk about ways to hire more adults with autism. The German software company SAP hosted the event and talked about how over the past five years it had hired 128 people on the autism spectrum and has a longer-term goal of having 1 percent (650 workers) of its total workforce occupied by people with autism. The autistic workers SAP hired say that they have benefited socially more than anything else; many of these young men and women lived with their parents, but without work they were isolated from a wider social network. The accommodations these companies offer include activities during break times—such as trampolines and ping-pong, video games, and couches for occasional naps—as well as light bulbs that don't bother people who are hypersensitive to light.

James Mahoney directs the Autism at Work Program at JPMorgan Chase. When I visited him in New York, he was eager to tell me that his initiative, which began in 2015, was not born of compassion and generosity. "We never said, 'let's do the right thing and be charitable.'" For Mahoney, fighting stigma certainly has nothing to do with pity, which he thinks is stigma clothed as compassion. "We never said we had jobs for people on the autism spectrum. . . . We said, 'we want talented people and maybe there is a group of talented people we haven't been hiring.'" For both Fieldhouse and Mahoney, the "normalization" of autism in the economy is a response to the labor market.

The problem, as Mahoney describes it, is that "capable people on the autism spectrum often get shut down because of the interview process; traditional interviews amplify the deficits of autism but not what the autistic person is actually good at." For example, an interviewer might write that the applicant was socially awkward, made poor eye contact, and gave long and rambling answers, and then end the interview without ever discovering that the person is one of the best Java coders in the city. Inspired by the Danish company Specialisterne, which was founded specifically in order to hire autistic software engineers, Mahoney and his colleagues wanted to create a separate autism recruiting track. So they partnered with a technology company in Delaware that had long-standing relationships with vocational rehabilitation centers.

First, they developed a new application process in which applicants answered skill-based questions provided by email. "There is a tendency to hire in our own image, and email helps avoid that bias," Mahoney said. Second, they launched a pilot study to evaluate the ability of four autistic employees, who had no prior experience in technology, to test mortgage banking software. Autistic and neurotypical employees did what is called "manual regression testing," which in the simplest terms looks for any functional problem that occurs after engineers introduce a new code. "After six months," Mahoney recalls, "the four autistic employees were equal to their typical peers in the quality of their testing, but the autistic employees were able to do their jobs 48 percent faster than their nonautistic peers." Other pilot studies proved even more successful, though there were of course some hiccups. Some managers continued to see autism as a deficiency and reserved the more basic work for autistic employees. The employees would finish their work so quickly that they became bored, played computer games, and gave the appearance of being unengaged with the work. The reality was that they were done with their work but did not know how to ask for more—a situation familiar to many schoolchildren with ADHD, and their parents, who receive high grades in their classes but critical evaluations of their behavior.

At the time Mahoney and I talked in 2018, there were ninety-one autistic employees hired through the program, but several others who worked at the company before the program started now felt empowered to disclose their diagnosis for the first time. The benefit of disclosure was additional social support—the same kind of support JPMorgan gave to the autism program hires, such as coaching and mentors at work, and what Mahoney called "buddies" outside of work (bowling trips and Minor League baseball games, for example). Mahoney's next plans are to expand the number of hires, in part by launching the program in other cities, such as recruiting from the CUNY campuses in the United States and the University of Bath in the UK. He's also eager to explore more flexible hours, especially if the employees are in countries where workers can receive health and retirement benefits if they work part-time, and to recruit people with other kinds of neurodiversity. He said, "There is a genuine desire to get different types of thinking in the room, and this doesn't mean that autism should be the only other way of thinking."

The movement known as "neurodiversity" illustrates how economics can play a role in destigmatizing a previously highly stigmatized condition. Advocates for neurodiversity modeled the movement explicitly after the social model of disability. This is the idea that it is the environment in which one lives, not the individual, that is responsible for disability.[15] In this view, a person who is blind is only disabled when there are sidewalk obstacles and an absence of tactile and auditory aids. Similarly, the disability of a person who is unable to speak, or is highly socially awkward, is mitigated by digital communication like email and telecommuting. Fortunately, for some people with disabilities, economies increasingly rely heavily on information services, such as the collection, analysis, and manipulation of data for marketing and other purposes, and they rely less on social skills and face-to-face interaction.

An increasing proportion of workers in the United States, the UK, and most G20 countries have alternative work schedules. This favors people who might otherwise be unemployed.[16] The Organisation for Economic Co-operation and Development (OECD) predicts that "such increased flexibility will provide greater opportunities for underrepresented groups to participate into the labour market, such as women, senior workers and those with disabilities."[17] Many scholars and policy makers consider such flexible work to be another way to exploit workers through "contingent work," given that part-time employees are often denied full benefits.[18] However, more creative kinds of work schedules make it possible for people with physical and mental disabilities to work, resisting norms that prevent them from becoming integral parts of a community. The move from manufacturing goods in factories toward flexible production, and the democratization of communication, have opened up a degree of community integration that was formerly inaccessible for people with mental illnesses and disabilities in general.

Research on the trajectories of autistic adults, and on employment opportunities in particular, lags behind research on children and special education.[19] Nonetheless, there is a growing body of literature that suggests people with autism, while continuing to face discrimination, are capable of succeeding in competitive inclusive employment,[20] especially if they had work experience as teenagers.[21] Kessler Foundation reports on National Trends in Disability Employment (nTIDE) show positive trends.[22]

But some worry that the association of autism with mathematical skills is reinforcing the stereotype initiated by the popular film *Rain Man* in 1988. "Selling autism as a brand," Susan Dominus noted in relation to the changing employment landscape for autistic adults, "likely perpetuates some generalizations—even stereotypes—in the name of overcoming bias, a complicated compromise, if a strategic one."[23] Alex Plank, an actor, autistic self-advocate, and consultant for television programming relating to autism, says that we shouldn't value only the kind of autism that involves extraordinary talent or genius. In fact, depending on the job, some people who are "lower functioning" may actually be more employable than those who are "higher functioning." "People with autism," Plank says, "do all sorts of things, just like everyone else." Commenting on the popular ABC television show about an autistic physician, *The Good Doctor*, he told me wryly, "We have the TV show 'The Good Doctor,' but we don't have 'The Good Grocery Store Bagger.'" The reality is that most people in supported employment programs for people with developmental disabilities participate in what is sometimes pejoratively called the "four Fs:" filing, flowers, food, and filth.

Isabel does not have the linguistic skills to engage in sustained conversation or argumentation, nor the social skills to detect nuanced aggression or seek out frequent social interaction. She would never have qualified for a diagnosis of Asperger's, the term that was associated with verbal skill and "high functioning" autism. But many people whom doctors characterize as "high functioning" have just as many, if not more severe, social impairments as people we might think of as "low functioning." In addition, bright and verbal people with Asperger's, who perhaps have undergraduate or graduate degrees, might expect—or their parents might expect—that they will find employment that demands far more social ability than they possess. In those cases, it's difficult to set one's sights lower. The same is true for the parents of so-called low functioning adults who set their sights higher.

One woman I interviewed in northern Virginia has a daughter who has been employed full-time at a grocery store not far from their home. She is encouraging her autistic daughter to quit her job bagging groceries because she thinks it is "beneath her." But her daughter loves bagging groceries. She is proud of how well she can organize the goods into bags, and she enjoys the repetition of the job and her interactions with repeat customers who know her by name. The majority of the workforce at Rising Tide, a car wash company in Miami that washes approximately 160,000 cars a year, is autistic. The repetitive tasks involved in cleaning are well suited to the skills and interests of many people with autism. If there is resistance, it's not from the employees, who by all accounts enjoy their jobs, but from parents who had higher hopes for their children.

Some years ago, Joyce and I tried to help Isabel get a job at a pharmacy. During a trial period, with support from a government-funded job coach, Isabel learned to stock shelves and clean. She did not think this job was demeaning because she had never learned that certain professions are stigmatized or associated with socioeconomic class. When Isabel, Joyce, and I met with the staff, her manager asked her to describe her job. Isabel said, "In the morning when I get to work I'm a cleaning lady." The manager admonished her, "You are *not* a cleaning lady! You are a retail associate." This is how children learn that there are some jobs more appreciated than others, not just in terms of money but in terms of their moral value.

Isabel volunteered for years in numerous jobs, contributing much but never receiving pay. We dreamed of her finding a job in the federal government because it would give her job security and benefits, but we also questioned our intentions. If we want her to be paid, and we view pay as a sign of success, are we accepting that her value as a person comes from her productivity? If she remains an unpaid volunteer, are we letting her be exploited for her free labor? And if we did find her a job that paid her minimum wage, was she being exploited for her cheap labor, since she had no other choice but to accept a low-paying job?

In addition to questioning the enormous disparities in pay in the United States among professions, we should also question the disparities in the social value of different kinds of work. The definition of economics that students learn in their introductory college courses is that individuals (and not communities) seek to maximize their gains with an ever-present insufficiency of means. Such a definition suggests that people who do not contribute economic value to themselves or families at a rate commensurate with that of the average members of society are unproductive and disabled. By these measures, most stay-at-home moms or dads are disabled since most of their work doesn't really count as productive labor. The homeless person who works day and night to scrape together enough food to eat is not, in this view, performing labor. Disability-studies scholars argue that this "productive rule" devalues people who do not produce as much as others, and makes it less likely that families will support them.[24] I do not think these scholars believe that in the Middle Ages, when there was no category for the disabled, and when people contributed what they could to their families, people with what we today call disabilities lived wonderful lives. But an individual's worth was not only what he or she could produce. No one worshipped at a shrine of limitless needs.

Sunaura Taylor is a scholar and activist who writes about the ways capitalism influences health and creates disabilities. Taylor is differently mobile. Because she was born with a condition called arthrogryposis multiplex congenita (a rare disease in which joints become permanently fixed), she has limited movement and uses a wheelchair. An accomplished artist and author, and one of the leading figures in disability studies today, Taylor uses her mouth for most things, including operating her smart phone and painting. She says that, growing up in Arizona, she suffered from the shame of being taken to healers because her "body was bad," but she did not imagine that she intrinsically lacked value to society, as a family member or as a citizen. She did believe, however, that she could create more value if she was more physically independent. And when she was finally able to do most things by herself, such as dressing and going to the bathroom, there was no great transformation in her life. What caused her the most discomfort was not her physical limitations but "the stigma others attached to needing help, and by the worry that these physical necessities could lead me into a life without choices."

One night in 2003, after participating in a protest for disability rights in Philadelphia, she went to a busy restaurant. There were no tables free, but she was able to get some food at a counter. Someone noticed she was having difficulty eating and said, "You can ask for help here. This isn't a place where we value independence"[25]—ironic, given that she was just steps from the place where the Declaration of Independence was signed. But she understood what this meant—her physical dependence was not necessarily a burden on others. It suggested that something had changed in America, that perhaps disabilities don't always produce isolation, that disabilities can connect people in relationships of care and reciprocity.

Taylor has recently embraced animal rights, including the rights of disabled animals to survive, in part because she compares her own oppression to that of nonhuman animals, analogous to the way colonial psychiatrists oppressed their "bestial" subjects in Africa.[26] Just as African colonial subjects were disabled—they were seen as inferior beings who could never rise to the level of European cultural and economic achievement and who should have been grateful for anything Europeans gave them—so too is she a victim of modernity. Raised to believe that independence and success equals work and wage labor, is she then supposed to believe that she has little value in this world beyond providing income for therapists, doctors, and nurses? Should she accept any job, however exploitative?

Taylor also asks whether we have the right "not to work." She does not mean the right to do nothing. She means the right not to engage in wage labor, whether one is an artist, an advocate, a volunteer, or a stay-at-home parent, among many other possibilities. In her landmark 2004 essay, "The Right Not to Work: Power and Disability," she wrote that "Western culture has a very limited idea of what being useful to society is" and that when people with disabilities cannot find employment, or they depend on others, they can feel as if they've failed. Speaking of people with disabilities, she said, "We often simply make inefficient workers," and "inefficient is the antithesis of what a good worker should be. For this reason, we are discriminated against by employers. We require what may be pricey adaptations and priceless understanding."[27] Taylor's claim to have the right not to work is purposely subversive as a challenge to the norm of autonomy that has long marginalized people with disabilities. Her story about receiving help in a restaurant is just as subversive, because it challenges independence, the fundamental ideological foundation of American society.

One expert on disability, Sara Hendren, believes that the stigma of both physical and psychological conditions can be addressed not only by refashioning employment and thinking more creatively about productivity but also by rethinking our built environment. Hendren is an artist and designer at Olin College of Engineering in Massachusetts, has close relatives with autism and bipolar disorder, and has a son with Down syndrome. More than a decade ago, after her son was born, she started taking him to various physical therapists where she first became familiar with devices like ankle braces, pressure vests, and crutches. She marveled at how, in that context, medical language had become a material language, concretized in objects. For example, the person who uses a wheelchair becomes not only "wheelchair-bound" but is also represented in signs posted at parking spots or on bathroom doors with a symbol of a wheelchair, as if the person and the chair were one. The effect of this imagery on one's sense of self can be profound and enduring, as Taylor suggested when she said her "body was bad."

Hendren told me, "It occurred to me that we could think about, that we could design, prosthetics in a way that might speak a different language about their users." Technology, she says, is so much about utility and function that engineers often forget that technology is also culture. She's helped design a new wheelchair symbol that replaces the rigid, mechanical image (the International Symbol of Access, or ISA) with one that is active and tilted forward, suggesting that the person and not the chair is in control. She designs wheelchair ramps that are artistic, beautiful, and can be used by both wheelchair users and skateboarders. To show the beauty of combining the art of movement with assistive technologies, she has collaborated with choreographer Alice Sheppard to design access ramps for dancers who are differently able and use wheelchairs. She has also worked on aesthetic modifications, like making prosthetic legs out of fine leather and polished wood.

Hendren recognizes that such changes are just a beginning. She compares the sleek design of new prosthetics to the design of Apple computers, calling it "smoothing work." In the case of eyeglasses, we've already achieved the goal of making prosthetics a more seamless part of everyday life. We often compliment people on their glasses even though we are publicly acknowledging a vision impairment. But we don't compliment people on their hearing aids or their wheelchairs, even though those are also assistive technologies. The next step is what disability scholars and advocates sometimes call "cripping," from the academic literature called "crip theory." Cripping reclaims the pejorative word "cripple" in the same way that other advocacy groups have reclaimed "queer" for queer theory, "fat" for fat studies, or "slut" for slutwalk, the movement to end victim-blaming in sexual violence. Cripping means that we see disability as a viable identity or culture, not as damage or deficit. Cripping also means questioning the norms that societies created to oppress people with disabilities in the first place. An example of cripping was when Taylor argued for the right not to work, or when Hendren and others took to the street with stickers of her new wheelchair icon design and placed them over the standard signs.

Hendren's experience raising a son with Down syndrome has also made her sensitive to the rise of selective abortions to eliminate the genetic condition because, she said, "it's as if your child's life is an affront to the logic of utility and efficiency and how people are valued for their economic worth." Her son, she says, "is living his best life all the time." She doesn't want to idealize him, or fashion a cliché story about victory in the face of serious disability, but she wanted me to know that he is "a thriving, happy person." "If he were to become a grocery bagger and love his job every day and feel a part of a thriving, happy community, then I will say 'success,' 100 percent."

Hendren and her husband live near public transportation to give their son more independence if he wants it, and she is grateful that the Boston subway payment system has become automated; her son, like many people with Down syndrome, struggles with mathematical calculations. The subway also hired red-shirted "ambassadors" who assist people with developmental and other disabilities. This kind of "service design" has parallels in Uber Assist, which helps people with a range of disabilities to become more mobile. Drivers are trained in how to interact with people with a range of disabilities. Most ski resorts now offer assisted skiing with instructors trained in specific conditions, like autism and ADHD. But Hendren is worried about the conflict between providing such opportunities and continuing selective abortions. Hendren said she is "haunted by the fact that those very possibilities are on a collision course with the optimization of pregnancy and the developing fetus." Her concern is that if children like her son are not even born, what does that say about how we define a good life and who deserves to have one?

The most memorable example of material assistance I've ever encountered was in Berlin, Germany, where I had gone to give a lecture. As I waited for a taxi in my hotel lobby, the concierge asked about my profession. I told him I studied autism, and he said, "We've made so many accommodations for people with autism in Germany, even in the brothels." I shot back, "What?! Autistic people are prostitutes?" "No," he said. "Sex workers now get training to help clients who have disabilities, since disabled people might want to go to sex workers just like anyone else." I didn't know how to think about this—ethically or legally. Eventually, however, I came to the conclusion that if a society was addressing the usually unspoken topic of sexuality for people with disabilities, this was great progress. The late anthropologist Robert Murphy, who became disabled by a neurodegenerative illness, wrote that differently mobile people often feel desexualized in a wheelchair even though they know there are many ways to experience the pleasures of sexual intimacy. Most people, he said, assume that someone in a wheelchair is asexual because they don't recognize that "a large majority of disabled people have the same urges as the able-bodied, and are just as competent in expressing them."[28]

There is dignity in risk, in having the opportunity both to succeed and to fail. There is dignity in being visible, in having the chance to be judged in a way you didn't expect. In fact, most of the positive stories I've heard about someone's struggles with disability and stigma involve some failures. Nearly every negative story about disability and stigma is about someone who has been sheltered, protected, and denied the opportunity to fail.

Just ask Reyma McCoy McDeid, an African American and autistic single mother, who is also a board member at the Washington-based Autistic Self Advocacy Network. "I was told I was a lost cause. People said, 'You won't do anything,' and definitely not college," she said. In foster care for much of her childhood, Reyma moved from family to family. She was non-speaking until she was five, and after that spoke in a monotone. She picked at her hair and rocked back and forth. She often got in trouble at school for behavioral issues, including flapping her hands and running into corners. "As a Black girl with autism, I was a unicorn," she said. "My biological family said I was retarded and made me a ward of the state of California."

When she was fifteen, she left foster care and moved with her mother and her mother's boyfriend to Rockford, Illinois, where her mother soon died from colon cancer. With no legal guardian, she went back into foster care, this time with a family that loaned her out for babysitting jobs and took away all the money she earned, including her federal disability benefits. "Despite being used and bullied, I managed to do well in high school," she said in a phone interview, and in 1998 she gained admission to Iowa State University. She eventually received two master's degrees, worked in community-based nonprofits, and in 2015 became the executive director of the Central Iowa Center for Independent Living, an organization that helps adults with disabilities, or who are homeless, to integrate into their communities. They offer social skills training and job coaching, among other things. "The problem," she told me, "is that we don't put people with developmental disabilities in the position to fail. But trial and error, succeeding and failing, are the normal parts of human experience. If you never fail, you won't grow or change. Everyone deserves to fail."

In 2018, Reyma ran for the Iowa House of Representatives, and lost.

Robert Perske coined the phrase "the dignity of risk" in 1972 when he was chaplain at the Kansas Neurological Institute, a state residential institution for people with intellectual disabilities. He wrote that there is, paradoxically, "a dehumanizing indignity in safety." Speaking of clients who were then called "retarded," he said that "overprotection endangers the client's human dignity, and tends to keep him from experiencing the risk-taking of ordinary life which is necessary for normal human growth and development."[29] At that time, children with intellectual disabilities were typically deemed uneducable, and in many countries they were protected in workshops where they wove baskets or made pottery. Even during Isabel's life, educators and potential employers have been skeptical about her abilities and warned us against setting her up for disappointment. We would say, "It's OK if she fails, but she might surprise you." Perske was surprised when he went to Sweden in the early 1970s and saw a man with Down syndrome operating a punch press at a metal factory, and other intellectually disabled adults assembling Volvo automobiles.

Perske didn't suggest that people with intellectual disabilities do such dangerous jobs, but he did suggest that these workers had a dignity and a right—the dignity of risk and the right to fail—so often denied to people in North America. Individual success and individual failure can be unabashedly capitalist concepts, as they are grounded in an ideology of freedom, autonomy, choice, and self-determination. But they can also be modes of compassion and inclusion.[30] Special Olympics is an example of how inclusion offers possibilities for people with disabilities to experience both victory and defeat. For every person who wins a medal, there are dozens who do not. Those who don't win still have the choice to continue to compete in the future or even to give up if they wish. They get to endure physical injuries, to cry, and to be angry or frustrated with themselves, just like any other athlete.

The Farrell family, in a suburb of Washington, DC, takes great pride in the struggles of their twenty-seven-year-old autistic son, Patrick, in large part because they compare Patrick's life with that of his late uncle, Raymond, who was born in 1928. Patrick's father, Joe, told me, "Raymond would definitely be diagnosed with autism if he had been born in the late twentieth century, and he was moderately disabled intellectually." Raymond's mother was, nonetheless, able to push him through Catholic school, and Raymond received a high school diploma despite completing few assignments or tests. Raymond's sister Anne (Joe's mom) remembered, "Mom did all his homework for him every night and then Raymond was able to copy it and hand it in. I doubt the school ever believed it was actually all his work." He had no diagnosis, no accommodations at school, and he preferred to stay inside while his sister and other neighborhood children played on lawns and in the street. "After high school," Joe said, "Raymond lived his entire life in his mom's house, and was independent only enough to walk to a corner store to buy a newspaper, and ride the subway all day long." He held only one job, at the Sealtest milk company, and he was fired within less than a week. His mother made no effort to find him work again and never applied for any government disability benefits on his behalf. "He didn't have any friends," Anne recollected. "But look at Patrick!" she said.

Patrick was born in 1993 on Long Island and was diagnosed with autism in 1995. Intensive early intervention and consistent and high quality special education programs made it possible for him to complete high school and eventually to receive a certificate from George Mason University LIFE, a Virginia state program designed to support job skills training and academic experiences for people with intellectual and developmental disabilities. He does paid clerical work four days a week for two federal offices, and volunteers at his local library on a fifth day. Unlike a sheltered workshop, which employs only disabled adults and pays them below minimum wage, these are jobs in which Patrick is working side by side with nondisabled workers and earns enough income to carry the roughly $800 in rent he pays in his supervised group home.

Patrick's achievements have been such a team effort that his parents, Pamela and Joe, remember the names of every one of his former teachers and therapists. When he was diagnosed with autism, they hit the ground running, arranging for government-funded therapies, meeting with school principals, and strategizing for the future. He had speech therapy and occupational therapy, and saw a child psychiatrist. He would have an aide by his side, what the school district called a "shadow," and therapists who helped him with behavioral modifications at home. Almost all of these supports were paid for or partially subsidized by the state or the federal government.

Joe worked for a company that administered government-funded loans, and Pamela was a stay-at-home mom. Pamela said, "I remember in the first grade, I'd just be at home waiting for that call to pick him up from school because he was screaming or had some other behavioral problem." Within a year, Pamela had developed enough experience navigating special education that she got a job as a teacher's aide at Patrick's school, and worked there as a paraeducator for the next eleven years. "It was the best thing we ever did," Joe said, "because now you're on the inside. And if a family came to me tomorrow and said my kid was just diagnosed, I'd tell them: first thing, one of you should go work for the school system. You hear things like 'you have no power over the school, and you can't pick the teacher who's best for your kid'—baloney! If you know how things work on the inside, you can do a lot."

Two of Patrick's fellow students, Lisa and Julie, had a lasting impact on him and his parents. Lisa and Julie were typically developing and popular kids in the school Patrick attended—Lisa is now in nursing school and Julie is in graduate school for industrial design—and they liked spending time with him. Pamela's eyes filled with tears as she said, "They never left his side all the way through high school." Their friendship with Patrick, although different from the friendships they had with their nondisabled peers, stopped bullies in their tracks and prevented him from being marginalized.

Pamela said, "Lisa and Julie did not make Patrick normal; they made it normal to be friendly with him."

Patrick rarely joined Lisa and Julie with their other friends in part because there seemed no reason to try and make Patrick fit in, and in part because they valued their distinctive relationship. Julie told me, "I could share things with Patrick that my other friends had outgrown or were maybe embarrassed to say they still liked—like watching Disney movies, which is good because it's not easy to have a conversation with Patrick. You don't just call him up and chat. But he's great to watch movies with." And when Julie went away to college she was surprised she didn't meet anyone who had a friend back home like Patrick. "Everyone," she said, "should have someone like Patrick in their life. He taught me so much about patience and empathy. I don't think he has any idea how important he is to me." As I listened to Julie, I thought about how much she and Patrick have to teach us about the possibilities for meaningful relationships between people who are neurotypical and people who are neurodiverse.

The Farrells don't see a clear boundary between the school, the home, and the community. Indeed, Patrick has benefited from the absence of such boundaries. Because Pamela knew what was happening with Patrick at school, she could provide continuity at home. And because Patrick was able to attend his local school, he would at least see, if not interact with, his peers at the park or the local swimming pool club. Patrick's social network also widened when he began to participate in Special Olympics basketball, soccer, and track and field. What's more, Lisa's and Julie's mothers are today among Pamela's closest friends.

Elizabeth Hassrick, a Drexel University sociologist with expertise in autism and education, studies how such relationships between schools, educators, parents, extended family, and clinicians influence one another and change the outcomes for people with autism. As a teacher in high-poverty neighborhoods in Oakland, on a Navajo reservation, and in Cameroon (as a Peace Corps volunteer), she marveled at the low expectations. "Twenty years ago, very different kinds of children were getting the identical services, in part because no one thought those kids could achieve anything.

And everyone blamed everyone else—bad parents, bad kids, bad teachers, etc." Now, she says, we live in a totally different world. "Increasingly, we don't see special education as a school within a school. We are developing a model of schooling based on the relationship between the child and the entire school, and even his community."

Hassrick says too much attention is paid to schools and too little on how children exist in a wider network that includes their homes, their communities, their park, pool, ice-skating rink, shopping mall, or movie theater—the places from which Patrick's uncle Raymond was so alienated. Hassrick says, "I've put all my eggs in the network basket." She is easily irritated when people tell autistic children to draw clear boundaries between those they call friends, family, or pets. "Who says your family cannot be your friends and that friends have to exist only outside the home? And who says a pet can't be your friend? Or that a person should live separate from their family after they turn eighteen?" For Hassrick, these are false boundaries that obscure the reality that we are all engaged in multiple interactions across boundaries, as when Lisa and Julie became friends with Patrick, when Pamela became part of the school, and when Lisa's and Julie's parents became good friends with the Farrell family. And if one doubts that Julie and Lisa can truly be friends with Patrick, we need only remind ourselves that "friend" is just a word and we can define it however we like.

Pamela remembers that when Patrick was three or four years old, a therapist asked her, "What do you want for Patrick in the future?" At that time, she couldn't think about the long term and said that she wanted him to play Little League baseball. "I don't know why that was my answer— maybe because baseball just seemed like the most 'normal' thing for a boy and I wanted him to be normal." Patrick didn't play baseball, but the Farrells are rewarded by what Patrick has done so far. They don't know what "normal" means anymore because Patrick is, simply, Patrick, and they try not to compare him to anyone, except perhaps to Raymond, to appreciate how far we've come in the United States.

"You know what?" Joe said. "Patrick loves the Special Olympics, he loves to work, he loves to play video games, he loves the Yankees and the

Redskins, he loves to ride the metro. And I don't have to worry about him taking illegal drugs or that he'll get a DUI—those things that many people have to worry about are off the table." "Patrick," Joe said, before he paused to gather his thoughts, "Patrick is good."

Many of the successes of people now employed, who in the past might very well have been confined in institutions, can be attributed to visibility and disclosure, to the open discussion and naming of a disability. When we hide a condition, we take away the chance to ask for help. Recently, when my wife and I met with a possible employer for Isabel, we said we wanted to talk about her disability. Perhaps in an attempt to be politically correct, the employer said that he didn't want to talk about disability since Isabel seemed capable of doing her job. Of course, he missed the point. The ability to perform a skill does not erase the disability; the job task is only one part of what makes someone a successful or unsuccessful worker. Do the hours and work conditions cause fatigue? Or increase the possibility for mistakes? Is the worker able to communicate with others about her needs? What are the physical and psychological challenges of the job as a whole? If her coworkers don't know about her disability, how will they understand her differences? Stigma is not eradicated when someone hides their distinctive personalities, skills, and challenges, or when someone pretends they don't see or don't need to see them. Hiding creates stigma while openness erases it.

I once saw stigma appear and disappear within seconds, when Isabel graduated from high school. She delivered a graduation speech, the first time anyone with a disability at the school had done so. The principal had expressed reservations about whether Isabel could do something so verbal and so high pressure, but Isabel herself insisted. Looking out into the spotlight, she told an audience of three thousand people—not in her school, but at the Daughters of the American Revolution Constitution Hall in Washington, DC, the largest concert hall in the city, just across the street from the White House—"When I was young, some people didn't think I would ever graduate from high school." When she started to speak, some students in the audience started to laugh. People who didn't know her were struck by the unusual rhythm of her voice, her singsong pattern. One could hear whispers and murmurs as well. But when she finally spoke the line "people with autism, like me," the room went quiet. The audience now had a way of understanding her, of seeing her as she wanted to be seen. And what had been strange suddenly made sense. She received a standing ovation.

ON THE SPECTRUM

Are you schizophrenic or cyclothymic or autistic,
or are you, perchance, a paranoid? No, we are not
trying to call you names. . . . We are merely trying
to classify your personality. You are almost sure
to be one or more of these. Don't Protest! . . . You
need not be ashamed, the best people fall into these
classifications.

"Now Everybody's Crazy," *Los Angeles Times,*
July 13, 1924[1]

There is a remarkable passage at the end of Nathaniel Hawthorne's 1850 *The Scarlet Letter* when, after a long absence, Hester Prynne returns to the scene of her crime. As her punishment for adultery, she had worn an embroidered red letter "A" on her breast, but after all those years not even the harshest judge would force her to continue wearing it. She decides, of her own free will, to keep it fastened to her blouse because, the narrator tells us, "the scarlet letter ceased to be a stigma which attracted the world's scorn and bitterness, and became a type of something to be sorrowed over, and looked upon with awe, yet with reverence too."

The village now saw her as a source of comfort and strength, not as a person stained with sin. When people suffered "the dreary burden of a heart," especially in matters of love or misplaced passion, they visited her cottage for counsel. They knew Hester would understand their pain. The goal of the punishment was to marginalize Hester from society; but by claiming "adultery" for herself, as if with the pride of a twenty-first-century LGBTQ advocate who has reclaimed the word "queer" from the bigots, she makes the letter a mark of dignity in experience rather than of shame.

Both Hester's original stigma and its transformation into a sign of self-worth derived from her ongoing struggle between her individual character and her society's expectations, a struggle Hester embraced by returning to her community. The question for us is whether we can win our own struggle and take ownership of the words and practices that exclude and discriminate. The many victories described in this book suggest that we can.

In the last century, mental health professionals, patients, advocates, and social scientists have repeatedly challenged many of the assumptions that underlie stigma. They have demonstrated that mental illnesses need not be divided into fictive and real ones; that there is no justification for separating illnesses of the mind from those of the body; and that mental illnesses are not always "abnormal" and disabling.

Of course, it is impossible to end stigma completely—every society can find something to demean and marginalize. But we can still resist, name, mute, and shape it. Stigma is not a thing but a process, and we can change its course.

One of these victories was the movement of psychiatry out of the asylums, the institutions that gave birth to the very idea of distinctly mental illnesses. Severely and chronically mentally ill people had long been identified, confined, disciplined, or treated. That's what asylums did. But people with less serious psychological problems in the general population, especially those who were still functional enough to work and maintain social relationships, went untreated. They kept their symptoms a secret or articulated their distress in the only way that was culturally acceptable, through bodily complaints such as fatigue, partial paralysis, and headaches. Yet by World War I, mental illnesses had become something other than just insanity or lunacy. American foot soldiers accepted the diagnosis of shell shock, and military officers accepted the diagnosis of neurasthenia, because those new labels, appropriate to their social class, gave a certain dignity to their pain.

Even reducing stigma for just a limited time during wars helped the least seriously affected people, both soldiers and civilians, the people with the so-called common conditions like anxiety and depression. Whereas in the early years of psychiatry the goal was to extend knowledge gained in the study of the more impaired to the less impaired, there is hope today that this process has reversed directions. Increased awareness of less serious forms of mental illnesses can make more serious illnesses less enigmatic and frightening.

Today, when someone wants their home or office to be neat and organized, they might say they are "a little bit OCD." The moody person says they are "a little bit bipolar," and the introvert says they are "on the spectrum." I don't believe that such phrases belittle the seriousness of these illnesses. For example, when comedian Jerry Seinfeld says that he is "on the autism spectrum" he does so with the full knowledge that many people with autism are profoundly intellectually disabled and need lifelong care. Similarly, when a student tells me that she has "PTSD" after taking a difficult final exam, she is not unaware that PTSD can involve severe and debilitating anxiety, and can sometimes lead to suicide.

Using the vocabulary of mental illness validates the growing acceptance that mental illnesses are a matter of degree and that they all exist on a spectrum. Most importantly, speaking these words more freely disarms the stigma of those illness labels by making them part of the general human condition, as Hester did when she continued wearing the letter "A." Hester's label, Hawthorne wrote, "seemed to give her the ability to see into people's hearts, exposing the outward guise of purity as a lie." Because

322   NOBODY'S NORMAL

everyone Hester met kept some kind of secret, her label conveyed to others not only that she would be sympathetic to them—as if the "A" was an ancient degree in clinical psychology—but also that she was more similar to them than different.

This emerging idea of the *spectrum* coincides with scientific studies questioning whether there are discrete mental disorders. During the time the DSM-III (1980–94) and DSM-IV (1994–2013) were in use, researchers and clinicians tended to talk about mental illnesses in categorical terms—one either had or did not have a particular mental illness. Echoing social movements such as those for transgender rights and neurodiversity, which view gender as continua rather than binaries and autism as a spectrum, the DSM-5 (2013–present) added a dimensional scoring component. The manual still uses names and categories to conceptualize groups of symptoms, to justify treatments and accommodations in work or school, and to prevent insurance fraud. But the dimensional model encourages clinicians to pay more attention to describing the severity and dynamics of a patient's various symptoms over time than assessing whether a patient meets every criterion for a specific disorder.

"Like most common human ills," the DSM-5 states, "mental disorders are heterogeneous at many levels, ranging from genetic risk factors to symptoms."[2] As one leading epidemiologist put it, "there is no evidence for the existence of true discrete mental illnesses that account for the patterns among symptoms in dimensional assessments."[3] In autism research, for example, scientists have shown that mild symptoms of autism are common in the general population and that family members of a person with autism often exhibit autistic traits. Yet only that one person may actually have the diagnosis, either because they need some sort of treatment or because the diagnosis drives an intervention like special education. With autism, as with many medical conditions—like hypertension and obesity—the boundary lines are drawn more by culture than by nature. Dividing human differences into distinct illnesses is like dividing up the color spectrum into distinct colors. While most of us can easily tell the difference between yellow and orange, we probably can't agree on exactly where yellow ends and orange begins because there is no single point at which one becomes the other. Similarly, the border between health and sickness is the judgment call we make about whether a person's symptoms are impairing their lives and warrant treatment.

A spectrum also presents an opportunity for people (and their health care providers) to negotiate perceptions of health over time, as symptoms change or improve. A spectrum not only challenges the diagnostic stability that so often underlies stigma—as if once labeled you are always labeled—but also the presumption that everyone with a particular diagnosis is the same. The spectrum is an invitation: it asks us to join the rest of the world on a continuum of suffering. It asks us to say, along with neurodiversity advocates, that both normality and abnormality are fictional lands no one actually inhabits.

Researchers, including the authors of the DSM-5, have now reframed the major diagnoses as spectrum disorders (e.g., the schizophrenia spectrum, bipolar spectrum, and obsessive-compulsive spectrum), as happened with autism more than a decade ago. Throughout the world, people with the most serious illnesses, like schizophrenia and bipolar disorder, exhibit a wide range of different symptoms and symptom severity, as well as diverse outcomes: some people with schizophrenia require residential placements while others, like the writer Elyn Saks, a dean and professor at the University of Southern California Gould Law School, are highly functional.[4] Kay Redfield Jamison, who has bipolar disorder, and survived a suicide attempt, became a successful psychologist and author. Temple Grandin, despite (or perhaps because of) her autism, is a leading animal rights activist, professor of animal science, and consultant and designer for the livestock industry. The more we encounter people like Saks, Jamison, and Grandin, the less likely we are to assume that the labels of schizophrenia, bipolar disorder, or autism are homogeneous entities, and the less likely we are to restrict them to a stereotype.

Another recent victory is the ongoing effort of activists to reclaim pejorative words that have long been used to demean and oppress. This effort is epitomized by academic movements with names like queer studies, fat studies, crip (from "cripple") studies, and neurodiversity. Taking the language of gay rights, some activists in fat studies even talk about "coming out" as "fat," to challenge discrimination by employers, doctors, insurers, and the financial interests of the weight-loss industry. None of these movements aim to make their constituencies "normal." Rather, like Hester, they seek to empower themselves on their own terms.

Resistance goes beyond seeking the rights and qualities of "normal" people or advocating for the appreciation of difference with slogans. Phrases in public awareness campaigns—like "Gay is Good," "Black is Beautiful," or the National Alliance on Mental Illness's campaign "CureStigma"—are intended to change attitudes, but those phrases still refer to and therefore reproduce preexisting categories of sexuality, race, and disease.[5] Slogans can, of course, have positive results, as can new mental illness words; the invention of "Asperger's" in the UK and the United States, and the new term for schizophrenia in Japan, "*togo shitcho sho*," illustrate these effects. Yet words can still reinforce lasting labels and behavior. One famous study of how powerful labels can be involved students with partial vision who, upon entering a school for the blind, stopped using their residual vision because they now considered themselves "blind."[6] Similarly, there is a substantial literature showing that people diagnosed with schizophrenia often come to see themselves in terms of the negative stereotypes to which they have been exposed all their lives. They may believe that they are dangerous and deserve to be feared.[7]

We should also resist the broken-brain model, which remains wedded to the feckless centuries-old struggle to disentangle disease and culture. My concern is that neuroscientific approaches to understanding and treating mental illnesses perpetuate stigma by reducing the complexity of illness experience, or our personalities, to the brain.[8] I am not questioning whether brain-based research might someday translate into new treatments, but whether it can actually remove obstacles to care and mitigate the pain caused by stigma. As the example of electroconvulsive therapy made clear, even when there is a highly effective treatment for a mental illness as a disorder of the brain, the treatment may not change stigma (and might even make it worse) because of the ongoing belief that the brain is the seat of the self and the soul. What good is an effective treatment if few people are willing to use it?

Of course, the staunchest advocates of biological psychiatry would react to such critical comments by saying that certainly they know that the brain interacts with culture, history, politics, and economics. However, as scholar Nikolas Rose writes, "It is not enough to simply acknowledge that social and environmental factors are important, and then to maintain that the research and explanation must focus on the neuronal architecture of the brain."[9] Indeed, aren't poverty and social stress just as important to depression as the hippocampus? Treating the hippocampus would not change a person's hunger, or their history of being discriminated against. Nor would it alter the fact that experience is always embedded in the larger contexts of our lives. In fact, experience itself changes the architecture of the brain.[10]

Equally, the focus on the brain risks dividing illnesses into those we can explain biologically from those we cannot. When that happens, we risk seeing the former as real—where there is observable or potentially observable evidence in laboratory tests—and the latter as fictive. In 2019, even a celebrated historian of science, Anne Harrington, wrote: "Among the very many people who present to a general practitioner or a psychiatrist with a mental affliction, some are (almost certainly) suffering from a real illness, one that is understandable (in principle) like any other medical complaint. By the same token, others are (almost certainly) not."[11] In this view, almost everyone with a mental illness, as well as the large number of people with conditions that do not have a clear medical finding—such as chronic pain, chronic fatigue, Gulf War syndrome, or chronic Lyme disease—is led to believe that their illnesses are somehow not real. What's more, many, if not most, people with a mental illness do not meet the full criteria for DSM disorders and have a constellation of symptoms that does not map neatly onto our current system of classification; their suffering is still as real as any other.

Those who privilege some conditions over others as more "real" also overlook that mental illness concepts are just frameworks, and temporary frameworks at that, because like all forms of sickness, they exist within the dynamics of history. When Asperger's disorder, for example, entered the DSM in 1994, the medical community accepted it as a "real" condition at a time when we desperately needed a less-stigmatizing term for certain forms of autism; the word "autism" was so frightening that doctors hesitated to make the diagnosis, often until children were school-age and had missed important opportunities for early interventions. But even as Asperger's became a common diagnosis, the very best neuropsychiatric testers admitted that they could never reliably distinguish Asperger's from other subtypes of autism. Asperger's persisted for cultural rather than for scientific reasons. Now the term is obsolete in clinical and research circles (and was removed from the DSM in 2013), but not because of any new scientific knowledge or because someone deemed it fictive. It is obsolete because "Asperger's" did its cultural work so well that it is no longer necessary. People can now have autism without shame.

Another temporary framework was neurasthenia, a condition we no longer diagnose. Characterized by symptoms like fatigue, irritability, and headaches, neurasthenia was certainly not fictive in the early twentieth century. It is only "fictive" today in the United States because the symptoms of neurasthenia are now grouped into new and different disease terms. We may not use the word "neurasthenia" anymore in the United States, but people still experience emotional hardship through fatigue, irritability, and headaches. And this may be the main value of the dimensional turn: to address symptoms rather than squabble over diagnostic labels and fictive versus real conditions, and to facilitate mental health research and treatment for a much larger population than could ever be represented by categorical symptom checklists.

Given all the variability across cultures and in the past, it would be foolish to assume that any current method of approaching mental illnesses is the best or only way. Every society is capable of making its own interpretations of behavior, its own mental illness categories, and its own stigma. For instance, in cross-cultural research on children with behavioral problems, Italian parents say that shy children are "difficult" while Swedish parents call shy children "undemanding." Italian parents sometimes praise moody and irritable children as "expressive" while Swedish and Dutch parents criticize such children as "difficult" because they demand so much attention.[12] Recall that in Namibia, the staff of the medical clinic that prescribed medicines to the Jun/oansi man Tamzo think of him as an individual with "schizophrenia," while at home he is the innocent victim of spiritual malevolence, suffering from a social rather than an individual illness. Yet he is the same person with the same symptoms. Although the meanings of Tamzo's symptoms could not be more different in the two contexts, they are equally meaningful and useful in both. He receives medicines in one and social support in the other.

Now imagine that a Jun/oansi hunter-gatherer from Namibia came to the United States and encountered something as unusual for him as vegetarians and vegans. In his society, the most highly valued item is meat. Not only does meat give life, but sharing meat is the primary means of establishing and maintaining social relationships. From his perspective, vegetarianism might be a mental disorder, since it would be debilitating and marginalizing. The description of the disorder—let's call it omnivore dysphoria—could even read as follows:

> *The essential feature of omnivore dysphoria is distress regarding eating patterns. There is a persistent fear of and desire to avoid meat consumption alone and in situations in which the individual's avoidance may be exposed to scrutiny by others. Impairment may be mild or affect every aspect of life, including phobic avoidance of social situations or activities that involve or symbolize the real or imagined trauma of meat consumption. The condition may interfere with the ability to form and sustain interpersonal relationships, and lead to social distress at the workplace. The individual experiences these conflicts as irreconcilable aspects of his or her personality, often justifying the position through a rigid ideology, philosophical mission, or higher purpose.*

This isn't a frivolous thought experiment. What one community sees as deviant, another may see as expected and socially appropriate.

There are communities in Micronesia, for example, that interpret mental disturbances not as deviance but as relational experiences that cement kinship ties. They struggle with medical professionals who tell them their pain is personal rather than social because emotional distress, in their view, is a mechanism to bring families closer together.[13] These societies teach us that mental illnesses need not tear families apart. In São Paulo, Brazil, people with the psychiatric complications of AIDS and degenerative neurological diseases seek to build their own narratives of disability. When they describe their lives, they emphasize resilience, endurance, and creativity. But they lose that ability when health professionals trained in the language of the DSM recast the person's illness in the language of disease.[14] Scientific classifications can sometimes impede our efforts to define ourselves, by ourselves.

Among the Salish Indians of Montana, depression is a terrible form of suffering but is not necessarily a disease. It is a disease only when one's sadness separates a person from family and friends. Depression, and surviving depression, authenticate Indian identity since "real Indians" have been beaten down into depression over years of domination by non-Indian oppressors.[15] By defining depression as something that has been imposed on them, the Salish reject depression as a disease of the self.

Each of these societies understands, in their own distinctive ways, how easily doctors can see sicknesses as moral failures of the individual, whether linking obesity to irresponsibility, lung cancer to smoking, liver failure to alcoholism, and so on. As the sociologist Jonathan Metzl reminds us, health and disease are continually changing ideological positions we can use to denigrate others: the unhealthy or abnormal people who have failed to live up to their obligation to conform to our culture's expectations. Metzl writes, "Every time we see someone smoking a cigarette and reflexively say, 'smoking is bad for your health,' what we really mean is 'you are a bad person because you smoke.' "[16] Patients themselves, whether they have a medical or a mental illness, thus experience illness not just as disease but as a kind of visibility, a condition that subjects them to a public's evaluation.[17]

The person battling substance abuse wonders: I'm an alcoholic, do people see me as weak, sinful, and unemployable? If my employer finds out that I have a history of depression, will it affect my chances for promotion? Are people seeing *me*, or just the stigma of mental illness? These are the disquieting ruminations the late nineteenth-century philosopher Friedrich Nietzsche dreamed would someday end: "To calm the imagination of the invalid, so that at least he should not . . . have to suffer *more* from thinking about his illness than from the illness itself—that, I think, would be something!"[18]

In this book, I have tried to show that stigma is a judgment that does not emanate from the person who is stigmatized. Rather, it comes from the stigmatizers, those who illuminate people who are suffering or deemed different with the harsh light of moral judgment and then, seeing only the shadows they created, mistake them for reality. Shadows then travel with the stigmatized, and usually with their families too. They become an extension of the person, like a second self that can seem impossible to shake, and that the stigmatized themselves may also come to see as real.

Mental health professionals still tend to reduce the historical and cultural complexity of barriers to mental health care to the word "stigma," as if the word is self-explanatory. When we reduce the barriers to care and the double suffering of the mentally ill to "stigma," discussions of the intricacies and variability of negative attitudes and beliefs, discrimination and prejudice, stop, like a black hole that absorbs the particulars of human experience. I hope that, even in some small way, I have shown that stigma need not be a conversation ender. It can be a conversation starter if it draws our attention to the often-invisible values and perspectives that we take for granted, invisible because they are so deeply embedded in our economic and social histories. It's also worth imagining what we would do if the word "stigma" didn't exist, or if every time we used it we were aware of its history. Perhaps, in its absence, we would have to confront the specific ways a given society brands and excludes those who do not conform. Perhaps we would then appreciate more fully that mental illnesses and their meanings are embedded in the particular worlds we have created and, therefore, have the power to change.

Consider that when children have difficulty sustaining attention in school, our first thought is to change the way they behave rather than to question the way we organize our classrooms and schools. When someone is homeless, our first thought is that the person has failed as an individual rather than to question the historical legacies of discrimination and inequality. When a person does not fit a preexisting or assigned sex or gender, our first thought is that the person has a mental or physical disease rather than to question our definitions of normality. Expectations of child behavior, discrimination, and gender conformity do not cause mental illnesses. But they do cause stigma. The challenge now is to learn from the past, and from other societies, and harness the creative power of culture to reduce both stigma and the fear of stigma. If culture put stigma and mental illness together, culture can surely begin to take them apart.

ACKNOWLEDGMENTS

Several years ago, on a long road trip, somewhere in the Shenandoah mountains, my wife, Joyce, said, "I've been thinking. You should write a book about stigma."

As a psychiatrist, Joyce had long heard doctors, therapists, and policy makers talk about the many barriers to mental health care, such as inadequate insurance, poverty, a shortage of mental health professionals, and insufficient psychiatric education among primary care doctors. She listened to them call for better psychotropic medications, better assessments for early diagnosis, broader insurance coverage, and awareness campaigns. "And only after they've made those recommendations," she said, "do they say 'and of course we also need to eradicate the major barrier to care, stigma.'"

In other words, the biggest problem sounded like an afterthought. Stigma was the obstacle one talked about only after all other possible explanations had been given, like the scientist who, after exhausting every quantifiable reason for a human behavior, shrugs their shoulders and says that whatever they can't explain must be due to culture. Joyce pushed me to write about the things we cannot measure or see in a laboratory, to think about stigma not as the residue left behind by other investigations but rather as a window into how culture shapes the science of the mind and our personal and social experiences of mental illnesses. I would never have embarked on this project without her.

Among the dozens of other people who gave me their intellectual and emotional support, my first thanks go to the amazing students I have worked with: Chloe Ahmann, Victoria Avis, Dana Burton, Michael Kaplan, and Caroline Pickering, each of whom brought their own perspectives and keen insights to every page of this book. Vindhya Ekanayake accompanied me on numerous interviews throughout Washington, DC; Mackenzie Fusco read every word I wrote and was my sounding board for matters large and small; Shweta Krishnan, a brilliant writer who knows how to turn the prosaic into poetry, helped me fine-tune the introduction; Abigail Pioch, Devin Proctor, and Maria Tapias de Pombo helped enormously, especially locating hard-to-find documents. Evy Vourlides, smart, big-hearted, and the most generous student I've ever known, boosted my confidence much more than she knows. For his attention to detail, I am doubly grateful to Dr. Jorge Benavides-Rawson for his expert counsel on medicine and medical anthropology. I am also indebted to my colleagues at the George Washington University: Celeste Arrington, Brenda Bradley, Alison Brooks, Alexander Dent, Ilana Feldman, Hugh Gusterson, Susan Johnston, Brandon Kohrt, Joel Kuipers, Chet Sherwood, Tadeusz Zawidzki, and especially Sarah Wagner, for commiserating and offering advice on the sometimes bumpy road from idea to publication.

For their generous help as interviewees or readers, I thank Julie Ansorge, Simon Baron-Cohen, Julia Bascom, Dr. Anne Becker, Dominique Pareja Béhague, Andy Bickford, Kai Blevins, Paul Bliese, Paul Brodwin, Rosalyn Carter, Col. Robert Certain, Naina Chernoff, John Cho, Kyungjin Cho, Lynn Conway, Patrick Corrigan, Peter Cryle, Dr. Jack Drescher, Dr. Charles Engel, Dr. Steven Epstein, Connor Farrell, Joseph Farrell, Pamela Farrell, Patrick Farrell, Elizabeth Fein, Michael Fieldhouse, Dr. Michael First, Brian Howard Freedman, Michele Friedner, Dr. Daniel Geschwind, Sander Gilman, Faye Ginsburg, Dr. C. T. Gordon, Olivia Grinker, Gerald Grob, Robert Grund, Cassandra Hartblay, Matt Harper, Elizabeth Hassrick, Sara Hendren, Steven Hinshaw, Dr. Harry Holloway, Dr. Beth Horowitz, Dr. Thomas Insel, Jenell Johnson, David Kieran, Eunjung Kim, Jerome Kim, Paul Kim, Junko Kitanaka, Arthur Kleinman, Rebecca Kling, Dr. Rishav

Koirala, Dr. Ellen Leibenluft, Dr. Sarah Lisanby, Louisa Lombard, James R. Mahoney, Michael Maloney, Reyma McCoy McDeid, Tey Meadow, Todd Meyers, Gowa-Onaiwu Morenike, Karen Nakamura, Ari Ne'eman, Theresa O'Nell, Francisco Ortega, Dr. Lawrence Park, Alex Plank, Dr. Daniel Pine, Eugene Raikhel, Laurence Ralph, Dr. Judith Rapoport, Rayna Rapp, John Read, Amanda Rioux, Samantha Rosenthal, Charles Samenow, Ralph Savarese, Ben Shephard, Stephen Shore, Steve Silberman, Jim Sinocchi, Dr. Andrew E. Skodol, Andrew Solomon, Mike Stanton, Elizabeth Stephens, Lucas Suarez-Findlay, Dr. Lucian Tatsa-Laur, Dr. Fred Volkmar, Dr. Timothy Walsh, Dr. Philip Wang, Dr. Simon E. Wessely, Dr. Rachel Yehuda, Debra Yourick, and Tyler Zoanni. Special thanks also go to Heli Meltsner for sharing with me the entirety of John Spiegel's papers from World War II.

Savannah Fetterolf, who has been helping me for many years to manage everything in my job, from egos to expenditures, made it possible for me to focus intensively on a book project. It is hard to express how much I value her calm temperament, generosity, and wit. Dr. Lance Clawson helped me shorten the text, refine my arguments, fact-check, and improve the clarity of my writing. I am grateful to him for the intelligence and wisdom he brought to bear on this often-difficult topic. Dr. Daniel Pine, who also read the book in its entirety, has for many years been one of my more constructive critics, as well as a friend. I deeply appreciate the fact that, despite his busy schedule, he is always just a phone call away.

To my agent, Anne Edelstein, I express deep gratitude for her faith in me, and for helping me find my nonacademic voice. I cherish her good judgment, pragmatism, and what probably amounted to dozens of hours on the telephone. Many thanks as well to the knowledgeable and insightful veteran editor, Jane Rosenman, for her enthusiasm and advice. And, of course, this book would not have been published without the confidence and support of my editor at W. W. Norton, Jill Bialosky. Also at W. W. Norton, I relied heavily on the advice of Nancy Palmquist and Drew Elizabeth Weitman.

Finally, for everything they have done for my career, I thank my family: my grandparents, the late Roy and Mildred; my late mother Florence and my father Dick; my sister, Jennifer; my children, Isabel and Olivia; and most of all, Joyce. My most treasured critic, Joyce is that rare kind of reader and editor with the uncanny ability to look at underdeveloped ideas, ill-chosen words, sentences in disarray, and paragraphs that have no reason to exist, and somehow find the marrow.

NOTES

Introduction: The Road Out of Bedlam

1. US government statistics on mental illness prevalence and treatment are available at: https://www.nimh.nih.gov/health/statistics/mental-illness.shtml#part_154788

2. National Institute of Mental Health statistics, retrieved May 10, 2019, from https://www.nimh.nih.gov/health/statistics/mental-illness.shtml

3. Approximately 20 percent of deaths from anorexia nervosa are from suicide. See Arcelus, J., et al. (2011). Mortality rates in patients with anorexia nervosa and other eating disorders: A meta-analysis of 36 studies. *Archives of General Psychiatry, 68*(7), 724–31.

4. Centers for Disease Control and Prevention. (2014). Youth risk behavior surveillance—United States, 2013. *Morbidity and Mortality Weekly Report, Surveillance Summaries, 63*(4), 1–172.

5. World Health Organization. (2004). *The global burden of disease: 2004 update.* Geneva: World Health Organization; there are numerous photo essays documenting such confinement. See, for example, Hammond, Robin. (2014). Breaking the chains of stigma. *Transition, 115,* 34–40.

6. U.S. Department of Health and Human Services. (1999). *Mental health: A report of the surgeon general.* Rockville, MD: U.S. Department of Health and Human Services, Substance Abuse and Mental Health Services Administration, Center for Mental Health Services, National Institutes of Health, National Institute of Mental Health.

7. Goffman, Erving. (1963). *Stigma: Notes on the management of a spoiled identity.* Englewood Cliffs, NJ: Prentice-Hall, 128.

8. Hoge, Charles W., et al. (2002). Mental disorders among U.S. military personnel in the 1990s: Association with high levels of health care utilization and early military attrition. *American Journal of Psychiatry, 159,* 1576–83; Hoge, Charles W., et

al. (2004). Combat duty in Iraq and Afghanistan, mental health problems, and barriers to care. *New England Journal of Medicine, 351,* 13–22.

9.   Carmichael, Rodney. (2019). Stressed out: How "Mind Playing Tricks on Me" gave anxiety a home in hip-hop. National Public Radio, May 29. Retrieved May 29, 2019, from https://www.npr.org/2019/05/29/726615663/geto-boys-mind -playing-tricks-on-me-anxiety-american-anthem

10.   College students and adolescents increasingly disclose psychiatric symptoms on social media, including symptoms of severe mental illness, possibly facilitating social support and referrals for treatment. See, for example: Moreno, Megan A., et al. (2011). Feeling bad on Facebook: Depression disclosures by college students on a social networking site. *Depression and Anxiety, 28,* 447–55; Mulfinger, Nadine, et al. (2019). Secrecy versus disclosure of mental illness among adolescents: II. The perspective of relevant stakeholders. *Journal of Mental Health, 28*(3), 304–11; Nasland, John A., et al. (2014). Naturally occurring peer support through social media: The experience of individuals with severe mental illness using YouTube. *PLOS One, 9*(10), 1–9.

11.   Schweik, Susan. (2014). In defense of stigma, or at least its adaptations. *Disability Studies Quarterly, 34*(1). Retrieved July 24, 2018, from http://dsq-sds.org/ article/view/4014/3539; Gleeson, Brendan. (1999). *Geographies of disability.* London: Routledge.

12.   Link, B. G., & Phelan, J. C. (2001). Conceptualizing stigma. *Annual Review of Sociology, 27,* 375.

13.   Collins, Francis, et al. (2003). A vision for the future of genomics research: A blueprint for the genomic era. *Nature, 422,* 841.

14.   De Boer, Hanneke M., et al. (2008). The global burden and stigma of epilepsy. *Epilepsy and Behavior, 12,* 540–46.

15.   As Ruth Benedict put it in 1932, "It is clear that there is not possible any generalized description of 'the' deviant—he is the representative of that arc of human capacities that is not capitalized in his culture. In proportion as his civilization has committed itself to a direction alien to him, he will be the sufferer." See Benedict, Ruth. (1932). Configurations of culture in North America. *American Anthropologist, 34*(1), 25.

16.   Office of the Surgeon, Multinational Force-Iraq, and the Office of the Surgeon General, United States Army Medical Command. (2006). *Mental Health Advisory Team (MHAT) IV. Final report. Operation Iraqi Freedom 05-07.*

17.   Addington, Jean, et al. (2015). Duration of untreated psychosis in community treatment settings in the United States. *Psychiatric Services, 66*(7), 753–56.

18.   Bettelheim, Bruno. (1979). *Surviving and other essays.* New York: Alfred A. Knopf, 111.

19.   On Hinshaw's experience, see Hinshaw, Stephen. (2017). *Another kind of madness: A journey through the stigma and hope of mental illness.* New York: St. Martin's Press. On Glenn Close's family, see her sister Jessie's memoir: Close, Jessie (with

Earley, Pete, & Close, Glenn). (2015). *Resilience: Two sisters and a story of mental illness.* New York: Grand Central Publishing.

20. Foucault, Michel. (1989). *Madness and civilization: A history of insanity in the Age of Reason* (Richard Howard, Trans.). New York: Routledge; Rose, Sarah F. (2017). *No right to be idle: The invention of disability, 1840s–1930s.* Chapel Hill: University of North Carolina Press.

21. Yang, Lawrence Hsin, et al. (2007). Culture and stigma: Adding moral experience to stigma theory. *Social Science and Medicine, 64,* 1529.

22. Tocqueville, Alexis de. (1899 [1835]). *Democracy in America* (Vol. 2). New York: Colonial Press, 332.

23. Silberman, Steve. (2001). The geek syndrome. *Wired,* December 1, 2001.

24. Conrad, Peter. (1992). Medicalization and social control. *Annual Review of Sociology, 18,* 209–32.

25. Kleinman, Arthur. (1988). *The illness narratives: Suffering, healing and the human condition.* New York: Basic Books, 3.

26. Grob, Gerald N., & Horwitz, Allan V. (2010). *Diagnosis, therapy, and evidence: Conundrums in modern American medicine.* New Brunswick, NJ: Rutgers University Press, 9.

Chapter 1: Every Man for Himself

1. Thomas, Elizabeth Marshall. (1958). *The harmless people.* New York: Vintage.

2. Groce, Nora Ellen. (1985). *Everyone here spoke sign language: Hereditary deafness on Martha's Vineyard.* Cambridge, MA: Harvard University Press.

3. Baynton, Douglas C. (1996). *Forbidden signs: American culture and the campaign against sign language.* Chicago: University of Chicago Press.

4. Experts in deaf studies still call other such "sharing sign communities" in the world (in Mexico, Bali, Israel, Ghana, Japan, and Jamaica, for example) "Martha's Vineyard Situations." See Kusters, Annelies. (2010). Deaf utopias? Reviewing the sociocultural literature on the world's Martha's Vineyard situations. *Journal of Deaf Studies and Deaf Education, 15*(1), 3–16.

5. Sacks, Oliver. (1989). *Seeing voices: A journey into the world of the deaf.* New York: Vintage.

6. Sahlins, Marshall. (2017 [1972]). *Stone Age economics.* London: Routledge, 37.

7. Dols, Michael. (1984). Insanity in Byzantine and Islamic medicine. *Dumbarton Oaks Papers, 38,* 135–48; see also: Dols, Michael. (1987). Insanity and its treatment in Islamic society. *Medical History, 31,* 1–14.

8. Dols, Insanity in Byzantine and Islamic medicine; Dols, Insanity and its treatment in Islamic society. See also Fabrega, Horacio, Jr. (1991). Psychiatric stigma in non-Western societies. *Comprehensive Psychiatry, 32*(6), 534–51.

9. Suh, Soyoung. (2013). Stories to be told: Korean doctors between hwa-byung (fire-illness) and depression, 1970-2011. *Culture, Medicine and Psychiatry, 37*(1),

81–104. Note that in the literature *hwa-byung* is also frequently transliterated as *hwabyeong.*

10. Bou-Yong, Rhi. (2004). *Hwabyung:* An overview. *Psychiatric Investigations, 1*(1): 21–24.

11. Suh, Stories to be told, 82.

12. Yoo, Theodore Jun. (2016). *It's madness: The politics of mental health in colonial Korea.* Oakland: University of California Press, 39.

13. See Kim Haboush, Ja Hyun. (1996). *The memoirs of Lady Hyegyŏng: The autobiographical writings of a crown princess of eighteenth-century Korea.* Berkeley: University of California Press.

14. Yoo, *It's madness,* 42.

15. Yoo, *It's madness,* 124, 153.

16. Spierenburg, Peter. (1996). Four centuries of prison history: Punishment, suffering, the body and power. In Norbert Finzsch and Robert Jütte (Eds.), *Institutions of confinement: Hospitals, asylums, and prisons in western Europe and North America, 1500–1900.* Cambridge: Cambridge University Press, 17–38.

17. Guarnieri, Patrizia. (2005). Madness in the home: Family care and welfare policies in Italy before Fascism. In Gijswijt-Hofstra, Marijke, et al. (Eds.), *Psychiatric cultures compared: Psychiatry and mental health care in the twentieth century: Comparisons and approaches.* Amsterdam: Amsterdam University Press, 312–30.

18. Haskell, Thomas L. (1985). Capitalism and the origins of the humanitarian sensibility, part 2. *American Historical Review, 90*(3), 547–66, 550.

19. Federici, Silvia. (2004). *Caliban and the witch: Women, the body and primitive accumulation.* Brooklyn: Autonomedia, 69.

20. Steuart, Sir James. (1966). *An inquiry into the principles of political oeconomy* (Vol. 1) (A. S. Skinner, Ed). Edinburgh, 67. Cited in Linebaugh, Peter. (2003). *The London hanged: Crime and civil society in the eighteenth century.* London: Verso, 99.

21. Scull, Andrew. (1993). *The most solitary of afflictions: Madness and society in Britain, 1700–1900.* New Haven, CT: Yale University Press, 26. Anderson, Michael. (1971). *Family structure in nineteenth century Lancashire.* Cambridge: Cambridge University Press.

22. Latin, the language of the church, was no longer the only vehicle to reach God. On all of these elements of modern individualism, see Macfarlane, Alan. (1979). *The origins of English individualism: The family, property, and social transition.* Cambridge: Cambridge University Press.

23. Grob, Gerald. (1983). *Mental illness and American society, 1875–1940.* Princeton, NJ: Princeton University Press, 27. As late as the 1880s, these institutions would still be brutal, in Europe and in the United States. When S. V. Clevenger came to the Cook County Lunatic Asylum in Chicago in 1883, he found that most of the patients had lice and were living in filthy conditions where they were straitjacketed, prescribed whiskey when sick, and died without any medical care. At Blackwell's lunatic asylum in New York in 1877, there was only one paid medical officer for more than 1400 female patients in a space designed for 900.

24. Marx, Karl. (1978 [1859]). A contribution to the critique of political economy [Preface]. In Robert C. Tucker (Ed.), *The Marx-Engels reader*. New York: W. W. Norton, 4.

25. Foucault, *Madness and civilization*, 48, 62.

26. Haskell, Thomas L. (1985). Capitalism and the origins of the humanitarian sensibility, part 1. *American Historical Review, 90*(2), 339–61.

27. See Gilman, Sander. (1982). *Seeing the insane*. Lincoln: University of Nebraska Press, 44–46.

28. Gilman, *Seeing the insane*, 47.

29. This view appears in countless documents, including in First Corinthians, in the New Testament: "If any of you think you are wise by the standards of this age, you should become 'fools' so that you may become wise. For the wisdom of this world is foolishness in God's sight." I Corinthians, 3, 18–19. "Lunatics" in literature and film have long served as the reflection of an insane society. Consider the 1946 Boris Karloff film *Bedlam*, about the insane residents of Bethlem asylum, in which the insane eventually apprehend the guards and doctors, put them on trial, and find them guilty of being sane.

30. Scull, Andrew T. (1979). *Museums of madness: The social organization of insanity in nineteenth-century England*. New York: St. Martin's Press, 18.

31. Graunt, J. (1662). *Natural and political observations mentioned in a following index, and made upon the bills of mortality ... with reference to the government, religion, trade, growth, ayre and the diseases of the said city*. London: J. Martyn, 22. Cited in Boulton, Jeremy, & Black, John. (2011). "Those, that die by reason of their madness": Dying insane in London, 1629–1830. *History of Psychiatry, 23*(1), 27–39.

32. Ray, Isaac. (1962 [1838]). *A treatise on the medical jurisprudence of insanity*. Cambridge, MA: Harvard University Press.

33. Report of the Limerick District Lunatic Asylum. (1867). Reprinted in Eghigian, Greg (Ed.), (2010). *From madness to mental health: Psychiatric disorder and its treatment in western civilization*. New Brunswick, NJ: Rutgers University Press.

34. Stone, Deborah A. (1984). *The disabled state*. Philadelphia: Temple University Press, 44–45.

35. Solomon, Andrew. (2001). *The noonday demon: An atlas of depression*. New York: Scribner, 300.

36. Fudge, Erica. (2006). *Brutal reasoning: Animals, rationality, and humanity in early modern England*. Ithaca, NY: Cornell University Press.

37. Animal metaphors for people with serious mental illnesses are also common in many other cultures. In parts of New Guinea some aberrant behaviors are called "*ahade idzi be*" ("a wild pig"), and the English phrase "going berserk" comes from the Old Norse term for a bear. See, for example, Newman, Philip L. (1964). "Wild man" behavior in a New Guinea highlands community. *American Anthropologist, 66*(1), 1–19.

38. Porter, Roy. (1998). Can the stigma of mental illness be changed? *Lancet, 352*, 1049.

39. Scott, Sir Walter (Ed.). (1814). *The works of Jonathan Swift*. Edinburgh: Archibald Constable, 554.

40. Gould, Stephen Jay. (1981). *The mismeasure of man*. New York: W. W. Norton, 394–99.

41. Mintz, Steven. (2004). *Huck's raft: A history of American childhood*. Cambridge, MA: Belknap Harvard.

42. Linebaugh, Peter, & Rediker, Marcus. (2001). *The many-headed hydra: Sailors, slaves, commoners, and the hidden history of the revolutionary Atlantic*. Boston: Beacon Press, 51.

43. Levine, Robert A. (1973). *Culture, personality, and behavior*. Chicago: Aldine, 254–65.

44. Federici, Sylvia. (2004). The great Caliban: The struggle against the rebel body. *Capitalism Nature Socialism, 15*(2), 7–16, 7.

45. Federici, The great Caliban, 188.

46. Martin, Emily. (2001). *Woman in the body: A cultural analysis of reproduction*. Boston: Beacon Press.

Chapter 2: The Invention of Mental Illness

1. Foucault, *Madness and civilization*, 213.

2. Sontag, Susan. (1978). *Illness as metaphor*. New York: Picador, 35.

3. Cited in Torrey, Edwin Fuller, & Miller, Judy. (2001). *The invisible plague: The rise of mental illness from 1750 to the present*. New Brunswick, NJ: Rutgers University Press.

4. Cross, Simon. (2012). Bedlam in mind: Seeing and reading historical images of madness. *European Journal of Cultural Studies, 15*(1), 19–34.

5. Quoted in Foucault, *Madness and civilization*, 146.

6. Gontard, Alexander von. (1988). The development of child psychiatry in 19th century Britain. *Journal of Child Psychology and Psychiatry, 29*(5), 569–88.

7. Observers in France echoed Howard. Foucault reproduces a letter written by the Bicêtre asylum bursar, appalled that criminals and poor people were housed together. He requested that "the prisoners be removed from Bicêtre, leaving only the poor, or indeed that the poor be sent elsewhere so that only the prisoners remain." And he continued: "If the latter is the preferred option, we could perhaps leave the mad where they are, as they are unfortunates of a different sort, who also bring horrible suffering to humanity." Foucault, Michel. (2006). *History of madness*. Khalfa, Jean (Ed.), Murphy, Jonathan, & Khlafa, Jean (Trans.). London: Routledge, 424–25.

8. Foucault, *Madness and civilization*, 213.

9. See Porter, Can the stigma of mental illness be changed?; Grange, K. M. (1961). Pinel and eighteenth century psychiatry. *Bulletin for the History of Medicine, 35*, 442–53; Charland, Louis C. (2010). Science and morals in the affective psychopathology of Philippe Pinel. *History of Psychiatry, 21*(1), 38–53.

10. Chilcoat, Michelle. (1998). Confinement, the family institution, and the case of Claire de Duras's *Ourika*. *L'Esprit Créateur, 38*(3), 6–16, 12.

11. Furst, Lillian R. (2003). *Idioms of distress: Psychosomatic disorders in medical and imaginative literature*. Albany: State University of New York Press, 23.

12. Grinker, Roy R., Sr. (1979). *Fifty years in psychiatry: A living history*. Springfield, IL: Charles C. Thomas, 69.

13. Reil, Johann. (1803). *Rhapsodieen über die Anwendung der psychischen Curmethode auf Geisteszerrüttungen*. Halle: In der Curtschen Buchhandlung, 205.

14. Marx, Otto M. (1990). German Romantic psychiatry, part 1. *History of Psychiatry, I*, 351–81, 365.

15. De Young, Mary. (2015). *Encyclopedia of asylum therapeutics: 1750–1950s*. Jefferson, NC: McFarland.

16. Levy, Norman, & Grinker, Roy R., Sr. (1943). Psychological observations in affective psychoses treated with combined convulsive shock and psychotherapy. *Journal of Nervous and Mental Disease, 97*(6), 623–37, 623.

17. Reil, *Rhapsodieen*, 7–8.

18. Marneros, Andreas. (2008). Psychiatry's 200th birthday. *British Journal of Psychiatry, 193*, 1–3.

19. Scull, Andrew. (1975). From madness to mental illness: Medical men as moral entrepreneurs. *European Journal of Sociology, 16*(2), 218–61; Keller, Richard C. (2005). Pinel in the Maghreb: Liberation, confinement, and psychiatric reform in French North Africa. *Bulletin of the History of Medicine, 79*(3), 459–99.

20. Foucault, *Madness and civilization*, 232.

21. Gamwell, Lynn, & Tomes, Nancy. (1995). *Madness in America: Cultural and medical perceptions of mental illness before 1914*. Ithaca, NY: Cornell University Press, 37.

22. Wright, David. (1997). Getting out of the asylum: Understanding the confinement of the insane in the nineteenth century. *Social History of Medicine, 10*(1), 137–55, 143.

23. Gilman, Sander. (2014). Madness as disability. *History of Psychiatry, 25*(4), 441–49, 444.

24. Charland, Louis C. (2007). Benevolent theory: Moral treatment at the York Retreat. *History of Psychiatry, 18*(1), 61–80.

25. Pinel used the word *écarts* to describe such differences—more precisely, "distinctions."

26. Mosse, George. (1982). Nationalism and respectability: Normal and abnormal sexuality in the nineteenth century. *Journal of Contemporary History, 17*, 221–46, 225.

27. See Gilman, Sander. (1999). *Making the body beautiful: A cultural history of aesthetic surgery*. Princeton, NJ: Princeton University Press.

28. Mosse, George L. (1985). *Nationalism and sexuality: Middle-class morality and sexual norms in modern Europe*. Madison: University of Wisconsin Press, 37.

29. Mosse, *Nationalism and sexuality*, 12; in 1828, George M. Burrows wrote: "The lamentable vice of masturbation is a frequent and formidable cause of insan-

ity." Cited in Porter, Roy. (1986). Love, sex, and madness in eighteenth-century England. *Social Research*, 53(2), 211–42, 222.

30. Parvin, T. (1854/1855). Review of European legislation for control of prostitution. *New Orleans Medical and Surgical Journal*, 11, 700–705.

31. Porter, Love, sex, and madness in eighteenth-century England, 228.

32. Darby, Robert. (2003). The masturbation taboo and the rise of routine male circumcision: A review of the historiography. *Journal of Social History*, 36(3), 737–52.

33. Money, John. (1985). *The destroying angel: Sex, fitness and food in the legacy of degeneracy theory, Graham crackers, Kellogg's Corn Flakes and American health history*. Buffalo, NY: Prometheus Books.

34. Whorton, James. (2001). The solitary vice: The superstition that masturbation could cause mental illness. *Western Journal of Medicine*, 175(1), 66–68.

35. Sokolow, Jayme A. (1983). *Eros and modernization: Sylvester Graham, health reform, and the origins of Victorian sexuality in America*. London: Associated University Presses.

36. Graham, Sylvester. (1834). *A lecture to young men, on chastity*. Providence, RI: Weeden and Cory, 25–26.

37. Mosse, *Nationalism and sexuality*, 32.

Chapter 3: The Divided Body

1. De Montaigne, Michel. (1903). *The journal of Montaigne's travels in Italy by way of Switzerland and Germany in 1580 and 1581* (3 vols.) (G. W. Waters, Trans.). London: John Murray.

2. The legacies of such views have been hard to shake. Under US laws, until 1990, American immigration officials were permitted to exclude homosexuals from immigrating. And as recently as 1986, the U.S. Supreme Court upheld a Georgia state law banning sodomy (oral or anal sex between any two consenting adults of whatever sex). It was overturned in 1998.

3. Laqueur, Robert. (1990). *Making sex: Body and gender from the Greeks to Freud*. Cambridge, MA: Harvard University Press. For a critical perspective on Laqueur's characterization of medieval sex, one less focused than Laqueur on continuities between ancient Greek medicine and the Middle Ages, see Cadden, Joan. (1993). *Meanings of sex difference in the Middle Ages: Medicine, science and culture*. Cambridge: Cambridge University Press.

4. Laqueur, Thomas. (2012). The rise of sex in the eighteenth century: Historical context and historiographical implications. *Signs: Journal of Women in Culture and Society*, 37(4), 802–13. Not surprisingly, most of the anatomical drawings in the Middle Ages were of women, not men, because women were the aberration to be explained.

5. Grinker, Roy R. (1994). *Houses in the rainforest: Farmers and foragers in Central Africa*. Berkeley: University of California Press.

6. Gettleman, Jeffrey. (2018). The peculiar position of India's third gender. *New York Times*, February 17, 2018.

7. Davies, Sharyn Graham. (2016). What we can learn from an Indonesian ethnicity that recognizes 5 genders. *U.S. News & World Report*, June 17, 2016.

8. Stip, E. (2015). RaeRae and Mahu: Third Polynesian gender. *Santé mentale au Québec, 40*(3), 193–208.

9. Laqueur, *Making sex*, 62.

10. Quoted in Ortner, Sherry B. (1972). Is female to male as nature is to culture? *Feminist Studies, 1*(2), 5–31.

11. Laqueur, *Making sex*, 213.

12. See Martin, Emily. (2001). *The woman in the body: A cultural analysis of reproduction*. Boston: Beacon Press.

13. Cited in Showalter, Elaine. (1980). Victorian women and insanity. *Victorian Studies, 23*(2), 157–81, 169.

14. Tosh, John. (2005). Masculinities in an industrializing society: Britain, 1800– 1914. *Journal of British Studies, 44*(2), 330–42, 336.

15. Chilcoat, Confinement, 13.

16. Chilcoat, Confinement, 13.

17. Scully, Pamela, & Crais, Clifton. (2010). Race and erasure: Sara Baartman and Hendrik Cesars in Cape Town and London. *Journal of British Studies, 47*, 301–23.

18. Qureshi, Sadia. (2004). Displaying Sara Baartman: "The Hottentot Venus." *History of Science, 17*, 233–57.

19. Gilman, Sander L. (1985). *Difference and pathology: Stereotypes of sexuality, race, and madness*. Ithaca, NY: Cornell University Press.

20. Comaroff, John, & Comaroff, Jean. (1991). *Of revelation and revolution, volume 1: Christianity, colonialism, and consciousness in colonial South Africa*. Chicago: University of Chicago Press.

21. Gilman, *Difference and pathology*, 107.

22. Porter, Love, sex, and madness in eighteenth-century England.

23. MacDonald, Michael. (1981). *Mystical Bedlam: Madness, anxiety and healing in seventeenth century England*. Cambridge: Cambridge University Press, 89.

24. Sontag, *Illness as metaphor*.

25. Showalter, Elaine. (1980). Victorian women and insanity. *Victorian Studies, 23*(2), 157–81, 170.

26. Showalter, Elaine. (1986). *The female malady: Women, madness, and English culture, 1830–1980*. New York: Pantheon.

27. Rose, *No right to be idle*.

28. Showalter, Victorian women and insanity, 177.

29. D'Emilio, John. (1983). Capitalism and gay identity. In Snitow, Ann, Stansell, Christine, & Thompson, Sharon (Eds.), *Powers of desire: The politics of sexuality*. New York: Monthly Review Press, 100–113.

30. Mosse, *Nationalism and sexuality*, 5.

31. Halperin, David. (1990). *One hundred years of homosexuality*. New York: Routledge.

32. See, for example, Cáceres, C. F. (1999). Sexual-cultural diversity in Lima, Peru. *Culture, Health and Sexuality, 6*, 41–47; Schiffter, Jacobo. (2000). *Public sex in a Latin society*. New York: Routledge; Parker, Richard G. (2009). *Bodies, pleasures, and passions: Sexual culture in contemporary Brazil* (2nd ed.). Nashville: Vanderbilt University Press; Kulick, Don. (1998). *Travesti: Sex, gender, and culture among Brazilian transgendered prostitutes*. Chicago: University of Chicago Press.

33. Halperin, *One hundred years of homosexuality*.

34. Rotundo, E. Anthony. (1989). Romantic friendship: Male intimacy and middle-class youth in the northern United States, 1800–1900. *Journal of Social History, 23*(1), 1–25.

35. Hacking, Ian. (1991). How should we do the history of statistics? In Burchell, Graham, Gordon, Colin, & Miller, Peter (Eds.), *The Foucault effect: Studies in governmentality*. Chicago: University of Chicago Press.

36. Arieno, Marlene A. (1989). *Victorian lunatics: A social epidemiology of mental illness in mid-nineteenth-century England*. London: Associated University Presses, 31.

37. Grob, Gerald. (2011). *The mad among us: A history of the care of America's mentally ill*. New York: The Free Press, 91.

38. Berrios, German E. (1996). *The history of mental symptoms: Descriptive psychopathology since the 19th century*. Cambridge: Cambridge University Press. Examples of mental illness terms include, in France, *délire de cotard* for mood disorders, *lypemania* for a cluster of symptoms associated with melancholia, and *délire emotif* or *folie lucide* for obsessive disorders; in Germany, *zwangsvorstellung* for obsessions, which was translated as "obsession" in England and "compulsion" in the United States.

39. Porter, Roy. (1990). Foucault's great confinement. *History of the Human Sciences, 3*(1), 47–54.

40. *Commissioners in Lunacy Annual Report* (1861), *18*, 77, cited in Arieno, *Victorian lunatics*, 115.

41. Grob, *Mental illness and American society*, 327.

42. Wright, David. (1997). Getting out of the asylum: Understanding the confinement of the insane in the nineteenth century. *Social History of Medicine, 10*(1), 137–55.

43. Bainbridge, William Sims. (1984). Religious insanity in America: The official nineteenth century theory. *Sociological Analysis, 45* (3), 223–39.

44. Deutsch, Albert. (1944). The first U.S. census of the insane (1840) and its use as pro-slavery propaganda. *Bulletin of the History of Medicine, XV* (5), 469–82.

45. Insanity in the Negro race. *Boston Courier*, June 15, 1843, col G.

46. Cited in Deutsch, The first U.S. census of the insane, 11.

47. See, for example, Jarvis, E. (1843). Insanity among the colored population of the free states. *American Journal of the Medical Sciences*, 268–82; Jarvis, E. (1843). On the supposed increase in insanity. *American Journal of Psychiatry, 8*(4), 333–64.

48. Jarvis, E. (1842). Statistics of insanity in the United States. *Boston Medical and Surgical Journal, 27*, 116–21; see also: Pasamanick, Benjamin. (1964). Myths regarding prevalence of mental disease in the American Negro. *JAMA: Journal of the American Medical Association, 56*(1), 6–17.

49. Deutsch, The first U.S. census of the insane, 480.

50. Bevis, W. M. (1921). Psychological traits of the southern negro with observations as to some of his psychoses. *American Journal of Psychiatry, 1*(69), 69–78.

51. Postell, William Dosite. (1953). Mental health among the slave population on southern plantations. *American Journal of Psychiatry, 110*(1), 52–54.

52. Kendi, Ibram X. (2017). *Stamped from the beginning: The definitive history of racist ideas in America.* New York: Bold Type Books.

53. Grinker, Roy R., & Spiegel, John P. (1963). *Men under stress.* New York: McGraw-Hill.

54. Kardiner, Abram. (2014 [1951]). *The mark of oppression.* New York: Martino.

55. Henderson, Carol E. (2002). *Scarring the black body: Race and representation in African-American literature.* Columbia: University of Missouri Press, 48.

56. Painter, Nell Irvin. (1996). *Sojourner Truth: A life, a symbol.* New York: W. W. Norton, 139, cited in Henderson, *Scarring the black body*, 48.

57. Henderson, *Scarring the black body*, 43.

58. Bromberg, Walter, & Simon, Franck. (1968). The "protest" psychosis: A specific type of reactive psychosis. *Archives of General Psychiatry, 19*(2), 155–60.

59. Metzl, Jonathan M. (2009). *The protest psychosis: How schizophrenia became a black disease.* Boston: Beacon Press, 210.

60. Du Bois, W. E. B. (1903). *The souls of black folk.* New York: Dover Publications, 2–3.

61. Blow, F. C., et al. (2004). Ethnicity and diagnostic patterns in veterans with psychoses. *Social Psychiatry and Psychiatric Epidemiology, 39*(10), 841–51.

62. Metzl, *The protest psychosis*, xi.

Chapter 4: The Divided Mind

1. Porter, Roy. (2015). Preface, in Haslam, John. *Illustrations of Madness* (Porter, Roy, Ed.). London: Routledge, xi.

2. Rosenhan, David. (1973). On being sane in insane places. *Science, 179*, 250–58.

3. Quoted and discussed in Decker, Hannah S. (2013). *The making of DSM-III: A diagnostic manual's conquest of American psychiatry.* Oxford: Oxford University Press, 178.

4. Decker, *The making of DSM-III*, 179.

5. McNally, Kiernan. (2016). *A critical history of schizophrenia.* New York: Palgrave Macmillan, 11.

6. Haslam, John. (1809). *Observations on madness and melancholy: Including practical remarks on those diseases.* London: J. Callow, 66–67.

7. Krauss, William C. (1898). The stigmata of degeneration. *American Journal of Insanity [Psychiatry], 55*(1), 55–88.

8. Cited in Barrett, Robert. (1998). Conceptual foundations of schizophrenia I: Degeneration. *Australian and New Zealand Journal of Psychiatry, 32*(5), 617–26, 620.

9. Barrett, Conceptual foundations of schizophrenia I, 618.

10. Barrett, Robert. (1996). *The psychiatric team and the social definition of schizophrenia: An anthropological study of person and illness.* Cambridge: Cambridge University Press, 191.

11. Barrett, *The psychiatric team and the social definition of schizophrenia,* 192.

12. Talbot, Eugene S. (1898). *Degeneracy: Its causes, signs, results.* London: Walter Scott, Ltd.

13. Dowbiggin, Ian. (1985). Degeneration and hereditarianism in French mental medicine 1840–90: Psychiatric theory as ideological adaptation. In Bynum, W. F., Porter, Roy, & Shepherd, Michael (Eds.), *The anatomy of madness: Essays in the history of psychiatry, volume I: People and ideas.* London: Tavistock, 209.

14. Albert Lemoine, cited in Dowbiggin, Degeneration and hereditarianism, 188–232, 209.

15. Barrett, Conceptual foundations of schizophrenia I, 623.

16. Cited in Barrett, *The psychiatric team and the social definition of schizophrenia,* 211.

17. Barrett, Conceptual foundations of schizophrenia I, 624.

18. Barrett, Robert. (1998). Conceptual foundations of schizophrenia II: Disintegration and division. *Australian and New Zealand Journal of Psychiatry, 32*(5), 617–26, 630.

19. See Trzepacz, Paula T., & Baker, Robert W. (1993). *The psychiatric mental status examination.* New York: Oxford University Press, 86–89.

20. Other, lesser known, tales described people in whom one self had become estranged from the other self, or whose minds had separated from their bodies. For example, in his 1771 novel, *The Sorrows of Young Werther,* Goethe promoted the idea that madness could be comprehended by listening to those who are mad, and that within each person there can exist both a sane and an insane self. See Thiher, Allen. (1999). *Neoclassicism, the rise of singularity, and moral treatment.* Ann Arbor: University of Michigan Press. On the ubiquity of dual selves in English literature, see Miller, Karl. (1985). *Doubles: Studies in literary history.* Oxford: Oxford University Press.

21. Akyeampong, Emmanuel. (2015). A historical overview of psychiatry in Africa. In Akyeampong, Emmanuel, Hill, Allan G., & Kleinman, Arthur (Eds.), *The culture of mental illness and psychiatric practice in Africa.* Bloomington: Indiana University Press, 24–49.

22. Quoted in Vaughn, Megan. (1983). Idioms of madness: Zomba Lunatic Asylum, Nyasaland, in the colonial period. *Journal of Southern African Studies, 9*(2), 218–38, 226.

23. John Colin Carothers, quoted in McCulloch, Jock. (1995). *Colonial psychiatry and "the African mind."* Cambridge: Cambridge University Press, 52.

24. Parle, Julie. (2003). Witchcraft or madness? The Amandiki of Zululand, 1894–1914. *Journal of Southern African Studies, 29*(1), 105–32, 112.

25. On the uses of witchcraft in colonial thought, see Smith, James. (2018). Witchcraft in Africa. In Grinker, Roy R., et al. (Eds.), *Companion to the anthropology of Africa.* Oxford: Wiley-Blackwell.

26. McCulloch, *Colonial psychiatry and "the African mind,"* 17.

27. Stoler, Anne. (1989). Rethinking colonial categories: European communities and the boundaries of rule. *Comparative Studies in Society and History, 31,* 134–61.

28. Swartz, Sally. (1995). The black insane in the Cape, 1891–1920. *Journal of Southern African Studies, 21*(3), 399–415.

29. Keller, Richard. (2001). Madness and colonization: Psychiatry in the British and French empires, 1800–1962. *Journal of Social History, 35*(2), 295–326.

30. Bloch, Sidney, & Reddaway, Peter. (1978). *Psychiatric terror: How Soviet psychiatry is used to suppress dissent.* New York: Basic Books; Ablard, J. D. (2003). Authoritarianism, democracy and psychiatric reform in Argentina, 1943–83. *History of Psychiatry, 14,* 361–76; Lu, S. Y., & Galli, V. B. (2002). Psychiatric abuse of Falun Gong practitioners in China. *Journal of the American Academy of Psychiatry and the Law, 30,* 126–30.

31. Ong, Aihwa. (1987). *Spirits of resistance and capitalist discipline: Factory women in Malaysia.* Albany: State University of New York Press.

Chapter 5: The Fates of War

1. Coco, Adrienne Phelps. (2010). Diseased, maimed, mutilated: Categorizations of disability and an ugly law in late nineteenth-century Chicago. *Journal of Social History, 44*(1), 23–37.

2. Quoted in Coco, Diseased, maimed, mutilated, 31–32.

3. Schweik, Susan M. (2009). *The ugly laws: Disability in public.* New York: New York University Press.

4. Grinker, Julius. (1912). Freud's psychotherapy. *Illinois Medical Journal, 22,* 185–95.

5. Geller, Jay. (1996). Le péché contre le sang: la syphilis et la construction de l'identité juive. *Revue Germanique International, 5,* 141–64.

6. Talbott, John E. (1997). Soldiers, psychiatrists and combat trauma. *Journal of Interdisciplinary History, 27*(3), 437–54; Reid, Fiona. (2014). "His nerves gave way": Shell shock, history and the memory of the First World War in Britain. *Endeavour, 38*(2), 91–100, 91.

7. Kleinman, *The illness narratives.*

8. Barham, Peter. (2004). *Forgotten lunatics of the Great War.* New Haven, CT: Yale University Press, 2.

9. *Washington Times Magazine.* (1900). Choose a wife as you would select live stock. December 9, 1900, 3.

10. *Chicago Record-Herald.* (1900). Doctor calls love a dream. December 9, 1900.

11. Loughran, Tracey. (2008). Hysteria and neurasthenia in pre-1914 British medical discourse and in histories of shell-shock. *History of Psychiatry, 19*(1), 25–46.

12. Cited in Shorter, Edward. (1992). *From paralysis to fatigue: A history of psychosomatic illness in the modern era.* New York: The Free Press, 75.

13. Marcus, Greil. (1998). One step back: Where are the elixirs of yesteryear when we hurt? *New York Times,* January 26, 1998.

14. Lutz, Tom. (1993). *American nervousness, 1903: An anecdotal history.* Ithaca, NY: Cornell University Press; see also: Beck, Julie. (2016). "Americanitis": The disease of living too fast. *The Atlantic,* March 11, 2016.

15. Grinker, R. R., Sr. (1963). A psychoanalytical historical island in Chicago (1911–12). *Archives of General Psychiatry, 8,* 392–404, 395.

16. Clevenger, S. B. (1883). Insanity in Chicago. *Chicago Medical Journal and Examiner, 47*(5), 449–63; see also: Rieff, Janice L., Keating, Durkin, & Grossman, James R. (Eds.). (2005). *Encyclopedia of Chicago.* Chicago: Chicago Historical Society.

17. Raffensperger, John G., & Boshes, Louis G. (Eds.). (1997). *The old lady on Harrison Street: Cook County Hospital, 1833–1995.* Chicago: Chicago Historical Society.

18. Duis, Perry R. (1998). *Challenging Chicago: Coping with everyday life, 1837–1920.* Urbana: University of Illinois Press, 334.

19. Barnes, J. K. (Ed.). (1870–1888). *Medical and surgical history of the War of Rebellion, 1861–1865* (6 vols.). Washington, DC: U.S. Government Printing Office *1*(1), 638–39, 711; 3, 884–85.

20. Calhoun, J. Theodore. (1864). Nostalgia as a disease of field service. *Medical and Surgical Reporter, 11,* 131; see also: McCann, W. H. (1941). Nostalgia: A review of the literature. *Psychological Bulletin, 38*(3), 165–82; Anderson, David. (2010). Dying of nostalgia: Homesickness in the Union Army during the Civil War. *Civil War History, 56*(3), 247–82; Clarke, Frances. (2007). So lonesome I could die: Nostalgia and debates over emotional control in the Civil War North. *Journal of Social History, 41*(2), 253–82; Anderson, Donald Lee, & Anderson, Godfrey Tryggve. (1984). Nostalgia and malingering in the military during the Civil War. *Perspectives in Biology and Medicine, 28*(1), 157–66; Starobinski, Jean, & Kemp, William S. (1966). The idea of nostalgia. *Diogenes, 14*(81), 103; Hall, J. K., Zilboorg, Gregory, & Bunker, Henry Alden (Eds.). (1944). *One hundred years of American psychiatry.* New York: Columbia University Press, 374.

21. Leese, Peter. (2002). *Shell shock: Traumatic neurosis and the British soldiers of the First World War.* London: Palgrave Macmillan, 17.

22. Reid, "His nerves gave way," 93.

23. Mosse, George L. (2000). Shell shock as a social disease. *Journal of Contemporary History, 35*(1), 101–8, 101–2.

24. Myers, Charles. (1915). A contribution to the study of shell shock. *Lancet, 185*(4772), 316–20.

25. Winter, Jay. (2000). Shell shock and the cultural history of the Great War. *Journal*

of Contemporary History, 35(1), 7–11, 10; see also: Lerner, Paul. (2009). *Hysterical men: War, psychiatry, and the politics of trauma in Germany, 1890–1930.* Ithaca, NY: Cornell University Press, 61.

26. De Young, *Encyclopedia of asylum therapeutics,* 202.

27. Winter, Shell shock and the cultural history of the Great War, 7.

28. Martinot, Alain. (2018). Les femmes de la grande guerre [women of the Great War]. *Cahier de Mémoire d'Ardèche et Temps Présent, 139,* 1–19.

29. Barham, *Forgotten lunatics of the Great War,* 182, 241.

30. Smith, Grafton Elliot, & Pear, T. H. (1918). *Shell shock and its lessons* (2nd ed.). Manchester, UK: Manchester University Press, 19.

31. Barker, Pat. (1991). *Regeneration.* New York: Plume, 48.

32. Barker, *Regeneration,* 48.

33. *Lancet,* October 31, 1914, quoted in Bogacz, Ted. (1989). War neurosis and cultural change in England, 1914–22: The work of the War Office Committee of Enquiry into "Shell-Shock." *Journal of Contemporary History, 24*(2), 227–56, 234.

34. Southard, E. E. (1919). *Shell-shock and other neuropsychiatric problems: Presented in five hundred and eighty-nine case histories from the war literature, 1914–1918.* Boston: W. M. Leonard.

35. Quoted in Boehnlein, James K., & Hinton, Devon E. (2016). From shell shock to PTSD and traumatic brain injury: A historical perspective on responses to combat trauma. In Hinton, Devon E., & Good, Byron (Eds.), *Culture and PTSD: Trauma in global and historical perspective.* Philadelphia: University of Pennsylvania Press, 161.

36. Crocq, Marc Antoine, & Crocq, Louis. (2000). From shell shock and war neurosis to posttraumatic stress disorder: A history of psychotraumatology. *Dialogues in Clinical Neuroscience, 2*(1), 47–55.

37. Pols, Hans, & Oak, Stephanie. (2007). War and military mental health: The US psychiatric response in the 20th century. *American Journal of Public Health, 97*(12), 2132–42.

38. Quoted in Lerner, *Hysterical men,* 61.

39. Macleod, Sandy. (2015). Australasian contributions to the "shell shock" literature of World War I. *Australasian Psychiatry, 23*(4), 396–98, 396.

40. Ellenberger, Henri F. (1970). *The discovery of the unconscious: The history and evolution of dynamic psychiatry.* New York: Basic Books, 95.

41. Lerner, *Hysterical men,* 26.

42. Freud, Sigmund (1957 [1917]). The sense of symptoms. In *The Standard Edition of the complete psychological works of Sigmund Freud, volume 16, 1916–1917.* Strachey, James (Ed.). London: Hogarth Press, 257–72.

43. Lerner, *Hysterical men,* 62.

44. Lerner, *Hysterical men,* 62.

45. Thomas Salmon, quoted in Shephard, Ben. (2000). *War of nerves: Soldiers and psychiatrists, 1914–1994.* London: Jonathan Cape, 101.

46. Ernst, Waltraud. (1991). *Mad tales from the Raj: Colonial psychiatry in South Asia,*

1800–1858. New York: Anthem Press; see also: Keller, Richard. (2001). Madness and colonization: Psychiatry in the British and French empires, 1800–1962. *Journal of Social History, 35*(2), 295–326.

47. Bogacz, War neurosis and cultural change in England, 227–56, 230.
48. Lerner, *Hysterical men*, 40.
49. Lerner, *Hysterical men*, 4–5. Many twentieth-century physicians agreed with Georg Groddeck, one of the pioneers of psychosomatic medicine, who wrote in 1923 of all diseases, psychological and physical, that "illness does not come from without; man creates it for himself, uses the outer world merely as an instrument with which to make himself ill." Groddeck, Georg. (1979 [1923]). *The book of the it*. Northport, AL: Vision Press. Susan Sontag cites Groddeck in *Illness as Metaphor* to suggest that physicians believed diseases were caused by the suppression of one's passions; in her words, "character causes the disease—because it has not expressed itself." Sontag, *Illness as metaphor*, 46.
50. Fassin, Didier, & Reichtman, Richard. (2009). *The empire of trauma: An inquiry into the condition of victimhood*. Princeton, NJ: Princeton University Press, 62.
51. Reid, "His nerves gave way," 93.
52. Some historians have lamented the fact that scholars have not adequately addressed the reasons behind the assumption in the British military that enlisted men and officers developed different illnesses in both world wars; see Shephard, Ben. (1999). "Pitiless psychology": The role of prevention in British military psychiatry in the Second World War. *History of Psychiatry, 10*, 491–524.
53. Barbusse, Henri. (1919). *Light*. Fitzwater Wray (Trans.). New York: E. P. Dutton.
54. Jones, Edgar. (2012). Shell shocked. *Monitor on Psychology, 43*(6), 18.
55. Shephard, Ben. (2001). *A war of nerves: Soldiers and psychiatrists in the twentieth century*. Cambridge, MA: Harvard University Press, 286.
56. Cited in Jones, Edgar, & Wessely, Simon. (2005). *Shell shock to PTSD: Military psychiatry from 1900 to the Gulf War*. Hove, UK: Psychology Press, 215.
57. House of Lords debates volume 39, February 10, 1920, April 28, 1920. London: HMSO. Quoted in Jones & Wessely, *Shell shock to PTSD*, 150.
58. Jones & Wessely, *Shell shock to PTSD*, 151.
59. Shephard, *War of nerves*, 55.
60. Reid, "His nerves gave way," 97.
61. McNally, Richard J. (2016). Is PTSD a transhistoric phenomenon? In Hinton & Good, *Culture and PTSD*, 117–34.
62. McNally, Is PTSD a transhistoric phenomenon?, 120–21.
63. Marlowe, David H. (2001). *Psychological and psychosocial consequences of combat and deployment: With special emphasis on the Gulf War*. Santa Monica, CA: RAND.
64. Arnold, Ken, Vogel, Klaus, & Peto, James. (2008). *War and medicine*. London: Wellcome Collection; see also: Allen, Arthur. (2007). *Vaccine: The controversial story of medicine's greatest lifesaver*. New York: W. W. Norton, especially chapter 4, War is good for babies, 115–59.

Chapter 6: Finding Freud

1. Shorter, Edward. (1997). *A history of psychiatry: From the era of the asylum to the age of Prozac.* New York: Wiley.

2. Gilman, Sander. (1987). The struggle of psychiatry with psychoanalysis: Who won? *Critical Inquiry, 13,* 293–313.

3. Grinker, Roy Richard, Sr. (1963). A psychoanalytical historical island in Chicago (1911–1912). *Archives of General Psychiatry, 8,* 392–404.

4. Grinker, Julius. (1912). Freud's psychotherapy. *Illinois Medical Journal, 22,* 185–95.

5. Grinker, R. R., Sr. Letter to Walter Freeman. December 8, 1965. Property of the author.

6. Rogow, Arnold A. (1970). *The psychiatrists.* New York: Putnam, 109. In another survey of the "most controversial living psychoanalysts," only three of the twelve vote-getters were American-born (John Rosen, Grinker, and Kubie). Rogow, *The psychiatrists,* 111.

7. Bassoe, Peter. (1928). Julius Grinker as a neurologist and as a man. Read before the Chicago Neurological Society, February 16, 1928. Property of the author.

8. Freud, Sigmund. (2010 [1930]). *Civilization and its discontents.* New York: W. W. Norton.

9. Gay, Peter. (1981). Introduction. *Bergasse 19: Sigmund Freud's home and offices, Vienna 1938: The photographs of Edmund Engelman.* Chicago: University of Chicago Press.

10. Grinker, A psychoanalytical historical island in Chicago, 392–404, 392.

11. U.S. Government, Bureau of the Census, Illinois, 1930 census.

12. Despite being a Jew, Grinker was appointed the first head of psychiatry at the university in 1930. The university made psychiatry a section within the Department of Medicine on the recommendation of Franklin McLean, MD, the former chair of medicine and head of clinics at the medical school, and a strong advocate for the establishment of departments of psychiatry in all universities, with or without medical schools. The University of Chicago would not have its own independent department of psychiatry until 1955.

13. Leff, Laurel. (2020). *Well worth saving: American universities' life-and-death decisions on refugees from Nazi Europe.* New Haven, CT: Yale University Press, 105–6.

14. Interview with Roy R. Grinker, Sr. Archives of the Chicago Institute for Psychoanalysis, cassette tape.

15. Gardener, LaMaurice. (1971). The therapeutic relationship under various conditions of race. *Psychotherapy: Theory, Research and Practice, 8*(1), 78–87.

16. Rogow, *The psychiatrists,* 73–76; 78. The survey and its significance are described in more detail in Luhrmann, T. M. (2000). *Of two minds: The growing disorder in American psychiatry.* New York: Alfred A. Knopf, 220–22.

17. Gould, Robert E. (1968). Dr. Strangeclass or how I stopped worrying about the theory and began treating the blue collar worker. *Journal of Contemporary Psychotherapy, 1*(1), 49–63.

18. The recollections of my grandfather's analysis with Freud derive from multiple sources. These include my own conversations with him, before his death in 1992, a taped interview lodged at the archives of the Chicago Institute for Psychoanalysis, and his written recollections in his book *Fifty Years in Psychiatry: A Living History*, and in the 1940 article by him, "Reminiscences of a Personal Contact with Freud" (*American Journal of Orthopsychiatry, 10*(4), 850–54). I also draw on letters between my grandfather and Freud lodged at the United States Library of Congress in the Sigmund Freud Collection. In addition, see Freeman, Walter. (1968). *The psychiatrist: Personalities and patterns.* New York: Grune and Stratton, 249–56; Weinberg, Jack. (1980). Roy R. Grinker, Sr.: Some biographical notes. *Journal of the American Academy of Psychoanalysis, 8*(3), 441–49; and Kavka, Jerome. (2000). Sigmund Freud's letters to R.R. Grinker Sr., 1933–1934: Plans for a personal analysis. *Psychoanalysis and History, 2*(2), 152–61.

19. Letter from Mildred Barman Grinker to Sigmund Freud, January 2, 1934. Archives of the Chicago Institute for Psychoanalysis.

20. Wortis, Joseph S. (1954). *Fragments of an analysis with Freud.* New York: Simon & Schuster.

21. *New York Times.* (1956). Tribute to Freud asks for him the "human privilege of error." April 21, 1956, 37.

22. Grinker, *Fifty years in psychiatry,* 174.

23. However, my grandfather did put his children in analysis—thirteen-year-old Joan (my aunt) and eleven-year-old Roy Jr. (my father). Both Joan and Roy Jr. would remember the analyses as "educational exercises," although my grandfather's letters to Freud suggested that they were therapeutic. He told Freud the children were "making great improvement."

24. R. R. Grinker to Sigmund Freud, February 18, 1936. Property of the author.

25. Property of the author. For other personal recollections of Freud, see Ruitenbeek, Hendrik M. (Ed.). (1973). *Freud as we knew him.* Detroit, MI: Wayne State University Press.

Chapter 7: War Is Kind

1. Glass, Albert J. (1966). Army psychiatry before World War II. In *Medical Department, United States Army, neuropsychiatry in World War II, volume I: Zone of interior.* Washington, DC: Office of the Surgeon General, Department of the Army, 3–23, 14.

2. Glass, Army psychiatry before World War II, 9.

3. Tuttle, Arnold Dwight. (1927). *Handbook for the medical soldier.* Baltimore: William Wood. Cited in Wanke, Paul. (1999). American military psychiatry and its role among ground forces in World War II. *Journal of Military History, 63,* 127–46, 130.

4. *Military Medical Manual* (2nd ed.). Harrisburg, PA: Military Service Publishing Co.

5. Jones & Wessely, *Shell shock to PTSD*, 67.

6. Bernucci, Robert J., & Glass, Albert J. (1966). Preface. In *Medical Department, United States Army, neuropsychiatry in World War II, volume I: Zone of interior*, xv–xviii, xvii.

7. Glass, Albert J. (1973). Preface. In *Medical Department, United States Army, neuropsychiatry in World War II, volume II: Overseas theaters*. Washington, DC: Office of the Surgeon General, Department of the Army, xvii–x.

8. Quoted in Bromberg, Walter. (1982). *Psychiatry between the wars, 1918–1945: A recollection*. Westport, CT: Greenwood Press, 153.

9. Gabriel, Richard A., & Metz, Karen S. (1992). *A history of military medicine, volume II: From the Renaissance through modern times*. Westport, CT: Greenwood Press, 250.

10. Bliss, G. (1919). Mental defectives and the war. *Journal of Psycho-Asthenics, 24*, 11–17. Cited in Smith, J. David, & Lazaroff, Kurt. (2006). "Uncle Sam needs you" or does he? Intellectual disabilities and lessons from the "Great Wars." *Mental Retardation, 44*(6), 433–37.

11. Smith & Lazaroff, "Uncle Sam needs you" or does he?, 434.

12. Davidson, H. A. (1940). Mental hygiene in our armed forces. *Military Surgeon, 86*, 477–81, 480.

13. Jones & Wessely, *Shell shock to PTSD*, 106. Walter Menninger cites the figure of 12 percent in "Wartime Lessons for Peacetime Psychiatry." University of Chicago Round Table. September 27, 1946. Audio available at: https://www.wnyc.org/story/wartime-lessons-for-peacetime-psychiatry. Retrieved May 18, 2018.

14. Jones & Wessely, *Shell Shock to PTSD*, 106.

15. Pols, Hans. (2011). The Tunisian campaign, war neuroses, and the reorientation of American psychiatry during World War II. *Harvard Review of Psychiatry, 19*, 313–20, 314.

16. Jones & Wessely, *Shell shock to PTSD*, 106; see also: Glass, Albert J. (1966). Army psychiatry before World War II. *Medical Department, United States Army, neuropsychiatry in World War II, volume I: Zone of interior*, 3–23, 7.

17. Herman, Ellen. (1995). *The romance of American psychology: Political culture in the age of experts*. Berkeley: University of California Press, 89.

18. Jones & Wessely, *Shell Shock to PTSD*, 106; see also: Shephard, *War of nerves*, 201.

19. Whitney, E. A., & MacIntyre, E. M. (1944). War record of Elwyn boys. *American Journal of Mental Deficiency, 49*, 80–85, cited in Smith & Lazaroff, "Uncle Sam needs you" or does he?, 435.

20. Scheerenberger, R. C. (1983). *A History of Mental Retardation*. Baltimore: Paul H. Brookes, 75; see also: Doll, Edgar A. (1944). Mental defectives and the war. *American Journal of Mental Deficiency, 49*, 64–66.

21. Brill, Norman Q., & Kupper, Herbert I. (1966). The psychiatric patient after discharge. *Medical Department, United States Army, neuropsychiatry in World War II, volume I: Zone of interior*, 729–33, 731.

22. Jaffe, Eric. (2014). *A curious madness: An American combat psychiatrist, a Japanese*

war crimes suspect, and an unsolved mystery from World War II. New York: Scribner, 130.

23. Menninger, William C. (1948). *Psychiatry in a troubled world.* New York: Wiley; see also: Glass, Army psychiatry before World War II, 3–23, 9.

24. Bond, Douglas D. (1973). General neuropsychiatric history. In *Medical Department, United States Army, neuropsychiatry in World War II, Volume II: Overseas theaters,* 851–79, 857.

25. Shephard, *War of nerves,* 213.

26. Jaffe, *A curious madness,* 139.

27. Appel, John. (1946). Incidence of neuropsychiatric disorders in the United States Army in World War II (preliminary report). *American Journal of Psychiatry,* 102(4), 433–36, 435.

28. Pols, The Tunisian campaign, 316.

29. Cited in Shepherd, *War of nerves,* and Lieberman, Jeffrey A. (2015). *Shrinks: The untold story of psychiatry.* New York: Back Bay Books, frontispiece.

30. Pols, The Tunisian campaign, 317.

31. Cited in Menninger, Walter W. (2004). Contributions of William C. Menninger to military psychiatry. *Bulletin of the Menninger Clinic,* 68(4), 277–96.

32. Glass, Col. Albert J. (1954). Psychotherapy in the combat zone. *American Journal of Psychiatry,* 110(10), 725–31, 727.

33. Pols, Hans. (1992). The repression of war trauma in American psychiatry after WWII. *Clio medica: Acta Academia Internationalis Historiae Medicinae,* 55, 251–76, 255–56.

34. Hadfield, J. A. (1942). War neurosis: A year in a neuropathic hospital. *British Medical Journal,* 1(4234), 281–85, 281.

35. Grinker, Roy R., & Spiegel, John. (1943). *War neuroses in North Africa.* New York: Josiah Macy Jr. Foundation for the Air Surgeon, Army Air Forces, 12. The book was declassified following the war and published in 1945 by the Blakiston Company, Philadelphia. An expanded edition was published in 1963 under the title *Men Under Stress,* by McGraw-Hill, New York.

36. *The doctor fights.* NBC Radio. August 7, 1945. Empire Broadcasting Corporation, vinyl (8 discs), 78 rpm.

37. Laurence, William. (1944). "Guilt feelings" pictured in fliers: Army Air Force psychiatrists tell associates of "mental X-rays" after missions. *New York Times,* May 17, 1944, 36.

38. Sargant, William, & Slater, Eliot. (1940). Acute war neuroses. *Lancet,* 236(6097), 1–2, 6.

39. Horsley, J. Stephen. (1936). Narco-analysis. *Lancet,* 227(5862), 55–56.

40. Drayer, Calvin S., & Glass, Albert J. (1973). Introduction. In *Medical Department, United States Army, neuropsychiatry in World War II, volume II: Overseas theaters,* 1–23, 8.

41. Drayer and Glass, Introduction, 17. However, in 1946, in a Chicago court case that received national attention, my grandfather did use narcosynthesis in Chi-

cago on a seventeen-year-old boy to extract a confession of murder. Kaempffert, Waldemar. (1946). "Truth Serum," reportedly used in Heirens case, is well known to psychiatrists. *New York Times*, August 4, 1946.

42. Mackenzie, DeWitt, Worden, Major Clarence, & Kirk, Major General Norman T. (1945). *Men without guns*. Philadelphia: Blakiston Company, 45.

43. National Broadcasting Corporation. (1946). Medicine serves America: Psychiatric objectives of our time, with Dr. Roy R. Grinker. December 11, 1946. 4 discs, 78 rpm. Property of the author.

44. Bérubé, Allan. (1991). *Coming out under fire: The history of gay men and women in World War Two*. New York: Plume, 152.

45. Severinghaus, E. L., & Chornyak, John. (1945). A study of homosexual adult males. *Psychosomatic Medicine, 7*, 302–5; Cornsweet, A. C., & Hayes, M. F. Conditioned response to fellatio. *American Journal of Psychiatry, 103*, 76–78; Solomon, Joseph C. (1948). Adult character and behavior disorders. *Journal of Clinical Psychopathology, 9*, 1–55; Kessler, Morris M., & Poucher, George E. (1945). Coprophagy in absence of insanity: A case report. *Journal of Nervous and Mental Diseases, 102*, 290–93.

46. Bérubé, *Coming out under fire*, 165–66.

47. Greenspan, Herbert, & Campbell, John D. (1945). The homosexual as a personality type. *American Journal of Psychiatry, 101*, 682–89.

48. Bérubé, *Coming out under fire*, 62–63.

49. Bérubé, *Coming out under fire*, 83.

50. Serlin, David. (2003). Crippling masculinity: Queerness and disability in U.S. military culture, 1800–1945. *Gay and Lesbian Quarterly, 9*(1–2), 149–79.

51. Homosexuals, Circular No. 3. War Department. Washington, DC, January 3, 1944. Papers of John Spiegel, courtesy of Heli Meltsner.

52. Estes, Steve. (2018). The dream that dare not speak its name: Legacies of the civil rights movement and the fight for gay military service. In Bristol, Douglas Walter, Jr., & Stur, Heather Marie (Eds.), *Integrating the U.S. military: Race, gender, and sexual orientation since World War II*. Baltimore: Johns Hopkins University Press, 198–218.

53. West, Louis Jolyon, Doidge, William T., & Williams, Robert L. (1958). An approach to the problem of homosexuality in the military service. *American Journal of Psychiatry, 115*(5), 392–401, 396.

54. West, Doidge, & Williams, An approach to the problem of homosexuality in the military service, 398.

55. Award-winning journalist Alix Spiegel, the granddaughter of John Spiegel, magnificently describes the role John Spiegel played in the removal of homosexuality from the DSM, as well as the details of his personal life. Spiegel, Alix. (2002). 81 words. Radio broadcast of *This American life*. National Public Radio. January 18, 2002.

56. Leed, Eric J. (1979). *No man's land: Combat & identity in World War I*. Cambridge: Cambridge University Press.

57. Grinker, Roy Richard. (2010). The five lives of the psychiatry manual. *Nature,* 468(11), 168–70; Grob, Gerald N. (1991). Origins of DSM-I: A study in appearance and reality. *American Journal of Psychiatry, 148*(4), 421–31. Houts, Arthur C. (2000). Fifty years of psychiatric nomenclature: Reflections on the 1943 War Department Technical Bulletin, Medical 203. *Journal of Clinical Psychology,* 56(7), 935–67.

58. Pols, The repression of war trauma in American psychiatry after WWII, 251–76, 256.

59. Grinker, *Fifty years in psychiatry.*

60. Grinker, *Fifty years in psychiatry.*

61. The phrase is often attributed to Canadian psychiatrist Chaim Shatan (1924–2001).

Chapter 8: Norma and Normman

1. Kinder, John M. (2015). *Paying with their bodies: American war and the problem of the disabled veteran.* Chicago: University of Chicago Press, 260–61; Terkel, Studs. (1984). *The good war: An oral history of World War II.* New York: The New Press.

2. Pols, The repression of war trauma in American psychiatry after WWII, 251–76, 261.

3. Pols, The repression of war trauma in American psychiatry after WWII.

4. On the challenges to postwar masculinity, see: Jeffords, Susan. (1989). *The remasculinization of America: Gender and the Vietnam War.* Bloomington: Indiana University Press.

5. *Chicago Daily News.* (1953). Cry for "normal" times stirs warning. November 17, 1953, 5.

6. Nisbet, Robert. (1945). The coming problem of assimilation. *American Journal of Sociology, 50*(4), 261–70, 263.

7. Gerber, Heroes and misfits, 548.

8. Pols, The repression of war trauma in American psychiatry after WWII, 263–64, emphasis mine.

9. Wartime lessons for peacetime psychiatry.

10. Wartime lessons for peacetime psychiatry. A major study commissioned by General Dwight D. Eisenhower in the late 1950s noted that "most of the young men who failed in WWII although normal at birth had suffered serious deprivations in childhood and adolescence." Ginsberg, E. (1959). *The ineffective soldier, volume 2: Breakdown and recovery.* New York: Columbia University Press.

11. Braceland, Francis J. George Neely Raines: A memorial. Unpublished eulogy. National Archives, Washington, DC.

12. Lundberg, Ferdinand, & Farnham, Marynia. (1947). *Modern woman: The lost sex.* New York: Harper and Brothers.

13. Blum, Deborah. (2011). *Love at Goon Park: Harry Harlow and the science of affection.* New York: Basic Books.

14. *New York Times.* (1973). The APA ruling on homosexuality. December 23, 1973.
15. Lieberman, Jeffrey. (2015). *Shrinks: The untold story of psychiatry.* New York: Little, Brown, 122.
16. Creadick, Anna. (2010). *Perfectly average: The pursuit of normality in postwar America.* Amherst: University of Massachusetts Press.
17. Hooton, Earnest. A. (1945). *Young man, you are normal.* New York: Putnam, 102.
18. Cited in *Smithsonian* magazine. https://www.smithsonianmag.com/history/reckless-breeding-of-the-unfit-earnest-hooton-eugenics-and-the-human-body-of-the-year-2000-15933294/#1oqqUTIrzMes26o0.99
19. Cantor, Nathaniel. (1941). What is a normal mind? *American Journal of Orthopsychiatry, 11,* 676–83, 682. On the rarity of the "normal," see also: Lunbeck, Elizabeth. (1994). *The psychiatric persuasion: Knowledge, gender, and power in modern America.* Princeton, NJ: Princeton University Press.
20. Cited in Cryle, Peter, & Stephens, Elizabeth. (2017). *Normality: A critical genealogy.* Chicago: University of Chicago Press, 333.
21. Passages about homosexual behavior reprinted in Kinsey, Alfred C., Pomeroy, Wardell R., & Martin, Clyde E. (2003). Sexual behavior in the human male. *American Journal of Public Health, 93*(6), 894–98. The authors wrote: "At least 37 percent of the male population has some homosexual experience between the beginning of adolescence and old age. This is more than one male in three of the persons that one may meet as he passes along a city street. Among the males who remain unmarried until the age of 35, almost exactly 50 percent have homosexual experience between the beginning of adolescence and that age." The original citation is Kinsey, Alfred C., Pomeroy, Wardell R., & Martin, Clyde E. (1948). *Sexual behavior in the human male.* Philadelphia: W. B. Saunders, 610–66.
22. Cryle & Stephens, *Normality,* 350.
23. Grinker, Roy R., Sr., Grinker, Roy R., Jr., & Timberlake, John. (1962). Mentally healthy young males (homoclites). *Archives of General Psychiatry, 6*(6), 405–53.
24. Murray, Henry A. (1951). In nomine diaboli. *New England Quarterly, 24*(4), 435–52.
25. *New York Times.* (1949). The patient at Bethesda. April 13, 1949, 28.
26. Rogow, Arnold A. (1963). *James Forrestal: A study of personality, politics, and policy.* New York: Macmillan; Hoopes, Townsend, & Brinkley, Douglas. (2000). *Driven patriot: The life and times of James Forrestal.* Annapolis, MD: Naval Institute Press, 10.
27. Hoopes & Brinkley, *Driven patriot.*
28. Werner, August A., et al. (1934). Involutional melancholia: Probable etiology and treatment. *JAMA: Journal of the American Medical Association, 103*(1), 13–16.
29. Interestingly, philosopher Nancy Sherman invokes a public reading of *Ajax,* staged by Theater of War Productions, as an analogy for the shame, suicidality, and urge for moral repair among veterans, in her 2015 book. Sherman, Nancy. (2015). *Afterwar: Healing the moral wounds of our soldiers.* Oxford: Oxford University Press.

30. Huie, William Bradford. (1950). Untold facts in the Forrestal case. *American Mercury, 71*(324), 643–52.

31. Pearson, Drew. (1949). Pearson replies: A communication. *Washington Post* (editorial). May 30, 1949.

32. *Washington Post* (editorial). May 23, 1949.

33. Group for the Advancement of Psychiatry. (1973). *The VIP with psychiatric impairment.* New York: Scribner, 1.

34. Group for the Advancement of Psychiatry, *The VIP with psychiatric impairment*, 1.

Chapter 9: From the Forgotten War to Vietnam

1. Truman, Harry S. (1948). Remarks at the National Health Assembly Dinner. Public Papers, Harry S. Truman, 1945–1953, May 1. Harry S. Truman Presidential Library and Museum. Retrieved November 27, 2018, from www.trumanlibrary.org

2. Brosin, in Wartime lessons for peacetime psychiatry.

3. Menninger, in Wartime lessons for peacetime psychiatry.

4. Rees, John Rawlings. (1945). *The shaping of psychiatry by war.* London: Chapman and Hall. Full text on-line, retrieved May 24, 2018, from https://archive.org/stream/shapingofpsychia029218mbp/shapingofpsychia029218mbp_djvu.txt

5. Wartime lessons for peacetime psychiatry.

6. Descartes, Rene. (1968). *Discourse on method and the meditations.* Sutcliffe, F. E. (Ed. and Trans.). Harmondsworth: Penguin.

7. McGaugh, Scott. (2011). *Battlefield angels: Saving lives under enemy fire from Valley Forge to Afghanistan.* Oxford: Osprey Publishing, 161.

8. Shephard, *War of nerves*, 342.

9. Ritchie, Elspeth Cameron. (2002). Psychiatry in the Korean War: Peril, PIES, and prisoners of war. *Military Medicine, 167*(11), 898–903.

10. The television show *M*A*S*H* brilliantly reflected the importance of psychiatry in its final episode when the lead character, surgeon Captain Hawkeye Pierce (played by Alan Alda), depressed and unable to work, returns to health only after a military psychiatrist helps him understand the traumatic source of his psychological disability.

11. Walaszek, Art. (2017). Keep calm and recruit on: Residency recruitment in an era of increased anxiety about the future of psychiatry. *Academic Psychiatry, 41,* 213–20.

12. In comparison to western Europe, psychoanalysis has always been unpopular in eastern Europe, especially in the USSR. Soviet psychologists were more interested in human consciousness than the unconscious, a patient's realities more than his fantasies. See, for example: Matza, Tomas. (2018). *Shock therapy: Psychology, precarity, and well-being in Postsocialist Russia.* Durham: Duke University Press, 46.

13. Funkenstein, D. H. (1965). The problem of increasing the number of psychiatrists. *American Journal of Psychiatry, 121*(9), 852–63.

14. Grinker, Roy R., Sr. (1982). Roy R. Grinker, Sr. In Michael Shepherd (Ed.), *Psychiatrists on psychiatry*. Cambridge: Cambridge University Press, 29–41, 37.

15. Grinker, Roy R., Sr. (1965). The sciences of psychiatry: Fields, fences, and riders. *American Journal of Psychiatry, 122*, 367–76; see also: Decker, *The making of DSM-III*, 8.

16. Berger, Milton Miles. (1946). Japanese military psychiatry in Korea. *American Journal of Psychiatry, 103*(2), 214–16.

17. Yoo, *It's madness*, 48.

18. Glass, A. J. (1953). Psychiatry in the Korean campaign: A historical review. *U.S. Armed Forces Medical Journal, 4*(11), 1563–83; see also: Norbury, F. B. (1953). Psychiatric admissions in a combat division in 1952. *Medical Bulletin of the U.S. Army, Far East, 1*(8), 130–33.

19. Yum, Jennifer. (2014). *In sickness and in health: Americans and psychiatry in Korea, 1950–1962*. PhD dissertation, Harvard University, Cambridge, MA, 79–100.

20. Yum, *In sickness and in health*, 106.

21. Gerber, David A. (1994). Heroes and misfits: The troubled social reintegration of disabled veterans in "The Best Years of Our Lives." *American Quarterly, 46*(4), 545–74.

22. Carruthers, Susan L. (2009). *Cold War captives: Imprisonment, escape, and brainwashing*. Berkeley: University of California Press, see chapter five, Prisoners of Pavlov: Korean War captivity and the brainwashing scare.

23. Ritchie, Psychiatry in the Korean War, 902.

24. Halliwell, Martin. (2012). American psychiatry, World War II and the Korean War. In Piette, Adam, & Rawlinson, Mark (Eds.), *The Edinburgh companion to twentieth-century British and American war literature*. Edinburgh: Edinburgh University Press, 294–303, 298.

25. *New York Times*. (1954). The fruits of brainwashing. January 28, 1954, 26.

26. Gallery, Rear Adm. D. V. Quoted in Carruthers, Susan L. (2018). When Americans were afraid of being brainwashed. *New York Times* (opinion page), January 18, 2018.

27. Carruthers, Susan L. (2009). *Cold War captives*. Los Angeles: University of California Press, 187.

28. Carruthers, *Cold War captives*, 18, 187.

29. Shephard, *War of nerves*, 343; Shephard says there were never more than twenty, but Allerton gives the number as twenty-three. Allerton, William S. (1969). Army psychiatry in Viet Nam. In Bourne, P. G. (Ed.), *The psychology and physiology of stress*. New York: Academic Press, 2–17, 9.

30. Jones, F. D., & Johnson, A. W. (1975). Medical and psychiatric treatment policy and practice in Vietnam. *Journal of Social Issues, 31*(4), 49–65.

31. Glass, Albert. (1974). Mental health programs in the armed forces. In Caplan, G. (Ed.), *American handbook of psychiatry*. New York: Basic Books, 800–809, 801.

32. Scott, Wilbur. (1990). PTSD in DSM-III: A case in the politics of diagnosis and disease. *Social Problems, 37*(3), 294–310, 297.

33. Marlowe, *Psychological and Psychosocial Consequences of Combat and Deployment,* 73; see also: Horowitz, M. (1975). A prediction of delayed stress response syndromes in Vietnam veterans. *Journal of Social Issues, 31*(4); Bourne, P. (1970). Military psychiatry and the Viet Nam experience. *American Journal of Psychiatry, 127,* 481–88; Jones, F. D., & Johnson, A. W. (1975). Medical and psychiatric treatment policy and practice in Vietnam. *Journal of Social Issues, 31*(4), 49–65. Richard McNally writes: "Ironically, historical scholarship has now confirmed that psychiatric casualties seldom occurred in the Vietnam War, relative to other wars: The rate of breakdown was only 12 cases per 1000 men. In contrast, the rate of psychiatric breakdown during the Korean War was 37 per 1000, and during World War II it ranged from 28 to 101 per 1000." McNally, Richard J. (2003). Progress and controversy in the study of posttraumatic stress disorder. *Annual Review of Psychology, 54,* 229.

34. Allerton, for example, reported that, over a twelve-month period between 1967 and 1968, army divisions in Vietnam (containing anywhere from 15,000 to 18,000 men) discharged on average only four patients a month for psychiatric reasons. Allerton, Army psychiatry in Viet Nam, 14–15.

35. Marlowe, *Psychological and psychosocial consequences of combat and deployment,* 86.

36. Marlowe, *Psychological and psychosocial consequences of combat and deployment,* 73.

37. Robert Huffman, cited in Marlowe, *Psychological and psychosocial consequences of combat and deployment,* 76.

Chapter 10: Post-Traumatic Stress Disorder

1. Lifton, Robert Jay. (1975). The post-war war. *Journal of Social Issues, 31*(4), 181–95, 183.

2. Associated Press. (1973). Cease-fire, peace bring official U.S. Thanksgiving. January 28, 1973.

3. Cited in Decker, *The making of DSM-III,* 8.

4. Ennis, Bruce J. (1972). *Prisoners of psychiatry: Mental patients, psychiatrists, and the law.* New York: Harcourt Brace Jovanovich.

5. Willis, Ellen. (1973). Prisoners of psychiatry. *New York Times,* March 4, 1973.

6. Rosenhan, On being sane in insane places.

7. Cahalan, Susannah. (2019). *The great pretender: The undercover mission that changed our understanding of madness.* New York: Grand Central Publishing.

8. Kety, Seymour S. (1974). From rationalization to reason. *American Journal of Psychiatry, 139*(9), 957–63, 959; see also: Spitzer, Robert L. (1975). On pseudoscience in science, logic in remission, and psychiatric diagnosis: A critique of Rosenhan's "On Being Sane in Insane Places." *Journal of Abnormal Psychology, 84*(5), 442–52.

9. Wilson, Mitchell. (1993). DSM-III and the transformation of American psychiatry: A history. *American Journal of Psychiatry, 150*(3), 399–410, 402.

10. Luhrmann, *Of two minds*, 225.

11. Charlton, Linda. (1973). One question marks Ford hearing. *New York Times*, November 2, 1973, 23.

12. Blairs, William M. (1968). Psychiatric aid to Nixon denied. *New York Times*, November 14, 1968. In 1972, Hutschnecker told the *Psychiatric News* that "there is no doubt in my mind that Jews have infected the American people with schizophrenia. Jews are carriers of the disease and it will reach epidemic proportions unless science develops a vaccine to counteract it." *Psychiatric News*. (1972). Physician claims Jews are schizo carriers. October 25, 1972. Washington, DC: American Psychiatric Association.

13. Cannon, James A. (1994). *Time and chance. Gerald Ford's appointment with history*. Ann Arbor: University of Michigan Press, 241. The quote is also in the *Congressional Record*.

14. Charlton, One question marks Ford hearing.

15. Charlton, One question marks Ford hearing.

16. Cited in Burkett, B. G., & Whitley, Glenna. (1998). *Stolen valor: How the Vietnam generation was robbed of its heroes and its history*. Dallas: Verity, 149. Original citation: Wicker, Tom. (1975). The Vietnam disease. *New York Times*, May 27, 1975. Wicker wrote: "The figure for heroin use overseas was reported by the *New York Times* two years ago. All the other statistics are from a comprehensive series of articles in *Penthouse Magazine*."

17. Hagopian, Patrick. (2009). *The Vietnam War in American memory: Veterans, memorials, and the politics of healing*. Amherst: University of Massachusetts Press, 53.

18. Scott, Wilbur J. (1993). *The politics of readjustment: Vietnam veterans since the war*. New York: Aldine de Gruyter.

19. Associated Press. (1968). Veterans find jobs faster. *New York Times*, May 3, 1968, 35.

20. Lamb, David. (1975). Vietnam veterans melting into society. *Los Angeles Times*, November 3, 1975, B1; see also: Musser, Marc J., & Stenger, Charles A. (1972). A medical and social perception of the veteran. *Bulletin of the New York Academy of Medicine, 48*(6), 859–69.

21. Borus, Jonathan. (1975). Incidence of maladjustment in Vietnam returnees. *Archives of General Psychiatry, 30*, 554–57. Borus wrote: "The data indicate that, in contrast to more subjective reports of widespread post-Vietnam readjustment difficulty, a relatively small minority of the veterans in this active-duty population had recorded indexes of either disciplinary, legal or emotional maladjustment during their initial reentry transition back to life in the United States. That the incidences of maladjustment indexes for Vietnam veterans were not greater than those of nonveteran controls in the same social milieu challenges assump-

tions that the Vietnam experience or the reentry transition itself are debilitating stresses for the majority of returning veterans."

22. Hoiberg, Anne. (1980). Military effectiveness of navy men during and after Vietnam. *Armed Forces & Society, 6*(2), 232–46; described in Wessely, Simon, & Jones, Edgar. (2004). Psychiatry and the "lessons of Vietnam": What were they and are they still relevant? *War and Society, 22*(1), 89–103, 97.

23. Marlowe, *Psychological and psychosocial consequences of combat and deployment,* xv.

24. Hierholzer, Robert, et al. (1992). Clinical presentation of PTSD in World War II combat veterans. *Hospital and Community Psychiatry, 43*(8), 816–20, 817.

25. Shatan, Chaim. (1972). Post-Vietnam syndrome. *New York Times,* May 6, 1972.

26. Brown, D. E. (1970). The military: A valuable arena for research and innovation. *American Journal of Psychiatry, 127*(4), 511–12.

27. Scott, Wilbur J. (1990). PTSD in DSM-III: A case in the politics of diagnosis and disease. *Social Problems, 37,* 294–310, 303.

28. Maier, Thomas. (1970). The army psychiatrist: An adjunct to the system of social control. *American Journal of Psychiatry, 126*(7), 163.

29. Perhaps the most important, data-driven, conclusion that no new category was necessary is: Helzer, John E., Robins, Lee N., & Davis, D. H. (1976). Depressive disorders in Vietnam returnees. *Journal of Nervous and Mental Disease, 168*(3), 177–85.

30. Wilson, John. (1994). The historical evolution of PTSD diagnostic criteria: From Freud to DSM-IV. *Journal of Traumatic Stress, 7*(4), 681–98.

31. Scott, *The politics of readjustment,* 3.

32. Grinker, Roy R., Sr. (1945). The medical, psychiatric and social problems of war neuroses. *Cincinnati Journal of Medicine, 26,* 241–59, 245.

33. Adler, Alexandra. (1945). Two different types of post-traumatic neuroses. *American Journal of Psychiatry, 102*(2), 237–40.

34. Andreasen, Nancy J. C., Norris, A. S., & Hartford, C. E. (1971). Incidence of long-term psychiatric complications in severely burned adults. *Annals of Surgery, 174*(5), 785–93.

35. Friedman, Matthew J., Keane, Terence M., & Resnick, Patricia A. (2007). *Handbook of PTSD: Science and practice.* New York: Guilford Press, 4.

36. Evans, Kathy M., et al. (2005). Feminism and feminist therapy: Lessons from the past and hopes for the future. *Journal of Counseling and Development, 83*(3), 269–77, 269–70.

37. Burstow, Bonnie. (2005). A critique of posttraumatic stress disorder and the DSM. *Journal of Humanistic Psychology 45*(4), 429–45, 430.

38. American Psychiatric Association. (1980). *DSM-III: Diagnostic and statistical manual of mental disorders.* Washington, DC: American Psychiatric Association, 236–39.

39. Green, B. L., et al. (1991). Children and disaster: Age, gender, and parental effects on PTSD symptoms. *Journal of the American Academy of Child and Adolescent Psychiatry, 30,* 945–51.

40. Desivilya, H. S., R. Gal, & Ayalon, O. (1996). Extent of victimization, traumatic

stress symptoms, and adjustment of terrorist assault survivors: A long-term follow-up. *Journal of Trauma and Stress, 9,* 881–89.

41. Yehuda, R., et al. (1997). Individual differences in post-traumatic stress disorder symptom profiles in holocaust survivors in concentration camps or in hiding. *Journal of Trauma and Stress, 10,* 453–63.

42. Kulka, R. A., et al. (1988). *Contractual report of findings from the National Vietnam Veterans' readjustment study: Volumes 1–4.* Raleigh, NC: Research Triangle Institute.

43. Schnurr, P. P., et al. (2003). A descriptive analysis of PTSD chronicity in Vietnam veterans. *Journal of Trauma and Stress, 16*(6), 545–53.

44. Griffith, James. (2014). Prevalence of childhood abuse among Army National Guard soldiers and its relationship to suicidal behavior. *Military Behavioral Health Journal, 2,* 114–22.

45. Black, S. A., Gallaway, M. S., & Bell, M. R. (2011). Prevalence and risk factors associated with suicide of army soldiers, 2001–2009. *Military Psychology, 23,* 433–51.

46. Breslau, Joshua. (2004). Cultures of trauma: Anthropological views of posttraumatic stress disorder in international health. *Culture, Medicine and Psychiatry, 28,* 113–26, 114.

47. Watters, Ethan. (2010). *Crazy like us: The globalization of the American psyche.* New York: The Free Press, 71; Theidon, Kimberly. (2013). *Intimate enemies: Violence and reconciliation in Peru.* Philadelphia: University of Pennsylvania Press.

48. McNally, Is PTSD a transhistoric phenomenon?

49. Hinton & Good, *Culture and PTSD.*

50. Wool, Zoë. (2015). *After war: The weight of life at Walter Reed.* Durham, NC: Duke University Press, 132.

51. Wool, *After war,* 151–55.

52. Hinton, Devon E., & Good, Bryon J. (2016). The culturally sensitive assessment of trauma: Eleven analytic perspectives, a typology of errors, and the multiplex models of distress generation. In Hinton & Good, *Culture and PTSD,* 50–113.

53. Hinton, Devon E., et al. (2010). *Khyâl* attacks: A key idiom of distress among traumatized Cambodia refugees. *Culture, Medicine and Psychiatry, 34,* 244–78.

54. Young, Allan. (1980). The discourse on stress and the reproduction of conventional knowledge. *Social Science and Medicine, 14*(3), 133–46.

55. Pupavac, Vanessa. (2002). Pathologizing populations and colonizing minds: International psychosocial programs in Kosovo. *Alternatives, 27,* 489–511.

Chapter 11: Expectations of Sickness

1. Stander, Valerie A., & Thomsen, Cynthia J. (2016). Sexual harassment and assault in the U.S. military: A review of policy and research trends. *Military Medicine, 181*(1), 20–27. The Department of Veterans Affairs defines MST as "psychological trauma, which in the judgment of a mental health professional employed by

the Department, resulted from a physical assault of a sexual nature, battery of a sexual nature, or sexual harassment which occurred while the Veteran was serving on active duty or active duty for training." See: Department of Veterans Affairs. (2010). *Military sexual trauma (MST) programming.* VHA Directive 2010-033. Washington, DC: Veterans Health Administration. Available at: http://www.va .gov/vhapublications/ViewPublication.asp?pub_ID=2272. Retrieved May 28, 2015.

2. Hagen, Melissa J., et al. (2018). Event-related clinical distress in college students: Responses to the 2016 U.S. presidential election. *Journal of American College Health,* DOI: 10.1080/07448481.2018.1515763, 1–5.

3. Sontag, *Illness as metaphor,* 3.

4. Hoge, C. W., et al. (2004). Combat duty in Iraq and Afghanistan, mental health problems, and barriers to care. *New England Journal of Medicine, 351,* 13–22.

5. Reimann, Carolyn A., & Mazuchowski, Edward L. (2018). Suicide rates among active duty service members compared with civilian counterparts, 2005–2014. *Military Medicine, 183*(3/4), 396–402.

6. Ronald C. Kessler, et al. (2014). Thirty-day prevalence of *DSM-IV* mental disorders among nondeployed soldiers in the US Army: Results from the army study to assess risk and resilience in soldiers in the US Army (Army STARRS). *JAMA Psychiatry, 71*(5), 504–13.

7. Nock, Matthew K., et al. (2013). Mental disorders, comorbidity and pre-enlistment suicidal behavior among new soldiers in the US Army: Results from the army study to assess risk and resilience in service members (Army STARRS). *Suicide and Life-Threatening Behavior, 45*(5), 588–99.

8. Williamson, Vanessa, & Mulhall, Erin. (2009). Invisible wounds: Psychological and neurological injuries confront a new generation of veterans. New York: Iraq and Afghanistan Veterans of America, 11.

9. Williamson & Mulhall, Invisible wounds, 12.

10. Petryna, Adriana. (2003). *Life exposed: Biological citizenship after Chernobyl.* Princeton, NJ: Princeton University Press, 175.

11. Young, Allan. (1995). *The Harmony of illusions: Inventing post-traumatic stress disorder.* Princeton, NJ: Princeton University Press.

12. Trivedi, Ranak B., et al. (2015). Prevalence, comorbidity, and prognosis of mental health among US veterans. *American Journal of Public Health, 105*(12), 2564–69.

13. Hoge, Charles W. (2010). *Once a warrior, always a warrior: Navigating the transition from combat to home, including combat stress, PTSD, and mTBI.* Guilford, CT: GPP Life, 178.

14. Chiarelli, Gen. Peter, interview with PBS *News Hour,* November 4, 2011.

15. Chiarelli, interview with PBS *News Hour.*

16. Paul Rieckhoff, executive director, Iraq and Afghanistan Veterans of America, interview with PBS *News Hour,* November 4, 2011.

17. Thompson, Mark. (2011). The disappearing "disorder": Why PTSD is becoming PTS. *Time* magazine, June 5, 2011.

18. Sherman, Nancy. (2015). *Afterwar: Healing the moral wounds of our soldiers.* Oxford: Oxford University Press, 14.

19. Junger, Sebastian. (2010). *War.* New York: Twelve, 40–41.

20. Engel, Charles C., Jr. (2004). Post-war syndromes: Illustrating the impact of the social psyche on notions of risk, responsibility, reason, and remedy. *Journal of the American Academy of Psychoanalysis and Dynamic Psychiatry, 32*(2), 321–34.

21. *Presidential Advisory Committee on Gulf War Veterans' Illnesses: Final Report.* December 1996. Washington, DC: U.S. Government Printing Office.

22. Murphy, F., Kang, H. K., & Dalager, N. (1999). The health status of Gulf War veterans: Lessons learned from the Department of Veterans Affairs health registry. *Military Medicine, 164*(5), 327–31.

23. Roy, M. J., et al. (1998). Signs, symptoms, and ill-defined conditions in Persian Gulf War veterans: Findings from the comprehensive clinical evaluation. *Psychosomatic Medicine, 60*(6), 663–68.

24. *Newsnight.* (1993). British Broadcasting Corporation. June 7, 1993, and July 5, 1993.

25. Durodié, Bill. (2006). Risk and the social construction of "Gulf War Syndrome." *Philosophical Transactions of the Royal Society of London, 361*(1468), 689–95.

26. Showalter, Elaine. (1997). *Hystories: Hysterical epidemics and modern culture.* New York: Columbia University Press, 19–20.

27. Wessely, Simon, & White, Peter D. (2004). There is only one functional somatic syndrome. *British Journal of Psychiatry, 185*, 95–96.

28. Ford, Julian, et al. (2001). Psychosomatic stress symptomatology is associated with unexplained illness attributed to Persian Gulf War military service. *Psychosomatic Medicine, 63*, 842–49, 847.

29. Bullman, Tim A., et al. (2005). Mortality in US Army Gulf War veterans exposed to 1991 Khamisiyah chemical munitions destruction. *American Journal of Public Health, 95*(8), 1382–88.

30. Goldberg, David. (1979). Detection and assessment of emotional disorders in a primary-care setting. *International Journal of Mental Health, 8*(2), 30–48.

31. Kroenke, Kurt, et al. (1994). Physical symptoms in primary care: Predictors of psychiatric disorders and functional impairment. *Archives of Family Medicine, 3*, 774–79.

32. Chrousos, G. P., & Gold, P. W. (1992). The concepts of stress and stress system disorders: Overview of physical and behavioral homeostasis. *JAMA: Journal of the American Medical Association, 267*(9), 1244–52.

Chapter 12: Telling Secrets

1. Plato. (2007). *The Republic.* New York: Penguin, 516.

2. Sontag, *Illness as metaphor,* 7.

3. Kinder, *Paying with their bodies,* 8.

4. Mintz, *Huck's raft,* 281.

5. *Mills v. Board of Education of District of Columbia.* (1972). U.S. District Court for the District of Columbia. 348 F. Supp. 866.

6. The formal name of the law is the Mental Retardation and Community Mental Health Centers Construction Act of 1963.

7. Goffman, Erving. (1961). *Asylums: Essays on the social situation of mental patients and other inmates.* New York: Doubleday Anchor, 386.

8. McNamara, Eileen. (2018). *Eunice: The Kennedy who changed the world.* New York: Simon & Schuster.

9. McNamara, *Eunice.*

10. Oosterhius, Harry. (2005). Outpatient psychiatry and mental health care in the twentieth century: International perspectives. In Gijswijt-Hofstra, et al. (Eds.), *Psychiatric cultures compared: Psychiatry and mental health care in the twentieth century: Comparisons and approaches.* Amsterdam: Amsterdam University Press, 248–74, 261.

11. Hopper, Kim. (1988). More than passing strange: Homelessness and mental illness in New York City. *American Ethnologist, 15*(1), 155–67.

12. Brodwin, Paul E. (2013). *Everyday ethics: Voices from the front line of community psychiatry.* Berkeley: University of California Press, 32.

13. Lamb, H. R. (1984). Deinstitutionalization and the homeless. *Hospital and Community Psychiatry, 35*(9), 899–907.

14. Lyon-Callo, Vin. (2001). Making sense of NIMBY: Poverty, power, and community opposition to homeless shelters. *City and Society, 13*(2), 183–209.

15. Roth, Alisa. (2018). *Insane: America's criminal treatment of mental illness.* New York: Basic Books.

16. See Sacks, Oliver. (2009). The lost virtues of the asylum. *New York Review of Books*, September 24, 2009.

17. Bloland, Sue Erikson. (2005). *In the shadow of fame: A memoir by the daughter of Erik H. Erikson.* New York: Viking, 22.

18. Friedman, Lawrence J. (1999). *Identity's architect: A biography of Erik H. Erikson.* New York: Scribner, 22–23, 208–20.

19. Friedman, *Identity's architect*, 210.

20. Bloland, *In the shadow of fame*, 87.

21. Friedman, *Identity's architect*, 212.

22. Sutter, John David. (2007). Once a shadowland. *The Oklahoman.* June 10, 2007. https://oklahoman.com/article/3064415/once-a-shadowlandbrspan-classhl2 today-patients-at-griffin-memorial-hospital-can-get-treatment-and-go-on-to -lead-productive-lives-the-states-oldest-mental-health-institution-was-span. Retrieved April 17, 2020.

23. Sheehan, Susan. (1982). *Is there no place on earth for me?* New York: Houghton Mifflin, 10.

24. Cited in Sheehan, *Is there no place on earth for me?*, 11.

25. Applebaum, Paul S. (1999). Law & psychiatry: Least restrictive alternative revis-

ited: Olmstead's uncertain mandate for community-based care. *Psychiatric Services, 50*(10), 1271–73.

26. Eyal, Gil, et al. (2010). *The autism matrix: The social origins of the autism epidemic.* Cambridge: Polity Press.

27. Srole, Leo, et al. (1962). *Mental health in the metropolis: The mid-town Manhattan study, volume 1.* Thomas A. C. Rennie Series in Social Psychiatry. New York: Blakiston.

28. Leighton, D. C., et al. (1963). Psychiatric findings of the Stirling County study. *American Journal of Psychiatry, 119,* 1021–26.

29. Bourdon, Karen H., et al. (1992). Estimating the prevalence of mental disorders in U.S. adults from the epidemiologic catchment area survey. *Public Health Reports, 107*(6), 663–68.

30. Bagalman, Erin, & Cornell, Ada S. (2018). Prevalence of mental illness in the United States: Data sources and estimates. Washington, DC: Congressional Research Service; Kessler, R. C., et al. (2005). Lifetime prevalence and age-of-onset distributions of DSM-IV disorders in the national comorbidity survey replication (NCS-R). *Archives of General Psychiatry, 62*(6), 593–602; Kessler, R. C., et al. (2005). Prevalence, severity, and comorbidity of twelve-month DSM-IV disorders in the national comorbidity survey replication (NCS-R). *Archives of General Psychiatry, 62*(6), 617–627.

31. Eyal, Gil, et al., *The autism matrix.*

32. Blashfield, Roger K., et al. (2014). The cycle of classification: DSM-I through DSM-5. *Annual Review of Clinical Psychology, 10,* 25–51, 41.

33. Bradley, Charles. (1937). The behavior of children receiving Benzedrine. *American Journal of Psychiatry, 94,* 577–81. But treating children with psychotropic drugs was highly controversial, and most pharmaceutical companies refused to fund research on stimulants until the 1970s. NIMH was virtually the only source of funding for any sort of pediatric psychopharmacology. Between 1937 and 1950 only a handful of papers were published about the use of stimulants in children.

34. Kefauver Hearings. (1961). *Administered drug prices. Report of the Committee on the Judiciary. United States Senate Subcommittee on Antitrust and Monopoly.* Washington, DC: U.S. Government Printing Office, 156.

35. Centers for Disease Control and Prevention. (2005). Mental health in the United States: Prevalence of diagnosis and medication treatment for attention deficit/hyperactivity disorder: United States, 2003. *MMWR: Morbidity and Mortality Weekly Report, 54*(34), 842–47.

36. Kolata, Gina. (1990). Researchers say brain abnormality may help to explain hyperactivity. *New York Times,* November 15, 1990, B18.

37. Nelson, Bryce. (1983). The biology of depression makes physicians anxious. *New York Times,* September 11, 1983.

38. Sullivan, P. F. (1995). Mortality in anorexia nervosa. *American Journal of Psychiatry, 152,* 1073–74.

39. Watters, *Crazy like us.*

40. Kravetz, Lee Daniel. (2017). The strange contagious history of bulimia. *New York* magazine (The Cut), July 31, 2017.

41. Mann, Traci, et al. (1997). Are two interventions worse than none? Joint primary and secondary prevention of eating disorders in college females. *Health Psychology, 16*(3), 215–25.

42. Mann, Are two interventions worse than none?, 224.

43. Davis, Lennard J. (2010). Obsession: Against mental health. In Jonathan M. Metzl & Kirkland, Anna (Eds.), *Against health: How health became the new morality.* New York: New York University Press, 121–32, 29.

44. Hinshaw, Stephen P., & Scheffler, Richard M. (2014). *The ADHD explosion: Myths, medication, money, and today's push for performance.* Oxford: Oxford University Press, 156.

45. Mandell, D. S., et al. (2009). Racial/ethnic disparities in the identification of children with autism spectrum disorders. *American Journal of Public Health, 99*(3), 493–98; see also: Blanchett, W. J., Klingner, J. K., & Harry, B. (2009). The intersection of race, culture, language, and disability implications for urban education. *Urban Education, 44*, 389–409.

46. Polyak, Andrew, Kubina, Richard M., & Girirajan, Santhosh. (2015). Comorbidity of intellectual disability confounds ascertainment of autism: Implications for genetic diagnosis. *American Journal of Medical Genetics. Part B: Neuropsychiatric Genetics, 168*(7), 600–608.

47. Some clinicians and researchers now even distinguish between syndromic autism and nonsyndromic (idiopathic) autism. Syndromic autism is increasingly a term of clinical utility for individuals with ASD associated with Down's, Angelman, Cohen, Williams, Fragile X, Rett, Cornelia de Lange, 22q11 deletion, and Prader Willi syndromes, among others. See Gillberg, Christopher, & Coleman, Mary. (2000). *The biology of the autistic syndromes* (3rd ed.). London: High Holborn House.

48. Rødgaard, Eya-Mist, et al. (2019). Temporal changes in effect sizes of studies comparing individuals with and without autism: A meta-analysis. *JAMA Psychiatry.* Published online August 21, 2019.

49. Sato, Mitsumoto. (2006). Renaming schizophrenia: A Japanese perspective. *World Psychiatry, 5*(1), 53–55.

50. Nishimura, Y., & Ono, H. (2006). A study on renaming schizophrenia and informing diagnosis. In Ono, Y. (Ed.), *Studies on the effects of renaming psychiatric disorders.* Tokyo: Ministry of Health, Labor and Welfare, 6–13. In Japanese.

51. Sartorius, Norman, et al. (2014). Name change for schizophrenia. *Schizophrenia Bulletin, 40*(2), 255–58.

52. Koike, Shinsuke, et al. (2015). Long-term effect of a name change for schizophrenia on reducing stigma. *Social Psychiatry and Psychiatric Epidemiology, 50*, 1519–26.

53. George, Bill, & Klijn, Aadt. (2013). A modern name for schizophrenia would diminish self-stigma. *Psychological Medicine, 43*, 1555–57.

54. There is a similar pattern in South Korea. Despite the Korean ideology of filial piety, Korea has the highest poverty rate for the elderly among OECD countries; many live alone or in institutions. See: Jeon, Boyoung, et al. (2017). Disability, poverty, and the role of the basic livelihood security system on health services utilization among the elderly in South Korea. *Social Science and Medicine, 178*, 175–83.

Chapter 13: An Illness Like Any Other?

1. Whitaker, Robert. (2010). *Anatomy of an epidemic: Magic bullets, psychiatric drugs, and the astonishing rise of mental illness in America.* New York: Crown, 280.
2. Lane, Christopher. (2007). *Shyness: How normal behavior became a sickness.* New Haven, CT: Yale University Press, 38.
3. Macalpine, Ida, & Hunter, Richard. (1966). The "insanity" of King George III: A classic case of porphyria. *British Medical Journal, 1*, 65–71, 71.
4. Andreasen, Nancy. (1984). *The broken brain: The biological revolution in psychiatry.* New York: HarperPerennial, 2.
5. Murray, C. J. (1994). Quantifying the burden of disease: The technical basis for disability-adjusted life years. *Bulletin of the World Health Organization, 72*(3), 429–45.
6. Rose, Nikolas. (1996). *Inventing ourselves: Psychology, power, and personhood.* Cambridge: Cambridge University Press, 109; see also: Gould, *The mismeasure of man.*
7. Hoogman, Martine, et al. (2019). Brain imaging of the cortex in ADHD: A coordinated analysis of large-scale clinical and population-based samples. *American Journal of Psychiatry, 176*(7), 531–42; Wannan, Cassandra M. J., et al. (2019). Evidence for network-based cortical thickness reductions in schizophrenia. *American Journal of Psychiatry, 176*(7), 552–63.
8. Rapoport, Judith L., et al. (1999). Progressive cortical change during adolescence in childhood-onset schizophrenia: A longitudinal magnetic resonance imaging study. *Archives of General Psychiatry, 56*(7), 649–54.
9. Kessler, Ronald C., et al. (2005). Lifetime prevalence and age-of-onset distributions of DSM-IV disorders in the national comorbidity survey replication. *Archives of General Psychiatry, 62*, 593–602.
10. Dawson, Geraldine, et al. (2018). Atypical postural control can be detected via computer vision analysis in toddlers with autism spectrum disorder. *Nature Scientific Reports, 8* (17008).
11. Marmar, Charles, et al. (2019). Speech-based markers for posttraumatic stress disorder in US veterans. *Depression and Anxiety.* Published online DOI: 10.1002/da.22890.
12. Kleinman, Arthur. (2019). *The soul of care: The moral education of a husband and doctor.* New York: Viking.
13. Hinshaw, Stephen P. (2007). *The mark of shame: Stigma of mental illness and an agenda for change.* Oxford: Oxford University Press, 86.

14. Insel, T., & Quirion, R. (2005). Psychiatry as a clinical neuroscience discipline. *JAMA: Journal of the American Medical Association, 294,* 2221–24.

15. Patel, Vikram, et al. (2011). A renewed agenda for global mental health. *Lancet,* 378(9801), 1441–42, 1441.

16. Collins, Pamela Y., et al. (2011). Grand challenges in global mental health. *Nature,* 475(7354), 27–30, 27. In full disclosure, when the authors were preparing the article, I was one of approximately 200 researchers the mhGAP group asked to submit opinions about the grand challenges.

17. Pandolfi, Mariella. (2003). Contract of mutual (in)difference: Governance and the humanitarian apparatus in contemporary Albania and Kosovo. *Indiana Journal of Global Legal Studies, 10*(1), 369–81, 381.

18. Ortega, Francisco, & Wenceslau, Leandro David. (2020). Challenges for implementing a global mental health agenda in Brazil: The "silencing" of culture. *Transcultural Psychiatry, 57*(1), 57–70.

19. Ticktin, Miriam. (2006). Where ethics and politics meet: The violence of humanitarianism in France. *American Ethnologist, 33*(1), 33–49, 39; see also: Ticktin, Miriam. (2011). *Casualties of care: Immigration and the politics of humanitarianism in France.* Berkeley: University of California Press.

20. Weissman, Myrna. (2001). Stigma. *JAMA: Journal of the American Medical Association, 285*(3), 261–62.

21. Dumit, Joseph. (2003). "Is it me or my brain?": Depression and neuroscientific facts. *Journal of Medical Humanities, 24*(1–2), 35–47.

22. Feder, Henry M., et al. (2007). A critical appraisal of "chronic Lyme disease." *New England Journal of Medicine, 357,* 1422–30; Marques, Adriana. (2008). Chronic Lyme disease: A review. *Infectious Disease Clinics of North America, 22,* 341–60.

23. Creed, F. (1999). The importance of depression following myocardial infarction. *Heart, 82*(4), 406–8; Barefoot, J. C., et al. (2000). Depressive symptoms and survival of patients with coronary artery disease. *Psychosomatic Medicine, 62*(6), 790–95.

24. Taylor, Stuart, Jr. (1982). CAT scans said to show shrunken Hinckley brain. *New York Times,* June 2, 1982.

25. Dumit, Joseph. (2004). *Picturing personhood: Brain scans and biomedical identity.* Princeton, NJ: Princeton University Press, 63.

26. Magliano, L., et al. (2004). Beliefs of psychiatric nurses about schizophrenia: A comparison with patients' relatives and psychiatrists. *International Journal of Social Psychiatry, 50,* 319–30.

27. Angermeyer, Matthias C., & Matschinger, Herbert. (2005). Causal beliefs and attitudes to people with schizophrenia: Trend analysis based on data from two population surveys in Germany. *British Journal of Psychiatry, 186,* 331–34.

28. Pescosolido, Bernice A., et al. (2010). "A disease like any other"? A decade of change in public reactions to schizophrenia, depression, and alcohol dependence. *American Journal of Psychiatry, 167*(11), 1321–30, 1324.

29. Nadesan, Majia Holmer. (2008). Constructing autism: A brief genealogy. In

Osteen, Mark (Ed.), *Autism and representation*. New York: Routledge, 78–95; see also: Ten Have, H. A. M. J. (2001). Genetics and culture: The geneticization thesis. *Medicine, Health Care and Philosophy, 4*, 295–304.

30. Silberman, Steve. (2015). *Neurotribes*. New York: Avery, 14.

31. Binder, Laurence M., Iverson, Grant L., & Brooks, Brian L. (2009). To err is human: "Abnormal" neuropsychological scores and variability are common in healthy adults. *Archives of Clinical Neuropsychology, 24*, 31–46.

32. Hilker, Rikke, et al. (2018). Heritability of schizophrenia and schizophrenia spectrum based on the nationwide Danish twin register. *Biological Psychiatry, 83*(6), 492–98.

33. This comparison is elaborated by Meehl, P. E. (1977). Specific etiology and other forms of strong influence: Some quantitative meanings. *Journal of Medicine and Philosophy, 2*, 33–53; see also: Murphy, Dominic. (2006). *Psychiatry in the scientific image*. Cambridge, MA: MIT Press, 118–19.

34. Benavides-Rawson, Jorge, & Grinker, Roy Richard. (2018). Reactive attachment disorder and autism spectrum disorder: Diagnosis and care in a cultural context. In Fogler, J. M., & Phelps, R. A. (Eds.), *Trauma, autism, & neurodevelopmental disorders: Integrating research, practice, and policy*. Switzerland: Springer Nature.

35. Richters, M. M., & Volkmar, F. R. (1994). Reactive attachment disorder of infancy or early childhood. *Journal of the American Academy of Child and Adolescent Psychiatry, 33*, 328–32.

36. Hanson, R. F., & Spratt, E. G. (2000). Reactive attachment disorder: What we know about the disorder and implications for treatment. *Child Maltreatment, 5*(2), 137–46.

37. Kim, Young Shin, et al. (2011). Prevalence of autism spectrum disorders in a total population sample. *American Journal of Psychiatry, 168*(9), 904–12.

38. Vickery, George Kendall. (2005). *A cold of the heart: Japan strives to normalize depression*. PhD dissertation, University of Pittsburgh, Department of Anthropology.

39. Weaver, Lesley Jo. (2019). *Sugar and tension: Diabetes and gender in modern India*. New Brunswick, NJ: Rutgers University Press, 84.

40. Kitanaka, Junko. (2012). *Depression in Japan: Psychiatric cures for a society in distress*. Princeton, NJ: Princeton University Press, 34.

41. Kitanaka, *Depression in Japan*, 36.

42. Sexton, Anne. The double image (lines 8–11). In *The complete poems*. New York: Mariner, 35.

Chapter 14: "Like a Magic Wand"

1. Electroconvulsive therapy. (1985). *NIH Consensus Statement, 5*(11), June 10–12, 1–23.

2. Centers for Disease Control and Prevention; https://webappa.cdc.gov/cgi-bin/broker.exe.

3. El-Hai, Jack. (2005). *The lobotomist: A maverick magical genius and his quest to rid the world of mental illness.* New York: Wiley, 116–17.

4. Dully, Howard, & Fleming, Charles. (2007). *My lobotomy.* New York: Three Rivers Press; Raz, Mical. (2013). *The lobotomy letters: The making of American psychosurgery.* Rochester, NY: University of Rochester Press; Whitaker, Robert. (2002). *Mad in America: Bad science, bad medicine, and the enduring mistreatment of the mentally ill.* New York: Basic Books.

5. Associated Press. (1949). Zurich, Lisbon brain specialists divide Nobel Prize for Medicine. *New York Times*, October 28, 1949.

6. Caruso, James P., & Sheehan, Jason P. (2017). Psychosurgery, ethics, and media: A history of Walter Freeman and the lobotomy. *Neurosurgical Focus, 43*(3), 1–8.

7. Paul Offit makes the comparison to Jeffrey Dahmer in his book *Pandora's Lab: Seven Stories of Science Gone Wrong*. Offit, Paul. (2017). *Pandora's lab: Seven stories of science gone wrong.* Washington, DC: National Geographic, 131–32.

8. Johnson, Jenell. (2011). Thinking with the thalamus: Lobotomy and the rhetoric of emotional impairment. *Journal of Literary and Cultural Disability Studies, 5*(2), 185–200, 191.

9. Braslow, Joel, cited in Johnson, Jenell. (2014). *American lobotomy: A rhetorical history.* Ann Arbor: University of Michigan Press, 54. See Braslow, Joel. (1997). *Mental ills and bodily cures: Psychiatric treatment in the first half of the twentieth century.* Berkeley: University of California Press, 162.

10. Quoted in Swayze, Victor W., 2nd. (1995). Frontal leukotomy and related psychosurgical procedures in the era before antipsychotics (1935–1954): A historical overview. *American Journal of Psychiatry, 152*(4), 505–15, 507.

11. Freeman, Walter, & Watts, James W. (1950). *Psychosurgery in the treatment of mental disorders and intractable pain.* Springfield, IL: Charles C. Thomas, 148.

12. Dreger, Alice Domurat. (2004). *One of us: Conjoined twins and the future of the normal.* Cambridge, MA: Harvard University Press.

13. Kaempffert, Waldemar. (1941). Turning the mind inside out. *Saturday Evening Post*, May 24, 1941, 19.

14. American Medical Association. (1941). Neurosurgical treatment of certain abnormal mental states: Panel discussion at Cleveland session. *JAMA: Journal of the American Medical Association, 117*(7), 517–27.

15. Panel discussion on neurosurgical treatment of certain abnormal mental states. The invited participants were Walter Freeman, M. A. Tarumianz, Theodore Erickson, J. G. Lyerly, H. D. Palmer, and Roy Grinker. The moderator was Paul Bucy. A condensed version was published: Neurosurgical treatment of certain abnormal mental states. *JAMA: Journal of the American Medical Association, 117*(1941), 517–26; the entire typescript of the discussion is conserved in the Freeman/Watts archives, box 16, folder 23 (referred to hereafter as "typescript" for brevity) at the George Washington University Gelman Library. The cita-

tions that were not published in the *JAMA* version will be quoted from this reference.

16. Johnson, *American lobotomy*, 35.

17. Solomon, Andrew. (2003). *Noonday demon*. New York: Scribner, 120–23.

18. Styron, William. (1988). Why Primo Levi need not have died. *New York Times*, December 19, 1988.

19. West, James L. W. (1998). *William Styron: A life*. New York: Random House.

20. Styron, William. (1992). *Darkness visible: A memoir of madness*. New York: Vintage, 84.

21. Cregan, Mary. (2019). *The scar: A personal history of depression and recovery*. New York: W. W. Norton.

22. Kennedy, Pagan. (2018). The great god of depression. *New York Times*, August 3, 2018.

23. From the Associated Press. (2003). Cited in Raak, Bill. Former U.S. senator Tom Eagleton dies at 77. St. Louis Public Radio (NPR), March 5, 2007. https://news .stlpublicradio.org/post/former-us-senator-tom-eagleton-dies-77#stream/0. Retrieved August 16, 2019.

24. Sackett, Russell. (1972). Positive v. negative in Tom Eagleton story. *Capital Times*, July 27, 1972.

25. Quoted in Giglio, James N. (2009). The Eagleton affair: Thomas Eagleton, George McGovern, and the 1972 vice presidential nomination. *Presidential Studies Quarterly, 39*(4), 647–76, 671–72.

26. On staring and disability, see: Garland-Thomson, Rosemarie. (2009). *Staring: How we look*. Oxford: Oxford University Press; Bogdan, Robert. (1990). *Freak show: Presenting human oddities for amusement and profit*. Chicago: University of Chicago Press.

27. Brown, Lydia X. Z. (2019). Autistic young people deserve serious respect and attention—not dismissal as the pawns of others. *Washington Post*, December 14, 2019.

28. Prendergast, Catherine. (2001). On the rhetorics of mental disability. In Wilson, J. C., & Lewiecki-Wilson, C. (Eds.), *Embodied rhetorics: Disability in language and culture*. Carbondale: Southern Illinois University Press, 45–60.

29. Bormann, Ernest G. (1973). The Eagleton affair: A fantasy theme analysis. *Quarterly Journal of Speech, 59*(2), 143–59.

30. McGinnis, Joe. (1972). I'll tell you who's bitter, my aunt Hazel. *Life* magazine, August 18, 1972, 30–31.

31. The quote from a story in *Family Circle* magazine in 1981 is cited in Thompson, Alex. (2015). Could America elect a mentally ill president? *Politico*, November/ December 2015. https://www.politico.com/magazine/story/2015/10/politics -mental-illness-history-213276. Retrieved January 8, 2020.

32. Sackeim, Harold A., Prudic, Joan, & Devanand, D. P. (2000). A prospective, randomized, double-blind comparison of bilateral and right unilateral electrocon-

vulsive therapy at different stimulus intensities. *Archives of General Psychiatry,* 57(5), 425–34.

33. Dukakis, Kitty, & Tye, Larry. (2006). *Shock: The healing power of electroconvulsive therapy.* New York: Avery, 190–91.

34. Sackeim, H. A. (1999). The anticonvulsant hypothesis of the mechanisms of action of ECT: Current status. *Journal of ECT, 15,* 5–26.

35. Prudic, J. (2005). Electroconvulsive therapy. In Saddock, B. J., & Saddock, V. A. (Eds.), *Comprehensive textbook of psychiatry.* (8th ed., vol. 2). Philadelphia: Lippincott Williams & Wilkins.

36. Singh, Amit, & Kar, Sujita Kumar. (2017). How electroconvulsive therapy works: Understanding the neurobiological mechanisms. *Clinical Psychopharmacology and Neuroscience, 15*(3), 210–21.

37. Luchini, Frederica, et al. (2015). Electroconvulsive therapy in catatonic patients: Efficacy and predictors of response. *World Psychiatry, 5*(2), 182–92. Kho, King Han, et al. (2003). A meta-analysis of electroconvulsive therapy efficacy in depression. *Journal of ECT, 19*(3), 139–47.

38. McCall, W. Vaugh. (2007). What does Star*D tell us about ECT? *Journal of ECT, 23*(1), 1–2.

39. Himwich, Harold E. (1943). Electroshock: A round table discussion. *American Journal of Psychiatry, 100,* 361.

40. Sackeim, H. A. (2000). Memory and ECT: From polarization to reconciliation. *Journal of ECT, 16*(2), 87–96.

41. Davis, Nicola, & Duncan, Pamela. (2017). Electroconvulsive therapy on the rise again in England. *Guardian,* April 17, 2017. https://www.theguardian.com/society/2017/apr/17/electroconvulsive-therapy-on-rise-england-ect-nhs. Retrieved May 1, 2019.

42. Whitaker, *Mad in America,* 106.

43. McCall, W. Vaughn. (2013). Foreword. In Ghaziuddin, Neera, & Walter, Gary (Eds.), *Electroconvulsive therapy in children and adolescents.* Oxford: Oxford University Press, ix–x.

44. Shorter, Edward. (2013). The history of pediatric ECT. In Ghaziuddin & Walter, *Electroconvulsive therapy,* 1–17.

45. Shorter, Edward. (2013). Electroconvulsive therapy in children. *Psychology Today,* December 1, 2013. Retrieved April 17, 2020, at https://www.psychologytoday.com/us/blog/how-everyone-became-depressed/201312/electroconvulsive-therapy-in-children

46. Harris, Victoria. (2006). Electroconvulsive therapy: Administrative codes, legislation, and professional recommendations. *Journal of the American Academy of Psychiatry and the Law, 34*(3), 406–11.

47. Smith, Daniel. (2001). Shock and disbelief. *The Atlantic,* February 2001. Retrieved April 21, 2020, from https://www.theatlantic.com/magazine/archive/2001/02/shock-and-disbelief/302114/

48. Cregan, *The scar.*

Chapter 15: When the Body Speaks

1. Ilechukwu, Sunny T. C. (1988). Letter. *Transcultural Psychiatric Review*, 25(4), 310–14.

2. Ilechukwu, Sunny T. C. (1992). Magical penis loss in Nigeria: Report of a recent epidemic of a koro-like syndrome. *Transcultural Psychiatric Review*, 29(1), 91–108, 96.

3. Epstein, Stephen. (1996). *Impure science: AIDS, activism, and the politics of knowledge*. Berkeley: University of California Press.

4. Dresser, Rebecca. (2001). *When science offers salvation: Patient advocacy and research ethics*. Oxford: Oxford University Press.

5. Fitzpatrick, Michael. (2009). *Defeating autism: A damaging delusion*. London: Routledge.

6. Hutchinson, Louise. (1959). Institute treats both body and mind in mental illnesses. *Chicago Sunday Tribune*, April 26, 1959, 13.

7. Freeman, Lucy. (1952). Studies link ills of body and mind: New psychosomatic institute at Chicago doing research into causes of tensions. *New York Times*, June 1, 1952, 19.

8. Stone, J. A., et al. (2010). Who is referred to neurology clinics?—The diagnoses made in 3781 new patients. *Clinical Neurology and Neurosurgery*, 112(9), 747–51; Stone, J., et al. (2009). Symptoms "unexplained by organic disease" in 1144 new neurology out-patients: How often does the diagnosis change at follow-up? *Brain*, 132(pt. 10), 2878–88.

9. Barsky, Arthur J., & Borus, Jonathan F. (1995). Somatization and medicalization in the era of managed care. *JAMA: Journal of the American Medical Association*, 274(24), 1931–34.

10. Bonhomme, Julien. (2016). *The sex thieves: The anthropology of a rumor*. Chicago: HAU Books.

11. Jackson, Michael. (1998). *Minima ethnographica: Intersubjectivity and the anthropological project*. Chicago: University of Chicago Press; Geller, A. (1997). Witch doctors torched after men see penises shrink. *New York Post*, March 8, 1997, 12. CNN. (1997). 7 killed in Ghana over "penis-snatching" episodes. January 18, 1997. Kamara, F. (2002). Blindman escapes mob justice for alleged penis snatching. *Daily Observer* (Gambia), April 30, 2002; Reuters. (1997). Senegal vigilantes slay suspected "genital thieves." *San Jose Mercury News* (California), August 2, 1997.

12. Bures, Frank. (2008). A mind dismembered: In search of the magical penis thieves. *Harper's*, June 2008, 60–65.

13. Dan-Ali, Mamir. (2001). "Missing" penis sparks mob lynching. *BBC News Online*, April 12, 2001: http://news.bbc.co.uk/2/hi/africa/1274235.stm. Retrieved October 7, 2019.

14. Gwee, A. L. (1968). *Koro*: Its origin and nature as a disease entity. *Singapore Medical Journal*, 9(1), 3–6.

15. Schdev, P. S., & Shukla, A. (1982). Epidemic *koro* syndrome in India. *Lancet*, 2(8308), 1161; Atalay, Haken. (2007). Two cases of *koro* syndrome. *Turkish Journal of Psychiatry*, 18(3), 1–4; Al-Sinawi, Hamed, Al-Adawi, Samir, & Al-Guenedi, Amr. (2008). Ramadan fasting triggering *koro*-like symptoms during acute alcohol withdrawal: A case report from Oman. *Transcultural Psychiatry*, 45(4), 695–704; Ang, P. C., & Weller, M. P. I. (1984). *Koro* and psychosis. *British Journal of Psychiatry*, 145, 355; Kim, Junmo, et al. (2000). A case of urethrocutaneous fistula with the koro syndrome. *Journal of Urology*, 164(1), 123.

16. Micale, Mark S. (1995). *Approaching hysteria: Disease and its interpretations*. Princeton, NJ: Princeton University Press, 182.

17. Kerckhoff, A. C., & Back, K. W. (1968). *The June bug: A study of hysterical contagion*. New York: Appleton-Century-Crofts.

18. Swanson, Randall, et al. (2018). Neurological manifestations among US government personnel reporting directional audible and sensory phenomena in Havana, Cuba. *JAMA: Journal of the American Medical Association*, 319(11), 1125–33, 1127.

19. Hurley, Dan. (2019). Was it an invisible attack on U.S. diplomats, or something stranger? *New York Times Magazine*, May 15, 2019.

20. Hurley, Was it an invisible attack?

21. Peikoff, Kira. (2014). My son almost lost his mind from strep throat. *Cosmopolitan*, October 1, 2014.

22. Swedo, S. E., et al. (1998). Pediatric autoimmune neuropsychiatric disorders associated with streptococcal infections: Clinical description of the first 50 cases. *American Journal of Psychiatry*, 155, 264–71.

23. PANDAS Network. 1 in 200 Children May Have PANDAS/PANS. Retrieved April 21, 2020, from http://www.pandasnetwork.org/understanding-pandaspans/statistics/

24. Dominus, Susan. (2012). What happened to the girls in LeRoy. *New York Times Magazine*, March 7, 2012.

25. Gulley, Neale. (2012). School's end clears up New York students' mystery twitching. Reuters, June 23, 2012. Retrieved July 18, 2019, from https://www.reuters.com/article/us-students-twitcnew-york-h/schools-end-clears-up-new-york-students-mystery-twitching-idUSBRE85M0DF20120623

26. Clauw, D. J., & Chrousos, G. P. (1997). Chronic pain and fatigue syndromes: Overlapping clinical and neuroendocrine features and potential pathogenic mechanisms. *Neuroimmunomodulation*, 4, 134–53; Fukuda, K., et al. (1998). Chronic multisymptom illness affecting air force veterans of the Gulf War. *JAMA: Journal of the American Medical Association*, 280(11), 981–88.

27. Donta, Sam T., et al. (2003). Cognitive behavioral therapy and aerobic exercise for Gulf War veterans' illnesses: A randomized controlled trial. *JAMA: Journal of the American Medical Association*, 289(11), 1396–1404.

28. Seagrove, J. (1989). The ME generation. *Guardian*, May 19, 1989.

29. Hawkes, Nigel. (2011). Dangers of research into chronic fatigue syndrome. *British Medical Journal, 342*, d3780.

Chapter 16: Bridging Body and Mind in Nepal

1. Kohrt, Brandon A., et al. (2008). Comparison of mental health between former child soldiers and children never conscripted by armed groups in Nepal. *JAMA: Journal of the American Medical Association, 300*(6), 691–702.

2. Kohrt, Brandon A., & Hruschka, Daniel J. (2010). Nepali concepts of psychological trauma: The role of idioms of distress, ethnopsychology and ethnophysiology in alleviating suffering and preventing stigma. *Culture, Medicine and Psychiatry, 34*(2), 322–52, 337.

3. On exorcisms in Nepal see: Peters, Larry. (1982). *Ecstasy and healing in Nepal: An ethnopsychiatric study of Tamang shamanism.* Malibu, CA: Undena Publications; Desjarlais, Robert. (1992). *Body and emotion: The aesthetics of illness and healing in the Nepal Himalayas.* Philadelphia: University of Pennsylvania Press.

4. Kohrt, Brandon A., et al. (2012). Political violence and mental health in Nepal: Prospective study. *British Journal of Psychiatry, 201*(4), 268–75.

5. World Health Organization. (2001). *World health report. Mental health: New understanding, new hope.* Retrieved March 27, 2019, from https://www.who.int/whr/2001/en/

6. Castañeda, Heide. (2011). Medical humanitarianism and physicians' organized efforts to provide aid to unauthorized migrants in Germany. *Human Organization, 70*(1), 1–10, 4.

7. "Minimally adequate care" is often generally defined as care in the previous twelve months, or at least one month of a medication, plus more than four visits to any kind of doctor, or more than eight visits with any professional including religious or spiritual advisor, social worker, or counselor. Wang, P. S., et al. (2007). Use of mental health services for anxiety, mood, and substance disorders in 17 countries in the WHO world mental health surveys. *Lancet, 370*, 841–50.

8. Thornicroft, Graham, et al. (2017). Undertreatment of people with major depressive disorder in 21 countries. *British Journal of Psychiatry, 210*(2), 119–24.

9. See, for example: Damasio, Antonio R. (2008 [1994]). *Descartes' error: Emotion, reason and the human brain.* New York: Random House.

10. Hsu, S. I. (1999). Somatisation among Asian refugees and immigrants as a culturally shaped illness behaviour. *Annals of the Academy of Medicine, Singapore, 6*, 841–45.

11. Ecks, Stefan. (2014). *Eating drugs: Psychopharmaceutical pluralism in India.* New York: New York University Press, 7.

12. Kohrt, Brandon, & Harper, Ian. (2008). Navigating diagnoses: Understanding mind–body relations, mental health, and stigma in Nepal. *Culture, Medicine and Psychiatry, 32*(4), 462–91, 479.

13. The method, called PhotoVoice, was first developed by public health workers to facilitate conversations about sensitive personal issues, and to give research subjects a way to actively participate in the research using their own images and voices. See: Wang, C., & Burris, M. A. (1997). Photovoice: Concept, methodology, and use for participatory needs assessment. *Health Education and Behavior, 24*, 369–87.

Chapter 17: The Dignity of Risk

1. Silberman, Steve. (2001). The geek syndrome. *Wired*, December 2001. Retrieved April 20, 2020, from http://www.wired.com/wired/archive/9.12/aspergers.html

2. Werner, Shirli, et al. (2018). "Equal in uniform": People with intellectual disabilities in military service in Israel. *International Journal of Disability, Development and Education, 65*(5), 569–79; Werner, Shirli, & Hockman, Yael. (2017). Social inclusion of individuals with intellectual disabilities in the military. *Research in Developmental Disabilities, 65*, 103–13.

3. Rubin, Shira. (2016). The Israeli army unit that recruits teens with autism. *The Atlantic,* January 6, 2016.

4. Kahana, Yossi. The IDF Has Room for All. Israel Forever Foundation. Retrieved April 10, 2019, from https://israelforever.org/interact/blog/the_idf_has_room_for_all/; Kinross, Louise. (2015). Israeli military opens training to disabled youth. *Bloom: Holland Bloorview Rehabilitation Hospital.* January 11, 2015. Retrieved April 10, 2019, from http://bloom-parentingkidswithdisabilities .blogspot.com/2015/01/israeli-military-opens-training-to.html

5. Giddens, Anthony. (1999). *The third way: The renewal of social democracy.* Cambridge: Polity Press.

6. Polanyi, Karl. (2001 [1957]). *The great transformation: The political and economic origins of our time.* Boston: Beacon Press.

7. Evans, Bonnie. (2017). The autism paradox. *Aeon.* Retrieved September 5, 2018, from https://aeon.co/essays/the-intriguing-history-of-the-autism-diagnosis; see also: Evans, Bonnie. (2017). *The metamorphosis of autism: A history of child development in Britain.* Manchester, UK: Manchester University Press.

8. Russell, Marta, & Malhorta, Ravi. (2002). Capitalism and disability. *Socialist Register, 38*, 211–28, 217–18.

9. Brucker, Debra L., et al. (2015). More likely to be poor whatever the measure: Working-age persons with disabilities in the United States. *Social Science Quarterly, 96*(1), 273–95.

10. Barnes, C., Mercer, G., & Shakespeare, T. (1999). *Exploring disability: A sociological introduction.* Cambridge: Polity Press.

11. Thornton, P., & Lunt, N. (1995). *Employment for disabled people: Social obligation or individual responsibility.* York, UK: Social Policy Research Unit, University of York.

12. Schall, Carol, Wehman, Paul, & McDonough, Jennifer L. (2012). Transition from

school to work for students with autism spectrum disorders: Understanding the process and achieving better outcomes. *Pediatric Clinics of North America, 59,* 189–202.

13. Dixon, K. A., Kruse, D., & Van Horn, C. E. (2003). *Restricted access: A survey of employers about people with disabilities and lowering barriers to work.* New Brunswick, NJ: Heldrich Center for Workforce Development, Rutgers University.

14. Anthony, William A., & Blanch, Andrea. (1987). Supported employment for persons who are psychiatrically disabled: An historical and conceptual perspective. *Psychosocial Rehabilitation Journal, 11*(2), 6–23.

15. Shakespeare, Tom. (2013). The social model of disability. In Davis, Lennard J. (Ed.), *The disability studies reader* (4th ed.). New York: Routledge, 214–21.

16. Meager, Nigel, & Higgins, Tim. (2011). Disability and skills in a changing economy. London: UK Commission for Employment and Skills, Briefing Paper Series.

17. Organisation for Economic Co-operation and Development (OECD). (2017). Future of work and skills. Paper presented at the Second Meeting of the G20 Employment Working Group, February 15–17, 2017.

18. Belous, Richard S. (1998). The rise of the contingent workforce: Growth of temporary, part-time, and subcontracted employment. *Looking Ahead, 19*(1), 2–24; Barker, Kathleen, & Christensen, Kathleen (Eds.). (1998). *Contingent work: American employment relations in transition.* Ithaca, NY: ILR Press; Thomason, Terry, Burton, John F., Jr., & Hyatt, Douglas E. (Eds.). (1998). *New approaches to disability in the workplace.* Madison, WI: Industrial Relations Research Association.

19. Wehman, Paul, et al. (2016). Employment for adults with autism spectrum disorders: A retrospective review of a customized employment approach. *Research in Developmental Disabilities, 53–54,* 61–72.

20. Wehman, Paul, et al. (2013). Supported employment. In M. Wehmeyer (Ed.), *The Oxford handbook of positive psychology and disability.* New York: Oxford University Press, 338–64.

21. Siperstein, G. N., Heyman, M., & Stokes, J. E. (2014). Pathways to employment: A national survey of adults with intellectual disabilities. *Journal of Vocational Rehabilitation, 41*(3), 165–78.

22. Kessler Foundation. (2018). National trends in disability employment (nTIDE). Retrieved April 21, 2020, from https://www.kesslerfoundation.org/content/ntide-january-2018-jobs-report-americans-disabilities-kick-new-year-sharp-gains-labor-market

23. Dominus, Susan. (2019). Open office. *New York Times Magazine,* February 21, 2019.

24. Taylor, Sunaura. (2004). The right not to work: Power and disability. *Monthly Review,* March 2004, 30–44.

25. Rothman, Joshua. (2017). Are disability rights and animal rights connected? *The New Yorker,* June 5, 2017.

26. Taylor, Sunaura. (2017). *Beasts of burden: Animal and disability liberation.* New York: The New Press.

27. Taylor, The right not to work, 43.

28. Murphy, Robert Francis. (2001). *The body silent: The different world of the disabled.* New York: W. W. Norton, 97.

29. Perske, Robert. (1972). The dignity of risk and the mentally retarded. *Mental Retardation, 10*(1), 24–26, 24.

30. Parsons, Craig. (2008). The dignity of risk: Challenges in moving on. *Australian Nursing Journal, 15*(9), 28.

Conclusion: On the Spectrum

1. Albert, Katherine. (1924). Now everybody's crazy. *Los Angeles Times,* July 13, 1924, B12.

2. American Psychiatric Association. (2013). DSM-5: *Diagnostic and Statistical Manual of Mental Disorders.* Washington, DC: American Psychiatric Association, 12.

3. Kessler, Ronald C. (2002). The categorical versus dimensional assessment controversy in the sociology of mental illnesses. *Journal of Health and Social Behavior, 43*(2), 171–88.

4. Hopper, Kim, et al. (Eds.). (2007). *Recovery from schizophrenia: An international perspective.* Oxford: Oxford University Press.

5. Halperin, David. (1997). *Saint Foucault: Towards a gay hagiography.* Oxford: Oxford University Press, 61; see also Corrigan, Patrick W. (2018). *The stigma effect: Unintended consequences of mental health campaigns.* New York: Columbia University Press.

6. Scott, Robert. (1969). *The making of blind men: A study of adult socialization.* New York: Routledge.

7. Corrigan, Patrick W., & Rao, Deepa. (2012). On the self-stigma of mental illness: Stages, disclosure, and strategies for change. *Canadian Journal of Psychiatry, 57*(8), 464–69.

8. Dumit, Is it me or my brain?

9. Rose, Nikolas. (2019). *Our psychiatric future: The politics of mental health.* Cambridge: Polity Press, 115.

10. See, for example: Sholz, Jan, et al. (2009). Training induces changes in white matter architecture. *Nature Neuroscience, 12*(11), 1370–71; Villarreal, Gerardo, Hamilton, Douglas, & Brooks, William M. (2002). Reduced hippocampal volume and total white matter volume in posttraumatic stress disorder. *Biological Psychiatry, 52*(2), 119–25.

11. Harrington, Anne. (2019). *Mind fixers: Psychiatry's troubled search for the biology of mental illness.* New York: W. W. Norton, 272–73.

12. Super, Charles M., et al. (2008). Culture, temperament, and the "difficult child": A study in seven western cultures. *European Journal of Developmental Science, 2*(1–2), 136–57.

13. Throop, Jason. (2010). *Suffering and sentiment: Exploring the vicissitudes of experience and pain in Yap.* Berkeley: University of California Press.

14. Biehl, Joao. (2005). *Vita: Life in a zone of social abandonment.* Berkeley: University of California Press.

15. O'Nell, Theresa. (1998). *Disciplined hearts: History, identity, and depression in an American Indian community.* Berkeley: University of California Press.

16. Metzl & Kirkland, *Against health*, 2.

17. Kleinman, Arthur. (1980). *Patients and healers in the context of culture: An exploration of the borderland between anthropology, medicine, and psychiatry.* Berkeley: University of California Press, 72–73.

18. Nietzsche, Friedrich. (1997 [1881]). *Daybreak: Thoughts on the prejudice of morality* (R. J. Hollingdale, Trans.). Cambridge: Cambridge University Press, 34.

INDEX